T0202473

Enterprise Systems Integration

Diogo R. Ferreira

Enterprise Systems Integration

A Process-Oriented Approach

 Springer

Diogo R. Ferreira
Instituto Superior Técnico
Technical University of Lisbon
Oeiras, Portugal

ISBN 978-3-662-51431-3   ISBN 978-3-642-40796-3 (eBook)
DOI 10.1007/978-3-642-40796-3
Springer Heidelberg New York Dordrecht London

Printed on acid-free paper

Springer is part of Springer Science+Business Media (www.springer.com)

Preface

Despite having been teaching enterprise systems integration for a number of years, I was unable to find a book that would cover the breadth of topics that I wanted to present to my students. Some books are too high level to convey a practical knowledge of the subject, while others do not raise above the low-level details of certain technological platforms. I wanted to have a book that would go across the landscape of integration concepts and technologies and yet provide an idea of how things work from the low-level systems to the high-level business processes in an organization.

Often, students and IT professionals alike are not fully aware of how technological solutions at the systems level have far-reaching consequences up to the higher levels of business processes in an organization, shaping the way activities and resources must be organized in order to reach a certain business goal or in order to deliver a certain service to the customer. Technology shapes business processes and sets the prospects as well as the limits of what organizations can do. This is not so apparent in computer science curricula where students are routinely asked to develop solutions from scratch, but it will come as a revelation when the student and IT professional realize that while everyone is developing solutions from scratch, someone will have to integrate everything together in order to create an application infrastructure that can support the desired business processes.

Integration has never been an easy topic to address, for several reasons. On one hand, integration has been mostly regarded as "patchwork," being highly dependent on the specific applications to be integrated. On the other hand, integration technologies keep constantly evolving, making any solution obsolete, or at least "old-fashioned," in a couple of years. However, when one looks at the technologies that have come one after the other, one starts noticing certain patterns, certain concepts that have been passed along from one technology generation to the next, and even though some concepts were abandoned along the way, others survived and were even improved as each new technology was introduced.

Today, the concepts and technologies associated with enterprise systems integration have matured to the point that now it is possible to see the connection between low-level systems and high-level business processes through a series of layers that include messaging, adapters, services, and orchestrations. It is always with a view towards supporting business processes that we address integration in this book. From messaging systems to data and application adapters, and then to services, orchestrations, processes, choreographies, and electronic data interchange, I will try to show how everything falls into place in the world of integration.

This book is intended for graduate students and IT professionals with some background in programming, database systems, and XML. These prerequisites are not absolutely essential, but they will help the reader in understanding certain topics and in appreciating the examples that are given throughout the book. Throughout the text, I have tried to abstain from my own views, and instead I decided that my mission would be to describe each topic as impartially and accurately as possible, so that the reader can assess the merits and advantages of the concepts and technologies being presented. Of course, the more knowledgeable the reader is in related fields, the better she or he will be equipped to make such assessment.

Due to its technological nature, it is impossible to teach integration in empty space, without referring to concrete tools and platforms. Unfortunately, every integration platform has its own idiosyncrasies, and choosing a particular platform to illustrate a given concept becomes a delicate decision. But rather than being my own decision, a set of circumstances determined that I would come in close contact with Microsoft BizTalk Server. Even though this platform is relatively complicated to set up (the interested reader is advised to follow the installation guides provided by the vendor), over the years I have found it to be a viable option to illustrate some of the main concepts associated with enterprise systems integration.

With some adaptions, the same concepts can be applied in other platforms, such as webMethods by Software AG, Oracle SOA Suite, or IBM WebSphere. The reader may find open-source alternatives in OpenESB, JBoss ESB, and, more recently, Apache ODE. There are other products which, despite not being mentioned here, may be worth considering as well. These integration platforms will certainly keep evolving, and as they expand in features and sophistication, I hope this book will continue to serve as a useful source of guidance in this exciting field.

Lisbon, Portugal   Diogo R. Ferreira
July 2013

Contents

Acronyms

API	Application Programming Interface
AS2	Applicability Statement 2
ASP	Active Server Pages
B2B	Business-to-Business
BAM	Business Activity Monitoring
BPMN	Business Process Model and Notation
BPEL	Business Process Execution Language
CA	Certification Authority
COM	Component Object Model
CORBA	Common Object Request Broker Architecture
CRM	Customer Relationship Management
CSV	Comma-Separated Values
DII	Dynamic Invocation Interface
DLL	Dynamic-Link Library
DSI	Dynamic Skeleton Interface
DTC	Distributed Transaction Coordinator
EDI	Electronic Data Interchange
ERP	Enterprise Resource Planning
FTP	File Transfer Protocol
HTML	Hypertext Markup Language
HTTP	Hypertext Transfer Protocol
IDL	Interface Definition Language
IFR	Interface Repository
IIS	Internet Information Services
JDBC	Java Database Connectivity
JMS	Java Message Service
JNDI	Java Naming and Directory Interface
JNI	Java Native Interface
JVM	Java Virtual Machine
LDAP	Lightweight Directory Access Protocol
LINQ	Language Integrated Query

MDN	Message Disposition Notification
MIME	Multipurpose Internet Mail Extensions
MSMQ	Microsoft Message Queuing
ODBC	Open Database Connectivity
OLE	Object Linking and Embedding
PGM	Pragmatic General Multicast
POP3	Post Office Protocol, version 3
REST	Representational State Transfer
RMI	Remote Method Invocation
RPC	Remote Procedure Call
S/MIME	Secure Multipurpose Internet Mail Extensions
SMTP	Simple Mail Transfer Protocol
SOA	Service-Oriented Architecture
SOAP	Simple Object Access Protocol
SQL	Structured Query Language
SSL	Secure Sockets Layer
TLS	Transport Layer Security
TPA	Trading Partner Agreement
UDDI	Universal Description Discovery and Integration
UML	Unified Modeling Language
URL	Uniform Resource Locator
WSDL	Web Services Description Language
XML	Extensible Markup Language
XSD	XML Schema Definition
XSLT	Extensible Stylesheet Language Transformations
WSDL	Web Services Description Language

Part I
Introduction

Chapter 1
Evolution of Enterprise Systems

The constant evolution of information technology means that organizations have systems of ever increasing complexity to support their business processes. Beyond a certain point, the coexistence of several systems used for different purposes, often in isolation from each other, creates enormous difficulties when it becomes necessary to integrate these systems in order to support end-to-end business processes.

This chapter presents an overview of the essential business functions in any business organization. These functions must be connected with each other in order to support business processes that traverse the whole organization. If each function is supported by a particular system, then connecting these functions becomes a problem of integrating their respective systems.

The evolution of enterprise systems has been such that at each attempt to support a given business function, a new problem appeared in the connection of that function to other business functions in the organization. A new generation of enterprise systems, known as Enterprise Resource Planning (ERP) systems, was created as an attempt to provide a single, common system to support a wide range of business functions, but even such approach did not eliminate the need for more specialized packages to support certain functions. As a result, ERP became one more system to be integrated alongside with other systems in the organization.

The fact that there will always be the need to integrate different systems in a business environment, regardless of how comprehensive each one of them is, led to the development of enterprise systems integration as an area of its own. This area deals with the problem of connecting all systems, providing asynchronous message exchange between them, and coordinating the execution of business processes on top of an infrastructure comprised of heterogeneous applications.

While in the past the main concern was the specific functionality of each system, in the present the focus is on the integration side, on connecting different systems, and in particular on developing each system as a set of services in order to make them more flexible, reusable, and easier to integrate with each other. As a result, this service-oriented approach plays a prominent role in the landscape of enterprise systems, and it shapes the way enterprise systems are built today.

D.R. Ferreira, *Enterprise Systems Integration*, DOI 10.1007/978-3-642-40796-3_1,
© Springer-Verlag Berlin Heidelberg 2013

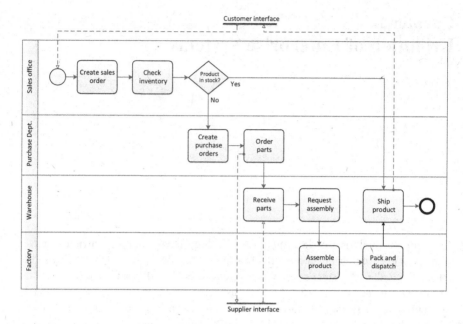

Fig. 1.1 Example of a simple business process

1.1   Essential Systems of a Business Organization

Essentially, every business organization has to deal with at least three interfaces: the interface to its customers, the interface to its suppliers, and the interface to its own employees. Through the interface to customers, sales orders come in; products or services go out; and payments come in. Through the interface to suppliers, purchase orders go out; materials, components, or services come in; and payments go out. Through the interface to employees, tasks go in and results come out; and payments, in the form of salaries, go out. Overall, and from an economic perspective, the net result of all revenues obtained and expenses incurred becomes the income generated by the business organization.

For the purpose of integration, the most interesting aspect is the information flow between these entities, i.e., between the company, its customers, and its suppliers, including the internal flow that is required to support end-to-end business processes. These processes may span the entire organization between the customer interface and the supplier interface, with every possible internal function in between. Figure 1.1 shows a simple example of a business process that crosses several organizational units. This could be the business process of a PC manufacturer who sells pre-configured models with certain specifications. When the customer orders the PC, the sales office checks if the product is available in stock. If so, it is immediately shipped from the warehouse. Otherwise, the parts must be ordered from suppliers and assembled at the factory, and finally the product is shipped.

Even in a simplified process such as this one, it is possible to imagine that there will be information flow across several systems:

- When the sales office creates a new sales order, it does so in an accounting system that will be later used for invoicing the customer (for simplicity, this is not shown in Fig. 1.1).
- When the sales office checks if the product is available in stock, it does so by using a warehouse system where the stock levels are kept up to date.
- When the purchase department creates one or more purchase orders, it does so in the accounting system that will be later used for payment to the supplier (for simplicity, this is not shown in Fig. 1.1).
- When the warehouse receives the parts, it updates the available quantities in the warehouse system.
- When the warehouse requests product assembly, it uses the factory system that manages production orders.
- The same factory system is used in the assembly line to assemble the product according to the requested specifications.
- Packing of the product may be supported by its own system.
- Shipping may be supported by a separate system as well.

In this scenario, there are several systems which must be used to support the business process, and this fact illustrates the need for integration. Basically, the output of one step becomes the input for another, and data must be provided to each system according to its own requirements. Integrating these systems not only facilitates the data flow, but also allows this process to be automated. Indeed, one can imagine all these steps be coordinated in an automated way, where the completion of one step triggers the execution of the next step in the same or in a different system. Integration then becomes a way of not only connecting systems to one another, but also of providing support to organizational processes.

In general, the following functions and systems can be recognized in any business organization [6]:

- Sales order processing—this entails several customer-facing functions and subsystems such as order entry, shipping, and invoicing. An incoming sales order is often the trigger for the whole process of order fulfillment, which includes all the interactions with the end customer between the moment the order is placed to the point when the product or service has been delivered and paid. Often, a company is seen as providing a better service to the customer if these customer-facing functions are properly integrated with each other. Automating the sales order processing also provides more efficiency and allows the company to handle much larger volumes of customer orders.
- Purchase order processing—this has to do with the acquisition of goods or services from suppliers. In a manufacturing scenario, for example, purchase order processing includes ordering, receiving, and paying for components or raw materials that are required to build the product to be delivered to the end customer. Often, the interaction with suppliers requires the use of specialized

systems to exchange documents—such as quotes, invoices, or payment records—in a standard format and in the correct sequence. Although it is almost invisible from the customer point of view, purchase order processing is associated with some of the hardest challenges with respect to integration, since it may require the integration of systems across organizational borders.

- Accounting—this is the backbone of any business organization and it is very common to see accounting-related activities intermingled with operational or production-related activities in a business process. An accounting system is usually divided into three subsystems: accounts receivable, accounts payable, and general ledger. The accounts receivable concerns the amounts that customers owe to the organization. The accounts payable concerns the amounts that the company owes to suppliers. The general ledger handles data from accounts receivable, accounts payable, and payroll information to determine the overall income and expenditure of the organization. In practice, when integrating business processes, the accounting function and its related systems appear most often as acts of invoicing and payment, from the customer side or to the supplier side.

In addition to these, there are other common business functions that are often in place, such as:

- Production—especially in manufacturing scenarios, this business function is connected to the actual manufacturing of goods, from raw materials, parts, or components, to the finished product. From an integration point of view, the most important aspect is to ensure that the right materials and product specifications are available at each step of the manufacturing process.
- Inventory—this business function may serve both the customer side and the supplier side, by storing finished products that will be sold to customers as well as raw materials, parts or components, which are required for the production process and have been bought from suppliers. In the integration of business processes, this function often appears in connection with queries to the stock levels of certain products or parts, as in the example of Fig. 1.1.
- Logistics—this usually refers to customer-side logistics but it may include supplier-side logistics as well. On the customer side, logistics is mainly concerned with shipping finished products to customer locations. This may be done by the company itself, in this case requiring the integration with an internal shipping system, or, as it is more and more common these days, this function may be performed by a third-party provider, in this case requiring a tight integration between systems at both organizations. To the supplier side, a similar integration may be required to ensure that the right materials will be available for the production process.

As described above, each of these functions is supported by one or more subsystems, which must be integrated in order to support organizational processes. The fact that these systems are usually built separately according to their own purpose makes it difficult to implement business processes on top of such heterogeneous infrastructure. In addition, this integration depends on how these systems have been built; their architecture, development platform, implementation, etc. all have an impact on how difficult it may become to integrate systems that were not devised to work together. Fortunately, over time system architectures have evolved to the point that today it is possible to combine system functionality in a plug-and-play fashion, as we will see in the next sections.

1.2 Evolution of System Architectures

In the early days of information systems (mainly 1970s and early 1980s), companies used to have large computer rooms where the mainframe (there were no stand-alone PCs at the time) occupied several cabinets, each approximately the size of a wardrobe. Databases were still not widely used and systems were based on files stored in magnetic tapes (these occupied a large portion of the computer room). There was also the possibility of storing data externally on punched cards, and these could be used for input/output as well. Most systems also had terminals where I/O could be provided in text mode.

The architecture of these early systems was such that there was only a single layer of application code on top of the operating system. The OS provided file storage, but the reading and writing of these files had to be managed by the application itself. With the rise of database systems, applications started relegating file storage to the database, so this became less of a concern. Applications could therefore focus on data operations alone, while interacting with the database through a relational interface such as the Structured Query Language (SQL). For the first time, there was a separation of the system architecture in two different layers, one dealing with application code and another dealing with data persistence through a database.

In the meantime, advances in personal computers resulted in more and more computing power being available to the client (users). Text terminals evolved towards full-fledged graphical terminals and turned into user workstations with advanced rendering capabilities. The possibility of having advanced user interfaces quickly prompted for the need to develop this layer independently from the application code. In essence, there could be several possible ways of rendering the same data, regardless of how these data were processed by the application code. The application layer became a core of application logic alone, supported on one end by a data layer which stores data in a database, and on the other end by a user interface layer to manage interaction with the end users.

By the 1990s, it was commonly accepted that every system architecture should comprise three layers: the data layer, the application layer, and the user interface layer. The rise of the Internet had a great impact in this conceptual arrangement, since the World Wide Web facilitated the development of applications where these layers were distributed across the network [9]. The need for distributed applications led, in turn, to the development and widespread use of distributed object technologies such as CORBA [29] and Java RMI [35]. These have been later superseded by Web services technology [8] and service-oriented computing [23].

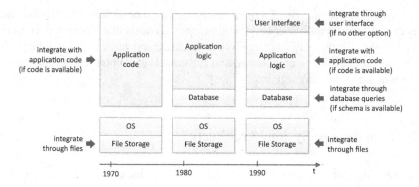

Fig. 1.2 Evolution of system architectures and integration possibilities

In a nutshell, this provides an overview of the evolution of enterprise systems in terms of their application architecture. Depending on this architecture, there may be different options for systems integration. For example, it is quite common to integrate applications with mainframes, or other commercial products where the database schema is not openly available, by means of so-called *flat files*, i.e., text files with a format that is compatible with the target system. If the database schema is available, then it may become easier to interact with the system database directly, and in this case to both read and write data to the application in the form of SQL queries. If the application code itself is available, then it is possible to achieve a tighter integration by writing additional code, or combining application code from different applications (this may require using one of the distributed or service-oriented technologies mentioned above). If neither the data layer nor the application layer is accessible, it may be possible to integrate via the user interface layer, by writing programs that simulate specific user behaviors to carry out particular tasks. This is certainly one of the least desirable ways to achieve integration, but it is actually becoming easier to do, especially when considering the fact that most applications provide a Web-based user interface that make use of standards such as HTML and HTTP; in this case it becomes rather simple to send requests and receive data from the application at the other end.

Figure 1.2 illustrates the evolution of system architectures across time. It becomes apparent that as system architecture evolved into a set of separate layers, also new opportunities appeared to achieve integration through each of these separate layers. So today there is the opportunity of integrating not only through files and application code as before, but also through at the data layer or at the user interface layer if needed. It should be noted, however, that integrating at the application layer is much different today than what it was in the past. If, in the past, this required coding in the same platform and language as the original application, today the application code can be abstracted as services than can be invoked from other platforms and languages. Also, service modularity and composition enables the reuse of functionality and the integration of new code in a much more flexible way than it was possible in the past. This is because system development methodologies have also evolved over the years in tandem with system architectures.

1.3   Integrating Several Applications Together

Now that we have briefly discussed the several ways in which it is possible to integrate with an existing application, we turn to the problems that arise in a scenario where several applications must be integrated together, in order to support a given business process. Figure 1.3 illustrates some of the links that are required to implement the business process shown earlier in Fig. 1.1. After a new sales order is created in the accounting system, part of the information in that sales order (e.g., the requested items, but not the customer address) is used to check for available quantities in the warehouse. If the product is not available, the warehouse can forward a request for assembly to the factory system. After production, the product enters the packing system and then goes to the warehouse, before eventually being shipped to the customer.

The process can be automated by integrating these systems and letting information flow automatically between them, from one stage of process to the next. Should the process be reconfigured according to business requirements, these links may have to be changed and also new links may have to be established; these are illustrated with dashed lines in Fig. 1.3. In this figure, a total of 10 links are shown. However, we should consider that integrating application A with application B is different from integrating B with A, since making A able to receive requests from B may require a different integration mechanism from making B receive requests from A. Therefore, each link in Fig. 1.3 may actually stand for two connections in opposite directions. In this scenario, since each system must be connected with every other, for N systems there will be a total of $N \times (N - 1)$ possible connections.

This illustrates a fundamental problem in the domain of enterprise systems integration. If one is to proceed by integrating applications in an ad-hoc fashion, the number of connections (i.e., integration mechanisms) that one must implement is of the order of $O(N^2)$. Clearly, a different approach is required, otherwise it would become impossible to implement business processes on top of heterogeneous infrastructures comprised of a large number of systems.

The solution to this problem is to centralize the logic of the process in an orchestrating node which can be configured and reconfigured according to the desired sequence of actions. Incidentally, this approach also reduces the number of required connections between applications. Rather than linking applications to each other, all applications are connected to the central orchestrator, which submits requests to each application according to the logic of the process. In this setup, the number of required connections is of the order of $O(N)$, and the process can be changed and configured much more easily (Fig. 1.4).

A second fundamental problem in the area of integration has to do with system availability at the precise moment when the interaction is needed. For a number

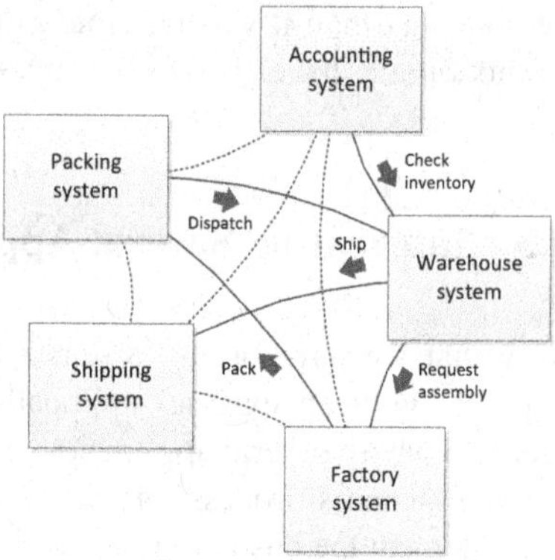

Fig. 1.3 Integrating
applications in an ad-hoc way

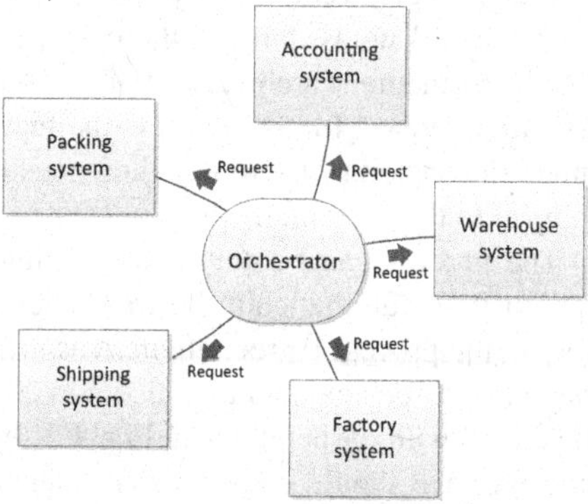

Fig. 1.4 Integrating
applications by means of an
orchestrator

of reasons, enterprise systems may not be available immediately upon request, and
the most common reason is that they are servicing or even overloaded by other
requests. Some systems may be used for tasks that are performed only once in a
while, whereas others may be absolutely central to the core business processes and
therefore are receiving requests all the time. Also, some systems are designated to
be online during part of the day and offline at other times for maintenance or batch
processing. Mobile applications running on wireless platforms may also be offline
or unavailable when located at remote sites.

An application that makes a request to another application cannot be waiting
for response for an unlimited amount of time. Such behavior would certainly block
other applications and create a chain of dependencies that would make the whole
organization work at the speed of its slowest system, or even slower.

For all of these reasons, applications need to communicate in an asynchronous
fashion. Rather than sending a request and blocking while waiting for the response,
each application should leave the request to be processed by the target application
and carry on with its own work. To implement such behavior, each application must
be provided with a message queue, much like a mailbox, from where it can fetch
and serve requests at its own pace, either in order of arrival or according to some

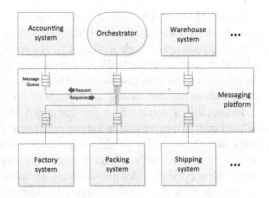

Fig. 1.5 Integrating applications through messaging

defined priority. When ready, the application deposits the response in the message queue of the original requester and proceeds to handle the next request.

Figure 1.5 illustrates the use of message queues for asynchronous messaging between applications. The orchestrator sends requests to each application queue in turn and waits for reply. The response comes back to the orchestrator in the same way as to any other application, through the use of its own message queue.

In fact, Fig. 1.5 illustrates some important facts about contemporary solutions to the problem of integration. In general, integration requires the use of a messaging platform in order to enable interaction and data exchange between applications; this is referred to as application-level integration. The use of a messaging platform opens up the possibility to connect each application to every other, but it does not say how processes are actually implemented. This is the job of an orchestrator, which relies on the messaging platform to coordinate message exchange between applications according to the intended process behavior; this is referred to as process-level integration. The combination of application-level integration and process-level integration is one of the key capabilities of current integration platforms.

1.4 Services: The Ultimate Solution?

For several years, if not decades already, system architects have been looking for ways to develop applications made of distributed components that interact across the network. Several technologies have been developed for this purpose, such as Remote Procedure Calls (RPC), the Common Object Request Broker Architecture (CORBA), and Java Remote Method Invocation (Java RMI). These technologies had much success and were used to build large-scale enterprise systems. Because of their ability to perform method invocations on remote applications, these technologies also became very useful for the purpose of integration at the application level.

Meanwhile, technology kept evolving, and while CORBA, RMI, and other similar technologies made use of their own transport protocols, there was a growing interest in making use of the World Wide Web and its associated technologies, especially HTTP and XML. For that reason, the concepts underlying CORBA, RMI, and others were eventually distilled, extended, and ported into a new generation of technology known as Web services [5]. However, some of the concepts associated with Web services are actually independent of the implementation technology, so the principles and benefits associated with using Web services were later collected and systematized into an abstract concept of *service* [11].

Essentially, a service is a self-contained block of functionality with a well-defined interface expressed in a standard format. The use of a service involves three roles: that of the *service provider* which offers a service implementation; that of the *service requester* which invokes and uses the service; and that of a *service registry* where the service provider publishes information about the service capabilities and the service interface, so that service requesters can find and invoke the service. This simple triangle and the fact that it can be implemented with readily available technologies have been the main success factors that explain the wide dissemination and use of service-oriented approaches.

The relevance of service-oriented approaches in the context of integration comes from the fact that the concept of service may be used to encapsulate the functionality of existing applications. In fact, a service may encapsulate a single application, only part of an application, or even a composition of several applications. Also, once a service is defined and ready to be invoked, other services may invoke that service; this opens up the possibility to create new services of higher level of complexity and abstraction on top of previously existing ones. The ability to create services that aggregate the functionality of other services to provide support for higher-level tasks is referred to as *service composition*.

Through the use of services, which expose the functionality of existing applications and combine the functionality of other services, it becomes possible to define each step in a business process as a service invocation. The ability to compose simpler services into more complex ones ensures that it will be possible to define a service at the right level of abstraction for any given task. Indeed, a wide range of services may be devised, from the lower-level services that simply expose the functionality of existing systems to higher-level services that implement the logic of business tasks. A business process can then be implemented as a series of services invocations. These invocations are carried out in a certain order, so that the output of previously invoked services becomes the input for newly invoked ones. The order and sequence in which services are invoked to implement a given business process is referred to as a *service orchestration*.

An important feature of service-oriented approaches is that not only services but also service compositions and service orchestrations can be exposed through a service interface. While service composition refers to the concept of nesting services into services, service orchestrations provide the possibility of nesting processes into processes, where each process is encapsulated and invoked as a service. This way it is possible to have lower-level processes or workflows connected with data exchange between applications, as well as processes that represent a sequence of high-level business tasks. A workflow of data exchange between applications may be invoked as a service as part of a business task in a higher-level process. In any case, the

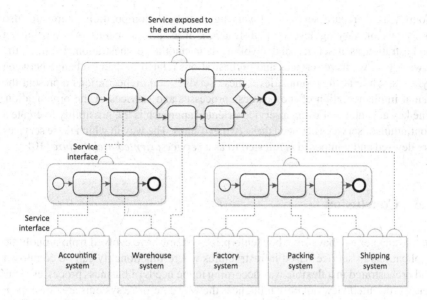

Fig. 1.6 Implementing business processes based on service orchestrations

implementation of these different processes is based on the same mechanism of implementing processes as service orchestrations.

Figure 1.6 illustrates a possible implementation of the example process shown earlier in Fig. 1.1, now based on service orchestrations. At the lowest level, we have the supporting systems that participate in this process. The functionality of these systems has been exposed as a set of services, which can be invoked in different steps of a business process. The high-level business process in this scenario begins by creating a sales order in the accounting system and checking if the product is available in stock. These two steps have been combined into a service orchestration, as can be seen in the lower-left corner of Fig. 1.6. Subsequently, this orchestration is exposed as a service to be invoked in the topmost process. If the product is available in stock, then it is shipped to the customer (top branch in Fig. 1.6), and for this purpose a specific service of the shipping system is invoked. Otherwise, if the product must be manufactured, a sequence of steps involving the warehouse and the factory is invoked. Part of this sequence has been abstracted as a service orchestration as well. The topmost process invokes these lower-level orchestrations as services and in turn exposes itself as a service; the whole business process is exposed as a service to the end customer.

This simple example illustrates several important features of service-oriented approaches. First, the idea is to have a single mechanism to invoke any system; that mechanism is the invocation of a service interface. Second, services can be orchestrated to implement business processes, and these service orchestrations can be exposed as services themselves. Third, orchestrating services and exposing the orchestration as a new service are effective ways to achieve service composition.

Fourth, as there are services of varying degree of composition, there are also processes of varying levels of abstraction; it is just a matter of exposing an orchestration as a service and invoking it in another orchestration. Fifth, at the lowest level we have services and orchestrations related to data exchange between systems, while at the topmost level these services and orchestrations represent the actual implementation of the business processes and services of the organization. The key advantage of using a service-oriented approach is the possibility to create a continuum of services between these two extremes. The way in which these services are devised and composed is referred to as a *service-oriented architecture* [10].

1.5   Conclusion

In this chapter, we have seen how enterprise systems have evolved from monolithic applications to service-based infrastructures where functionality can be composed and orchestrated in a flexible way according to the needs of business processes. This service-oriented view not only influences the way enterprise systems are developed, but also facilitates their integration with each other. Through the use of service interfaces, integration can be achieved at the application logic layer rather than at the data layer or at the user interface layer. Services can be orchestrated, and also interaction with these services should be performed in an asynchronous fashion. In the forthcoming chapters, we will delve into asynchronous messaging and service orchestrations, but before we will introduce the integration platform that will be used in practical examples throughout the book.

Chapter 2
Introduction to BizTalk Server

In the previous chapter we have seen that enterprise systems can be integrated at different application layers, from files to database, application logic, and even at the user interface layer if there is no other option (Fig. 1.2 on page 8). The simplest, most rudimentary way to integrate two systems would be through files. If one system is able to export data in a known format, and another system is able to import data in some format, be it the same or different than the first, then this would suffice to integrate the two systems at the most basic level. In fact, in all current platforms for systems integration, no matter how sophisticated they are, the first step is to define the data formats. These are often called *schemas*.

If the data format used by the source application is different from the one used by the target application, then there are two different schemas, and there needs to be a way to translate the data from one to the other. Current integration platforms support this concept through the use of *transformation maps*.

The critical and common feature of today's integration platforms is the ability to develop integration solutions as sequence of data exchanges between systems. Even if these systems use different data formats, it is possible to describe their integration as a series of steps in which data is read from one system, transformed into another format, and sent to a second system, and so on, until there is a data flow between all systems that have to be integrated to support a given business process. This data flow and transformation between systems can be specified as an *orchestration*.

Finally, data can not only be exported and imported through system files, but it may also be possible to fetch those data from an application, or to deliver the data to another application, through other means, for example some network protocol. Each system may support its own data exchange protocols, and it may as well support standard communication protocols, such as e-mail, FTP, and HTTP. While coordinating the data flow between systems, it becomes necessary to use some protocol to connect with each system. The way in which an integration platform connects to an existing system in order to fetch or deliver data is referred to as a *port*.

Schemas, maps, orchestrations, and ports are the type of *artifacts* from which contemporary integration solutions can be built. In this chapter, we present an

D.R. Ferreira, *Enterprise Systems Integration*, DOI 10.1007/978-3-642-40796-3_2,
© Springer-Verlag Berlin Heidelberg 2013

integration platform that, in a similar way to other state-of-the-art platforms, has all of these features: it provides the ability to define schemas; it provides the ability to define transformation maps between schemas; it provides the ability to implement orchestrations by specifying the data flow between systems; and it provides the ability to configure the way in which the orchestration connects to each system through the use of ports.

This platform, known as Microsoft BizTalk Server or simply BizTalk, is one of several commercial products that make use of similar concepts to provide the capability of developing integration solutions based on orchestrations. Throughout the book, we will make use of this platform to illustrate key concepts associated with each integration technology. A particular feature of BizTalk Server is the use of an internal *message box* through which all messages and data go through. So, instead of communicating directly with applications, an orchestration dispatches and receives data through the message box. As we will see, this also provides the possibility of bypassing orchestrations altogether, and of integrating applications directly at the messaging level. This fits well with the approach in the following chapters, where we will study integration solutions both at the messaging and at the orchestration level. For now, we will delve into the inner workings of BizTalk Server.

2.1   The Message Box

The message box of BizTalk Server is a publish–subscribe system that receives messages from publishers and dispatches them to subscribers. In this context, a publisher is usually defined as a receive port through which BizTalk receives messages. It can also be an orchestration intending to dispatch messages to external systems; in this case, the orchestration publishes the message on the message box, and the message box dispatches it to the intended subscribers. A subscriber is usually a send port through which BizTalk dispatches messages to external applications. The send port can be configured in such a way that if a certain message appears in the message box, it is sent out through that send port.

Multiple send ports may subscribe to the same kind of message; in this case, a copy of the message is sent through each of those send ports. An orchestration may also play the role of subscriber: if a message of interest appears in the message box, the message is routed to the orchestration. Figure 2.1 illustrates how the message box mediates the interaction between publishers and subscribers. Whereas receive ports and send ports are distinct entities, a single orchestration may play the role of both publisher and subscriber, when it needs to send and receive messages at different points in time. In particular, the following steps represent an example of the typical behavior of messages across the message box:

1. A receive port collects data from an external (source) application and publishes a message in the message box.

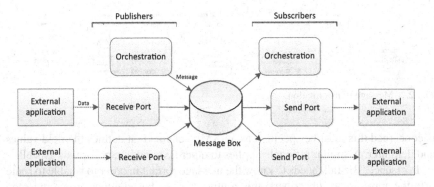

Fig. 2.1 The message box as a publish–subscribe mechanism

2. The message box determines the subscribers for the incoming message—in this case, an orchestration—and forwards the message to that orchestration.
3. The orchestration receives the message and transforms it to another format.
4. The same orchestration then acts as a publisher by placing the new, transformed message in the message box.
5. The message box determines the subscribers for the new message—now it will be a send port—and dispatches the message through that send port to a second (target) application.

In practice, the behavior of the message box is implemented by means of a BizTalk service that is always running in the background, and all messages are stored in a database. The database system used by BizTalk Server is Microsoft SQL Server, so naturally there is a strong dependency between both products. The fact that all messages are stored in a database allows for advanced monitoring capabilities, either by tracking the load and rate of data exchanges between systems (e.g., number of orders processed), or by aggregating the actual content of messages in order to obtain meaningful business indicators (e.g., total sales). The latter is often referred to as Business Activity Monitoring (BAM).

2.2 Schemas and Transformation Maps

In general, all messages that enter or exit the message box need to have a known format. This format does not necessarily have to be based on XML, but in any case it is specified by means of an XML schema. For example, an external system may be able to produce data in text format; a typical example is Comma-Separated Values (CSV), where different fields or values are separated by a delimiter, in this case a comma. The CSV format is popular since it can be easily imported or exported from spreadsheet applications. Even if the message is in CSV format, as far as BizTalk

Fig. 2.2 Message transformation

is concerned this must be specified as an XML schema that defines the field values
and delimiter. A similar rationale applies to other text and binary formats as well.

In essence, BizTalk needs to know the message format in order to be able to route
it to the appropriate subscribers; this routing may be based either on the message
type or on the actual message content. Another reason to provide BizTalk with all
the details regarding message structure is the need to transform messages from one
format into another. When the applications that need to be integrated use different
formats, a message transformation must be done by accommodating the elements
of the source message into the structure of the target message. This is achieved by a
transformation map. Since message schemas are based on XML, it becomes natural
to define transformation maps based on XSLT.

Figure 2.2 illustrates the concept of a transformation map between a source and a
target schema. The transformation map is defined at the level of schemas so that the
same transformation can be applied to all messages with the same source schema.
Upon arrival of the source message, a new target message can be created with
the same structure as the target schema. In other words, the source message is an
instance of the source schema and the target message is a newly created instance
of the target schema. The elements of the target message will be filled with values
from the source message, in the way specified by the transformation map.

Besides copying values from the source message to the target message, an
interesting feature of BizTalk and other similar platforms is the possibility of
applying mathematical, string, and other kinds of operators to the source values
and then use the results to fill out elements in the target message. In the context
of BizTalk, such operators are called *functoids*. There are string functoids to
concatenate strings, to extract part of a string, etc.; mathematical functoids provide
arithmetical operations such as summing, subtracting, and multiplying values;
logical functoids provide the capability of expressing logical conditions such as
testing for equality and comparing values; advanced functoids provide the ability to
count elements, loop through elements, and so on; and many other types of functoids
are available as well. These functoids extend the original capabilities of XSLT.

Functoids can also be linked together such that the output of one functoid
becomes an input for another. For example, if the message is an order with several
items, where each item has a quantity and a unit price, then multiplying quantities
by unit prices and then summing everything provide the total price for the order.
Using functoids, this can be implemented with a loop functoid that iterates over
items, a multiplication functoid that receives as input a quantity and a unit price,
and finally a cumulative sum functoid to sum all terms and provide the result.

Although some very sophisticated functionalities can be implemented by means of functoids—such as accessing a database, executing custom code, and launching an external program—it is good practice to leave these tasks to an orchestration, where such operations can be specified and changed in a more flexible way. In practice, it is not expected to find application logic implemented within a transformation map, although the range of functionality provided by functoids would make it possible to do so.

2.3   Ports, Pipelines, and Adapters

Messages that are produced by external applications and that are intended to BizTalk arrive to the message box through receive ports. On the other hand, messages produced by BizTalk and that are intended to external applications are sent from the message through send ports. The send port is therefore the counterpart of the receive port. As explained above in Sect. 2.1, receive ports are publishers of content in the message box, while send ports are subscribers. There does not have to be a one-to-one mapping between receive ports and send ports; on the contrary, an arbitrary number of receive ports and send ports may exist. In the simplest of applications, however, there will be at least one receive port and one send port.

Let us imagine that application A needs to be integrated with application B, in the sense that B must receive data from A. A solution based on BizTalk would have a receive port to get the data from A and a send port to deliver the data to B. In addition, the send port to B would be configured to subscribe to the kind of messages produced from A. Note that, in general, there may be other receive ports and send ports already configured, so it is important to specify exactly what each send port is subscribing to. If it becomes desirable that a third application C also receives the data from A, then it is just a matter of creating a new send port to C. This kind of flexibility could not be achieved if applications A and B had been integrated directly through some means.

Going a bit further in this example, one may have that applications A, B, and C all use different schemas. In addition, the message box may need to have the message in a fourth schema in order to correctly parse and route the message from A to the appropriate subscribers. To achieve this, each send port and receive port may contain a transformation map. In the case of a receive port, the map transforms an incoming message so that it arrives to the message box in a different schema. In the case of a send port, the map transforms an internal message into another schema before sending it to the external application. The transformation map is an optional component in both receive ports and send ports: it could be that the receive port transforms the incoming message into a schema that is readily understandable by both the message box and applications B and C; or it could be that there is no need to transform the incoming message and that it has to be transformed only when being delivered to either application B or C. Again, this provides more flexibility than would be possible if these applications had been integrated directly.

Besides transformation maps, another component that both send ports and receive ports may contain is the *pipeline*. Pipelines can be used for several purposes, namely: to validate messages; to encode and to decode messages; to divide a message into several parts; to convert between XML and plain text; to encrypt or to decrypt messages; and to digitally sign or to verify the signature in a message. Here too, the concept of *send pipeline* and *receive pipeline* must be distinguished.

A receive pipeline can be used to:

- decode the message (e.g., if the message arrives by an e-mail protocol such as POP3, it may be necessary to use a MIME or S/MIME decoder to decode the message parts),
- disassemble the message (i.e., to split an incoming message into several parts; this is usually based on the message schema, where a certain XML element is associated with the beginning of a new message part; in this case, every time such element appears, a new message is created, so the disassembler component of a receive pipeline is an effective way to split an incoming message into N parts, where each part becomes a new message that enters the message box),
- validate the message (by comparing and ensuring that its structure is consistent with that of an existing, previously defined schema),
- resolve the external party (through the use of digital certificates, if the message has been digitally signed this component can verify that signature).

On the other hand, a send pipeline can be used to:

- assemble the message (here, assembling means just converting the message to another format, typically converting an XML message to a plain text format),
- encode the message (if, for example, the message is to be sent by an e-mail protocol such as SMTP, it may be necessary to use a MIME or S/MIME encoder to encode the message content; if a digital signature is required, this can also be done at this stage).

Figure 2.3 depicts the several stages of receive and send pipelines. For receive pipelines, the message gets decoded, disassembled, validated, and resolved. For send pipelines, the message gets assembled and encoded. These stages are optional, i.e., it is not mandatory to encode or decode messages, assemble or disassemble, etc. These should be used according to the requirements of the integration solution. However, the order of these stages is fixed (hence the name of pipeline), which means that if some stages are used, they must be used in the order depicted in Fig. 2.3. By default, if no pipeline components are used, the message passes through the pipeline without change. Pipelines can therefore be seen as providing a limited and specialized processing at the moment when the message is being received or sent.

An interesting and useful feature of BizTalk pipelines, from the business perspective, is the possibility of disassembling messages. Consider an order message comprising several items (such as a book order comprising several books). Then the disassemble stage of a receive pipeline allows the incoming order (message) to be split into several items (messages) for separate processing; this can be useful,

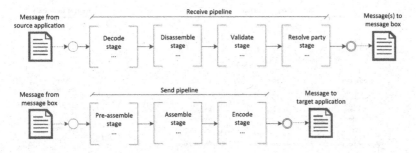

Fig. 2.3 Anatomy of receive and send pipelines

for example, to launch multiple instances of a process that checks the available stock of a given item. Also, note that the validate stage, if used, appears after the disassemble stage, which means that each item message will be validated separately. Unfortunately, the assemble stage of a send pipeline does not support the reverse operation, which would be to aggregate several parts into a single message; however, the send pipeline provides the possibility of additional processing in its pre-assemble stage, where it is possible to make use of custom processing, for example to add or remove data according to the requirements of the target application.

In summary, each port—be it a send port or receive port—has two components: an optional transformation map and a pipeline. In receive ports, messages go through the receive pipeline and then get transformed, if needed, before reaching the message box; in send ports, messages coming from the message box undergo transformation and then go through the send pipeline. In addition, the port needs to know how to connect to the external application, either to fetch the data (in a receive port) or to transmit the data (in a send port). A third component that is always present in each port (and this one is mandatory) is an *adapter*.

Above, we have mentioned the possibility of exchanging messages through e-mail, for example. In this case, the receive port can use POP3 while the send port uses SMTP. BizTalk includes several possible adapters, including adapters for data exchange through SMTP and POP3. Many other protocols, such as HTTP and FTP, are also supported by special-purpose adapters. Also, it is possible to simply read or write the data to disk files; this is provided by the file adapter. In any case, the port must know how to fetch or dispatch data to the external application, so it becomes necessary to choose one of the available adapters for use with each port.

It is now possible to have a complete look at the inner workings of receive ports and send ports, which is provided in Fig. 2.4. Essentially, a port has at least one adapter, one pipeline, and optionally a transformation map. Receive ports are slightly more complex than send ports in the sense that they may contain several *receive locations*. The interest of having several receive locations is to have the possibility of receiving messages through different adapters; a receive location

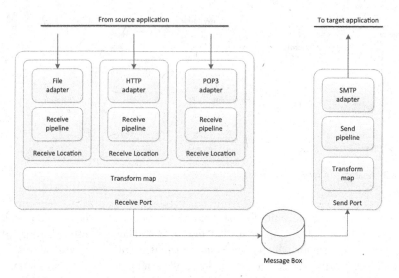

Fig. 2.4 Anatomy of receive ports and send ports

includes an adapter and a receive pipeline. The transformation map, if included in a receive port, applies to the message that comes from any of the receive locations.

In a send port, there is one adapter, one send pipeline, and possibly one transformation map as well. The choice of adapter is limited to the available adapters for send ports; these are in general the same as in receive ports, except when there are different protocols for receiving and for sending messages (as in the case of e-mail). Finally, note that the transformation map is the last component to be applied when a message enters the message box, but it is the first component to be invoked when a message exits through a send port. In a similar fashion, and on the other side, the adapter is the component that is closest to the external applications.

2.4   Orchestrations

Even though applications can be integrated through send ports, receive ports, and the publish–subscribe mechanism available in the message box, this does not provide the most convenient way to devise large integration solutions involving many applications and message exchanges between them. Since each subscriber must be configured separately, in a large scenario it becomes difficult to manage all the exchanges and data flow that takes place between applications. As explained in Sect. 1.3, it becomes useful to have a single point of control—an orchestrator—where all exchanges can be easily configured and changed if necessary.

This is precisely the purpose of using orchestrations: to define the integration between applications as a process, where at each step a different application is

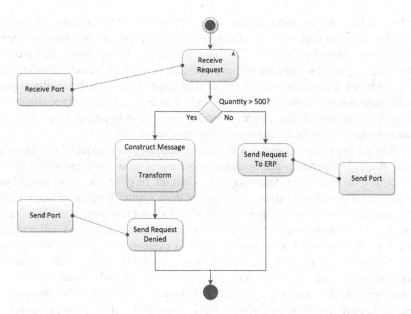

Fig. 2.5 Example of a simple orchestration

invoked, and where the output from one application is passed on as input to another application. In between, it is also possible to transform messages from one schema to another, to suit the requirements of each application. An orchestration therefore defines the message flow between all applications, so that a change of scenario leads to a change in the orchestration, without the need to reconfigure each application.

In BizTalk, orchestrations are created through the use of *shapes*, where each shape represents a certain kind of action. There are shapes to send and to receive messages; these are the most commonly used. There are also shapes to create, transform, and manipulate the content of messages; and there are shapes to control the flow of the orchestration, such as deciding between alternative branches, running parallel branches, looping, terminating the orchestration, and throwing exceptions. Figure 2.5 shows an example of a simple orchestration, which is often used as a first tutorial when introducing BizTalk.

The orchestration represents the following purchase order scenario: when the company runs out of a certain item (e.g., printer cartridges), a new request is created, specifying the desired product and quantity to be purchased. When the request is received by BizTalk, the orchestration in Fig. 2.5 decides whether to approve the request or not. If approved, the request is sent directly to the company's ERP system (branch on the right-hand side). Otherwise, if it is denied, the original message is transformed into a new message and sent back to requester (branch on the left-hand side). In this simple scenario, the rule for approving a purchase request is based on the requested quantity: if the quantity exceeds 500 units the request is denied, otherwise it is approved and forwarded to the ERP system.

To build such orchestration, several shapes are needed. The first shape is a receive to get the purchase request. Typically, an orchestration begins by a receive shape, which triggers the whole process. This first receive is different from other receive shapes that may appear along the orchestration; we say that it is an *activating* receive since it creates a new instance of the orchestration. In this example, the arrival of each new request at the receive port connected to the receive shape triggers a new instance of this orchestration. Several orchestration instances may be active simultaneously, while their execution is managed separately.

Following the receive, there is a branching condition that requires the use of a decide shape. In general, a decide shape may have several branches, with each of them corresponding to a different logical condition. In principle, these conditions will be mutually exclusive, so that only one of them applies for a given input. Even if the conditions are not mutually exclusive, this does not represent a problem since, in practice, the conditions are evaluated from left to right, so execution will proceed through the first branch having a condition that evaluates to true. By convention, the rightmost branch is an "else" case, meaning that it will be executed if no other branches are selected. This ensures that at least one branch will execute.

Following the decision shape, the right-side branch simply dispatches the request message through a send shape connected to a send port. On the left-side branch, the message is transformed and sent through another send shape connected to a send port. For the message transformation, there are actually two different shapes, since the transform shape is inside a construct message shape. The construct message shape is necessary since the transform shape will fill the content of a newly created message. This new message, with a different structure from the original request, will be dispatched through the send shape that comes immediately afterwards.

The transform shape uses a transformation map, as explained in Sect. 2.2, to fill in the elements of a target message based on the content of a source message. In this scenario, the source message is the original request, and the target message is the denied request message. To inform the requester that a particular request has been denied, it is not necessary to repeat all the details of the request. If there is a unique request number, or if it can be safely assumed that there are no two requests for the same product with the same quantity, it suffices to include that info in the denied request message in order to inform the requester of which request has been denied. Hence, the transformation map may specify that only the request number or only the product and quantity are to be included in the target message.

As a general rule, messages are immutable variables that cannot be changed during orchestration execution. For example, it is not possible to transform the initial request message into a denied request message; rather, a new message must be created, and that is precisely the purpose of the construct message shape. The advantage is that all messages that have been created at some point in the orchestration (and this includes the initial message that triggered the orchestration as well) are kept in their original form and can be used at any later step. Their original content cannot be changed outside the scope of a construct message shape.

2.5   BizTalk Applications

The four kinds of artifacts presented in the previous sections—schemas, transformation maps, pipelines, and orchestrations—are the basic building blocks for
developing integration solutions based on BizTalk. Together, they define how the
solution will behave: the schemas define what kind of messages will be sent and
received, the transformation maps define how messages from one schema can be
transformed into another schema, the pipelines define how messages can be encoded
or decoded to fit the requirements of external applications, and orchestrations
implement the desired message flow between those applications. These artifacts
work in tandem with each other and together they constitute a *BizTalk application*.

Essentially, a BizTalk application is a software package; it takes the form of
a library of compiled code, which contains all the artifacts required to run the
application. Here, running the application means actually sending messages and
receiving messages through ports, as well as running the message flow described in
the orchestration, if there is one. However, contrary to other types of applications, a
BizTalk application is not a stand-alone executable; rather, it is a library that must
be installed in the BizTalk run-time platform, and that will be run by the BizTalk
services. The act of installing a new BizTalk application in the BizTalk run-time
platform is referred to as the *deployment* of the BizTalk application.

Therefore, there are two separate phases to make a BizTalk application ready to
run: one is to compile all artifacts into a library, and the other is to deploy the library
to the BizTalk run-time platform. In this context, compiling means compiling actual
code. The fact is that an orchestration, which is typically specified in graphical form
as in Fig. 2.5, is translated by BizTalk into C# code. This code is compiled, together
with the remaining artifacts, into a .NET assembly library (DLL). Deploying this
library means installing it in the operating system and registering it in the BizTalk
run-time platform. Typically, the user will then configure the send and receive ports,
if they have not been configured earlier, and will start the application. From this
moment on, the BizTalk application is ready to receive messages.

Figure 2.6 illustrates the typical behavior of a BizTalk application at run-time.
When the application starts, all receive ports and send ports become enabled; and
when a new message arrives through a receive port, the message is published in the
message box. If the message has a recognized schema, and there are subscribers for
that schema, the message is forwarded to those subscribers. A subscriber may be a
send port or an orchestration; for an orchestration to be a subscriber, it must have
a receive shape that is active at that point (i.e., waiting for a message) and that is
configured to receive messages with such schema.

Here, two scenarios must be distinguished: either the receive shape belongs to a
running instance of an orchestration, or it is an activating receive (see Sect. 2.4) that
triggers the whole orchestration (i.e., it creates a new instance of that orchestration).
In any case, be it an orchestration that was already running or an orchestration
that has just been instantiated by the arrival of the incoming message, for the
orchestration the incoming message is a newly created variable that is an instance

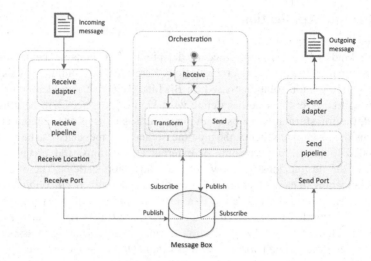

Fig. 2.6 Typical behavior of a BizTalk application

of a known schema. This variable may be provided as input to transformations, or it may be sent to an external application through the use of a send shape.

While a receive shape makes the orchestration behave as a message subscriber, the send shape makes the orchestration behave like a message publisher, as shown in Fig. 2.6. Send ports are message subscribers, so if a message with the appropriate schema appears in the message box, it will be dispatched through send ports that subscribe to that schema. Usually, an orchestration includes at least a specification of the *logical ports* that it uses to receive and send messages. A logical port can be seen as a placeholder for a *physical port* that has not been configured yet. The physical port has all the configurations that are necessary to fetch/deliver the message from/to its actual location. After deployment of a BizTalk application, one of the tasks that an administrator must do before starting the application is to create and configure the physical ports, as shown on the left- and right-hand sides of Fig. 2.6. Alternatively, but not as often done, the physical ports can be configured at design-time, when the orchestration is being developed.

2.6 Business Rules

In the example of Sect. 2.4, the decision to approve or deny a purchase request was made automatically based on the quantity value. Even though such rule may seem unrealistic in a real-world scenario, it serves well the purpose of illustrating the kind of decisions that can be embedded into an orchestration. However, including this rule by means of a decide shape has a severe inconvenient: should the rule be

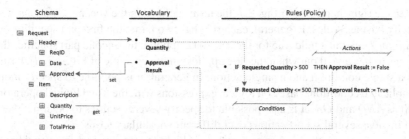

Fig. 2.7 Specification of business rules

changed, it will be necessary to recompile and redeploy the orchestration. In a sense, the rule is hard-coded in the orchestration, and it is not easy to change it.

In addition, it is quite likely that these rules will be changed by business people, rather than technical developers, so it would be very convenient to provide the possibility of configuring these rules outside the development environment of BizTalk applications, and being able to change them for running orchestrations, without the need to interrupt or redeploy them. Indeed, BizTalk provides such possibilities through the use of *business rules*.

The business rule component of BizTalk is provided as a separate application for business users. These can configure the rules to be invoked by an orchestration during run-time. Since rules are defined in an external component, it is possible to configure and change them independently of the orchestration which invokes them. In fact, rules can be changed at any time before an orchestration actually invokes them. The deployment of a new version of business rules implies that any subsequent call to those rules will make use of the latest version. Rules can be invoked in an orchestration by means of the *call rules* shape.

The use of business rules requires, first of all, that a *business vocabulary* is created. A vocabulary is a set of terms that can be used to define business rules. In the previous example, *quantity* would be a relevant term. Each term gives meaning to a certain value that can be read from, or written to, a message. To that end, it is necessary to specify the exact message element where the value will be read from or written to. Since messages are instances of a given schema, the vocabulary contains a set of definitions of each term and its corresponding schema element.

Figure 2.7 illustrates the relationship between schemas, vocabulary, and rules. The terms in a vocabulary have a direct relationship to schema elements, and this relationship may involve a *get* (read value from element) or a *set* (write value to element) operation. In Fig. 2.7 there is one example of each: the term *Requested Quantity* is read from the schema element *Request/Item/Quantity*, while *Approval Result* is written to the schema element *Request/Header/Approved*. For simplicity, both elements belong to the same schema, but it could be that these terms refer to elements in different schemas. In general, it is possible to define vocabulary terms involving get or set operations over the elements of any available schema.

On the right-hand side of Fig. 2.7, the terms defined in the vocabulary are used to specify business rules. In general, each rule has two parts: the first part specifies the *conditions* that must hold true for the rule to be applied; the second part specifies the actions to be carried out when the rule applies. In the example of Fig. 2.7, each rule has a single condition and a single action. In general, it is possible to specify more complicated conditions based on logical expressions with the usual logical operators such as *AND* and *OR*. It is also possible to specify several actions to be done; these will involve several set operations over different vocabulary terms.

A set of rules define a business policy, which can be invoked from within an orchestration by means of the call rules shape. This shape is straightforward to configure: basically, it needs to know which policy (set of rules) will be invoked, and which messages will be provided as input. Naturally, these messages must already exist in the orchestration at the time when the rules are invoked; either they have been received by the orchestration, or they have been constructed during the orchestration. Additionally, the messages must be instances of the same schemas that have been used to define the vocabulary. For example, to invoke the rules in Fig. 2.7 it is necessary to provide as input the request message, since the vocabulary terms that are used in the rules have been defined based on the request schema.

The result of invoking a business policy is—should any of the rule conditions apply—a set of actions performed over the input messages. The set operation associated with a vocabulary term effectively changes the value of the corresponding message element, so this is an exception to the general principle that messages are immutable across the orchestration. Through the use of set operations, it becomes possible to change the content of messages, so that the forthcoming steps in the orchestration will see the new content.

A typical application of a business policy is to set the price, or discount, for a certain product or customer. For example, a 3-for-2 promotion could state that when buying two products, the third is for free. In this case, it would be useful to have a rule based on the product and quantity ordered. Another example is to set the price based on customer status, so that regular and premium customers have different discounts; this discount can also be implemented by the use of an appropriate rule. In any case, the invocation of the business policy sets the price or discount outside of the orchestration, but henceforth to be used within the orchestration.

It should be noted that in the previous example of the purchase request (Fig. 2.5), the use of a business policy does not replace the need for a decide shape in the orchestration. In fact, the insertion of a call rules shape between the initial receive and the decide shape in Fig. 2.5 can be used to determine whether the request should be approved or not, according to the business rules in Fig. 2.7. However, these rules just set the value of the *Approved* element in the original message request; it will be necessary to use a decide shape to test whether this value is actually true or false. The orchestration can then proceed either to the left or to the right branch in Fig. 2.5. So, in conclusion, business rules are not a way to avoid decisions in an orchestration, they are just a way of making those decision rules more explicit and easier to change without having to redeploy the orchestration.

2.7 Conclusion

BizTalk Server is an example of a state-of-the-art platform for enterprise systems integration. With this platform, integration solutions can be built as a collection of artifacts, each having a different purpose: schemas are used to specify the structure of messages to be exchanged with external applications; transformation maps are used to create new messages from existing ones, where new messages may contain the same data but in a different format; pipelines are a means of applying specialized processing tasks over messages that are about to enter or exit the message box; and, finally, orchestrations are a way to implement the process behavior associated with message exchanges between applications.

Modern platforms for enterprise systems integration provide the ability to develop integration solutions based on these or similar artifacts. The ability to specify schemas, transformation maps, and orchestrations is present in other platforms as well. So, while BizTalk has certainly its own particularities, the features that have been presented here are sufficiently representative and pervasive in other integration platforms. The key capability of these platforms is the ability to develop integration solutions based on orchestrating the message exchanges between systems.

In effect, the run-time environment for such orchestrations is, in general, and as is the case with BizTalk, a messaging infrastructure. This type of infrastructure is absolutely critical to enable the implementation of orchestrations on top of heterogeneous systems. The required features and capabilities of such messaging infrastructures are a topic to be discussed in detail throughout the next chapter.

Part II
Messaging

Chapter 3
Messaging Systems

One of the essential principles in enterprise systems integration is the use of asynchronous communication between applications. This is because applications cannot afford to interact synchronously, i.e., to block while waiting for the response from other applications. Such behavior would not only decrease the overall performance, but it would also bring the organization to a stand-still, either by mutual deadlock of applications or by an amount of load that would make applications stop servicing requests. An environment comprising several applications that communicate synchronously would, at best, operate at the speed of its lowest component.

Enterprise systems must therefore communicate asynchronously, to allow each application to respond to requests at its own pace, while other applications proceed with their own work. In a sense, this is similar to the use of mail: rather than phoning someone, which would require that person to be immediately available to speak on the phone, one may choose to send a letter or e-mail instead, allowing the recipient to handle the message when available. Of course, following the same analogy, someone must take care of sending the letter or e-mail from the sender to the recipient; both the sender and the recipient expect this to be done reliably, so that the message does not become lost somewhere along the way.

Messaging systems fulfill a similar purpose: they provide the means for asynchronous communication between sender and receiver, and they also provide reliability in message delivery. The features and capabilities of messaging systems are relatively standardized to the point that different systems, or systems developed by different providers, may provide the same interface to applications. Such is the goal of the Java Message Service (JMS), which is a platform-neutral, Java-based interface for messaging systems. On the other hand, it becomes useful to look at how a particular messaging system is implemented, and for that purpose this chapter presents an overview of Microsoft Message Queuing (MSMQ) as well.

Although MSMQ does not conform to the JMS interface, it can be easily integrated with BizTalk and it provides a different perspective of how messaging systems can be implemented. But even if JMS and MSMQ have different implementations, they share a set of common concepts that are pervasive to all messaging systems. These fundamental concepts of messaging systems are explained next.

D.R. Ferreira, *Enterprise Systems Integration*, DOI 10.1007/978-3-642-40796-3_3,

3.1 Fundamental Concepts

In Chap. 1, Fig. 1.5 illustrated the need for a messaging platform in order to support asynchronous communication between applications. The fundamental concept behind such messaging platform is the use of message queues, with one queue for each application, which works as a "mailbox" for that application. There are other fundamental concepts associated with messaging systems, and it becomes useful to have a broad view of these concepts before focusing on any messaging system in particular, for two reasons: on one hand, particular messaging systems can be seen as essentially different implementations of the same common concepts; on the other hand, a given messaging system may not implement all of these concepts, so it becomes possible to have an idea of the extent of functionality when compared to the full range of capabilities that are often associated with messaging systems.

Figure 3.1 illustrates the basic principle of data exchange between applications through asynchronous messaging. The sender, or source application, creates a new message with the desired data, to be sent to the target application. In the source application, the data is stored in files or memory according to internal data structures. When writing the data to a message, those data must be converted to a schema that can be understood by the target application. The message is delivered by the source application to the message channel, so that the channel will dispatch it to the target application. Information about the recipient, as well as other info such as message priority, and expiry date, are not part of the actual content of the message, but are written on the message envelope.

The channel routes and forwards the message to the target application, just like a post office takes care of sending a letter to the intended recipient. In principle, the routing is based on the information contained in the message envelope alone, but in the case of messaging systems there is also the option of determining the route or recipient based on the actual message content. When the message arrives at the destination, the channel delivers it to the receiving end. The target application then has access to the envelope, to the message, and to its content. The message content must be in a schema that can be understood, but once the data is read, those data may be stored in some internal data structures of the target application.

The way that the source application stores the data internally may be different from the way the target application does it. What these applications should agree on is on the use of a given channel and a certain message schema. If this cannot be done, because the applications have been developed independently and there is no way to change them in order to make them use a common schema, then the message system may provide message translation capabilities in order to convert the schema used by the source application into that used by the target application. This effectively corresponds to the use of transformation maps.

Overall, the mechanisms and capabilities available in messaging systems can be divided into six groups, i.e., into those that pertain to *channels*, *messages*, *pipelines*, *routers*, *translators*, or *endpoints* [15]. These represent the fundamental concepts associated with messaging systems.

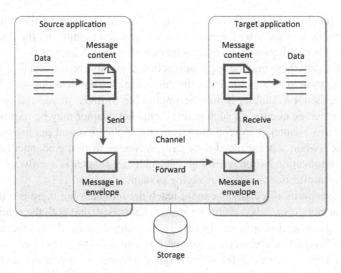

Fig. 3.1 Data exchange between applications through messaging

3.1.1 Channels

Essentially, channels correspond to the message queues available or created in the messaging system. Sending a message means that a source application asks the messaging system to deliver a message to the message queue of the target application. For this purpose, each channel (queue) has a unique name within the messaging system. Also, a channel guarantees persistence so that no message is lost in its route between sender and receiver (this is the reason for having the storage component associated with the channel in Fig. 3.1).

Channels can be point-to-point, i.e., connecting one sending application to one receiving application, or they may be publish–subscribe, in which case the sender is referred to as *publisher* and the receivers are called *subscribers*. Message queues are appropriate for point-to-point messaging, since each queue usually belongs to a single, determinate target application. Different senders may dispatch messages to the same queue, but the queue is usually read by a single receiver. To implement the publish/subscribe paradigm, where there can be several receivers for the same message, messaging systems typically provide a different mechanism—called a *topic*—which admits several subscribers. When a publisher sends a message to a topic, every subscriber of that topic receives a copy of the message.

Between a sender and a receiver, a channel may be used to transmit several kinds of messages. Alternatively, there may be different channels for different kinds of messages. Also, there may be special-purpose channels, such as a channel for dropping off invalid messages, or to drop off messages that could not be delivered (for this purpose, there is usually a dedicated channel called the *dead-letter channel*). It is the job of an administrator to keep monitoring the dead-letter channel to check if there were messages that could not be delivered.

In some cases, there may be applications that are unable to interact directly with a messaging system. For example, in the case of legacy applications for which the source code is not available, it may be impossible to make them send or receive data from message queues. In such cases, a channel adapter may be required. The purpose of this adapter is to read data from the application and publish messages in a channel (when sending), and to receive messages from the channel and write data to the application (when receiving). The channel adapter is a software layer in between the application and the messaging system.

In other scenario, if a channel cannot reach the recipient but there is a different channel that can do so, it is possible to *bridge* channels so that both the sending and the receiving application appear to be using a common channel when in fact it is a set of channels bridged, or connected, together. It is also possible, at least conceptually, to bridge channels across different messaging systems, so that a channel in one platform or administrative domain may work as an extension of another channel in a second platform or administrative domain. An example would be to have a sending application in Java publishing messages using JMS and a receiving application in C# consuming messages through MSMQ; in this case, a bridge between message channels in JMS and MSMQ would be required.

3.1.2 Messages

A message can be seen as a package of data that travels through a channel. Semantically, the message may carry a document, a command, or an event. For example, an invoice can be regarded as a document that contains a full description of the products that were ordered; it can also be interpreted as a command for the customer to pay for the order; and it may mean that the products have been shipped and in this case it serves as an event. In any case, a message typically has a *header* (in a mail system, this can be seen as the *envelope*) and a *body* (its actual content).

The message header contains metadata such as information about the sender, the destination, and the message priority. Usually the message header is used only by the messaging system for routing purposes and is ignored by the applications. On the other hand, the message body contains application data. The content of the message body is used by applications and is usually ignored by the messaging system. However, in some scenarios it may be useful to have the messaging system determine the routing of messages based on the actual content of the message body; such practice is known as *content-based routing*, to be explained ahead.

In a request–response interaction between two applications, the request message is usually a command and the response message may contain one or more documents. While a channel is used to deliver the request to the target application, another channel must be used for the source application to receive the response.

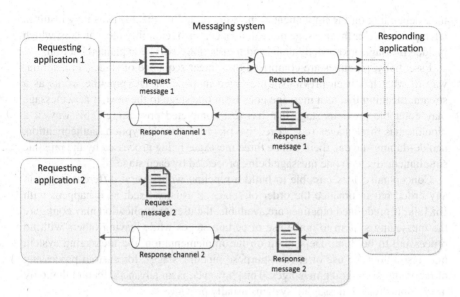

Fig. 3.2 Request–response interaction with the response channel being specified in the request

This a analogous to what would happen in a mail system, where each user has its own mailbox: the mailbox where the request message is dropped is different from the mailbox where the response is returned. In other words, each requester has its own mailbox where the response should be delivered; this is illustrated in Fig. 3.2.

When sending messages, it is possible to specify additional parameters such as *time to live* or *expiry date*. These parameters will be stored in the message header, as header fields. If the message is not delivered within the specified time frame, it ends up being redirected to the dead-letter channel. These and other advanced features depend to some extent on the particular messaging system being used. In general, these features can be configured when the message in being created in the messaging system, by specifying the appropriate values for the header fields. At the receiving end, if desired, applications have access to the message header and it is possible to read the values of all header fields. Usually, however, the receiving application will be mainly interested in the content of the message body.

3.1.3 Pipelines

Pipelines, in a similar way to what happens in BizTalk (see Sect. 2.3), are intended to perform specialized processing tasks as the message enters or exits the message channel. These tasks include message encryption or decryption, authentication based on digital certificates, and *de-duping*, i.e., removing duplicate messages. The need for message de-duping in messaging systems can be explained by the fact that, depending on the implementation, some reliability mechanisms may result in attempts to deliver the message more than once. Such reliability mechanisms, which include message acknowledgments and transactions, will be explained later on.

Essentially, pipelines are comprised of a linear sequence of stages, in a similar way to what has been previously presented in Fig. 2.3. The pipeline works as a stream, meaning that as a message goes from one stage to the next, a new message may enter the previous stage that has just completed processing. This way, if a pipeline has three stages (e.g., a receive pipeline with decryption, authentication, and de-duping stages), there can be three messages being processed by the pipeline simultaneously, with one message being processed by each stage.

Conceptually, it is possible to build a pipeline with several different stages in any order, but in practice the order of stages is usually fixed, as it happens with BizTalk. If predefined pipelines are available, the user or application may configure the messaging system to make use of certain stages while leaving others with no processing to be done. Depending on the implementation, the messaging system may also allow the use of special-purpose pipeline stages, for custom processing of incoming or outgoing messages. This, however, is an advanced feature that only more sophisticated messaging systems usually provide.

Another kind of processing tasks that pipelines may provide is the possibility of *splitting* and *aggregating* messages. These concepts are equivalent to disassembling and assembling messages, respectively, as discussed in Sect. 2.3. Splitting means creating several messages out of a single message, by dividing the original message in parts. With messages whose content can represented by an XML schema, the parts may correspond to several occurrences of a certain XML element. A typical example is that of an order with several items, where each item must be processed individually as if it were a separate message.

However, when splitting items coming from the same order, it may be necessary to include and replicate the original order number in each item. This allows to merge the items again after processing, for example to produce a shipping order with all items. This merging corresponds to the concept of aggregation, which is the counterpart of splitting. Typically, an aggregation stage works in conjunction with a previous splitting stage, as illustrated in Fig. 3.3.

Aggregation brings additional problems, such as knowing how many messages should be aggregated, or how long the aggregation should wait for message parts until it finishes and wraps up those parts as a single output message. Also, some notion of *correlation* between messages must exist, e.g., only items coming from the same order should be aggregated in a new shipping order (the important concept of correlation will be discussed ahead in Sect. 3.4).

In practice, given that pipelines work by processing a stream of messages, it becomes difficult to implement aggregation since, in some cases, this would require knowing which messages or how many messages will arrive in advance. For this reason, some messaging systems provide splitting capabilities but do not provide aggregation capabilities in pipelines. However, the same effect can sometimes be obtained by other means such as implementing the behavior in an orchestration, if the messaging system includes support for orchestration logic.

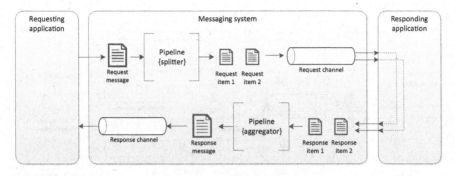

Fig. 3.3 Message splitting and aggregation through pipelines

3.1.4 Routers

Basically, routers are the components of a messaging system that decide the ultimate destination of messages. Given that different messages may be handled by different applications, routers allow this decision to be embedded in the messaging system itself, so that sending applications just publish messages, and receiving applications just wait for the messaging system to deliver them, without having to embed routing logic in any of the applications. Placing the routing logic inside the messaging system also provides a centralized point of control for the whole integration solution.

In an analogy with a mail system, a messaging system may also route messages according to the metadata contained in the message header or envelope. But, in addition to that, a messaging system may also decide the routing of messages according to the actual content found in the message body. This is known as *content-based routing* and it allows applications to publish messages without specifying the recipient. The message system itself will decide what to do with such kind of message.

There are therefore three options for routing messages between applications. At this point, we know that either the sending application specifies the recipient, in which case the routing logic is embedded in the sender; or the messaging system decides the recipient, in which case the routing logic is embedded in the system. The third option is to have no routing logic at all, and the messaging system just broadcasts messages to every possible recipient. In this case, each target applications will decide what to do with the message, either handle or just ignore it.

For this third option it becomes useful to have a special component called a *message filter*. Each target application may have a message filter that decides which messages actually go through the filter and reach that recipient. The use of message filters is a way to simplify the routing logic at the messaging system (it just broadcasts messages) and still have some level of control on which messages reach a given destination. Usually, more sophisticated routing mechanisms are preferred.

One such mechanism is *dynamic routing*, in which receiving applications may themselves configure, at run-time, the rules that determine which messages they will

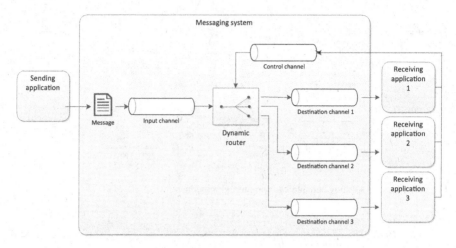

Fig. 3.4 Dynamic routing of messages according to run-time rules

receive. This is effectively a way to implement the publish/subscribe paradigm by
letting target applications decide which messages they are interested in. Since each
application defines its own rules, the rules for different applications are not mutually
exclusive, so any N-out-of-M (with $0 \leq N \leq M$) applications may receive a copy
of the same message. This routing approach will require a special-purpose *control
channel*, through which applications send their subscription rules to the messaging
system. This is illustrated in Fig. 3.4.

Another routing approach which becomes especially important in the context
of integration is *process-based routing*. Put simply, this means having a process
manager—or orchestrator—coordinating the interactions between several applications. Figure 3.5 illustrates this concept. After a triggering message is received from
Application A, the process manager creates and initiates the execution of a new
process instance. This process may implement, for example, a linear sequence of
interactions with applications B, C, and D such that the first action is to send a
request to Application B and wait for a response, then to Application C and wait
for response, and then finally to Application D. The idea is that the process logic
can be changed in a flexible way to implement any desired behavior.

Compared to other routing mechanisms, process-based routing has the distinctive
advantage of allowing the implementation of more sophisticated behavior in a
flexible way, while providing a central point of control where the process logic
can be configured. On the downside, process-based routing may constrain the
performance of the messaging system by requiring all messages to go through that
central point. In practice, this effectively represents a problem of process-based
integration platforms which, when subject to heavy loads in terms of number and
rate at which incoming messages arrive, may have difficulties responding in a timely
fashion, or may even run out of available resources, especially memory.

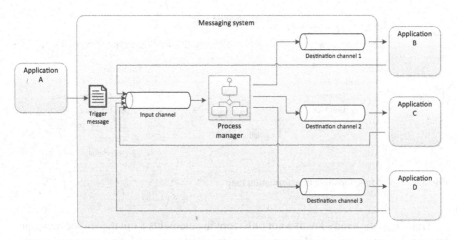

Fig. 3.5 Routing of messages through a process manager

It is therefore a common practice in integration platforms to keep loaded in memory only those process instances which are currently active. Other instances showing no activity for a certain period of time may be unloaded and saved to persistent storage, usually a database. In BizTalk Server, this is precisely what happens when, for example, an instance of an orchestration is waiting to receive a message that is taking too long to arrive. In this case, BizTalk will unload that instance from memory and load it back to memory when the message arrives. Such behavior is referred to as *dehydration* (when unloading from memory) and *rehydration* (when reloading). The act of dehydrating and rehydrating an orchestration instance does not usually result in any noticeable decrease in the performance of that instance.

3.1.5 Translators

In messaging systems, translators provide the ability to convert message content from one structure into another. Since each application may have its own requirements regarding the messages it is able to receive, a translator becomes useful to create messages that are in a proper format to be processed by the target application. A translator is specified in terms of metadata: it must know the structure of the source message, it must know the structure of the target message, and it must know how to fill in the content of the target message based on the content of the source message. In general, the structure of messages is specified by means of schemas, and the translation is specified by means of a schema transformation. So the preferred way to implement translators is by means of transformation maps.

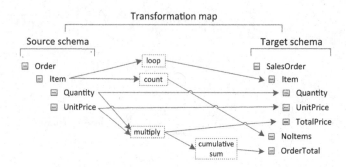

Fig. 3.6 Use of functoids in a transformation map

Transformation may involve not only copying elements from the source message to the target message, but also carrying out computations with data from the source message in order to create the results that are to be stored in the target message. A typical example is when the source message is a sales order with several items, each with a quantity and unit price, and the target message needs to store the number of items, the total price for each item (i.e., multiplying unit price by quantity), and the total price for the order (the sum of all the previous multiplications). Such capabilities are usually attained through the use of special functions in the transformation map. In BizTalk, as explained in Sect. 2.2, these functions are known as functoids. Figure 3.6 illustrates the use of functoids to implement the above example.

A functoid may have one or more inputs, and one output. The loop functoid replicates all occurrences of a given element from the source message into the target message. The counting functoid, as the name implies, counts the number of occurrences of a given element. The multiplication is an example of a functoid that has more than one input. Also, the output of this functoid is being used for two different purposes: one is to fill in the total price of each item, and the other is to serve as input to a cumulative sum functoid which sums up the results of all multiplications. Many other functoids exists, from string operations such as concatenation and substring extraction, to advanced functionalities such as database lookup.

Besides being able to transfer data from a source message to a destination message, a translator can also be used as a *content filter* or as a *content enricher*. In a content filter, only the minimal required data are transferred to the target message, and everything else from the source message is omitted. Such filtering finds application where an application *A* would not like to share sensitive data with application *B* but still needs to send some minimal information so that application *B* can carry out its job. On the contrary, a content enricher achieves the opposite effect of augmenting a target message with additional data that is not available in the source message, and that cannot be computed from the data available in the source message. Such enrichment usually involves fetching data from external sources, and it is used to meet the requirements of the target application.

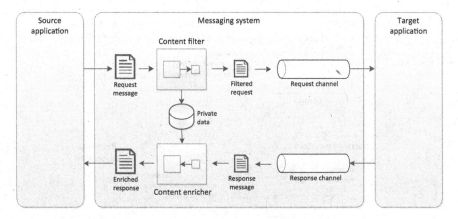

Fig. 3.7 Use of content filter and enricher to protect private data

Figure 3.7 illustrates the use of a combination of content filter and content enricher to interact with a remote application without having to disclose the full message data. For example, a reseller (source application) may want to ask a supplier (target application) whether it has some product in stock. The original request message contains the details about the product and also about the customer that requested such product from the reseller. The details about the customer are to be kept private, so these data are filtered out from the request. When the supplier returns the response, the customer details are filled back into the message through a content enricher. As another example, a company may ask a third-party logistics partner to deliver some package without disclosing its actual contents. For this purpose, the company sends only the package identifier, while the package details are filtered out. Afterwards, when the partner confirms that the package has been delivered, it returns the same package identifier, and the company is able to retrieve the information about the products that have just been delivered.

Such filtering and enriching of message data can be accomplished in a more flexible way through the use of orchestrations, but this may require capabilities that are beyond those that are typically available in a messaging system. To implement the same behavior in an orchestration, one would have to (1) receive the request message, (2) interact with a database in order to store the private data, (3) filter the request message via a transformation map, (4) send the filtered request to the target application, (5) wait for the response to arrive, (6) query the database to in order to fetch the private data, and (7) enrich the response through a second transformation map. Such orchestration would require at least four receives, three sends, and two transforms, but it would make the integration logic more explicit and easier to manage than what would happen if the logic is embedded in translation components. In general, it is good practice to implement the integration logic in an orchestration, if possible, rather than through the use of advanced capabilities of translators.

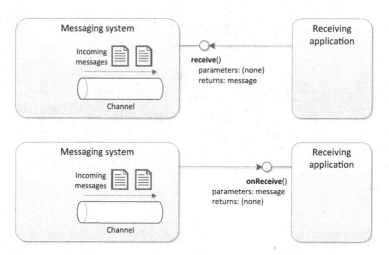

Fig. 3.8 Polling vs. callback when receiving messages

3.1.6   *Endpoints*

The concept of endpoint has to do with the way applications connect and interact with the messaging system. An endpoint refers to the application code that is used exclusively to create messages and send them through the messaging system, as well as receiving messages and accessing their content. When sending messages, the interaction between the application and the messaging system is usually a synchronous call: the application simply invokes a method to send messages. On the other hand, when receiving messages there are two possible behaviors: either the application keeps *polling* the messaging system to check whether a new message has arrived, or the messaging system itself invokes a *callback* method on the application to deliver messages whenever new messages arrive.

The difference between polling and callback is in who invokes whom; when polling, the application invokes a synchronous method on the messaging system, and this method blocks until a new message arrives in the channel. When using callback, it is the messaging system which invokes a synchronous method on the application to deliver a newly arrived message; the message is passed as a parameter to the callback method, and this method should return as soon as possible in order to release the corresponding thread in the messaging system. Figure 3.8 illustrates the two endpoint behaviors. Usually, the polling method implemented by the messaging system receives no parameters and returns a reference to a message object, while the callback method implemented by the application receives a reference to the message as input parameter and returns nothing.

Another possibility is to have transactional endpoints that support message transactions between the application and the messaging system. Here, it should be noted that the concept of transaction applies only in the context of an endpoint and should not be used to denote interactions between end applications. Such end-to-end inter-actions can only be regarded as being transactional in the sense that applications at both ends use transactional endpoints, and the messaging system itself may provide reliability mechanisms between endpoints as well, to ensure for example that mes-sages cannot be lost. In any case, a message transaction refers always to a interaction between an application and the messaging system alone. The topic of transactions is sufficiently important to be explained in a separate section, as comes next.

3.2 Message Transactions

In database systems, the concept of transaction is associated with a set of operations that are performed as a single unit and that must leave the database in a consistent state [27]. In messaging systems, a similar concept applies: a transaction is a set of send and/or receive operations that are performed as a single unit and that must not leave the system in any intermediate, inconsistent state; either the whole set of operations succeed, or the message system must revert to the last, previous consistent state. In particular, the successful execution of a message transaction comprising send and/or receive operations implies that:

1. the application has successfully consumed all messages that it intended to receive;
2. the application has successfully produced all messages that it intends to send.

Here, it should be noted the careful choice of words. The messages are *consumed*, meaning that they have been received and removed from their original channel or queue. Also, about the messages that the application *produced* and intends to send: these messages will be sent to their destination only after the transaction completes successfully. Such behavior is necessary to ensure that, should the transaction fail, the messaging system can revert to the previous state. A transaction that fails therefore results in the following behavior:

1. all messages that have been consumed by the application are placed back again in their original queues;
2. all messages that have been produced are discarded by the messaging system.

This is conceptually equivalent to a transaction *rollback*. By returning the mes-sages that have been consumed to their original queues, and discarding messages that have been produced, this results in the state of the messaging system that existed before the transaction had begun. Such recovery approach, however, has some implications on the interactions that can actually be supported through transactions. Since a message transaction involves a set of send and/or receive operations, one must consider the following scenarios:

- A message transaction that comprises only send operations—this creates no problem from the recovery point of view; in case the transaction fails, all

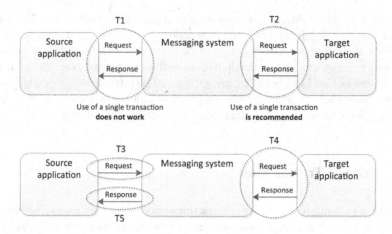

Fig. 3.9 The use of transactions in a request–response scenario

messages will be discarded. The messaging system will not initiate the actual send operation before the transaction commits.

- A message transaction that comprises only receive operations—this creates no problem as well; in case the transaction fails, all messages that have been received are returned to their original queue. After the transaction commits, however, there is no turning back, and the messages have disappeared from the messaging system.
- A message transaction that comprises receive operations and send operations, in this order—this creates no problem and is actually a common scenario for the use of message transactions. An application that receives a message and must produce another message in response should in fact do so within the context of a transaction, so that, if something fails in between, on restarting the application the original request is again available in the queue and the application can try again. This way, it is guaranteed that no request is lost or is left without response.
- A message transaction that comprises send operations and receive operations, in this order—if the messages to be received are responses to the messages that are to be sent, then this will not work, because the messages to be sent will not be sent until the transaction commits, and the transaction will not commit until the responses are received. In a request–response scenario, the transaction will not complete. In such scenario, the use of transactions is unnecessary since reliability can be ensured by a transaction at the receiving end (previous scenario above) and by the inherent mechanisms of the messaging system.

Figure 3.9 illustrates the problem of using a single message transaction in a request–response scenario. The source application expects to send a request and receive a response; however, the request will not reach the target application until the transaction commits. Without receiving the request, the target application will not produce the response, so transaction T1 will never complete. In Fig. 3.9, the use of two individual transactions T3 and T5 solves the problem, and ensures that no message is lost. Transaction T4 ensures that the request will not be left without response, while transaction T5 ensures that the source application will not miss the response. Transaction T3 makes the source application sure that the request was sent and will eventually reach the target application. The three transactions T3, T4, and T5 fall into the first three admissible scenarios described above.

3.3 Message Acknowledgments

Besides transactions, messaging systems implement other reliability mechanisms such as messages acknowledgments. Basically, an acknowledgment is confirmation that a message was successfully received at its destination. The acknowledgment itself is a special-purpose message with several possible meanings. Usually, it indicates whether a message that was to be delivered to a target application was successfully received by that application; in some cases, the acknowledgment may also indicate that the message was not only received but also processed without errors by the target application. Usually, message acknowledgments are for internal use of the messaging system, but they may be accessible to the sender as well, if the messaging systems provides that feature. This is illustrated in Fig. 3.10.

A message acknowledgment may be *implicit*, meaning that it is generated by the messaging system itself as soon as the message is delivered. The other option is to have *explicit* acknowledgments, which means that the target applications must themselves confirm that they received the message correctly by invoking a method on the messaging system to generate the acknowledgment. An explicit acknowledgment is often taken to mean that the target application not only received the message but processed it correctly as well. All of this happens regardless of whether the message is delivered in polling or callback mode, as shown earlier in Fig. 3.8. Also, when acknowledgments are used, a transaction is considered to have completed successfully only when all consumed messages have been acknowledged.

While acknowledgments are typically used to signal positive events (i.e., message received successfully), some systems use acknowledgments to signal negative events as well. For example, if the messaging system cannot route the message to the destination, or if the message remains in the destination channel without ever being received, the messaging system may generate an acknowledgment to signal that fact. The purpose of a negative acknowledgment is to inform the original sender that something that went wrong with the message, so the use of negative acknowledgments is more relevant in scenarios where the sender can have access to the acknowledgment. In general, we will refer to an acknowledgment as a positive event that is accessible to the messaging system only.

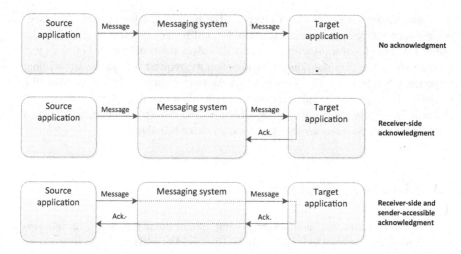

Fig. 3.10 Use of acknowledgments in messaging systems

3.4   Message Correlation

In message acknowledgments, as well as in many practical scenarios which involve
request–response interactions, there needs to be a mechanism to allow applications
to *correlate* messages, such that they will know that a message that has just arrived
is related to another message that was previously sent or received. Figure 3.11
illustrates the need for correlation. In this scenario, a source application sends three
independent requests to a target application, which is expected to return a response
for each request. Since the requests are independent, they will be handled separately
and the responses may be produced in any order; a response may be returned to the
sender as soon as the target application has finished handling the corresponding
request. Now, as the source application receives a response, it must be able to
determine the original request that the present response refers to.

In a messaging system, every message has a unique identifier (*message id*) which
can be used to keep track of the message as it is routed through the system. The
message id is unrepeatable in the sense that even if a second message has the
exact same content as a previous message, the second message will have a different
message id. In a scenario where an application receives a message and resends it
to another application, there will be two messages with different message ids. In
general, the message id can be assumed to be a sequential number that is assigned
to each new message created in the messaging system. Whenever an application asks
the messaging system to create and send a new message, the sequential number is
increased and its value is attached to the new message. Having unique message ids
is essential in order to be able to identify each message and, if necessary, refer to it
later, even if that message is no longer in the messaging system.

In a request–response scenario, an application that is responding to a previously
received request (which is no longer in the message system) may refer to that request

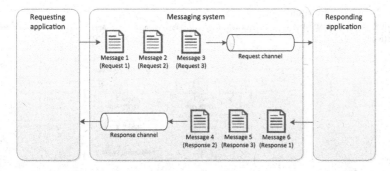

Fig. 3.11   Need for correlation in request–response interactions

using its message id. However, the response to that request has its own message id, which is naturally different from the message id of the original request. Therefore, to be able to refer to the original request, the application needs to make use of a second message field, called *correlation id*. The correlation id, if included in a message, contains the value of the message id of another message to which the present message is correlated. So, while the message id is always different for every new message, the correlation id may contain the message id of any previous message. This way it becomes possible to send a response (a new message with a new message id) which is correlated to a previous request (because the correlation id is the message id of the original request).

In the example of Fig. 3.11 there are six messages, each with its own message id. Messages 1 to 3 do not have to use a correlation id. However, messages 4 to 6 must use a correlation id since they are responses to previous requests. In this example, message 4 has a correlation id with value 2 since it is a response to message 2; message 5 has a correlation id equal to 3 since it is a response to message 3; and message 6 has correlation id with value 1. One can see that such mechanism can be used not only in request–response scenarios, but also in interactions that involve any set of messages. Using the correlation id to refer to the message id of a previous message allows an application to keep sending and receiving messages that are all correlated, regardless of the direction in which these messages are exchanged.

Figure 3.12 shows a different example of a chain of interactions. In this example, application *A* submits a request to application *B* which, in turn, creates a request to application *C*; then this triggers a request from application *C* to application *D*. When *D* responds to *C*, then *C* responds to *B*, and finally *B* responds to *A*. These exchanges are all triggered by the request from application *A*, and all messages are numbered sequentially in the order they have been created in the messaging system. For such scenario to work, there needs to be a correlation between every pair of request and response. Message 4 is a response to message 3, so it must use this value as its correlation id; in the same way, message 5 is a response to message 2, and message 6 is the response to message 1. Messages 1 to 3 (the requests) do not use a correlation id; messages 4 to 6 use as correlation id the message id that corresponds to the original request. In this scenario, there are three separate correlations.

Fig. 3.12 Use of correlation in chained request–response interactions

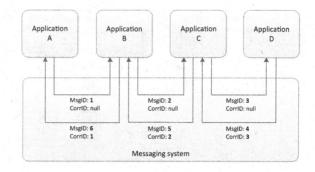

3.5 The Java Message Service

In the previous sections, we have seen the wide range of concepts and capabilities that are typically associated with messaging systems. In this and the next section we will have a look at actual messaging systems that implement those features. In this section we will delve into the JMS and in the next into MSMQ. There are other messaging systems as well, but these two examples provide an idea of how different the implementations can become; also, these two examples cover the two main platforms in use today. In particular, the JMS has a wide support in the industry, with several Java-based products implementing this standard.

The JMS is, in effect, a standard. It is not a messaging system, but rather a standard application programming interface (API) for messaging systems. A first version of the JMS standard was released in 2001; the second version (version 1.1) released in 2002 has remained since then and is in widespread use today, with a wide range of both commercial and open-source products that implement the standard. Basically, the JMS standard is intended to provide a common interface through which (Java-based) applications can interact with a messaging system, regardless of its underlying implementation. So, rather than having to adapt to a messaging system, an application can be prepared to operate through JMS regardless of the particular messaging system being used.

JMS provides two distinct types of messaging: *queues* and *topics*. These are referred to in the JMS standard as types of *destinations*. Queues are intended for point-to-point (one-to-one) communication between applications, while topics provide the concept of publish/subscribe where one application may send a message to several other applications (one-to-many). In the parlance of JMS, applications that send messages are called *producers* and applications that receive messages are called *consumers*. Producers and consumers are also referred to as *clients*, while the messaging system that implements the JMS interface is called *JMS provider*.

In point-to-point communication, applications make use of queues, where only one consumer receives each message. The consumer may or may not be online, so a message may remain in the queue for a relatively long period of time until it is eventually received by the consumer. JMS messages may have attributes such as expiry time or *time-to-live* that determine the maximum time that the message should be in the queue without being received. Messages that go past their expiry date or time-to-live are discarded by the messaging system.

Also, all messages in JMS are acknowledged upon receipt. This receipt may be implicit or explicit, as explained in Sect. 3.3. For the moment we will focus on implicit acknowledgments, since this is the default in JMS. The acknowledgments are for internal use of the messaging system only, i.e., they do not reach the sender of the message. In addition, acknowledgments are strictly positive, meaning that an acknowledgment is generated when the message is successfully received, and no acknowledgment is generated if the message is not received.

In publish/subscribe communication, application use topics, for which there may be multiple consumers. Each consumer receives a copy of the message that arrives at the topic. However, the default behavior here is that a consumer receives the message only if it is online and has an active subscription to the topic; if the consumer goes offline or deactivates the subscription, the default behavior of JMS is to stop delivering messages to that consumer. This behavior can be change through the use of *durable subscriptions*, where JMS stores messages for that consumer, in case it is currently offline. This choice of behavior must be done explicitly by the consumer; otherwise, given the potentially large number of subscribers to a topic, this would require the messaging system to store messages for all of them.

3.5.1 The JMS API

The JMS API defines a set of Java class interfaces, with predefined methods, that the messaging system must implement in its own set of classes. For example, the MessageProducer interface defines the signature of the method send() that is used to dispatch a message to a given destination; for that purpose, the method send() has a parameter of type Message that is used to refer to the message to be sent. On its turn, Message is another interface that specifies the methods to get and set the properties and content of a message. The interfaces in the JMS API work in such a way that each interface has its own methods, and these methods have input and output parameters that are references to objects that implement other interfaces.

The use of the JMS API begins by obtaining a reference to an object that implements the ConnectionFactory interface. Such object must have been previously created and must be readily accessible for applications to initiate connections to the messaging system. Indeed, according to JMS, an application must first open a connection to the messaging system before doing anything else, such as sending or receiving messages. The ConnectionFactory interface is perhaps the simplest of all JMS interfaces: it just defines a createConnection() method to be invoked by applications in order to open such kind of connection. In order to accept the connection, the messaging system may require some form of authentication based on username and password; in this case, createConnection() may be provided with those two input parameters. Otherwise, the method can be called without any input

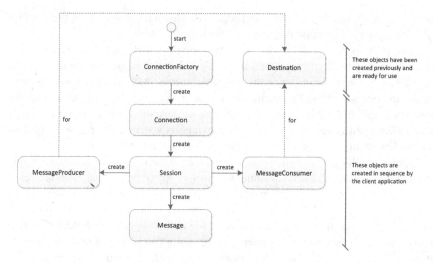

Fig. 3.13 Diagram illustrating the use of JMS interfaces

parameters, and a default identity is used. In either case, createConnection() returns a reference to an object that implements the Connection interface.

To keep track of all these interfaces and their relationships, Fig. 3.13 illustrates the sequence associated with the usage flow of JMS. From the connection factory, the application opens a connection to the messaging system, and with that connection creates one or more sessions. A session can be regarded as a period of activity during which the application sends and receives messages. In general, these messages will be sent to, or received from, preexisting destinations (queues or topics). It is also possible for an application to create destinations dynamically at run-time within a session, but these destinations are temporary and, at most, they will last until the connection is closed. The use of temporary queues or topics is not very common, since this would require other applications to learn about their existence in order to use them; an example is when a source application sends a request that specifies a temporary destination where the target application should send the response to. More usual is to make use of preexisting destinations that have already been created and are ready for use by applications.

Within a session, an application can create message producers and message consumers for use with particular destinations. It may also create messages to be sent through message producers. Creating a message producer means invoking the createProducer() method of the Session interface, which returns a reference to an object that implements the MessageProducer interface. This object is created within the messaging system, and a reference to the object is handed over to the client application. The procedure is analogous for creating message consumers and messages as well. As explained above, after creating a message producer and a message object, the message can be sent by invoking the send() method of the MessageProducer interface. This method receives a reference to the message object as input parameter;

the reference to the destination is unnecessary since it has already been specified when the message producer was created through the Session interface.

The MessageConsumer provides a receive() method to fetch messages from a destination. Again, the destination has already been specified when the message consumer was created. The receive() method is a blocking call that returns only when a new message is available at the destination. Alternatively, JMS also supports asynchronous receives through the use of a callback interface known as MessageListener. This interface has a single method onMessage() that is to be implemented by the client application and that is invoked by the messaging system to deliver messages to the application. In this case, a reference to the message object is passed as input parameter to the onMessage() method call. The JMS standard specifies that messages are received in serial order within a session, so the messaging system will not invoke the onMessage() method until the session has completed the previous call.

A connection factory object and, optionally, one or more destination objects are created before applications start using the messaging system. So the first problem that a JMS-compliant messaging system must address is how to provide client applications with references to those objects that already exist. This is usually attained by letting applications retrieve such references from a directory service. Basically, the messaging system creates the object that implements the ConnectionFactory interface and registers that object in a directory service. Applications perform a lookup operation on the directory service to retrieve the connection factory and initiate a connection to the messaging system. A similar scenario applies to destination objects: these are in general created by an administrator that registers the objects in the directory service. Applications can then lookup the destinations they want to use. According to the JMS standard, such directory service should implement the Java Naming and Directory Interface (JNDI), which is another standard API.

In the above description, and also in Fig. 3.13, the presentation of the JMS interfaces was slightly simplified to abstract from the details that are specific to the different types of destinations, namely queues and topics. Although the logic of the API is similar in both cases, the fact is that working with queues or topics requires the use of different JMS interfaces. In the case of queues, the interfaces ConnectionFactory, Connection, Session, MessageProducer, MessageConsumer, and Destination correspond, respectively, to QueueConnectionFactory, QueueConnection, QueueSession, QueueSender, QueueReceiver, and Queue. In the case of topics, the same interfaces correspond, respectively, to TopicConnectionFactory, TopicConnection, TopicSession, TopicPublisher, TopicSubscriber, and Topic. However, it is still correct to refer to the common interfaces ConnectionFactory, Connection, Session, etc., since these are parent interfaces (super-interfaces) of the specific interfaces that apply to queues and topics. In particular:

- ConnectionFactory is the parent interface of QueueConnectionFactory and Topic-ConnectionFactory;
- Connection is the parent interface of QueueConnection and TopicConnection;
- Session is the parent interface of QueueSession and TopicSession;

- MessageProducer is the parent interface of QueueSender and TopicPublisher;
- MessageConsumer is the parent interface of QueueReceiver and TopicSubscriber;
- finally, Destination is the parent interface of Queue and Topic.

Given this interface hierarchy, an object that implements a sub-interface also implements the corresponding super-interface. For example, an object that implements TopicPublisher also implements MessageProducer; and similarly in other cases.

3.5.2 How to Use JMS

From the perspective of client applications, interacting with a JMS-compliant messaging system is straightforward. Typically, applications will implement the following behavior:

1. Use JNDI to retrieve an object that implements the ConnectionFactory interface.
2. Use the ConnectionFactory object to create a Connection object. This opens a connection to the messaging system but, at this stage, message delivery is still disabled.
3. Use the Connection object to create one or more Session objects.
4. Use JNDI again to lookup one or more references to Destination objects.
5. Use the Session object and the Destination references to create MessageProducer and MessageConsumer objects.
6. To send messages, use Session to create a Message object, and use a MessageProducer to send the message. To receive messages, initiate the delivery of messages on the Connection and use a MessageConsumer to receive the message.

The application code that is needed to perform these operations and to send a message is shown in Listing 3.1. Line 4 obtains a reference to the directory service that can later be used to lookup objects. The first object to be retrieved is the connection factory (lines 6–7); in this example, we assume the object has been registered in the directory service with the name "MyConnectionFactory." Lines 8–11 create the connection and the session objects. When creating the session, the two parameter values in line 11 specify that the session is non-transactional and that message acknowledgments are to be generated implicitly. In line 12, the application retrieves a destination object (queue) from the directory service, which in this example has been registered with the name "MyQueue."

Up to line 12, the code is quite general in the sense that this would be the behavior of any application that intends to use a JMS queue, either to send or to receive messages. In the particular example of Listing 3.1, the application will send a text message and this behavior is shown in lines 14–17. Here, the application creates a message producer (line 14) by passing the reference to the queue that it intends to use. A new message, in this case a text message, is created in line 15, and in line 16 the application sets the message content. Finally, in line 17 the application uses the message producer to send the message to the queue.

Listing 3.1 Application code to send a text message using JMS

```
1   import javax.naming.*;
2   import javax.jms.*;
3
4   Context jndiContext = new InitialContext();
5
6   QueueConnectionFactory queueConnectionFactory =
7           (QueueConnectionFactory) jndiContext.lookup("MyConnectionFactory");
8   QueueConnection queueConnection =
9           queueConnectionFactory.createQueueConnection();
10  QueueSession queueSession =
11          queueConnection.createQueueSession(false, Session.AUTO_ACKNOWLEDGE);
12  Queue queue = (Queue) jndiContext.lookup("MyQueue");
13
14  QueueSender queueSender = queueSession.createSender(queue);
15  Message message = queueSession.createTextMessage();
16  message.setText("This is a text message.");
17  queueSender.send(message);
```

Listing 3.2 Application code to receive a text message using JMS

```
1   import javax.naming.*;
2   import javax.jms.*;
3
4   Context jndiContext = new InitialContext();
5
6   QueueConnectionFactory queueConnectionFactory =
7           (QueueConnectionFactory) jndiContext.lookup("MyConnectionFactory");
8   QueueConnection queueConnection =
9           queueConnectionFactory.createQueueConnection();
10  QueueSession queueSession =
11          queueConnection.createQueueSession(false, Session.AUTO_ACKNOWLEDGE);
12  Queue queue = (Queue) jndiContext.lookup("MyQueue");
13
14  QueueReceiver queueReceiver = queueSession.createReceiver(queue);
15  queueConnection.start();
16  Message message = (TextMessage) queueReceiver.receive();
17  String text = message.getText();
```

At the other end, the application code needed to receive the message is analogous and is shown in Listing 3.2. Indeed, the first part, up to line 12, is equal to that of Listing 3.1; the difference is in lines 14–17. Here, the receiving application creates a message consumer for the queue in line 14, and in line 15 the application enables message delivery to this consumer. In line 16, the application fetches a message from the queue by invoking the receive() method of the message consumer. This is a blocking call that will return a reference to a message object when a new message is available in the queue. In line 17, the application retrieves the message content.

Instead of using a blocking call, the application may receive the message through a callback interface. This requires the application to implement the MessageListener interface which, as previously explained, has a single method onMessage() that is to be invoked by the messaging system every time a new message arrives. In this case, the messaging system delivers the message to the application by invoking the callback method onMessage(), passing a reference to the message object as input parameter. An implementation of the MessageListener callback interface is shown in

Listing 3.3 Implementation of callback interface to receive messages asynchronously

```
1   class TextListener implements MessageListener
2   {
3           public void onMessage(Message message)
4           {
5                   TextMessage message = (TextMessage) message;
6                   String text = message.getText();
7           }
8   }
```

Listing 3.4 Application code to receive message asynchronously

```
1   QueueReceiver queueReceiver = queueSession.createReceiver(queue);
2   TextListener textListener = new TextListener();
3   queueReceiver.setMessageListener(textListener);
4   queueConnection.start();
```

Listing 3.3. Here, the onMessage() method simply converts the input message to an appropriate class, and then retrieves the message content as before.

However, in addition to implementing the MessageListener interface, the application must also make the messaging system aware of that implementation, so that the messaging system will invoke this particular onMessage() method when a new message arrives. Such is attained by creating a listener object and registering that object in the messaging system, through the MessageConsumer interface, as shown in Listing 3.4. After creating the message consumer in line 1, the application creates a listener object (line 2) from the class defined in Listing 3.3. Then in line 3 of Listing 3.4 the application sets this object as the callback listener for the message consumer. In line 4, message delivery becomes enabled, so the messaging system will invoke the listener as soon as a new message is present in the queue.

3.5.3   JMS Messages

Messages are defined in JMS as comprising three main parts: the *header*, a set of *properties*, and the *body*. JMS requires all messages to have a number of standard fields in their header. These are used by the producer, which sets fields such as destination, priority, and correlation id. The same header fields can be read by the consumer; and they can also be used by the messaging system itself, for example to record whether the delivery of the same message has been attempted before. In essence the header fields that are part of every JMS can be summarized as follows:

- JMSDestination specifies the queue or topic that the message should be delivered to;
- JMSDeliveryMode specifies whether the message should be delivered in persistent or non-persistent mode; non-persistent mode requires less resources, but the message may be lost if there is a failure in the messaging system; the persistent mode ensures reliability at the expense of requiring the messaging system to store and keep track of the message;

- JMSMessageID is a unique identifier; all messages created in the messaging system have a different message id, even if they have exactly the same content as previous message;
- JMSTimestamp records the date and time at which the message has been handed over to the messaging system to be sent to its destination;
- JMSCorrelationID may be used to establish a correlation to a previous message; in this case, it contains the message id of that previous message;
- JMSReplyTo specifies the destination to which responses to the present message should be sent to;
- JMSRedelivered is to be read by the consumer; it indicates whether the messaging system has attempted to deliver the same message before;
- JMSType is an arbitrary, application-defined name that can be used by applications to distinguish between different "types" of messages, where this type has an application-defined meaning;
- JMSExpiration sets a date and time after which the message will be discarded by the messaging system, in case it has not been received by that time;
- JMSPriority defines the message priority in a range from 0 to 9, with 9 being the highest priority; when arriving at a destination, a message with higher priority will be place ahead of messages with lower priority; this way the consumer will receive messages in decreasing order of priority.

In addition to these standard header fields, a JMS message may contain a set of additional properties. These properties are optional fields that can be included in the message header. They may be some of the optional, extended fields that JMS defines; they may be also some specific fields defined by applications; or they may be specific fields used by the messaging system itself. In any case, properties are name–value pairs, where the name is a string and the value can be any of the basic Java types. There are specific methods of Message to set properties of particular types, for example setBooleanProperty() and getBooleanProperty() allow setting and getting the value of a boolean property.

With regard to the set of message properties defined in JMS, which are optional extensions to the standard header fields, they can be summarized as follows:

- JMSXUserID identifies the user who sends the message, if some sort of authentication mechanism is used;
- JMSXAppID identifies the application which sends the message;
- JMSXDeliveryCount records the number of attempts which the messaging system has done to deliver the message; for a message that is being delivered for the first time, this number is 1;
- JMSXGroupID identifies the group of messages to which this message belongs, if indeed the message belongs to a group of messages that should be taken together;
- JMSXGroupSeq identifies the sequence number of this message in that group;
- JMSXProducerTXID identifies the transaction in which the message was produced;
- JMSXConsumerTXID identifies the transaction in which the message was received;
- JMSXRcvTimestamp is the time and date at which the message was received;

- JMSXState records the internal state of the message in the messaging system; this is of interest for the messaging system only, and depends on the implementation of the messaging system.

Finally, the message body may contain different kinds of content: in a TextMessage the body contains a string; in a StreamMessage the body can be written and read as a sequential stream that stores primitive Java types; in an ObjectMessage the body may contain any serializable Java object; and in a MapMessage the body contains a set of name–value pairs in a similar way to the message properties discussed above, although here the application has complete control over the content.

3.5.4   Message Acknowledgments in JMS

As discussed in Sect. 3.3, an acknowledgment is a confirmation that a message has been received by the target application. In JMS, such acknowledgment can be done either implicitly (with AUTO_ACKNOWLEDGE) or explicitly (with CLIENT_ACKNOWLEDGE). An implicit acknowledgment means that the acknowledgment will be generated automatically once the message is successfully delivered to the target application. An explicit acknowledgment means that it must be the target application that generates the acknowledgment. A third acknowledgment mode (DUPS_OK_ACKNOWLEDGE) is available, which is an implicit mode that is intended to ease the work of the session with regard to acknowledgments.

When creating a session, the client application specifies the acknowledgment mode as in line 11 of Listing 3.1. If AUTO_ACKNOWLEDGE is chosen, then the session itself will automatically acknowledge messages as soon as the client application receives them. On the other hand, if CLIENT_ACKNOWLEDGE is specified, then the client application must explicitly invoke the acknowledge() method of the Message interface after receiving the message. Such explicit acknowledgment means that the application not only received the message but also processed it successfully, so the messaging system can consider that its job is done.

The third mode (DUPS_OK_ACKNOWLEDGE) is another kind of implicit acknowledgment (as AUTO_ACKNOWLEDGE) where, again, the session will automatically acknowledge the messages received. However, in the DUPS_OK_ACKNO-WLEDGE mode, the session is not required to generate the acknowledgment immediately. This is intended to allow the session implementation to become simpler, and to make the processing of multiple messages become faster. Instead of generating the acknowledgment immediately, the session is allowed to generate it at any time after the message has been received. However, if the session takes too long to do this, the messaging system may attempt to deliver the same message a second time, hence the designation of DUPS_OK_ACKNOWLEDGE, i.e., this mode should be used only by applications which are prepared to handle duplicate messages.

3.5.5 *Transactions in JMS*

Transaction support in JMS is very similar to the transaction mechanisms described earlier in Sect. 3.2. Basically, a transaction takes place between a client application and the messaging system. In sending a message from a producer to a consumer, transaction support is provided in three stages: (1) a message transaction at the producer guarantees that the message is delivered to the messaging system in a reliable way; (2) the reliability mechanisms of the messaging system guarantee that the message is not lost on the way to its destination; (3) a second message transaction at the consumer guarantees that message is reliably received by the target application.

As explained in Sect. 3.2, a transaction that includes only send operations, only receive operations, or receive and send operations (in this order) can run correctly. However, a transaction that performs send and receive operations while expecting to receive responses to requests that were sent within the same transaction will not work. This is because the messaging system will not deliver messages to their destination until the transaction successfully completes.

In the case of transaction rollback, all messages that have been produced to be sent are discarded, and all messages that have been consumed are returned to their original queues. These messages will be redelivered with the header field JMSRedelivered set to true, and the property JMSXDeliveryCount increased by one. If the session or connection is closed during a running transaction, the transaction is rolled back by the messaging system.

To create a transactional session, the client application must indicate that option when creating the session. For this purpose, the first parameter of the createSession() method of the Connection interface must be set to true. When working with queues, this means setting the first parameter of createQueueSession() to true in line 11 of Listing 3.1. If set to true, then the second parameter, which pertains to acknowledgments, is ignored. In a JMS transactional session, the message acknowledgments will be generated automatically when the transaction commits.

3.6 Microsoft Message Queuing

Microsoft Message Queuing (abbreviated as MSMQ) is a messaging system that has been part of the Windows operating system almost since its inception. It is perhaps not very common for users to know that a full-fledged messaging system is readily available in that operating system, but the fact is that applications can rely on MSMQ to implement asynchronous message exchanges with other local and remote applications. This way, MSMQ can also be used to develop distributed and asynchronous applications in the Windows platform. Features such as guaranteed delivery, efficient routing, security, transactions, and priority are already provided by MSMQ, so there is no need to reimplement them in applications.

In MSMQ, the application that produces a message is simply called the *sender*, and the application that consumes it is called the *receiver*. The communication channel between sender and receiver is always a *queue*, and the most common scenario is to use queues for one-to-one communication. MSMQ also supports one-to-many interactions through a reliable IP multicast protocol known as Pragmatic General Multicast (PGM). In this case, the message is sent to an IP multicast address which, in turn, can be attached to one or more queues. A message sent to an IP multicast address will be inserted in all queues that have been associated with that address. For the receiver, the behavior is the same in any case: it just fetches a message from a queue. It is interesting to note that while JMS provides the concept of topic to support the publish–subscribe paradigm, MSMQ uses only queues and relies on network-level facilities to implement that paradigm.

In MSMQ, messages may be delivered in express mode or in recoverable mode. In express mode, messages are stored in memory, so they may be lost if the system fails. In recoverable mode, MSMQ ensures reliability by saving messages to persistent storage until they are successfully received.

An interesting characteristic and architectural difference of MSMQ when compared to other messaging systems is that a message may travel across several machines until it reaches its destination queue. In each machine, there is a component known as *Queue Manager* that checks whether the message is to be delivered to a local or to a remote queue. If the message is intended for a local queue, the Queue Manager inserts the message in that queue; otherwise, the message is placed in an *outgoing queue* from which it will be dispatched to another machine. As soon as the local Queue Manager is able to establish contact with the remote machine, it hands the message over to the Queue Manager running on that machine, and the remote Queue manager proceeds in the same way. Figure 3.14 illustrates the procedure. An outgoing queue is a temporary queue created automatically by the Queue Manager to store one or more messages to be dispatched to a remote Queue Manager; the outgoing queue disappears as soon as the messages have been dispatched. This kind of behavior is known as *store and forward*, as opposed to *direct routing* which applies when the message is immediately delivered to a local destination queue.

The outgoing queue is just one special kind of queue used by MSMQ for routing purposes, but there are others. The *dead-letter queue* is used to store messages that could not be delivered to the intended destination queue. The *queue journal*, if enabled, stores a copy of every message delivered to a queue. The *computer journal* does the same but for all messages arriving in all queues in the local machine. Besides journals, there are also *report queues* that can be used for monitoring purposes; as a message is being routed to its final destination, a tracking message is created and sent to the report queue every time the message passes through a different machine. Finally, *administration queues* are used to store message acknowledgments.

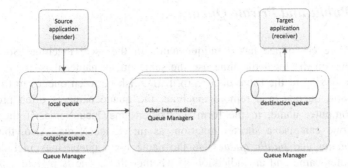

Fig. 3.14 Message routing across Queue Managers in different machines

3.6.1   Message Acknowledgments in MSMQ

Message acknowledgments in MSMQ are also different from other messaging systems in that there can be positive and negative acknowledgments, and these become accessible to the original sender of the message. When sending a message, the source application specifies the administration queue to be used to store the acknowledgments; after sending the message, the same application can receive the acknowledgments that arrive on that administration queue. Even if everything runs without error, the source application may choose to receive more than one positive acknowledgment: first, an acknowledgment that the message arrived at the destination queue and, second, an acknowledgment that the message has been successfully received by the target application. On the other hand, if the message does not arrive at the destination queue, or if the message is not received by the target application, a negative acknowledgment is generated and this may happen for several reasons, which are indicated in the acknowledgment itself, such as:

- The destination queue does not exist or has been removed.
- The destination queue is full and no more messages can be added.
- If security features such as encryption and digital signatures are being used, a negative acknowledgment may be generated if the queue manager at the receiving end is unable to decrypt the message or to validate its signature.
- Since a message may traverse several Queue Managers, a negative acknowledgment may be generated if the message exceeds a maximum hop count.
- A mismatch between message and destination queue in terms of transaction queue may generate a negative acknowledgment as well. In particular, a non-transactional queue can only receive non-transactional messages, a transactional queue must receive transactional messages.
- If a maximum time to reach the destination queue or a maximum time to be retrieved from the destination queue is specified in the message, then if the message does not reach the queue or is not received by the target application within that time frame, a negative acknowledgment is generated.
- Other particular errors, such as an access denied being encountered at any stage during message routing, may also originate negative acknowledgments.

3.6.2   Public and Private Queues

In MSMQ, every queue has a unique name in the local machine. So if two applications on the local machine use the same queue name, it is assumed that they are referring to the same queue. To distinguish between queues in the local machine and queues in a remote machine, the queue name is often preceded by the computer name, in the form: ComputerName\QueueName. If the queue is local, one can use a shorter notation, as in: .\QueueName. Also, there are *private queues* and *public queues*, so the name for a queue may include both the computer name and an indication of whether the queue is private, as in the form ComputerName\PRIVATE$\QueueName or .\PRIVATE$\QueueName if the queue is local. If PRIVATE$ is missing in the queue name, it is assumed that the queue is public.

The most common scenario is to use private queues, i.e., queues that are only known to the applications that use them. In general, a private queue is accessible only to applications that know the complete name of the queue. Through the use of public queues, it is possible for applications to discover queue names which they did not know about. For this purpose, the queue name is published in Active Directory, a directory service based on LDAP that is available in Windows server systems. In this context, Active Directory plays the same role for MSMQ as JNDI does for JMS by allowing applications to discover and use existing queues.

3.6.3   Distributed Transactions in MSMQ

Besides an optional directory service, which may be used to register and discover information about public queues, MSMQ relies on another external component to manage distributed transactions. In fact, in the Windows operating system, transactions are managed by an independent component known as Distributed Transaction Coordinator (DTC). This component is able to manage transactions that cross several systems, such as messaging systems, databases, and file systems. The DTC service provides a transaction scope for such distributed transactions, and MSMQ can use the DTC to support message transactions between client applications and the local Queue Manager. In the communication between Queue Managers, MSMQ makes use of its own reliable transfer mechanisms.

Figure 3.15 illustrates the use of the DTC service in connection with message transactions. As explained in Sect. 3.2, a message transaction takes place between an application and the messaging system, and such transaction may include multiple receive and send operations. In the example of Fig. 3.15, there are two simple transactions: one to send a message, and another at the receiving end to receive the message. In both cases, the client application initiates the transaction by contacting the transaction coordinator, which provides a transaction scope to be used in all operations that belong to the transaction. When the client application asks the local Queue Manager to send a message within a transaction, the Queue Manager registers

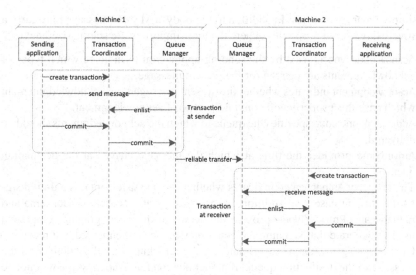

Fig. 3.15 Use of an external transaction coordinator in message transactions

(enlists) itself in the transaction coordinator, in order to be notified of when the transaction commits or rollbacks, so that it can take appropriate actions in response to those events. When the client application informs the transaction coordinator that it intends to commit the transaction, the transaction coordinator will ask all systems involved in the transaction to commit their work.

If the destination queue is on another machine, the local Queue Manager will route the message to the remote Queue Manager, either directly or through other, intermediary Queue Managers. At the receiving end, the client application initiates a second transaction following the same behavior as described for the sending application. In this case, the client performs a receive operation to fetch the message. Once the Queue Manager receives the request from the transaction coordinator to commit the transaction, the message is permanently removed from the queue and the transaction cannot be rolled back any more. To revert the effects of a transaction that has already committed, a client application will have to initiate a new transaction and perform a set of operations that are the logical undo of the previous ones.

3.6.4 The Structure of MSMQ Messages

Unlike JMS, where messages are clearly divided into header, properties, and body, in MSMQ the whole content of messages is a set of name–value pairs called properties. In this context, the *body* is just one of the properties in a message, and its value may be empty or it may contain basic data types, text, serializable objects,

or simply an array of bytes. In addition to the body, a MSMQ message may carry a
relatively large set of properties, where the most important are summarized next:

- AcknowledgeType is used by the sending application to indicate which types of
  acknowledgments are desired for the present message.
- Acknowledgment indicates whether the present message is an acknowledgment, in
  which case this property will contain the type of acknowledgment.
- AdministrationQueue specifies the queue to which the acknowledgments should be
  delivered.
- ArrivedTime provides the time at which the message arrived at the destination
  queue.
- The property Authenticated indicates whether the message contains a digital signature. In that case, two additional properties—AuthenticationProviderName and
  AuthenticationProviderType—provide the details of the cryptographic component
  used to generate that signature. When a message is authenticated, the receiving
  Queue Manager attempts to validate the digital signature before delivering the
  message to the destination queue. If authentication fails, the message will not be
  delivered; in this case, it is possible to generate a negative acknowledgment to
  indicate an authentication failure.
- The properties Body, BodyType, and BodyStream concern the body of the message.
  Setting the body content through the Body property is perhaps the easiest way, as
  it can be set to any object (its type will be specified in the BodyType property).
  However, when using the Body property, the content will be serialized and
  formatted in XML (unless a different formatter is specified by means of the
  Formatter property). This means that when the receiving application retrieves the
  message, it must be able to understand the message body in the serialized format
  used by MSMQ (there is some support to ease this task, of course). To preclude
  MSMQ from formatting the body content, the sending application may choose
  to write the content directly to the body, as if it would be stream; in this case,
  the application retains full control of how the content will be serialized in the
  message body. Using the BodyStream property, it is possible to write content to
  the message body as a stream; at the receiving end, the application reads data
  from the BodyStream as a stream as well. In this scenario, MSMQ does not
  interfere with the way the message body is serialized and formatted. It should
  be noted that the body of a MSMQ message is limited to a maximum size of
  4 MB.
- CorrelationId specifies the message id of a previous message to which the
  present message is related to. This is typically usually in request–response
  scenarios as explained in Sect. 3.4. Another use for the CorrelationId property is
  in acknowledgments. If the present message is an acknowledgment, then this
  property contains the id of the original message that this acknowledgment refers
  to.
- DestinationQueue is set by the sending application by providing a reference to the
  destination queue that the present message should be sent to.

- DestinationSymmetricKey is used by applications that require the message to be encrypted. In this case, this property contains the key that was used to encrypt the message and that can also be used to decrypt it (hence the name of *symmetric* key). Of course, sending the decryption key along with the message itself would be a useless security measure, since anyone who would intercept the message would be able to decrypt it. Therefore, the symmetric key is itself encrypted with the public key of the receiving Queue Manager. This Queue Manager, which will be the only component that is able to decrypt the symmetric key, will use the key to decrypt the message before placing it in the destination queue. In a similar way to what happens with message authentication, failure to decrypt the message may generate a appropriate negative acknowledgment.
- If message authentication is being used, DigitalSignature will contain the digital signature for the present message. Another property called HashAlgorithm specifies which hashing algorithm was used to create the digital signature. On the other hand, when message encryption is being used, EncryptionAlgorithm specifies the algorithm that was used to encrypt the message.
- Formatter specifies how the message body will be formatted after being serialized. By default, the body will be formatted in XML, as explained above about the Body property. However, the sending application may choose to write the message body directly as a stream. In this case, before sending the message it will be important to specify that the body content is in binary format, and the Formatter property can be used for this purpose as well.
- The Id property contains the message id that distinguishes the present message from every other. In MSMQ, the message id is generated by combining a machine identifier (the machine where the message was created) with a unique identifier for the message within that machine. This way every MSMQ message is guaranteed to have a unique message id: two messages created within the same machine will have different message ids because the message identifier within that machine will be different; and two messages created in different machines will also have different ids because the machine identifier will be different. MSMQ generates a unique message id for every message, be it a regular message, an acknowledgment, or a report.
- The Label property contains an arbitrary, application-defined value that can be used by applications for their own purposes. The message label does not need to be unique; multiple messages may have the same label. In practical scenarios, it can be used to identify messages of a certain type. It plays the same role as the JMSType field in JMS messages.
- MessageType indicates whether the present message is a regular message, an acknowledgment, or a report. Note that if the message is an acknowledgment, the exact type of acknowledgment can be retrieved from the Acknowledgment property. Report messages are used when reporting is enabled; in this case, MSMQ will send a report message (to a dedicated report queue) each time the original message enters or leaves a Queue Manager.
- Priority specifies the message priority, from highest to lowest, on a scale of eight levels. Actually, the scale goes from 0 to 7, with 7 begin the highest priority,

and the default level being 3. Messages of higher priority will be inserted in the destination queue ahead of messages of lower priority, so that higher-priority messages are received first. This means that the messages in a queue may have to be shifted or moved in order to accommodate for an incoming message of higher priority. For messages with the same priority, they are placed in the queue according to their arrival time.

- Recoverable is a property that specifies whether the present message is to be delivered in express mode or in recoverable mode. As explained in the beginning of this section, in express mode the messages are stored in memory and may be lost due to system failure. In recoverable mode, the message is stored locally at every machine along the route, until it is forwarded to the next machine.

- In a request–response interaction, if the present message represents the request, then the ResponseQueue property specifies the queue to which the response should be sent. Typically, the response message will include the CorrelationId property, in order to include the message id of the original request.

- If the message is digitally signed, SenderCertificate contains the public-key certificate of the sending application so that the digital signature can be verified.

- SentTime specifies the time at which the sending application handed over the message to the local Queue Manager for delivery.

- SourceMachine contains the name of the machine where the message was created.

- The property TimeToBeReceived specifies a time limit for the message to be received from the destination queue. This includes the time spent on routing the message to the destination queue together with the time spent on waiting in the queue to be received. If the time limit is reached before the message is actually consumed, the message is sent to the dead-letter queue.

- The property TimeToReachQueue works in a similar way to TimeToBeReceived but it applies only to the time spent on routing the message. If the message does not reach the destination queue within the given time limit, it is sent to the dead-letter queue. If the message does reach the destination queue within the time limit, then TimeToReachQueue produces no effect.

- TransactionId applies to messages that have been sent within a transaction. In this case, the property contains the transaction identifier for the sending transaction. In a similar way to the message id, the transaction identifier is produced as a combination of the machine identifier and sequential transaction number. This sequential number has a limited range, after which it goes back to the beginning and starts all over again. For this reason, transaction identifiers are not guaranteed to be unique. However, the receiving application can make use of two additional message properties—IsFirstInTransaction and IsLastInTransaction—to determine when a message initiates or completes a running transaction.

It should be noted that some of the above properties are set by the sending application, while others are set by the MSMQ infrastructure. For example, the sending application specifies the message body, the destination queue, the desired acknowledgments, the priority, etc.; on the other hand, the messaging system fills in other details, such as message id, arrival time, source machine, etc. So at the receiving end, the receiver has access not only to the properties set by the sender, but also to the array of properties set by the messaging system itself.

3.6.5 How to Use MSMQ

Although the native MSMQ API is accessible to several programming languages, the easiest way to use MSMQ is through a higher-level API such as the one provided for .NET languages, namely C#. In fact, the System.Messaging namespace provides a convenient set of classes that allow .NET applications to use message queues and to send and receive messages through MSMQ. Usually, the queues will be created manually by a system administrator, but it is possible for applications to create queues programmatically as well. In the following example we illustrate both possibilities and some common tasks when using MSMQ.

To illustrate the use of MSMQ, we consider a purchasing scenario in a company, where each purchase order is described by the following data elements: the product and quantity to be purchased, and the date and time of the purchase order. The structure of such purchase orders can be captured in a C# class such as the one in Listing 3.5, where there is a class property of type string to store the product, another class property of type int to store the quantity, and a DateTime object to store the date and time of the purchase order. The three class properties have get and set methods, and the class constructor initializes the Date property with the current date and time.

In this example, the goal is to show how a purchase order (an instance of the class above) can be exchanged between two applications using MSMQ. The sender will write the purchase order data, and the receiver will read the data. The purchase order will be transmitted from sender to receiver through a private, local message queue. We will develop both applications as command-line applications in C#.

Listing 3.6 shows the code for the sender. The program has a namespace (line 4) which is the same as for the PurchaseOrder class (Listing 3.5). The sender in Listing 3.6 has also a single class (line 6) and the method Main() (line 8) that will be invoked when the program runs. In line 2 the program imports the namespace that provides the interface to MSMQ. One of the classes defined in that namespace is MessageQueue, used in lines 10, 15, 20, and 39. In line 11, a string variable provides the name of the queue. The "@" symbol before the string indicates that the string is to be taken literally, or "as is," without escape characters (the backslashes are part of the queue name). In line 12 the program checks whether the queue already exists. If it does, then line 15 obtains a reference to the queue. Otherwise, line 20 creates the queue in the local machine, as specified in the queue name.

In line 26, the program creates an instance of the PurchaseOrder class, and in lines 29 and 32 the product and quantity to be purchased are read from the command line. Line 34 just prints the date and time of the purchase order, which have been initialized in the class constructor. In line 36, the program creates a new message, and by passing the PurchaseOrder object as input parameter, the constructor for the

Listing 3.5 A class representing the purchase order to be exchanged between applications

```
1    using System;
2
3    namespace MSMQSolution
4    {
5        public class PurchaseOrder
6        {
7            public string Product { get; set; }
8            public int Quantity { get; set; }
9            public DateTime Date { get; set; }
10
11           public PurchaseOrder()
12           {
13               Date = DateTime.Now;
14           }
15       }
16   }
```

Message class will use an XML formatter to serialize the object into the message body. This could have been done explicitly, by setting the Body property in a similar way to what happens with the Priority property in line 37. In line 39, the program sends the message to the queue by invoking the Send() method of the MessageQueue class. The second parameter passed as input to the Send() method will be used to set the message label, another property that could have been set explicitly as well.

The sending application in Listing 3.6 has an infinite loop starting on line 23. This means that the program will keep creating new purchase orders and asking the user for the product and quantity details before sending the purchase order to the queue. Since the date and time for the purchase order is being initialized in the class constructor in Listing 3.5, it may be some time before the user provides the details and the purchase order is sent to the queue. In this scenario, it would be preferable to set the Date property for the purchase order only after the user provides all the details. However, this is meant only as a simple example to illustrate the use of MSMQ; in a real-world application, the queue name would also have to be configured in another way instead of being hardcoded in the program at line 10.

Running the program in Listing 3.6 will result in a new message being placed in the destination queue. If the receiving application is offline, then the message will remain in the queue waiting to be consumed, and in that period of time it is possible to inspect its content through the MSMQ management console. If no security features, namely encryption, are being used then the message body will be accessible and its content will be similar to the XML document shown in Listing 3.7 (this has been obtained from an actual run of the sender application above). From Listing 3.7 it is clear that the XML formatter has structured the message body in a way that resembles the original structure of the PurchaseOrder class.

The message format in Listing 3.7 might seem very convenient from the point of view of a software developer who wants to integrate applications based on the exchange of XML messages, as it happens with platforms such as Microsoft BizTalk described in Chap. 2. However, as we will see in the next chapter, in practical integration scenarios it becomes more convenient to define the message structure as

Listing 3.6 Application code for the sender of purchase orders

```
1   using System;
2   using System.Messaging;
3
4   namespace MSMQSolution
5   {
6       class Program
7       {
8           static void Main(string[] args)
9           {
10              MessageQueue mq;
11              string queueName = @".\private$\purchaseorders";
12              if (MessageQueue.Exists(queueName))
13              {
14                  Console.WriteLine("Opening queue: {0}", queueName);
15                  mq = new MessageQueue(queueName);
16              }
17              else
18              {
19                  Console.WriteLine("Creating queue: {0}", queueName);
20                  mq = MessageQueue.Create(queueName);
21              }
22
23              while (true)
24              {
25                  Console.WriteLine("Create a new purchase order");
26                  PurchaseOrder PO = new PurchaseOrder();
27
28                  Console.Write("Product: ");
29                  PO.Product = Console.ReadLine();
30
31                  Console.Write("Quantity: ");
32                  PO.Quantity = int.Parse(Console.ReadLine());
33
34                  Console.WriteLine("Date: {0}", PO.Date);
35
36                  Message msg = new Message(PO);
37                  msg.Priority = MessagePriority.Normal;
38
39                  mq.Send(msg, "PurchaseOrder");
40                  Console.WriteLine("Message has been sent!");
41              }
42          }
43      }
44  }
```

Listing 3.7 Message body formatted in XML

```
1   <?xml version="1.0"?>
2   <PurchaseOrder xmlns:xsd="http://www.w3.org/2001/XMLSchema"
3                  xmlns:xsi="http://www.w3.org/2001/XMLSchema-instance">
4       <Product>printer cartridge</Product>
5       <Quantity>3</Quantity>
6       <Date>2012-04-10T12:22:43.0410156+01:00</Date>
7   </PurchaseOrder>
```

a schema to be used by applications, rather than letting the MSMQ XML formatter decide the structure based on the actual data to be transmitted. Therefore, in Sect. 4.7 we will write the message body directly through the use of the BodyStream property, retaining full control of the body content, rather than writing that content by setting the Body property, which in turn relies on a message formatter.

Listing 3.8 Application code for the receiver of purchase orders

```
1    using System;
2    using System.Messaging;
3
4    namespace MSMQSolution
5    {
6        class Program
7        {
8            static void Main(string[] args)
9            {
10               string queueName = @".\private$\purchaseorders";
11               Console.WriteLine("Receiving on queue: {0}", queueName);
12
13               MessageQueue mq = new MessageQueue(queueName);
14
15               System.Type[] types = new Type[] { typeof(PurchaseOrder) };
16               mq.Formatter = new XmlMessageFormatter(types);
17
18               while (true)
19               {
20                   Message msg = mq.Receive();
21                   Console.WriteLine("Received new message!");
22
23                   PurchaseOrder PO = (PurchaseOrder)msg.Body;
24                   Console.WriteLine("Product: {0}", PO.Product);
25                   Console.WriteLine("Quantity: {0}", PO.Quantity);
26                   Console.WriteLine("Date: {0}", PO.Date);
27               }
28           }
29       }
30   }
```

Listing 3.8 shows the code for the receiving application. The program uses the same namespace (line 4) as before. Like the sender, the receiver is implemented as a single class (line 6) with a Main() method (line 8). The queue name is stored in a string variable (line 10) as before. The program opens the queue on line 13; here it is assumed that the queue already exists. However, before the program receives a message from the queue, it must be aware that the message body will be formatted in XML, as a serialized PurchaseOrder object. Therefore, the receiver tells MSMQ to use an XML formatter (line 16) based on the structure of the PurchaseOrder class (line 15). Then it enters an infinite loop in line 18, where it waits for messages to arrive (Receive() on line 20 is a blocking call). Once a new message is fetched from the queue, the program retrieves the message body and casts it into a PurchaseOrder object (line 23). The rest is just printing the purchase order data (lines 24–26).

It is interesting to note that besides Receive(), MSMQ provides a Peek() method which retrieves a message without actually removing it from the queue. Since the message remains in the queue, a subsequent call to Peek() will return the same message, unless a message of higher priority has arrived in the meantime. Both the Receive() method and the Peek method are blocking calls, i.e., either a message is available in the queue and the method call returns immediately with a reference to the message object, or the queue is empty and in this case the application thread will block until a new message arrives.

Listing 3.9 Application code for asynchronous receive in MSMQ

```
1   using System.Messaging;
2
3   namespace MSMQSolution
4   {
5       class Program
6       {
7           private static void MyReceive(Object source, ReceiveCompletedEventArgs asyncResult)
8           {
9               MessageQueue mq = (MessageQueue) source;
10              Message msg = mq.EndReceive(asyncResult.AsyncResult);
11              Console.WriteLine("Message: " + (string)msg.Body);
12              mq.BeginReceive();
13          }
14
15          static void Main(string[] args)
16          {
17              ...
18              MessageQueue mq = new MessageQueue(queueName);
19              ...
20              mq.ReceiveCompleted += new ReceiveCompletedEventHandler(MyReceive);
21              mq.BeginReceive();
22          }
23      }
24  }
```

3.6.6 Receiving Messages Asynchronously

As with JMS, MSMQ also provides a way for applications to receive messages asynchronously, and the mechanism is, as usual, based on implementing a callback method. However, whereas in JMS the receiver must implement the callback interface MessageListener together with its callback method onMessage() (as in Listing 3.3 on page 56), in the MSMQ API provided to .NET applications the receiver uses one of its own methods as an *event handler* that will be invoked when a new message arrives. This event handler must adhere to a certain function prototype, and in order to be invoked by MSMQ it must be registered as a handler for the ReceiveCompleted event. In addition, the receiver must explicitly call the BeginReceive() method to initiate the asynchronous receive of a new message.

Listing 3.9 shows the application code that would have to be used to receive messages asynchronously. Lines 7–13 define the method that will be invoked by MSMQ to notify the application of incoming messages. This method must conform to the following guidelines: it must return void and it must have two input parameters, one of type Object and another of type ReceiveCompletedEventArgs. The first parameter provides a reference to the MessageQueue object; the second parameter provides a set of data associated with the ReceiveCompleted event. The program in Listing 3.9 obtains a reference to the MessageQueue (line 9) and then uses that reference to complete the receive operation and fetch the message from the queue (line 10).

It is worth noting that when MSMQ invokes an event handler for the ReceiveCompleted event, it does not actually deliver the message but only notifies the receiving application that a new message arrived at the queue. The application itself must

Listing 3.10 Application code to receive and send messages within MSMQ transaction

```
1   MessageQueueTransaction trans = new MessageQueueTransaction();
2   trans.Begin();
3   ...
4   MessageQueue mq1 = new MessageQueue(...);
5   Message msg1 = mq1.Receive(trans);
6   ...
7   MessageQueue mq2 = new MessageQueue(...);
8   Message msg2 = new Message(...);
9   mq2.Send(msg2, trans);
10  ...
11  trans.Commit();
```

invoke the EndReceive() method to fetch the message from the queue (line 10). The input parameter passed to EndReceive() ensures that the application will retrieve the exact same message that caused the ReceiveCompleted event to be raised. After that, the application has a reference to the message object and may access the message body as usual (line 11). To keep receiving messages asynchronously, the application makes a call to BeginReceive() in line 12. This method must be called after EndReceive() in order to initiate a new asynchronous receive.

In the Main() function, the application performs two important tasks. The first task is to register the method that will serve as an event handler for the Receive-Completed event (line 20). This is done using the standard mechanism of events and event handlers available in the C# language. Basically, the syntax Event += new EventHandler(method) registers a method as an event handler for the specified event. Conversely, the syntax Event -= new EventHandler(method) removes the method as an event handler for the event. The second important task performed in the Main() function is to initiate the asynchronous receive with a call to BeginReceive(). From this moment on, MSMQ knows that the application is ready to receive a message.

3.6.7   Using MSMQ Transactions

Besides the distributed transactions described earlier in Sect. 3.6.3, it is possible to make use of message-only transactions that run within and are managed by MSMQ alone. Not every queue supports transactions; for this purpose, queues must be marked as being transactional when they are created. Then it is just a matter of creating a new transaction, perform the usual receive or send operations on queues, and commit the transaction. Listing 3.10 illustrates the procedure.

In line 1 a new transaction object is created. A reference to this object must be passed to every receive or send operation within the transaction. This is visible in lines 5 and 9, where the transaction object is provided as a parameter to receive and send operations. In principle these operations will take place in different queues, and Listing 3.10 illustrates that on lines 4 and 7. When all the desired operations within the transaction have been performed, the application calls the Commit() method (line 11) to complete the transaction and make its effects permanent. Alternatively, the application may invoke the Abort() method to cause rollback of the transaction.

Listing 3.11 Application code to request acknowledgments for sent message

```
1  MessageQueue mq = new MessageQueue(...);
2  Message msg = new Message(...);
3  msg.AcknowledgeType = AcknowledgeTypes.FullReceive;
4  msg.AdministrationQueue = new MessageQueue(...);
5  mq.Send(msg);
```

3.6.8 Using Acknowledgments

As explained in Sect. 3.6.1, MSMQ supports a wide range of acknowledgments, especially in the case of negative acknowledgments. Depending on the scenario at hand, an application may be interested in receiving some, but not all, of these acknowledgment types. The common practice in MSMQ is to specify which acknowledgments should be generated for each sent message. Also, the application must specify the queue where the acknowledgments are to be returned. All of these specifications are configured in the message itself, as illustrated in Listing 3.11.

In line 1 the application obtains a reference to the message queue and in line 2 creates a new message object. The type of acknowledgments desired for this message are specified in line 3 and stored in the message property AcknowledgeType. The MSMQ API available to .NET applications simplifies the task of specifying the acknowledgments by dividing positive and negative acknowledgments into different groups, namely positive arrival acknowledgments, positive receive acknowledgments, negative arrival acknowledgments, and negative receive acknowledgments. In this context, "arrival" means reaching the destination queue.

In the example of Listing 3.11, line 3, the application is interested in both positive and negative receive acknowledgments, hence FullReceive is specified. This means that a positive acknowledgment will be generated if the message is received from the destination queue (but not peeked), and a negative acknowledgment will be generated if an error occurs or when the time limit specified in the TimeToBeReceived property expires. Both kinds of acknowledgment are returned to the sending application via the administration queue specified in line 4. When the message is handed over to the Send() method in line 5, it carries all the information that MSMQ needs to generate and return the acknowledgments to the sending application.

3.7 Conclusion

In this chapter we have covered a lot of ground on messaging systems, from the fundamental concepts that underlie this kind of systems to advanced capabilities such as transactions and message acknowledgments. Before the advent of process-oriented integration platforms, and when network facilities where not as ubiquitous as they are today, messaging systems were a fundamental tool to integrate applications in a reliable and asynchronous way. Today, this technology still plays a key role in enterprise systems integration, but at a more infrastructural or supporting level, rather than at the core of the integration logic. Current integration platforms build upon messaging systems to implement integration logic over a mature and reliable infrastructure. However, in contrast with messaging systems, current platforms provide mechanisms to develop a complete integration solution as a centralized point of control where the integration logic can be changed and managed in a more flexible way. Using messaging systems alone, as has been done in the past, results in the integration logic being scattered and embedded in each application, making it difficult to reconfigure the whole solution in order to support new business processes. In the next chapter, we will make a step in this direction by explaining how message brokers differ from traditional messaging systems. This will be a change in paradigm that opens the way to understand the integration platforms available today.

Chapter 4
Message Brokers

The messaging systems described in the previous chapter can be seen as an integration infrastructure based on message queues that applications can use to communicate with each other asynchronously. The use of such infrastructure has several advantages. One is that all applications use the same interface (the messaging system API) to communicate with each other, rather than having to integrate each application with the custom API of other applications. The second advantage is that the use of message queues decouples applications from each other by allowing each application to handle requests at its own pace, without blocking other applications. And the third advantage is that applications can rely on the mechanisms of the messaging system that provide guaranteed delivery, efficient routing, storage, etc. without having to implement those mechanisms themselves.

However, from the point of view of integration, the use of a messaging system alone does not suffice, since it leaves up to the applications the decision of how they will interact with each other. If application A is configured to send messages to application B, and B is configured to send messages to application C, then if the need arises to change the sequence of interaction between these applications, it will be necessary to reconfigure the behavior of each application. In such scenario, the integration logic is distributed across applications, and changing this logic requires not only reconfiguring several applications but also checking that the new configuration works as expected. In a large infrastructure comprising many heterogeneous applications, such effort may be cumbersome and also error-prone.

Message brokers are different from messaging systems in that they themselves control how applications will interact with each other. Rather than letting each application decide the destination for a message, it is the message broker who will decide which application the message should be sent to. In this scenario, the sending application simply produces and delivers the message to the message broker which, in turn, will route the message according to its own rules. These rules can be as simple as specifying the subscribers for each kind of message, hence the connection between message brokers and the publish–subscribe paradigm. However, the simple fact that these rules are stored in a single place changes the nature of the integration solution and provides much more flexibility when the integration logic needs to

D.R. Ferreira, *Enterprise Systems Integration*, DOI 10.1007/978-3-642-40796-3_4,
© Springer-Verlag Berlin Heidelberg 2013

be reconfigured. In this scenario, it becomes much easier to modify the interaction between applications, as this can be done at the message broker, by rewiring them in order to implement a different business process.

Already in Sect. 3.1 we discussed the concept of content-based routing, where a messaging system is configured to route messages to different destinations according to the actual message content. This can be based not only on the type of message, but even for messages of the same type it may be the case that some have an attribute with a certain value and should be forwarded to one queue, while others have a different value for the same attribute and should be routed to another queue. A more sophisticated routing mechanism was presented in Fig. 3.5, where a process manager controls the sequence of interactions and the flow of data between applications. This provides much more flexibility in implementing the desired behavior and at the same time provides a single point of control. The downside is that, under heavy load, the process manager may become a performance bottleneck, since all traffic must pass through that routing component.

In the messaging technologies described in Sect. 3.5 (JMS) and Sect. 3.6 (MSMQ) we have not seen such mechanisms as content-based routers or process managers since they are usually reserved for message brokers, i.e., systems which not only provide the messaging infrastructure, as messaging systems do, but also provide capabilities for configuring the whole interaction between applications. In this context, both JMS and MSMQ can be regarded as belonging to the category of messaging systems, whereas a system such as the one presented in Chap. 2 (BizTalk) belongs to the category of message brokers. There are other integration platforms with capabilities similar to those of BizTalk Server, and all of them provide process-based routing on top of a messaging infrastructure.

4.1 Message-Level vs. Orchestration-Level Integration

A message broker is a composite system that comprises a messaging platform and an orchestrator, as illustrated in Fig. 4.1. Using a message broker, it is possible to integrate applications at two different levels: at the level of the messaging platform, or at the level of the orchestrator. At the level of the messaging platform, messages are routed between applications according to the publish–subscribe rules configured in the platform. If an application is configured as being a subscriber for a certain kind of message (or for a message that obeys certain criteria), then the message will be forwarded to that application. The publish–subscribe rules are stored in the messaging platform itself; applications connected to that platform have no control over that configuration and it is possible to change the interaction between applications just by changing the configuration in the messaging platform.

The same publish–subscribe mechanism can be used to integrate applications via the orchestrator. Here, the orchestrator is automatically configured as a subscriber for the messages that the orchestration is waiting to receive. Also, when the orchestration specifies that a certain message should be sent to an application,

Fig. 4.1 Message-level and orchestration-level routing in a message broker

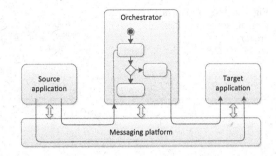

that application is automatically configured as a subscriber for that message. So the orchestrator works together with the messaging platform by configuring the publish–subscribe rules that enable the orchestration to work as expected. In other words, the publish–subscribe rules are configured automatically in the messaging platform in order to support the behavior defined in the orchestration.

As a result of these mechanisms, applications can be integrated in two different ways. One way is to use the messaging platform alone and manually configure a set of publish–subscribe rules in the messaging platform. These rules are *static* and, if needed, they must be changed by a system administrator. Another way is to develop an orchestration, and the publish–subscribe rules will be configured automatically in the messaging platform when the orchestration is *deployed*. Deployment means installing and configuring the orchestration in the message broker, both in the orchestrator and in the messaging platform, so that everything is prepared for the orchestration to run. In this case, the publish–subscribe rules are *dynamic* and they will be reconfigured automatically if the orchestration is changed and redeployed.

4.2 Publish–Subscribe with Message Filters

Perhaps the simplest way to implement a publish–subscribe system is through the use of message filters. The concept of message filter has been briefly described in Sect. 3.1 as a special kind of router. Basically, a message filter is a component that can be associated with a receiving application; the application will receive a message only if the message complies with the condition specified in the filter. If each application connected to the messaging platform has its own filter, then message routing between applications becomes as simple as iterating through all filters and checking whether the message produced by a sending application complies with the conditions in any of those filters. The filters which yield a positive result will let the message go through to the corresponding receiving application.

Figure 4.2 illustrates this concept. A message that enters the messaging platform will be inspected in order to determine which filter conditions hold true. In the example of Fig. 4.2, a message will be forwarded to application *A* if the property Customer has the value XYZ; it will be forwarded to application *B* if Price is

Fig. 4.2 Use of filters to
route messages in a message
broker

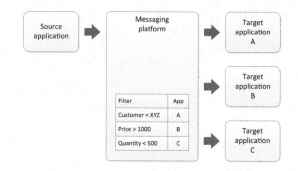

over 1,000; and it will be forwarded to application C if Quantity is less than 500.
These conditions are independent and, in general, they do not have to be mutually
exclusive, so the same message may be forwarded to n-out-of-m applications, where
$n \leq m$. In particular, it may happen that none of the conditions hold true (i.e.,
$n = 0$); in this case, the message is not delivered to any destination. Although such
behavior may be the intended one for a given message, the message broker is likely
to generate an error or warning if such situation occurs. For example, this is the
reason why BizTalk generates the error "no subscribers found."

The use of message filters requires the message broker to inspect an incoming
message in order to retrieve the property values that are needed to evaluate the filter
conditions. In the example of Fig. 4.2, Customer, Price, and Quantity are properties to
be retrieved from the message body. Clearly, the message broker must know how to
find these properties in the message. Usually, the message schema will be available
to the broker (in case, for example, transformations are needed) so it would not
be difficult to inspect the message content. However, for performance reasons, it
is a good idea to facilitate the access to the required properties, so that the message
broker spends as little time as possible in the processing of each message. This leads
to the concept of *promoted properties*, as explained next.

4.3   Promoted Properties

When the routing of messages is to be decided based on the actual message content,
as in the example of Fig. 4.2, it becomes necessary to provide the message broker
with all the properties required for evaluating the filter conditions. Rather than
requiring the message broker to go through the whole message content in order to
find those properties, it is more convenient to bring those properties to the forefront
of the message, where they can be accessed more easily. This can be done, for
example, by writing those properties in the message header, so that the message
broker can read them without having to open and go through the message body.

To understand this concept, an analogy can be established with a traditional mail system. Instead of sending a letter to the destination specified in the envelope, suppose that the destination is to be determined based on some information contained in the letter itself. In this scenario, the postman would have to open the letter and read its content in order to find that info. Rather than allowing this to happen, it is more convenient to write that information outside in the envelope, so that the letter can be delivered without being opened.

The same principle applies to the messaging platform in a message broker. For routing purposes, it is more convenient to make the required properties easily accessible, rather than requiring the message broker to read and retrieve them from the message body. Making properties (that are inside the message body) accessible from the outside is referred to as *property promotion*.

Property promotion is a mechanism that should be used with care. In general, it is possible to promote all properties in the message body. However, properties should not be promoted because they *can* be promoted, but because they *must* be promoted. The way in which property promotion is implemented depends on the particular message broker being used but, in its simplest form, promoting a property may imply writing additional message headers. These headers inform the message broker that the message carries properties that are required for content-based routing. The presence of such headers also instructs the message broker to read and use those property values. If the message contains promoted properties that are not being used for message routing, then the message broker undergoes unnecessary work and delay while processing the message.

Therefore, system developers and integrators should have a good understanding of promoted properties and what they are used for, in order to avoid making suboptimal decisions which may have an impact on the performance of the message broker and of the integration solution overall.

In BizTalk, the use of promoted properties is implemented by means of a special-purpose *property schema*, as illustrated in Fig. 4.3. A property schema defines which properties will be used for message routing. The conditions specified in a message filter must refer to properties defined in a property schema. So, in a sense, a property schema defines the vocabulary to be used by message filters. A different matter is how to obtain the values for these promoted properties; this is done by establishing a relationship between the elements in a message schema and the properties defined in a property schema.

For example, suppose that an incoming message (e.g., a purchase request) has an element Qty used to denote the quantity of the product to be purchased. Also, suppose that this information is used to route the purchase request in the following way: if the quantity exceeds 500 units the request is denied and is routed back to the original sender; otherwise, the request is approved and forwarded to an ERP system. (This is similar to the example that was used in Sect. 2.4 to present a simple orchestration; here we resort to the same scenario to illustrate the use of content-based routing at the message level.) In this scenario, it would be necessary to create a property schema and to define a promoted property, e.g., Quantity. Then, in a second step, it would be necessary to establish a relationship between the Qty element in

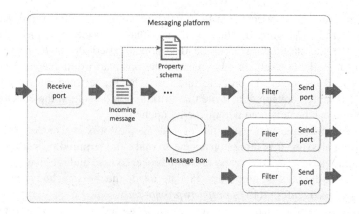

Fig. 4.3 Use of property schemas in BizTalk

the purchase request schema and the Quantity promoted property. This is equivalent to *promoting* the Qty element, and such promotion has two effects:

• The first is that the value for the Qty element will be brought to the forefront of the message, so that the message broker can read it without having to read and parse the message body.
• The second effect is that, as a new purchase request enters the messaging platform, the value of the Qty element will be used to set the value of the Quantity property defined in the property schema.

In general, the name of the promoted property (Quantity in this example) does not have to match the name of the element (Qty) which provides the value for that property. However, the names used to specify the filter conditions (e.g., Quantity ≤ 500) must be the names of properties defined in the property schema.

After reading the promoted properties in the message and setting the value for the corresponding properties in the property schema, these properties can now be used to evaluate the filter conditions. Figure 4.3 illustrates the use of property schemas in connection with filters at each send port. As explained in Sect. 2.3, a send port has an adapter, a pipeline, and an optional transformation map. In addition, a send port may have another optional component, which is the message filter. The filter contains a set of logical expressions, each yielding a result of true or false. These expressions are based on the values of properties defined in a property schema, and they can be combined with logical AND and OR operators. The filter condition may therefore comprise several expressions on different properties.

The concept is similar to that presented in Fig. 4.2, but while in Fig. 4.2 the filter condition for each target application had a single expression, in practice the conditions may be composed of several expressions connected by logical operators. Another difference between Figs. 4.2 and 4.3 is in the place where these filter conditions are actually stored. In Fig. 4.2 these appear to be stored together, somewhere inside the messaging platform, while Fig. 4.3 shows that, in BizTalk, the filter conditions are actually stored in the filter within each send port.

4.4 Orchestration-Level Integration

In enterprise systems integration, the behavior of an integration solution can often be implemented in different ways. In the previous section, a solution that checked the quantity of a purchase request and decided where to send that request was implemented at the messaging level based on message routing mechanisms. The same behavior can be implemented at the orchestration level, with much more flexibility. At the orchestration level the solution is not confined to the publish–subscribe paradigm and, in principle, it is possible to implement any kind of interaction between applications. In this context, the message routing mechanisms of the messaging platform are essential in order to ensure that the orchestration runs as expected. The key feature of an orchestrator is that it allows specifying the interaction between applications at a different level, on top of the messaging platform.

When using an orchestrator, the messaging platform is configured in such a way that the orchestrator becomes a subscriber for all messages that the deployed orchestrations are waiting to receive. On the other hand, the orchestrator also becomes the producer of messages that are to be delivered to target applications. In this context, the orchestrator publishes and subscribes messages just like a regular application. The difference is the close connections that exist between the orchestrator and the messaging platform, especially in terms of receive and send ports: the ports defined in an orchestration can be *bound* to specific ports that exist in the messaging platform, so that receiving or sending a message at the orchestration level has the same effect as routing messages at the messaging level.

Figure 4.4 illustrates the use of an orchestration to implement the behavior of the same scenario as before, where a purchase request is received and the decision of what to do with it depends on some property of that request, in this case the quantity specified in the Qty element. To implement this scenario, the orchestration has the following steps:

1. It receives the purchase request through a receive port.
2. It checks whether the Qty element in the purchase request is greater than 500, and then:

   a. If so, it transforms the request into a denied request message and sends it through a send port back to the original requester (left branch).
   b. If not, then it just forwards the message to the ERP system through another send port (right branch).

3. In either case, the orchestration has nothing left to do afterwards and terminates.

It is worth noting that the transformation on the left branch can be attained by a transformation map, so the use of a transformation map in the orchestration effectively dispenses the use of a transformation map in the send port. This mere detail is quite significant, as it shows that the use of an orchestration brings visibility to components of the integration solution that would otherwise be embedded in the

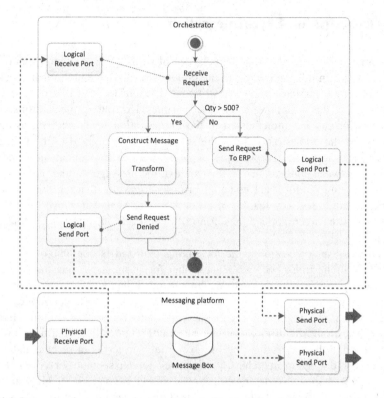

Fig. 4.4 Integration through an orchestrator on top of a messaging platform

messaging platform. Also, in the orchestration the send port can be changed while keeping the same transformation, whereas at the messaging platform changing to another send port would require configuring the transformation map in the new send port. These are just some examples of the advantages in using an orchestration rather than relying solely on the mechanisms of the messaging platform.

Figure 4.4 also illustrates the connections between ports in the orchestration and ports in the messaging platform. At the orchestration level, ports are referred to as *logical ports*, and they specify the points of entry and exit of messages in the orchestration. In the messaging platform, ports are referred to as *physical ports* and they contain all the required configurations (in terms of protocols and addresses) to communicate with the application associated with that port. After an orchestration has been deployed, but before it can actually run, it is necessary to establish a connection between each of its logical ports and a physical ports existing, or to be created, in the messaging platform. Such connection between a logical port and physical port is referred to as a *port binding*.

When a message enters a physical receive port, if that port is bound to a logical port, then the message is forwarded to the orchestration containing that logical port, as in Fig. 4.4. Likewise, when the orchestration sends a message through a logical send port, the message is sent through the physical send port that is bound to that logical port. For physical ports that are not bound to logical ports, the messaging platform will make use of its own routing mechanisms, as described in the previous section. In particular, a physical send port that is not bound to a logical port will need to have a filter in order to subscribe to messages.

4.5 Distinguished Properties

In the example of Fig. 4.4, the orchestration receives a purchase request and decides whether to deny the request (left branch) or to forward it to the ERP system (right branch). The decision is based on the value of the Qty element in the incoming message, so the orchestration must have access to this element in order to determine how to proceed. Contrary to what happens in the messaging platform (Sect. 4.3), where the properties to be accessed for the purpose of message routing must have been promoted, at the orchestration level there is no need to promote such properties, since the orchestration has full access to the actual message content.

As explained in Sect. 3.1, and as shown in Sects. 3.5 and 3.6, a message has two main parts known as header and body. While the header is used by the messaging platform for routing purposes, the body carries the actual content that is of interest to applications. This is similar to a traditional mail scenario in which the information in the envelope is used by the post office to deliver a letter to its destination; but once the letter arrives at the destination, the receiver will throw away the envelope and focus on its actual content. The same happens with the messaging platform and the orchestrator: while the messaging platform will use the message header to route the message, the orchestrator will be working with the actual message body in order to implement the desired integration logic.

Therefore, the orchestrator can make use of any content available in a message to implement the orchestration logic. For example, if a message needs to be transformed to another schema, the orchestration can use a transformation map to create a new message with the same content but with a different structure. However, some elements in particular may play a critical role in determining how the orchestration will be executed, as is the case with the element Qty in the example of Fig. 4.4. To allow the use of expressions such as Qty > 500 in the orchestration, those elements need to be marked in a special way, so that the orchestrator knows that Qty refers to a specific element in the purchase request message. An element that is marked for this purpose is called a *distinguished property*. Essentially, distinguished properties are message elements that can be used in expressions throughout an orchestration, to determine how the orchestration will be executed at run-time.

Distinguished properties, contrary to promoted properties, do not pose a problem from the performance point of view. The use of promoted properties requires the messaging platform to retrieve and store them for routing purposes, and this may result in a slight increase in the time required to handle each message at run-time. On the other hand, distinguished properties have no significant impact on performance; they are used at design-time to specify how the behavior of an orchestration may change depending on the actual content of messages. Regardless of how this content affects the orchestration flow, it does not require any additional processing, since that content (the message body) is available to the orchestration in any case.

To summarize, promoted properties are used at the message level to implement message routing based on filters associated with send ports. Distinguished properties are used at the orchestration level to specify how the orchestration will behave at run-time according to the content of messages. In both cases, the message content is used to determine the behavior of the integration solution. However, at the message level one can only make use of publish–subscribe mechanisms, while at the orchestration level there is a wide range of constructs allowing to implement any form of desired behavior, as we will see in later chapters.

4.6   Correlations

In Sect. 3.1 we explained the concept of process-based routing which relies on a process manager to coordinate the interaction between applications, as illustrated in Fig. 3.5. The purpose of this process manager is exactly the same as that of an orchestrator in a message broker, and just as a process manager is able to execute multiple instances of the same process, so an orchestrator is able to execute multiple instances of an orchestration. As an example, in Fig. 4.4 the first step in the orchestration is to receive a purchase request from a receive port. This means that the orchestration is triggered every time a purchase request arrives at that receive port. Triggering the orchestration means creating and starting a new orchestration instance. Each orchestration instance has a life of its own and is independent from other instances. In particular, there will be instances where the purchase request will be denied because the quantity exceeds 500, and other instances where the request will be accepted because the quantity is lower. Also, in general, some instances may run successfully while others may end in error, and some instances may take long to complete while others may be rather quick. It all depends on the particular data and conditions that an orchestration instance finds at run-time.

For a better understanding of the concept of orchestration instance, an analogy can be established with an order placed in an online bookshop. As the customer enters a new order, a new instance of an order processing orchestration is triggered. This orchestration may consist in, for example, fetching the books from the warehouse, packing them, and shipping them to the customer. Each order originates an instance of this orchestration that is independent from other instances being created by the orders of the same or different customers. For example, a customer may check the status of an order at any time, and each order has its own status. Also, an order may be canceled without affecting the processing of other orders. Since orders are handled as separate process instances, they can be managed independently.

When a customer wants to check the status of an order, a small but important problem arises: the customer must be able to identify the order whose status is to be retrieved. Naturally, providing the title of the ordered book does not suffice, since many customers may have ordered the same book. Perhaps providing the title together with the customer info may suffice, if the customer did not order the same book more than once. In any case, a precise, unambiguous way of identifying the customer order is needed in order to locate the correct orchestration instance in the midst of all instances for all book orders. This is not just a problem of choosing an appropriate identifier as when selecting a primary key for a relational database table; the problem of identifying a particular orchestration instance may appear several times during the execution of that instance, and it has far-reaching implications with respect to the inner workings of a message broker.

Figure 4.5 illustrates the problem by means of a simple orchestration which, at a certain point, sends a request and receives a response from an external system. To begin with, three messages enter the messaging platform through the first receive port shown in the left side. These three messages trigger three instances of the same orchestration, all of which will do exactly the same thing: they will send a shipping request to a logistics provider application, they will receive the response from that application, and they will send an confirmation to the customer. At the point shown in Fig. 4.5, the three instances have already sent the shipping request to the logistics provider and are now waiting for a response. When the first response comes in, which orchestration instance should it be sent to?

Clearly, there needs to be a mechanism for *correlating* the present response with a previously sent request. Such correlation is necessary in order to determine which orchestration instance is the correct recipient for each response. This becomes a matter of determining the subscriber for an incoming message, and therefore must be dealt with at the message level, in much the same way as explained in Sect. 4.2. In particular, it will be necessary to use promoted properties (explained in Sect. 4.3) to correlate a response with a previous request based on some property or properties. In the context of a correlation, the set of promoted properties that are used to correlate messages is referred to as the *correlation id*.

In a relational database, it is often easier to create a new column to serve as the primary key for a table, rather than selecting a subset of existing columns, which is not guaranteed to yield a unique identifier. The same scenario applies to correlation ids: often it becomes easier to create a new element in the message schemas just for the purpose of serving as a correlation id, rather than using an identifier based on the existing message elements, which are not guaranteed to be unique. In the example of the online bookshop from above, when a customer wants to check the status of an order, a suitable identifier must be provided to identify the desired process instance. For this purpose, it is common to have a unique order id, which can be used to identify the process instance without having to resort to other order data.

In any case, regardless of the actual message elements that are selected to serve as a correlation id, these elements must be promoted so that the orchestration instance can be determined at the message level.

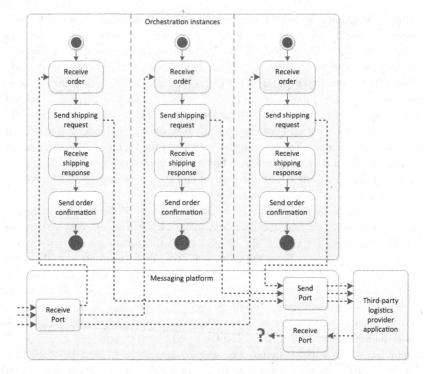

Fig. 4.5 Need for correlation in an orchestration with a request–response interaction

For the moment, let us assume that each orchestration instance shown in Fig. 4.5 has a unique order id. For simplicity, it can be assumed that this order id is provided in the original order message that triggered the whole orchestration. When an orchestration instance creates the shipping request, it includes the order id as a promoted property to serve as correlation id. The orchestration then sends the shipping request through the messaging platform, which reads the promoted properties that are being used as correlation id. In the future, any incoming message that arrives at the messaging platform having the same values for the same promoted properties will be forward to the same orchestration instance.

The scenario in Fig. 4.5 can therefore be implemented in the following way:

1. In the initial order message that triggers the whole orchestration, provide a unique order id value that can be used in correlations within the orchestration.
2. In the schema for the shipping request to be sent to the logistics provider, include an additional element to store the order id. Also in the schema for the shipping response, include an additional element to store the order id.
3. Create a property schema to define the promoted property that will be used as correlation id. We assume that this promoted property will be called OrderId.

4. Promote the order id elements of step 2. In both the shipping request and the shipping response, establish a relationship to the OrderId property defined in the property schema created in step 3.
5. In the orchestration, create a new correlation based on the OrderId property. This correlation will be used at two points in the orchestration: when the shipping request is being sent, and when the shipping response is being received.

In the BizTalk platform, step 5 is a bit more intricate because it requires several sub-steps. In particular, BizTalk makes a distinction between the concepts of *correlation type* and *correlation set*. Basically, a correlation type is an artifact that specifies the properties on which the correlation will be based. In this example, there is a single property called OrderId. So, by defining a correlation type with OrderId, it becomes possible to create correlations based on that property. To create an actual correlation that can be used in the orchestration, it is necessary to define a correlation set. Therefore, a correlation set can be seen as an instance of a previously defined correlation type. In general, it is possible to create several correlation sets from the same correlation type; this would mean having several correlations across the orchestration, all of which are based on the OrderId property.

After creating the correlation type and at least one correlation set, which represents the actual correlation, the next sub-step is to indicate where the correlation will be used in the orchestration. The point where the correlation is first used is the point where the correlation set will be *initialized*. In this example, the correlation set will be initialized when the shipping request is being sent. Subsequent actions within the same correlation are said to *follow* the same correlation set. In this example, the correlation set will be followed when the shipping response is being received. No other actions in this orchestration initialize or follow correlations.

Although the correlation is being initialized when the shipping request is sent, it would be possible to initialize it even earlier, at the point where the initial order is received. This is because the order id is assumed to be available at that point, so it would be possible to initialize the correlation set immediately. On the other hand, it would also be possible to extend the use of the same correlation to later actions, such as to the point when the order confirmation is sent to the customer. In other words, all the actions in the orchestration of Fig. 4.5 could be performed within a correlation, although that is not necessary. The point at which the correlation is strictly required is when receiving the shipping response, since at this point it is necessary to determine the orchestration instance that the response is intended for. For this to work, the correlation must have been initialized previously, so it is required also when sending the shipping request. However, nothing precludes the same correlation to be used at other points in the orchestration as well.

This shows that the use of correlations is not confined to request–response scenarios, and in fact they can be extended to include any set of interactions with the outside world. Examples are a request that results in multiple responses, or a sequence of several request–response pairs within the same correlation.

Another important and often misunderstood issue has to do with receive actions. The first receive in an orchestration is the action that triggers the orchestration, so that when a message is received, a new orchestration instance is created. As explained in Sect. 2.4, such kind of receive is called an *activating* receive. Clearly, no actions can precede an activating receive, since before that the orchestration has not been instantiated yet. However, after the activating receive it is possible to have other receive actions, as in the example of Fig. 4.5 where the orchestration receives the shipping response. Obviously, such kind of receive is non-activating, since the orchestration instance is already running. Now, if a receive is non-activating, then it must follow a correlation; otherwise, the messaging platform would be unable to forward messages to that running orchestration instance.

The conclusion is that a receive action must either be the initial, activating receive in an orchestration (and there is a single activating receive in an orchestration), or be a non-activating receive which follows a correlation (several such receives may exist in an orchestration). In the latter case, the correlation must have been previously initialized by a previous action, usually a send. Developers often find it strange that they have to make such an elaborate decision when using something as simple as a receive action. Hopefully, this section has contributed to clarify why such decision is necessary: it has to do with the fact that several instances of the same orchestration may be running at the same time on top of the messaging platform. The activating receive creates such instances; the non-activating receive requires correlation to determine which instance a message is intended for.

4.7   Using Asynchronous Messaging

In the previous sections we have explained that a message broker is a combination of a messaging platform and an orchestrator, such that the orchestrator works on top of the messaging platform, i.e., it coordinates the exchange of messages between applications connected to the messaging platform. In this context, the messaging platform has been presented as a messaging system similar to those described in Chap. 3. In practice, however, the features provided by a messaging system and by the messaging platform of a message broker are slightly different.

On one hand, there is no need for a message broker to replicate the functionality and reliability mechanisms of a messaging system; if such capabilities are required, the message broker can be integrated with an existing messaging system, such as a JMS provider or MSMQ. On the other hand, the message broker extends the capabilities of traditional messaging systems by making use of the concepts of receive and send ports. Receive ports are entry points of messages in the messaging platform, i.e., they are message publishers, and they are connected to applications that produce messages. Send ports are message subscribers, and they are connected to applications that consume messages. Therefore, a message broker works according to the publish–subscribe paradigm, while traditional messaging systems typically support point-to-point communication through channels or queues.

In addition, a message broker is able to coordinate message exchange between applications through an orchestrator, and for that purpose it is necessary to configure the port bindings between the logical receive and send ports in an orchestration and the physical receive and send ports created or available at the messaging level.

Despite these differences, it is possible to use messaging systems of the kind described in Chap. 3 in combination with a message broker. For this purpose, it is possible to specify that a physical receive port is connected to a messaging system, so that it receives messages from a message queue. Similarly, it is possible to specify that a send port is connected to a messaging system, so that it sends messages from a message queue. The queue from which messages are received and the queue to which messages are sent may be in the same or in different message systems. In the latter case, one can see the potential of using a message broker to create a bridge between different messaging systems.

In Sect. 2.3 (Fig. 2.4) we have seen that both receive and send ports comprise an adapter, a pipeline, and an optional transformation map. (Furthermore, in Sect. 4.3 we have seen that a send port may contain an optional message filter as well.) The adapter in a port is the component that specifies the protocols and parameters to connect to the source (in case of a receive port) or the target application (in case of a send port). As explained in Sect. 2.3, a message broker typically includes a set of predefined adapters, so configuring the adapter for use in a port becomes a matter of selecting one of the existing adapters. In particular, there are adapters for messaging systems. For example, BizTalk includes an adapter for MSMQ that allows receive ports and send ports to connect to message queues.

To configure the MSMQ adapter in a receive port, one basically specifies the queue name and whether the message should be received within a transaction or not. When configuring the MSMQ adapter in a send port, a lot more options are available; besides the queue name and transaction support, one can specify the priority of the message to be sent, whether it should be sent in express or recoverable mode, whether acknowledgments should be generated, etc. In general, all those message properties that can be configured by a sending application using MSMQ can also be configured in the MSMQ adapter of a send port.

However, there is one important difference in an application that communicates with BizTalk through MSMQ, as opposed to an application that communicates with another application through MSMQ. When two applications exchange messages through MSMQ, as described in Sect. 3.6, it is possible to use the Body property. In this case, the sender application sets the Body property and the receiver retrieves the content of that property. During transmission, MSMQ automatically formats the body content into an XML message (an example is shown in Listing 3.7 on page 69). When using an integration platform such as BizTalk, such automatic formatting interferes with the processing of messages because the message broker is expecting an XML message with a user-defined schema, rather than the schema used by MSMQ. In fact, in integration platforms such as BizTalk, developing a new solution begins by defining the schemas of messages that will go across the message broker. If MSMQ is allowed to wrap the message content into a new, previously undefined schema, then the message broker will be unable to handle the message correctly.

Listing 4.1 Application code to send a message to BizTalk through MSMQ

```
1    string requestMsg = File.ReadAllText("PurchaseRequest.xml");
2
3    string queueName = @".\private$\requests";
4    MessageQueue queue = new MessageQueue(queueName);
5
6    Message queueMsg = new Message();
7
8    StreamWriter writer = new StreamWriter(queueMsg.BodyStream);
9    writer.Write(requestMsg);
10   writer.Flush();
11
12   queue.Send(queueMsg);
```

Clearly, something must be done in order to avoid having MSMQ interfere with the message content. In particular, the message body must be written to the message in such a way that it reaches the message broker without having been changed or reformatted. The solution to this problem is to write the message body through the BodyStream property rather than through the Body property. When writing to the BodyStream property, the content is written directly to the message body, as if it would be a file or stream. At the receiving end, the message broker reads the message body data through the BodyStream property as well. This way, it is possible to have the message content arrive at the message broker intact.

The only problem with this approach is that the source application must guarantee that the body content adheres to the schema that the message broker is waiting for. This is easy to achieve if the source application has access to an example of the message to be sent. For this purpose, it is possible to create a sample instance from the predefined schema and provide it to the source application, so that this application has only to modify the data elements and send the whole message to the message broker, in the body stream. The procedure is illustrated in Listing 4.1.

This example is based on the same scenario as in Sect. 4.4, particularly Fig. 4.4 on page 82. Here we suppose that the physical receive port in Fig. 4.4 is connected to a message queue, and Listing 4.1 shows the application code for the source application that sends a message to that queue. For this purpose, we assume that an instance of the purchase request schema is available in an XML file (line 1). For simplicity, we also assume that such instance already contains the correct data to be sent. Now it is a matter of opening the specified queue (lines 3–4), creating a new message (line 6), writing the message body (lines 8–10), and sending the message (line 12). The main difference to the example of Listing 3.6 on page 69 is that the message body is being written directly as a stream through the BodyStream property. Line 8 opens the stream, line 9 writes the content, which comes from line 1, and line 10 ensures that the content has actually been written to the message object before sending it on line 12. This way, the message broker (BizTalk) will receive the exact same content as in the XML file specified in line 1.

If the Qty element in the purchase request contains a value that is less than or equal to 500, then the orchestration in Fig. 4.4 will approve the request and forward it to the ERP system (right-side branch). Assuming that the send port is connected to

Listing 4.2 Application code to receive a message from BizTalk through MSMQ

```
1   string queueName = @".\private$\requestsaccepted";
2   MessageQueue queue = new MessageQueue(queueName);
3
4   Message queueMsg = queue.Receive();
5
6   StreamReader reader = new StreamReader(queueMsg.BodyStream);
7   string requestMsg = reader.ReadToEnd();
8
9   Console.WriteLine(requestMsg);
```

a message queue, then the application code at the receiving end should do something similar to Listing 4.2 to retrieve the message and its content.

In lines 1–2 the application just opens the message queue where the message sends the message to. In line 4, there is a synchronous receive, but an asynchronous receive, as in Listing 3.9 on page 71, could be used as well. The important feature is in lines 6–7, where the application reads the message body. Again, this is done by accessing the body content as a stream, through the BodyStream property. In this example, the application just reads the entire body content (line 7) and writes it to the command line. A real ERP system would probably store the purchase request in a database or handle it in some other way.

4.8   Conclusion

Message brokers provide the possibility of implementing the integration logic outside the applications and in the integration platform itself. This provides a much-desired centralized point of control, where the integration logic can be maintained and changed according to business needs. A message broker differs from a traditional messaging system in that it makes extensive use of the publish–subscribe paradigm, and it includes an orchestrator to coordinate message exchanges between applications. The desired behavior can be implemented by means of orchestrations which define the routing of messages between receive ports and send ports in the underlying messaging platform.

Although orchestrations represent a process-oriented and flexible way to implement the integration logic, it is possible to integrate applications through a message broker without the use of orchestrations. In this case, the integration solution will rely on the publish–subscribe mechanisms of the messaging platform alone, and for this purpose it becomes necessary to define message filters to specify which messages should be sent through each send port. The use of transformation maps in receive and send ports also allows messages to be transformed if necessary. A disadvantage of this approach is that the overall behavior is embedded in the messaging platform and is not as easy to understand as in the case of an orchestration.

In conclusion, as far as the external applications are concerned, the same behavior can be implemented at the messaging level or at the orchestration level. For solutions at the messaging level, it becomes necessary to promote certain message properties in order to evaluate filter conditions and determine which send ports the message should be sent to. The message properties that must be promoted are the ones that are used to define the filter conditions. For solutions at the orchestration level, it is necessary to promote certain message properties as well, in order to determine which orchestration instance the message should be sent to. In this case, the message properties that must be promoted are the ones that are used to establish a correlation with a previous message belonging to the same orchestration instance.

The last section (Sect. 4.7) has shown how to connect a message broker with a messaging system, so that the broker receives messages from and sends messages to a message queue, which provides asynchronous interaction with the external applications. The same section also explained how the applications should write and read the message body in order to exchange messages with a predefined schema.

In the same way as messaging systems can be connected to a message broker, other kinds of systems can be connected to a message broker as well. We have already discussed that such connection can be made through the use of adapters in receive and send ports. In the next chapters, we will have a closer look at the concept of adapter and at the way other systems—namely databases and Web services—can be invoked from within an orchestration running in the message broker.

Part III
Adapters

Chapter 5
Data Adapters

Integration is an effort to bring heterogeneous applications to interoperate with each other. Had these applications been devised to interoperate with each other in the first place, there would be no need for integration. Integration is therefore something that is typically done after applications have already been developed and deployed in the organization. Through time, as the organization evolves and changes, it is likely that new applications are developed, acquired, upgraded, replaced, etc., leading to a heterogeneous landscape of information systems. It is in this scenario that system integrators must come up with solutions to connect applications, old and new, in order to implement the desired business processes. So while developers keep creating applications according to particular business requirements, it is the job of system integrators to ensure that it is possible to implement processes that span the whole organization on top of those heterogeneous applications.

The job of a systems integrator would be much easier if all applications were developed using the same technology. In this case, by mastering such technology it would be possible either to change the application code or to develop new code in order to make applications interoperate. However, technologies keep changing all the time, and applications from different technology generations will coexist in an organization. Some of these technologies can be so old that there are no longer any developers or any system integrators with experience in the technology or having the appropriate tools to keep working with it. However, such applications are still in use because they fulfill some business need for which a newer application is not available. Such applications are referred to as *legacy systems*.

Often a legacy system can only be regarded as a black box. Knowledge of how it works on the inside is unavailable, and both the source code and the documentation may be missing as well. The only way to integrate with such applications is through the mechanisms of input and output available to the users. This is certainly the worst-case scenario, since then the integration must be done either manually or through an adapter that simulates the behavior of a user. Fortunately, applications are usually developed according to a common and well-known architectural model—namely, the three-tier model—which provides several possibilities for integration. It is these possibilities that we explore in this and the next chapter.

D.R. Ferreira, *Enterprise Systems Integration*, DOI 10.1007/978-3-642-40796-3_5,
© Springer-Verlag Berlin Heidelberg 2013

Fig. 5.1 Integration
approaches at different
application layers

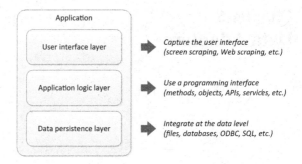

5.1   The Three-Tier Model

The three-tier model is an architectural pattern that reflects a common practice
in software engineering. Essentially, applications are developed according to a
common architecture that comprises three different layers: the data persistence
layer, the application logic layer, and the user interface layer. The user interface layer
refers to the application functionality that has to do exclusively with user interaction
such as displaying data and receiving user commands. At the opposite end, the data
persistence layer is where the data reside; at this layer, persistence is usually attained
by storing data in files or in a database. The application logic layer is where the
application manipulates entities (or objects) and executes program logic.

As an example, a purchase order may be regarded as a different entity at each
layer: at the user interface layer, it is a set of data that the user can visualize on the
screen and possibly change by means of certain commands; at the application logic
layer, it is an object (i.e., a class instance) with certain data attributes; and at the data
persistence layer, it is a row in a database table that stores all purchase orders.

Figure 5.1 illustrates the layers in a three-tier model, suggesting that each
application layer actually represents a different possibility for integration. At the
data persistence layer, it is possible to integrate through files or through a database;
at the application logic layer, one integrates with application code directly in order
to perform the desired operations; and at the user interface layer, it is possible to
access and submit data using the same I/O mechanisms available to end users.

Such possibilities can be put into practice only under certain assumptions. For
example, to integrate through files, one assumes that the file format used by the
application is known and documented. To integrate through a database, one assumes
that the database schema is known and that there are sufficient privileges to access
and change the data. To integrate at the application logic layer, one must have either
the original source code for the application or a programming interface to invoke its
functionality. If none of these assumptions hold, then the only remaining option is to
integrate via the user interface, by developing an adapter that simulates the behavior
of a user that reads data and sends commands. Clearly, this is the least desirable
option, since the user interface may not provide a convenient way to access data and
to invoke the full range of application functionality.

An easier and more flexible approach is to integrate at the data layer. Integrating through files seems rather primitive but it can be quite effective; also, the use of standard file formats can facilitate this task. On the other hand, if a relational database system is being used, then there are several mature technologies that can be used to connect and interact with the database from any programming language. In either case, some care must be taken in order to avoid unpredictable application behavior. If the application logic is not completely known, then feeding the application with data through the data layer may cause exceptions, bugs, or other forms of undesired behavior. Therefore, integration at the data layer must be based on solid knowledge about how the application processes the data.

The ideal option is to integrate at the application logic layer. Here one can have complete control of how the application functionality will be invoked. This is also the option that requires the deepest knowledge about the application internals, since it may involve programming the application to do something it was not originally prepared to do. If the source code is available, then this becomes more of a software engineering issue. Typically, the source will not be available, but a suitable application programming interface (API) will be provided by the application developer. In this case, one has to learn the API in order to develop an adapter.

Often the purpose of an adapter is just to provide a different API on top of the proprietary application API. This is especially the case for applications that have a rather comprehensive and complicated API, when only a subset of the application functionality will actually be used for integration. In this case, the adapter works as a software layer that provides a simplified API to interact with the application.

The way in which APIs can be built on top of other APIs can be seen at work in other application layers as well, namely at the data layer where there are several alternative APIs, as well as database APIs that build on top of one another. Also at the user interface layer, it is possible to build an adapter that interacts with the user interface and exposes an API to other applications. From this perspective, an adapter can be seen as a software layer that brings the problem of integration to the level of application logic, regardless of how data is actually exchanged with the application, be it through the data layer, through the application logic layer, or through the user interface layer. In this chapter we will be mostly concerned with adapters at the user interface layer and at the data layer, leaving adapters at the application logic layer to be studied in the next chapter.

5.2   Capturing the User Interface

In an organization, there may be applications for which no source code is available, no documentation is available, no APIs are provided, no experience with the programming language exists, the technological platform is obsolete, integration is not supported, etc. In this scenario, the only option is to integrate through the user interface layer, by using the same I/O mechanisms as those available to the users.

This involves reading data from whatever mechanism the application has to display them (e.g., text boxes), and sending commands through whatever user interface elements that the application provides (e.g., buttons). Clearly, the implementation of an adapter for the user interface layer is very dependent on the particular UI features provided by the application. In some cases, the more sophisticated the user interface, the more difficult it will be to grab data from that UI in an automated way.

As with other application layers, integration at the user interface layer is only possible under certain assumptions. For example, some very old systems such as the first generation of computer mainframes (dating from the 1960s) had no user interface at all; instead, data I/O was based on punched (perforated) cards. Teletype devices (a kind of typewriter with communication capabilities) were also used as a command line interface to mainframe computers, but still the output was printed on paper. In the 1970s, mainframes started having client terminals with text-mode user interfaces. Later, during the 1980s, these client terminals were replaced by personal computers equipped with terminal emulation software. It was only in the 1990s that enterprise systems acquired graphical user interfaces (GUIs). After 2000, proprietary GUIs were discontinued in favor of Web-based user interfaces.

From this brief overview of how user interfaces evolved over the years, it becomes apparent that a user interface adapter may not be a straightforward thing to develop. Integrating with punched cards is out of question, and fortunately it will be hardly necessary, as enterprise systems have evolved well beyond that. On the other hand, a text-mode user interface may not be too difficult to integrate with, if the communication protocol is well documented; in this case, the adapter can work in a similar way to a terminal emulator, while providing external applications with a convenient API to access the system.

Graphical user interfaces, despite being more sophisticated, can be harder to integrate with, since it is not easy to capture the layout of a GUI and interact with its elements in an automated way. In some cases, this can be made easier by resorting to features of the operating system, such as querying the graphical elements that are currently being presented on the screen. In the Windows operating system, for example, it is possible to write a native application (in C/C++) that retrieves a handle to an application window that is being displayed on the screen, and from that handle it is possible to retrieve a further set of handles for the GUI elements within that application window. Such kind of approach is referred to as *screen scraping* and it can be used to capture any data that is currently being displayed on the screen.

Figure 5.2 illustrates the kind of elements that may be present in a GUI. After retrieving a handle to the main application window, it is possible to retrieve a handle to each of the GUI elements contained in that window. (In general, a GUI is built as a hierarchy of windows that contain other windows.) The user interface may include data-displaying elements (such as grid controls), data input elements (such as text boxes), and also action elements (such as buttons). After retrieving the handles to those elements, it is possible to fill in data and send commands to the application by sending system events to the main application window. This is done by calling special functions available in the operating system API. The events that are sent to the application are the same as those that would be generated if a user was

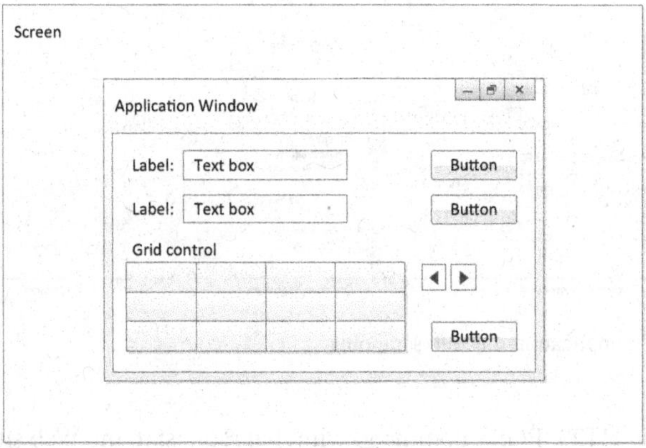

Fig. 5.2 Examples of graphical user interface elements

interacting with the application. This kind of adapter can be the most difficult to implement and it depends on the capabilities and API of the underlying operating system.

Fortunately, GUIs have evolved to become less platform-dependent, as developers started adopting more standard technologies. With the advent of the World Wide Web, application vendors started putting less effort on developing proprietary, native interfaces, and turned instead to lighter, Web-based user interfaces based on HTML and associated technologies, which can be displayed in any standard Web browser. In this case, the content is transmitted over the standard HTTP protocol, so it becomes fairly easy to write an adapter that opens a HTTP connection to a Web server, parses the HTML content, and submits new content through the use of HTTP commands.

In fact, this is the principle behind Web crawling applications and Web robots that collect data from the Web in an automated way. This can be used for either useful purposes (such as Web indexing and search) and unfortunately for malicious purposes as well (such as collecting e-mail addresses for spamming). In enterprise systems integration, and especially in cases where the integration logic requires interacting with external systems available on the Web, the use of adapters to automatically query Web sites and other resources on the Web is a normal procedure and can be implemented from any programming language.

A simple example is when the postal code for a certain address is required; typically, this can be fetched from some Web site or service available on the Web, so an adapter can be written to fetch these data automatically at run-time. What the adapter would do is open a HTTP connection to the Web site, request the Web page that contains the data, and parse the HTML content in the response. Alternatively, if the postal code must be retrieved by filling out some online form, the adapter can also perform this task automatically by assembling a request with the given postal

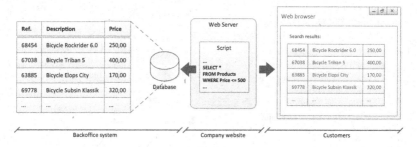

Fig. 5.3 A sample application for Web scrapping

address, send an HTTP POST command with that request to the Web site, and again retrieve the response and parse the HTML content.

Here we present a simple example of a Web-based application that serves as an online catalog for the bicycles being sold in a bike store. The prices are stored in a database somewhere in the backoffice of the company, but the information is made available to the public via the company Web site. This scenario is illustrated in Fig. 5.3, where a script running at the Web server retrieves all bicycle models that meet certain search criteria, e.g., price below a certain value. The results are transmitted to the client and rendered in the form of a HTML table.

Listing 5.1 shows an excerpt of C# code that illustrates how to connect to the Web server and retrieve the Web page (lines 1–5), as well how to extract the results from the HTML table using regular expressions (lines 7–12). The URL is hard-coded in line 1 but it could be generated dynamically by string concatenation with values obtained at run-time. Line 2 creates the HTTP request and line 3 sends the request to the Web server. Lines 4 and 5 read the response, which contains the HTML code for the Web page. It is possible that this HTML contains a lot of code that is used only for the purpose of rendering the Web page. The relevant data will be found inside a table with three columns and an unknown number of rows. In this example, we use regular expressions to retrieve all occurrences of the pattern specified in line 7. Line 8 obtains a collection of all such occurrences, and line 9 iterates through those occurrences in order to print them to the command line in line 11.

To devise such regular expression, the application developer must retrieve the Web page manually at least once, in order to inspect its content. In particular, there should be no other instances of table rows with three divisions (where a table division is delimited by <td>...</td>) that could be mistakenly interpreted as a result. If there are, then the regular expression must be changed in order to find only those table rows that contain the results that are of interest to the application.

Different techniques can be used to parse HTML content to find the desired data. The simplest way is to use substring search but this can become quite cumbersome if the HTML code contains nested structures. A more robust and powerful way is to use regular expressions as in the example of Listing 5.1. Still a third option is to use an XML parser to find the desired elements, although this will be possible only if the Web page is well formed, for example by following the XHTML standard.

Listing 5.1 Application code to retrieve Web page and parse HTML content

```
1   string url = "http://bikestore.com/search.php?maxprice=500";
2   WebRequest request = WebRequest.Create(url);
3   WebResponse response = request.GetResponse();
4   StreamReader reader = new StreamReader(response.GetResponseStream());
5   string html = reader.ReadToEnd();
6
7   Regex rx = new Regex(@"<td>.*</td><td>.*</td><td>.*</td>");
8   MatchCollection matches = rx.Matches(html);
9   foreach (Match match in matches)
10  {
11      Console.WriteLine(match.Value);
12  }
```

In conclusion, the move towards Web-based user interfaces actually facilitates the development of adapters at the user interface layer. Over the years, the user interface went from text-mode to full-fledged native GUIs (which are difficult to integrate with) and then back to text-mode, Web-based interfaces, with the important difference that now these UIs rely on standard content and communication protocols. The focus on standards has also had a profound impact on the remaining application layers, namely at the data layer, as we will see ahead in Sect. 5.4.

5.3   Integrating Through Files

Some legacy applications have a closed architecture and do not make use of a standard data layer such as a relational database or, if they use, such database is not accessible. Still, they read and write data to files that are kept somewhere in the system, such as in a hard drive or in another storage device. If the location and content of these files are documented or otherwise known, then this represents an opportunity for integration that may become easier to implement than integrating at the user interface layer. If one has access to the data files that the application is using, then it may be possible to exchange data with the application by having an adapter read and write data to those files. Like when reading and writing data to an application database, one must be careful to ensure that such file I/O does not disrupt the application behavior. Still, if such integration is possible, then it becomes an interesting possibility to be considered, since most of the current integration platforms have specialized file adapters to handle a variety of file formats.

The first issue to be considered is whether the legacy application reads and writes files in text mode or in a binary format. If a binary format is being used, then special-purpose file adapters and pipelines may be required to correctly serialize and de-serialize the data. If the binary format is known or documented, it may be laborious but not at all difficult to develop such an adapter. However, if the binary format is unknown, then this is usually a sufficient reason to abandon all attempts to integrate through files and try to integrate at another application layer instead.

Ref.	Description	Price
68454	Bicycle Rockrider 6.0	250,00
67038	Bicycle Triban 5	400,00
63885	Bicycle Elops City	170,00
69778	Bicycle Subsin Klassik	320,00

```
68454;Bicycle Rockrider 6.0;250,00        68454   Bicycle Rockrider 6.0    250,00
67038;Bicycle Triban 5;400,00             67038   Bicycle Triban 5         400,00
63885;Bicycle Elops City;170,00           63885   Bicycle Elops City       170,00
69778;Bicycle Subsin Klassik;320,00       69778   Bicycle Subsin Klassik   320,00
```

Fig. 5.4 Data represented in a database table, in a delimited flat file, and in a positional flat file

The scenario is quite different if the legacy application stores data in text mode. In this case, even if the file format is not documented, the data content is plainly readable and it is not difficult to identify and figure out how the application stores the different data fields. In fact, it is very common for legacy applications to be able to accept or produce data in text files, and this type of files are typically referred to as *flat files*. Applications typically use one of the following two possible mechanisms to organize their data in flat files: *delimited flat files* or *positional flat files*.

5.3.1 Delimited and Positional Flat Files

Delimited flat files separate the data fields with a special character, such as a comma (,) or a semicolon (;). This allows the application to store data in a structure that is similar to a relational database table. Basically, each line in the text file contains a number of comma- or semicolon-separated values. Each line is conceptually equivalent to a database record, and the file may contain several such lines (records). In general, each line contains the same number of data fields. This is the basis for the well-known CSV (Comma-Separated Values) format. However, it is possible to use any character as delimiter, other than comma and semicolon. The use of a tab stop, for example, leads to the TSV (Tab-Separated Values) format.

Figure 5.4 shows a set of data represented in a delimited flat file format. Here we used a semicolon to separate the data fields, in order to avoid a clash with the comma that is being used in the values for price. Had we used a comma to separate the values, it would appear that each line had four data fields rather than three. In practice, in a large data set such clashes cannot be avoided, no matter what delimiter is chosen. In such cases, one must indicate that a certain occurrence of the delimiter character is to be interpreted as belonging to the data itself, and not as a separator. For that purpose, it is common to use an escape character such as a backslash (\) before the character occurrence. For example, in a comma-separated file the price value 250,00 would be represented as 250\,00.

The problem with this approach is that it requires inserting escape characters throughout the data, which may be quite inconvenient in large data sets. In addition, the escape character itself may happen to occur in the data, meaning that such occurrences of the escape character must be escaped as well. Another approach is to enclose the data values with double quotes, such as "250,00." In this case, the comma will not be interpreted as a separator since it occurs within the double quotes. However, if the data itself contains double quotes then these are escaped by the double quote symbol itself (e.g., " is represented by "" inside a data field). This again requires inserting escape characters through the data.

An alternative approach that does not require the use of special separator symbols is provided by positional flat files. These specify that each data field begins at a fixed position in each line. Figure 5.4 shows an example. Here, the first 8 characters are reserved for the product reference number, the next 26 characters are reserved for the description field, and the rest of the line is used to store the price. (Given that the description can be rather long, whereas the price value is more self-contained, a better solution would be to leave the description for last, where it can occupy an arbitrary number of characters.) So, the product reference number begins at position 1, the description begins at position 9, and the price begins at position 35. These positions apply to every line, hence the name of positional flat file.

While positional flat files do not have the sort of problems that occur with special symbols in delimited flat files, they do have the major disadvantage of limiting the size or length of each data field. In the above example, the description field is limited to 26 characters. Anyway, this is not a decision that the systems integrator has to do; in practice, such decision has already been made by system developers and what is left to do is to use the correct file adapter to be able to both read and write data files in the same format as expected by the legacy application.

An important issue to mention about flat files, both delimited and positional, is that they usually do not include any self-explaining data headers. So, while in Fig. 5.4 we know that the first data field is the product reference number, the second data field is the description, and the third is the price, in practical scenarios the systems integrator has to discover this from some sample data. This becomes an especially difficult task if the legacy application makes use of some additional data fields whose purpose is unclear. In this case, a useful idea is to run the application in several testing scenarios in order to discover the purpose of those data fields.

5.3.2 Using XML Files

One of the major advantages of using XML instead of flat files is precisely the fact that XML tags serve as self-explanatory labels for the various data fields contained in the file. In addition, and this is well known, the nesting of XML tags into other XML tags provides the possibility of building much more complex structures than in plain text files (this is the main reason why plain text files are often called "flat" files). A more complex structure will require more complex processing, but this is made easier by the fact that each data field is delimited by its own tag. A well-designed XML structure is able to accommodate much more than the flat content shown in Fig. 5.4. In fact, in an XML file it is possible to associate a record with a set of other records by nesting their corresponding XML elements.

To begin with a simple example, Fig. 5.5 shows in the left-hand side the same content of Fig. 5.4 but now represented as an XML file. There is a single *root element* called Catalog and below this root element there are several Product

```
<?xml version="1.0"?>
<Catalog>
  <Product ref="68454">
    <Description>Bicycle Rockrider 6.0</Description>
    <Price>250,00</Price>
  </Product>
  <Product ref="67038">
    <Description>Bicycle Triban 5</Description>
    <Price>400,00</Price>
  </Product>
  <Product ref="63885">
    <Description>Bicycle Elops City</Description>
    <Price>170,00</Price>
  </Product>
  <Product ref="69778">
    <Description>Bicycle Subsin Klassik</Description>
    <Price>320,00</Price>
  </Product>
</Catalog>
```

```
<?xml version="1.0"?>
<xs:schema id="Catalog"
          xmlns:xs="http://www.w3.org/2001/XMLSchema">
  <xs:element name="Catalog">
    <xs:complexType>
      <xs:choice minOccurs="0" maxOccurs="unbounded">
        <xs:element name="Product">
          <xs:complexType>
            <xs:sequence>
              <xs:element name="Description" type="xs:string" />
              <xs:element name="Price" type="xs:string" />
            </xs:sequence>
            <xs:attribute name="ref" type="xs:string" />
          </xs:complexType>
        </xs:element>
      </xs:choice>
    </xs:complexType>
  </xs:element>
</xs:schema>
```

Fig. 5.5   A sample XML file together with its corresponding XSD definition

elements. These Product elements all have a similar structure: there is an attribute called ref to store the product reference number, and there are two nested elements, Description and Price, to store the remaining data fields. Such nesting of elements can be used to build complex hierarchical structures in an XML file. In general, an XML element can have a number of attributes and contain either plain text or other XML elements.

On the right-hand side of Fig. 5.5 there is another XML document, whose purpose is to define the structure of the XML document on the left. The document on the right-hand side has also a root node and several nested elements with different attributes; so, in essence, it conforms to the general structure of an XML document. The difference between the XML document on the left-hand side and the one on the right-hand side is that the elements on the left have been defined by the user or are application-defined, whereas the elements on the right are defined by the XML Schema standard (abbreviated as XSD for XML Schema Definition), which establishes an XML structure that can be used to define other XML documents.

The first element that appears in the XSD definition (xs:schema) provides an identifier for this definition and also defines where the namespace xs: comes from. So every element that is preceded by xs: is a building block defined in the XML Schema standard. Such elements include the xs:schema element itself, the xs:element elements that appear throughout the definition, as well as xs:complexType, xs:choice, xs:sequence, xs:attribute, etc. It is curious to note that the XSD element that is used to define the elements in other XML documents is called element. At first this may seem confusing, but it is just a result of the fact that XSD allows defining the structure (elements) of XML documents using some special-purpose elements of its own.

For example, the definition on the right-hand side of Fig. 5.5 says that any XML document that is an instance of this definition will have a root element (xs:element) called Catalog and inside this root element there will be a *complex type*. Such complex type includes an arbitrary (unbounded) number of Product elements. In turn, each of these Product elements is also a complex type that contains a sequence of two elements: Description and Price, both of type string. The Product element also contains an attribute ref of type string.

In practice, the XSD definition is a XML document that defines the structure of another XML document. Because they are both XML documents, and because they both need to have a clear structure, they make use of the same XML mechanisms. The structure of any XML document can be defined by an XSD definition. The XSD definition is itself an XML document whose structure is defined by a standard.

This scenario has not always been like this. In the beginning, when XML was developed, there was a general idea that the structure of an XML document would be defined using a special-purpose language called document type definition (DTD) which was quite different from XML itself. This meant that whoever understood the mechanisms of XML documents did not necessarily understand how to define them, if they were not familiar with the language of DTDs. This all changed when XML-based languages for schema definition were developed; then knowing the basic mechanisms of XML was enough to both use and define XML documents, fostering the wide dissemination of XML itself. Currently, XSD definitions are largely preferred over DTD definitions.

There is also another reason why XML documents are defined using an XML-based language, and that has to do with the possibility of using the same kind of *parser* to process both XML documents and their definitions. If the languages were different, then it would be necessary to have a parser for XML documents, and another parser to process a DTD definition. With an XML document being defined by an XSD definition which is an XML document in itself, it becomes possible to reuse the same logic to parse both kinds of documents.

Nowadays, XML parsing is needed in so many applications that most programming languages already include libraries to parse XML and facilitate the development of applications that make use of XML documents. In addition, there are a number of third-party XML parsers that can be used freely. With such possibilities, it is no surprise that new applications are developed with XML in mind. For older applications which do not make use of XML, it is relatively easy to convert their data into an XML structure, regardless of where the data comes from, be it from a relational database, flat files, or other sources.

5.3.3 Canonical Data Formats

When integrating through files, the same data may have to be converted across several formats, be it plain text, XML, or other. Also, each application may have its own format, and for the purpose of implementing the integration logic between applications, it may be necessary to convert to yet another format that is more convenient for processing. All of these factors can combine to create a scenario similar to that of Fig. 5.6, where each application to be integrated has its own format, and yet for the purpose of integration none of these formats is the most

Fig. 5.6 Use of a canonical
format which all other
formats can be converted into

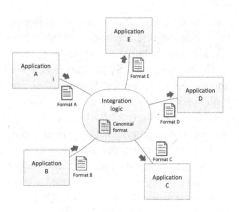

convenient, hence an additional, canonical format is used. It may be the case that the
canonical format coincides with the format of one of these applications, but usually
the integration logic will have to combine data coming from multiple applications,
and therefore a more complete format may be required to accommodate those data.
This new format that is defined only for the purpose of integration, and which all
other formats can be transformed into, is referred to as a *canonical format*.

In the scenario of Fig. 5.6, every document coming from each source application
will have to be transformed into the canonical format, and every document going
to each target application will have to be transformed from the canonical format
to the corresponding target format. Such transformations are not depicted here, but
they have been introduced in Sect. 2.2 in connection with BizTalk Server, and in
Sect. 3.1.5 as well, from a conceptual point of view.

The schemas that are defined in a BizTalk solution are usually created to
represent the structure of data coming from or going to external applications. These
will be the schemas of messages that come through receive ports or go through
send ports, so they are equivalent to the proprietary data formats of each application
in Fig. 5.6. On the other hand, there are usually additional schemas in order to
combine and allow processing of data as a whole. These schemas are typically used
only within orchestrations, for the purpose of collecting all the necessary data to
subsequently create new messages to be sent to each application. These schemas
that are hidden within the orchestration but play a key role in implementing the
integration logic can be regarded as canonical formats.

A canonical format may be hidden inside an orchestration for several reasons.
The first is that such format is of no real use for external applications, since it is not
an appropriate target format. The second reason is that, even if external applications
would be able to handle the canonical format, most likely it would be undesirable
to grant access to those data by external applications. After all, a message in a
canonical format may contain private or business data that is not to be disclosed to
external applications; instead, only those data that are necessary for the interaction
are actually transmitted. Figure 5.7 illustrates this concept. A canonical format used
within the orchestration is transformed to a particular request format and sent to

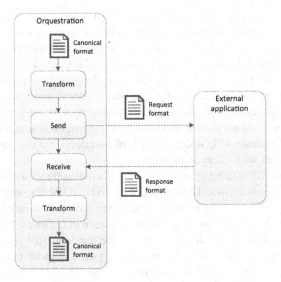

Fig. 5.7 Orchestration-level transformation between canonical and target formats

an external application; the application returns a response in a proprietary format, which is then transformed back into the canonical format.

This kind of logic can be used, for example, in a scenario where it is necessary to fetch additional data from an external application in order to complete the canonical message. The data that are used to create the request to the external application come from the canonical message, but not all data in the canonical message will end up being included in the request. When the external application returns the response, the data contained in that response will be used to enrich the content of the canonical message. This kind of behavior can be seen as an orchestration-level implementation of the behavior depicted in Fig. 3.7 on page 43. Here, the message transformations are playing the role of content filter (when creating the request) and of content enricher (when processing the response).

We will now move to the issue of exchanging data with applications at the data layer, but using a database rather than files. As we will see, it is possible to retrieve data from a database in XML (Sect. 5.5) and the same pattern of request–response applies when an orchestration interacts with a database (Sect. 5.6).

5.4 Database Access APIs

Rather than using files, nowadays most enterprise applications are built on top of some sort of database where data can be stored and managed with improved reliability and efficiency. The use of a database relieves an application from having to deal with several concerns regarding data persistence, such as where and how data is stored. Instead, the application just interacts with the database, and the database takes care of committing and retrieving data from persistent storage.

For applications that are built on top of a database, the most common scenario is to have a relational database and the possibility of interacting with this database using SQL. In this context, SQL is just the query language; i.e., it is the language that the application uses to specify the data that it wants to read or write. Besides specifying the queries in SQL, the application must have some way of submitting the queries to the database system and to retrieve the results. These mechanisms are provided by a database API, which is a set of functions that the database system provides to interact with client applications.

Now, the interesting thing about database APIs is that they have been standardized. For example, the Open Database Connectivity (ODBC) standard defines a programming interface for use with the C language. This API is independent of any particular database system, and an application written in C can use ODBC to query data from any database system that implements the standard. This allows application developers to replace the underlying database system without having to change the application code, since the interface to the database system remains the same. A similar database API exists for Java-based applications, and it is called JDBC (Java Database Connectivity). Today, virtually every programming language has one or more standard APIs through which applications written in that programming language can interact with a relational database system.

Despite the fact that there are different database APIs for every programming language, these APIs share some common concepts. Therefore, using a database API in one programming language versus using a different database API in another programming language becomes mainly a matter of syntax. Typically, interacting with a relational database system through a database API requires the following steps, regardless of the actual API being used:

1. Opening a connection to the database system—This requires specifying the machine where the database system is located (it is usually in a remote machine, possibly using a different operating system), as well as a username, password, and the name of the database that the application needs to use or access.
2. Preparing the SQL query to be sent to the database—Sometimes, the query is fixed and can be hardcoded in the application itself. Other times the query is to be built dynamically according to some user input, as in Fig. 5.3 on page 100 where the products to be returned are only those with a price up to 500. In this case, the user specifies a price limit and that limit must be taken into account in the query; therefore, the application can only build the exact query at run-time.
3. Sending the SQL query to the database—This usually consists in calling a specific function of the database API in order to execute the desired SQL query. The exact function to be called may depend on the type of query being performed. For example, a SELECT statement requires calling a function that returns a cursor to fetch the results. On the other hand, an INSERT, UPDATE or DELETE can be done with another function that returns only a success code.

4. Fetching and iterating through the results—A fundamental but often poorly understood feature of database APIs is the need to iterate through the results rather than fetching everything at once. When querying a database, the result is a relation with data that may not fit the working memory (after all, databases are typically used to store large amounts of data). For this reason, the application is given a cursor which can be used to iterate through the results and fetch each row at a time. Then, from each row, the values for each column can be easily accessed by name or position index.

5. Closing the connection—This seems trivial, and indeed it is just a matter of calling the appropriate function, but the absence of this step can have dramatic consequences. Database systems have a maximum number of possible connections, and therefore applications must be rather conservative and careful in making use of those connections. Each application that opens a connection should also close it; otherwise, other applications (or other instances of the same application) may be unable to connect to the database, which may cause them to crash or bring them to a standstill. Some database systems will close connections that remain idle for a long time, but even then there may be times at which the database is inaccessible to other applications. Also, even if the connection limit can be increased indefinitely, the underlying operating system will reach its limits when the number of connections becomes too high. For these reasons, it is imperative that application programmers (and system integrators as well) make sure that all database connections will eventually be closed. In object-oriented programming languages with automated garbage collection (e.g., Java) this may be easier to ensure, since it is just a matter of inserting a call to the appropriate function in the class destructor. In any case, either implicitly or explicitly, the API function that closes the database connection must be invoked.

Interacting with a database through an API can therefore be summarized as comprising the following five main steps: opening the connection, preparing the query, executing the query, iterating through the results, and closing the connection. As explained above in step 2, usually the desired query is known beforehand, except for one or more parameters that the user will provide at run-time. After constructing the SQL query as a string (step 2), the query is sent to the database system where it will be compiled and executed (step 3). In case it is necessary to perform the same query multiple times with different parameter values, then it becomes inefficient to compile the query for every run, when only some parameter value has changed. In this case, it is possible to use *prepared statements*. A prepared statement is a SQL query whose overall structure is known but which includes some parameters that can be set at run-time. For example, the query in Fig. 5.3 on page 100 could be implemented as a prepared statement with the form:

SELECT * FROM Products WHERE Price <= ?

where the question mark is a placeholder for a parameter value. This statement can be compiled by the database beforehand, so that in subsequent executions all that is left to do is to set the parameter values and execute the statement without having to compile it again. A prepared statement is therefore a precompiled SQL query which can be executed efficiently multiple times with different parameter values. The use of prepared statements does not change the procedure described above in steps 1–5. Rather, it is a different way of performing steps 2–3, where in step 2 the application prepares the SQL statement and sets its parameters, and in step 3 the application sends the SQL statement for execution in the database system. There are specialized functions to perform these tasks in every database API.

The above steps 1–5 describe the main procedure through which an application can connect and interact with a database, and software engineers make use of this procedure to develop applications. Alternatively, in some object-oriented programming languages it is possible to make use of object-relational mappings that provide easier access to the data from the application code. One way of creating such mapping is through the use of Language Integrated Query (LINQ) in C#, as we will see ahead. In any case, the mechanisms that are available to applications developers can also be used by system integrators to integrate with an application at the data layer. Therefore, a study of the main database APIs is of interest also to system integrators. In the following paragraphs, we will present a brief overview of the main database APIs, mainly from the perspective of the steps described above. The fact is that it is possible to recognize these same steps when working with different database APIs in several programming languages, be it C, Java, C#, PHP, etc.

5.4.1   Using ODBC

Listing 5.2 illustrates the kind of application code that is necessary in order to perform a database query using ODBC. The code is written in C++ and was developed for the Windows platform. For those who are familiar with Windows programming, it is not surprising to find several *handles* throughout the code, such as HENV, HDBC, and HSTMT. Basically, a handle is similar to a pointer to an object that has been created inside the Windows kernel. There are many types of objects that can be created in this way, and hence there are different types of handles as well. In the example of Listing 5.2 we see a handle for the OBDC environment (HENV in line 1), a handle for a database connection (HDBC in line 4), and a handle for a SQL statement (HSTMT in line 8). These objects exist in the Windows kernel while the program is running and are eventually freed in lines 32, 34 and 35, respectively. The ODBC API is not object-oriented; it was originally developed having the C language in mind, and therefore these handles are being passed as input parameters to function calls such as SQLConnect() (line 6), SQLExecDirect() (line 13), SQLBindCol() (lines 22–24), and SQLFetch() (line 26). The ODBC API includes these and other functions.

In Listing 5.2 the program begins by retrieving a handle to the ODBC environment (lines 1–2). This is basically an initialization of the ODBC driver within the application. In lines 4–6, the program creates and opens a connection to the

Listing 5.2 Application code to perform a database query through ODBC using C++

```
1    HENV env;
2    SQLAllocEnv(&env);
3
4    HDBC conn;
5    SQLAllocConnect(env, &conn);
6    SQLConnect(conn, "BikeStore", SQL_NTS, "user", SQL_NTS, "password", SQL_NTS);
7
8    HSTMT stmt;
9    SQLAllocStmt(conn, &stmt);
10
11   char sqlquery[] = "SELECT * FROM Products WHERE Price <= 500";
12
13   RETCODE error = SQLExecDirect(stmt, sqlquery, SQL_NTS);
14
15   if (error == SQL_SUCCESS)
16   {
17           int ref;
18           char description[80];
19           float price;
20           int lenOut1, lenOut2, lenOut3;
21
22           SQLBindCol(stmt, 1, SQL_C_SLONG, &ref, 0, &lenOut1);
23           SQLBindCol(stmt, 2, SQL_C_CHAR, description, 80, &lenOut2);
24           SQLBindCol(stmt, 3, SQL_C_FLOAT, &price, 0, &lenOut3);
25
26           while(SQLFetch(stmt) == SQL_SUCCESS)
27           {
28                   printf("%d %s %f", ref, description, price);
29           }
30   }
31
32   SQLFreeStmt(stmt, SQL_DROP);
33   SQLDisconnect(conn);
34   SQLFreeConnect(conn);
35   SQLFreeEnv(env);
```

database system. For this purpose, it is necessary to provide the name of the ODBC data source, together a username and password, to the SQLConnect() function. (In Windows, this ODBC data source must have been previously created and configured in the operating system, through the control panel.) The values for these parameters are provided as null-terminating strings, hence the use of SQL_NTS for each of them. Lines 8–9 create a statement; this could have been a prepared statement but instead the program here uses a hardcoded SQL query (line 11). In line 13, the query is executed on the database without any further preparation.

Assuming that the query runs successfully (line 15), lines 26–29 contain a loop that fetches each row from the results and prints the data to the standard output. The actual values being printed in line 28 are those of a set of local variables defined in lines 17–19, namely ref, description, and price. These variables are bound to the three columns of each row in the results (lines 22–24). The function SQLBindCol() establishes a binding between a table column and a local variable, so that each time a new row is fetched from the table, the variable is updated with the value in that column. Here, "table" refers to the results of a statement that has been previously executed. The binding mechanism is illustrated in Fig. 5.8.

Fig. 5.8 Binding between table columns and local variables in ODBC

The function SQLBindCol() in lines 22–24 of Listing 5.2 seems rather complicated only because of the number of parameters it requires. The first parameter is a handle to the statement, the second parameter is the column index, and the third parameter specifies the C-language data type that the incoming data should be converted to. In ODBC, there is a one-to-one mapping between the data types that can be used in a database and the corresponding C data types, so it is important to use local variables of a type that is compatible with the data types used in the database. Assuming that the product reference number is stored as an integer, the description is stored as a string, and the price is stored as a real number in the database, then one should choose appropriate C types as in lines 17–19 of Listing 5.2.

The fourth parameter of SQLBindCol() is a pointer to the local variable. The fifth parameter is the maximum number of bytes that can be stored in the local variable, and it is used only for data with variable length, such as character or binary data. The sixth and final parameter in SQLBindCol() will contain the actual number of bytes that have been written to the local variable. That result will be stored in the variables lenOut1, lenOut2, and lenOut3, which have been declared in line 20.

In line 33, the program closes the connection to the database.

In addition to the basic features presented here, the ODBC API provides several other features that have been introduced over successive versions of the standard. For example, it is possible to run and manage database transactions using ODBC. The AUTO_COMMIT option that is usually switched on by default in most database systems can be switched off with a call to SQLSetConnectOption(conn, SQL_AUTOCOMMIT, 0). Transactions can be committed or aborted with SQL-Transact(conn, SQL_COMMIT) and SQLTransact(conn, SQL_ROLLBACK), respectively. Furthermore, ODBC has support for retrieving information (metadata) about the database or table schema, for example by calling SQLDescribeCol() to obtain the name and type of a table column. These and other functions can be invoked using a similar logic to the function calls in the example of Listing 5.2.

Listing 5.3   Application code to perform a database query through JDBC using Java

```
1    try
2    {
3            Class.forName("com.mysql.jdbc.Driver");
4            Connection conn = DriverManager.getConnection(
5                    "jdbc:mysql://localhost/bikestore", "user", "password");
6
7            Statement stmt = conn.createStatement();
8
9            ResultSet rset = stmt.executeQuery(
10                   "SELECT * FROM Products WHERE Price <= 500");
11
12           while(rset.next())
13           {
14                   System.out.println(
15                           rset.getInt("Ref") + " " +
16                           rset.getString(2) + " " +
17                           rset.getFloat("Price"));
18           }
19   }
20   catch(SQLException sqle)
21   {
22           System.out.println("SQLException: " + sqle);
23   }
24   finally
25   {
26           stmt.close();
27           conn.close();
28   }
```

5.4.2   Using JDBC

Java Database Connectivity (JDBC) is a Java-based API to integrate with relational database systems. Much like ODBC, it supports querying and modifying data as well as retrieving metadata. Communication with the database system follows the same steps as before, namely: opening a connection, creating a query statement, executing the statement on the database, retrieving the results, and closing the connection. In many respects, JDBC can be regarded as the Java counterpart of ODBC. Perhaps the most noticeable differences are in the fact that JDBC is an object-oriented API and in the fact that JDBC uses exception handling to deal with errors.

Listing 5.3 illustrates the application code that is needed to interact with a database through JDBC. First of all, it is necessary to load the JDBC driver; this is done with a call to Class.forName() in line 3, which causes the specified Java class (i.e., the JDBC driver) to be instantiated dynamically, at run-time. Lines 4–5 open the connection to the database by specifying a URL with the location and name of the database, along with a username and password for authentication. Line 7 creates a statement; this could have been a prepared statement, but for the sake of simplicity there are no parameters here, as the query is hardcoded in line 10. The fact that the statement is created from the connection object (line 7), and the query is executed through the statement object (line 9) illustrates how an object-oriented API such as JDBC makes it possible to write much clearer code than with ODBC.

Listing 5.4 Example of a prepared statement in JDBC

```
1    PreparedStatement stmt;
2    stmt = conn.prepareStatement(
3            "SELECT * FROM Products WHERE Price <= ?");
4
5    stmt.setFloat(1, 500);
6
7    ResultSet rset = stmt.executeQuery();
8    while(rset.next())
9    {
10           System.out.println(
11                   rset.getInt("Ref") + " " +
12                   rset.getString(2) + " " +
13                   rset.getFloat("Price"));
14   }
15
16   stmt.close();
```

The method executeQuery() (line 9) returns a reference to another object of type ResultSet. This is basically an iterator that works as a cursor over the results of the query. The iterating loop in lines 12–18 fetches each row at a time and prints the results to the standard output. In each row there are three column values: Ref, Description, and Price. Lines 15 and 17 retrieve the column value by name, whereas linc 16 retrieves the value by column index. This is just to illustrate that column values can be retrieved in one of these ways.

In lines 20–23, the program contains a catch block that is intended to handle any JDBC exception that may occur during program execution. The most common error is when it is not possible to connect to the database (the server may be down, the network may be down, the maximum number of connections may have been exceeded, the database may have been dropped, the user may have lost privileges, etc.). In this example, the program just prints the exception to standard output. In any case, with or without the occurrence of exceptions, the database connection must be closed. This is ensured by the finally block in lines 24–28: this block always executes, regardless of whether an exception has occurred or not. Even if the statement or connection has been closed before, attempting to close it again will not cause any harm, since the JDBC standard defines this situation as a no-op (no operation).

Listing 5.4 illustrates the use of a prepared statement in JDBC. Here, rather than creating a regular Statement object (as in line 7 of Listing 5.3), the program creates a PreparedStatement (line 1 of Listing 5.3). This object will be used to prepare a query (line 2) with a single parameter, as indicated by the question mark in the expression of line 3. To set this parameter, one must call an appropriate function, depending on the parameter type. In line 5, the program sets parameter 1 to 500, which is given as float value through setFloat() for compatibility with the column type in the database table. The parameter numbered 1 corresponds to the first question mark in the prepared statement; should there be more parameters in the prepared statement, these would be referred to as 2, 3, etc. In line 7, the program executes the query; there is no need to provide an expression here, since it has been already prepared through the statement. Then in lines 8–14 the program iterates through the results in the same way as before. Line 16 closes the statement; this has the effect of releasing any resources associated with this statement, as well as closing the result set that was obtained from executing the statement.

5.4.3 Types of JDBC Drivers

To connect with a particular database system using JDBC, it is necessary to have an appropriate *driver*. Usually, this driver is provided by the database system vendor. The need for an application to use a JDBC driver was only briefly mentioned in Sect. 5.4.2. However, in Listing 5.3 it is apparent that the program is making use of a JDBC driver to connect to MySQL (lines 3–5). Although this is of no concern to the application, there are actually different types of JDBC drivers. Being aware of the different kinds of drivers is useful to understand how database APIs are built, and this view can serve as a source of inspiration when developing application adapters.

Basically, JDBC drivers are built in layers, and the different types of JDBC drivers can be distinguished by the number of software layers that exist between the client application and the database system. Figure 5.9 illustrates the different types of JDBC drivers. A JDBC type 1 driver is a driver that relies on a JDBC-ODBC bridge to connect to the database system. The JDBC API is indeed quite similar in its usage logic to the ODBC API, so creating a bridge (or adapter) between the two is not too difficult, and several implementations are already available. Therefore, this is perhaps the easiest way to develop a JDBC driver, provided that an ODBC driver is available for the database system.

A JDBC type 2 driver is a driver that does not rely on ODBC or other third-party drivers. Instead, the type 2 driver is a layer of Java code that can directly invoke the client API of the database system. In other words, most database system have their own client APIs; an ODBC or a JDBC type 2 driver is a software layer that knows how to communicate with the database system using its client API, but exposes a standard API such as ODBC or JDBC to the outside world. For an application that uses a JDBC type 2 driver, this usually requires a client-side library to be installed in the local machine. This client-side library will connect to the database system on a remote machine through some network protocol.

A JDBC type 3 driver is used in a scenario where there is no database client software installed in the local machine. Rather, the JDBC type 3 driver communicates through the network with the remote machine where the database system, or an application server that connects to the database system, is available. If there is an application server between the client and the database system, then the communication with the application server can be made independently of the specific database system being used. However, this requires the application server to use some driver to connect to the database system, so for the application it seems that it is connecting directly to the database system, when in fact the requests are going through the application server and its own database driver.

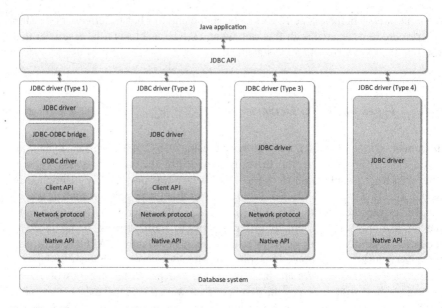

Fig. 5.9 Different types of JDBC drivers

A JDBC type 4 driver is able to perform function calls directly on the database system using its own native, proprietary protocol. A JDBC type 4 driver converts JDBC function calls into database function calls. It is therefore database-specific, and it provides the best performance, since there are no other software layers between the client application and the database system. Typically, a type 4 JDBC driver can be provided by the database vendor alone. For example, Microsoft provides a JDBC type 4 driver for their SQL Server database system.

5.4.4 Database APIs in Windows

As with the different types of JDBC drivers, in the Windows platform there are also several possible ways of connecting an application to a database system through different stacks of software layers. The fundamental database API and the first to be available on Windows was ODBC, but over time additional APIs have been included to facilitate application development. Some of the newer database APIs that are available on Windows were developed to provide a uniform interface not only to database systems but also to other data sources, such as message stores, directory services, spreadsheet documents, and several kinds of legacy data. The idea was that applications could use the same API to query different data sources regardless of the actual system the data are stored in. The API that was developed to implement this

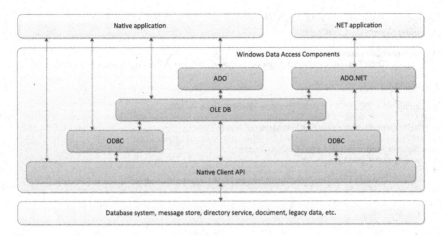

Fig. 5.10 Database APIs in the Windows platform

idea is known as OLE DB and, contrary to what the name suggests, it can be used to query data sources other than database systems.

Figure 5.10 illustrates the software stack in the Windows platform. The ODBC drivers work with database systems only, and they use the native API of those systems to implement and expose the standard ODBC API to applications. For data sources that have no ODBC driver, the application can interact with them through their native client APIs, as shown in the far left of Fig. 5.10 (e.g., it is possible to use a native API to retrieve data from a spreadsheet file).

Besides the native client API and the ODBC API, the third main option in the Windows platform is to use the OLE DB API. In the terminology of OLE DB, the "driver" (i.e., the software component that implements the OLE DB API and provides access to the data source) is referred to as a *provider* and the client application that needs to access the data is referred to as a *consumer*. Originally, OLE DB was meant as an alternative to ODBC, since an OLE DB provider can be implemented directly on top of a native client API, and today there are OLE DB providers for a wide range of systems. However, there is also an OLE DB provider for ODBC, which means that OLE DB can work on top of ODBC to provide access to all ODBC data sources. Both of these options are illustrated on the left side of Fig. 5.10.

A fourth database API that is available on Windows is ADO, which is basically a simplification of OLE DB to facilitate the development of database applications in programming languages other than C/C++. Due to the intricacies of the Component Object Model (COM) in the Windows platform, the OLE DB API is accessible to native applications written in C/C++ only. However, there are several other programming languages in the Windows platform, and these are unable to work with interface pointers and other advanced COM features required to make use of OLE DB. Therefore, the ADO API was developed to make OLE DB providers accessible to those languages. For these reasons, ADO works exclusively on top of OLE DB.

Listing 5.5 Example of using the .NET data provider for SQL Server in C#

```
1   using System.Data.SqlClient;
2
3   SqlConnection conn = new SqlConnection(
4         "Data Source=localhost;Integrated Security=SSPI;Initial Catalog=BikeStore");
5
6   conn.Open();
7
8   string sql = "SELECT * FROM Products WHERE Price <= 500";
9
10  SqlCommand cmd = new SqlCommand(sql, conn);
11
12  SqlDataReader reader = cmd.ExecuteReader();
13  while (reader.Read())
14  {
15        Console.WriteLine("{0} {1} {2}", reader["Ref"], reader["Description"], reader["Price"]);
16  }
17
18  reader.Close();
19  conn.Close();
```

5.4.5   Database Access in the .NET Framework

A different type of applications that exist in the Windows platform are .NET applications. Rather than being compiled to native code, .NET applications are compiled to an intermediate language that runs in a controlled environment— the .NET framework—which provides advanced features such as code safety, garbage collection, and exception handling. These .NET applications have their own database API, which is called ADO.NET. Despite the similarity in the designations of ADO and ADO.NET, the latter is a different API and has a separate implementation from ADO. The implementation of ADO.NET includes a data provider for OLE DB, a data provider for ODBC, and a couple of data providers for specific database systems, namely SQL Server and Oracle. Therefore, using these providers that are already included in the .NET framework, a .NET application can choose whether to connect to a data source through OLE DB, ODBC, or a native client API. These possibilities are illustrated in the right-hand side of Fig. 5.10.

In any case, the API that the .NET application needs to use is very similar in terms of function calls. In essence, only the software library to be included (in order to select the appropriate data provider) is different. Listing 5.5 illustrates the use of the .NET data provider for SQL Server. Basically, the program opens a connection (lines 3–6), creates a SQL query (lines 8–10), executes the query (line 12), iterates through the results (lines 13–16), and finally closes the connection (lines 18–19).

The ADO.NET API is object-oriented and in the particular case of the provider for SQL Server (included in line 1), all class names are preceded by the "Sql" prefix (e.g., SqlConnection, SqlCommand, and SqlDataReader). Should the program make use of the data provider for ODBC, the namespace to be included would be System.Data.Odbc and the class names would be preceded by "Odbc" (e.g., OdbcConnection, OdbcCommand, and OdbcDataReader). The same applies to the

OLE DB provider, whose namespace is System.Data.OleDb and the prefix is "OleDb." Apart from the change in names, the program logic would be exactly the same.

5.4.6   Using LINQ

Up to this point, we have seen how it is possible to use different database APIs in different programming languages to execute a SQL query over a database. For this purpose, the SQL query is embed in the application code. One problem with these approaches is that there is no checking of the SQL query at compile time; i.e., the application code may compile successfully and yet the SQL query embedded in the code may be wrong or may not work, something that can only be discovered at run-time, when the application is already running.

This problem has led IT vendors to think about ways to develop applications in which both the application code and the SQL queries embedded in the code can be compiled seamlessly in one step. In the .NET framework, this effort resulted in the development of LINQ as an extension to .NET languages such as C#. Basically, LINQ extends C# with SQL-like operators in such a way that the query is written in C# code and can be checked by the compiler.

For this to happen, the compiler must be aware of the data structure that is being accessed, and therefore the data schema must be somehow "lifted" to the level of application code. This is achieved by an automated procedure that inspects the data source and generates a number of C# classes to represent the data structure. The query can then be written in the programming language as an operation over those classes. Since this data abstraction mechanism is an integral part of LINQ, this technology is regarded as a kind of *object-relational mapping*.

The first step when using LINQ is to create a connection to the data source. (Here we are assuming that the data source is a relational database, but in practice LINQ can be used to connect to a variety of data sources other than relational databases, such as XML files, CSV files, object-oriented databases, and online services.) From this connection, an automated procedure associated with LINQ is able to inspect the data source and generate a number of classes to represent the data structure. The first class to be created is a DataContext. This class connects to the data source and is able to retrieve the entities (i.e., tables) found in the data source. Then there is also a separate class to represent each of these entities. The attributes of these classes correspond to the columns in a database table. Querying these attributes equates to querying the corresponding database table.

All these classes are generated automatically by LINQ and they can be used directly in application code. Listing 5.6 provides an example. In line 3, the program instantiates the BikeStoreDataContext which is a subclass of DataContext generated automatically by LINQ. Instantiating this class is equivalent to opening the connection to the database. Then lines 5–8 contain the query. There are no string delimiters here, since the query is written in C# (or an extension thereof). The query

Listing 5.6 Example of querying a database using LINQ in C#

```
1    using System.Linq;
2
3    BikeStoreDataContext db = new BikeStoreDataContext();
4
5    var query =
6            from product in db.Products
7            where product.Price < 500
8            select product;
9
10   foreach(var result in query)
11   {
12           Console.WriteLine("{0} {1} {2}", result.Ref, result.Description, result.Price);
13   }
```

syntax is reminiscent of SQL: the select, from, and where clauses are present, albeit in a different order, where the select comes last.

In line 6, product is an object that represents a row in table Products. This table is accessed via the DataContext object; hence the use of db.Products, where db is the DataContext object created earlier in line 3. Line 7 specifies that only those rows with price up to 500 will be returned, where Price is an attribute of the product object. The complete product object, with all its attributes, is returned as a result in line 8. Then lines 10–13 show the typical loop that is used to iterate through the results. Using result as an alias for every returned record, line 12 just prints each column value to the standard output. Note that, here too, the column values are being accessed as attributes of the result object.

Overall, the program in Listing 5.6 appears to be shorter and simpler than previous examples with other APIs, but it must be recalled that there is an additional amount of automatically generated code that is not shown here. More importantly, in contrast with previous examples there is no embedded SQL code in Listing 5.6; rather, the query is specified using language constructs in lines 5–8. This means that the query is assured to be well formed at compile time, even before the program is run. Naturally, this kind of mechanism introduces new possibilities and improved reliability to programs and adapters for integration at the data layer.

5.5   Returning Data in XML

In modern integration platforms, the integration logic is implemented using message brokers and orchestrations to coordinate the exchange of messages between applications. To facilitate processing, these messages are usually expressed in XML. In Sect. 5.3.2 we have already discussed the advantages of using XML when compared to other formats, namely flat files. However, when describing the database APIs for integration at the data layer in Sect. 5.4, in every example the program just fetches the results one by one with a loop and prints the data to standard output without any special format. Clearly, for the purpose of integration it would be useful if these data would come out in some sort of XML structure.

Listing 5.7 Example of using RAW mode

```
1   SELECT *
2   FROM Products
3   WHERE Price <= 500
4   FOR XML RAW
5
6   <row Ref="68454" Description="Bicycle Rockrider 6.0" Price="250.00" />
7   <row Ref="67038" Description="Bicycle Triban 5" Price="400.00" />
8   <row Ref="63885" Description="Bicycle Elops City" Price="170.00" />
9   <row Ref="69778" Description="Bicycle Subsin Klassik" Price="320.00" />
```

One possibility would be to write the program in such a way that it produces an XML structure as it loops through the results. This would require defining an appropriate XML structure for the data that is being retrieved from the database, and also making sure that the program would create and fill the XML structure correctly. Fortunately, there is no need to go through such effort since most database systems provide the possibility of returning the query results in XML form. Such feature is not yet standardized, so the functionality that allows data to be returned in XML is implemented in different ways across database systems from different vendors. Here we will focus on the example of SQL Server and on the SQL extensions that it provides to return data in XML.

Conceptually, the mechanism provided by SQL Server to return data in XML form is quite simple. Basically, it is a matter of inserting the clause FOR XML at the end of the SQL statement (SELECT ... FROM ... WHERE ... FOR XML ...). Using the FOR XML clause, it is possible to make the database system generate XML in several different ways. The problem with this approach is that, while it is easy to get the data in some XML structure generated automatically by the database system, it can get fairly complicated for the client application to have full control over that XML structure so as to specify how exactly that structure should be.

For this reason, SQL Server provides four different modes to generate the XML structure: FOR XML RAW, FOR XML AUTO, FOR XML EXPLICIT, and FOR XML PATH. While the first two modes (RAW and AUTO) are intended to let the database system decide the XML structure to be returned, the last two modes (EXPLICIT and PATH) provide the client with full control over that XML structure. However, the latter are significantly more complicated to use than the former, so we will dedicate some attention to each of these modes in the following paragraphs.

5.5.1   Using the RAW Mode

The RAW mode is the simplest option of all: it just generates one <row> element for each record in the results of the SQL query. Listing 5.7 shows an example of a query using FOR XML RAW (lines 1–4) together with the results (lines 6–9). In the results, there is one XML element per record and the column values are included as attributes of that element. These attributes have been given the same names as the corresponding table columns.

Listing 5.8 Example of using RAW mode with ELEMENTS

```
1   SELECT *
2   FROM products
3   WHERE Price <= 500
4   FOR XML RAW('product'), ELEMENTS
5
6   <product>
7     <Ref>68454</Ref>
8     <Description>Bicycle Rockrider 6.0</Description>
9     <Price>250.00</Price>
10  </product>
11  <product>
12    <Ref>67038</Ref>
13    <Description>Bicycle Triban 5</Description>
14    <Price>400.00</Price>
15  </product>
16  <product>
17    <Ref>63885</Ref>
18    <Description>Bicycle Elops City</Description>
19    <Price>170.00</Price>
20  </product>
21  <product>
22    <Ref>69778</Ref>
23    <Description>Bicycle Subsin Klassik</Description>
24    <Price>320.00</Price>
25  </product>
```

The RAW mode can be customized in order to change the name of the <row> element, and also to insert the column values as sub-elements rather than attributes of the <row> element. Listing 5.8 illustrates the use of both options. Again, the query (lines 1–4) is presented together with the corresponding results (lines 6–25). Here, the row element <product> has been given the name specified in the FOR XML clause, and the use of ELEMENTS has the effect of including the column values as sub-elements of <product>. This provides some, although limited, degree of control over the XML structure generated by the database system.

5.5.2   Using the AUTO Mode

The AUTO mode is intended to let the database system decide on a proper XML structure for the output data. This XML structure will be based on the actual data to be returned and also on the way the query is specified. Using the AUTO mode in a trivial query, such as the one that has served as an example before, is illustrated in Listing 5.9. Apparently, the difference towards the RAW mode (Listing 5.7) is not very meaningful, since only the row element has been renamed to Products. However, the fact that this row element has been given the same name as the table that appears in the query is already a sign of how the AUTO mode operates.

The full potential of the AUTO mode can only be appreciated in more complicated queries, where the database systems succeeds in accommodating the output data in an appropriate XML structure. For example, a query which involves a join of two tables, where each record of the first table is paired with multiple records of the

Listing 5.9 Example of using AUTO mode

```
1    SELECT *
2    FROM Products
3    WHERE Price <= 500
4    FOR XML AUTO
5
6    <Products Ref="68454" Description="Bicycle Rockrider 6.0" Price="250.00" />
7    <Products Ref="67038" Description="Bicycle Triban 5" Price="400.00" />
8    <Products Ref="63885" Description="Bicycle Elops City" Price="170.00" />
9    <Products Ref="69778" Description="Bicycle Subsin Klassik" Price="320.00" />
```

second table, is likely to result in the creation of an element for each record of the first table with several sub-elements for each record in the second table.

We can build such an example by adding another table to our sample database. Up to this point we have been using a Products table with columns Ref for product reference number, Description for the product description, and Price. Assuming that the company has several stores, we can add a table to keep the stock level of each product in each store. This new table will be called Stocks and it will have the column Ref for product reference number, the column Store to identify each store, and the column Available to record the available quantity of each product in each store. The resulting database schema then comprises the following tables: Products(Ref, Description, Price) and Stocks(Ref, Store, Available).

To illustrate the use of the AUTO mode, we will retrieve the available quantity for each product in each store. To make the results more easily understandable, we will include the product description along with its reference number. The example is presented in Listing 5.10 where the query is in lines 1–4 and the results are in lines 6–25. Here it is apparent that there are two sets of row elements: those that come from the Products table, and those that come from the Stocks table; and since there are several records of Stocks associated with each record of Products (a consequence of the fact that each product is available in multiple stores), the <Stocks> elements are nested in the <Products> elements. As before, the system has decided to place column values as attributes with the same name in each of those elements.

For comparison, Listing 5.11 presents the results (in lines 6–17) that would be obtained using the RAW mode. Here, there is no clue about the one-to-many relationship between Products and Stocks that is represented hierarchically in Listing 5.10. Rather, the query in Listing 5.11 returns a flat structure where each <row> element corresponds to a different record in the results. Even if RAW mode is used together with ELEMENTS as in Listing 5.8, this does not produce the results of Listing 5.10; rather, the attributes in lines 6–17 of Listing 5.11 become sub-elements but there is no nesting of elements from Stocks into elements from Products.

5.5.3 Using the EXPLICIT Mode

The EXPLICIT mode is one of two modes (together with PATH) that provide complete control over the XML structure to be returned by the SQL query. Of all the four

Listing 5.10   A second example of using AUTO mode

```
1    SELECT Products.Ref, Products.Description, Stocks.Store, Stocks.Available
2    FROM Products, Stocks
3    WHERE Products.Ref = Stocks.Ref
4    FOR XML AUTO
5
6    <Products Ref="63885" Description="Bicycle Elops City">
7      <Stocks Store="Main" Available="0" />
8      <Stocks Store="City 1" Available="2" />
9      <Stocks Store="City 2" Available="3" />
10   </Products>
11   <Products Ref="67038" Description="Bicycle Triban 5">
12     <Stocks Store="Main" Available="2" />
13     <Stocks Store="City 1" Available="4" />
14     <Stocks Store="City 2" Available="1" />
15   </Products>
16   <Products Ref="68454" Description="Bicycle Rockrider 6.0">
17     <Stocks Store="Main" Available="1" />
18     <Stocks Store="City 1" Available="3" />
19     <Stocks Store="City 2" Available="0" />
20   </Products>
21   <Products Ref="69778" Description="Bicycle Subsin Klassik">
22     <Stocks Store="Main" Available="5" />
23     <Stocks Store="City 1" Available="3" />
24     <Stocks Store="City 2" Available="4" />
25   </Products>
```

Listing 5.11   The previous example in RAW mode

```
1    SELECT Products.Ref, Products.Description, Stocks.Store, Stocks.Available
2    FROM Products, Stocks
3    WHERE Products.Ref = Stocks.Ref
4    FOR XML RAW
5
6    <row Ref="63885" Description="Bicycle Elops City" Store="Main" Available="0" />
7    <row Ref="63885" Description="Bicycle Elops City" Store="City 1" Available="2" />
8    <row Ref="63885" Description="Bicycle Elops City" Store="City 2" Available="3" />
9    <row Ref="67038" Description="Bicycle Triban 5" Store="Main" Available="2" />
10   <row Ref="67038" Description="Bicycle Triban 5" Store="City 1" Available="4" />
11   <row Ref="67038" Description="Bicycle Triban 5" Store="City 2" Available="1" />
12   <row Ref="68454" Description="Bicycle Rockrider 6.0" Store="Main" Available="1" />
13   <row Ref="68454" Description="Bicycle Rockrider 6.0" Store="City 1" Available="3" />
14   <row Ref="68454" Description="Bicycle Rockrider 6.0" Store="City 2" Available="0" />
15   <row Ref="69778" Description="Bicycle Subsin Klassik" Store="Main" Available="5" />
16   <row Ref="69778" Description="Bicycle Subsin Klassik" Store="City 1" Available="3" />
17   <row Ref="69778" Description="Bicycle Subsin Klassik" Store="City 2" Available="4" />
```

modes available (RAW, AUTO, EXPLICIT, and PATH), the EXPLICIT mode is perhaps the most complicated and less understood. This is because the XML generation in EXPLICIT mode involves in two different steps:

- The first step is to produce an intermediate table with the output data. This intermediate table must be created according to certain requirements, and the need to present the output data according to these requirements is what makes the EXPLICIT mode especially difficult to use. However, once the structure of this intermediate table is understood, using the EXPLICIT mode becomes much easier.
- The second step is an automatic translation of the data in the intermediate table to an XML structure. For this step to be done automatically, most of the work

Listing 5.12 Desired XML output for a query over the Products table

```
1    <Product Ref="63885">
2      <Description>Bicycle Elops City</Description>
3      <Price>170.00</Price>
4    </Product>
5    <Product Ref="67038">
6      <Description>Bicycle Triban 5</Description>
7      <Price>400.00</Price>
8    </Product>
9    <Product Ref="68454">
10     <Description>Bicycle Rockrider 6.0</Description>
11     <Price>250.00</Price>
12   </Product>
13   <Product Ref="69778">
14     <Description>Bicycle Subsin Klassik</Description>
15     <Price>320.00</Price>
16   </Product>
```

Fig. 5.11 Intermediate table to generate the XML data in Listing 5.12

Tag	Parent	Product!1!Ref	Description!2	Price!3
1	NULL	63885	NULL	NULL
2	1	63885	Bicycle Elops City	NULL
3	1	63885	NULL	170.00
1	NULL	67038	NULL	NULL
2	1	67038	Bicycle Triban 5	NULL
3	1	67038	NULL	400.00
1	NULL	68454	NULL	NULL
2	1	68454	Bicycle Rockrider 6.0	NULL
3	1	68454	NULL	250.00
1	NULL	69778	NULL	NULL
2	1	69778	Bicycle Subsin Klassik	NULL
3	1	69778	NULL	320.00

must have been done in the previous step, and this is effectively what happens in practice. The intermediate table that is a result of the previous step describes an XML structure (the nodes and relationships between them) in tabular form. Then the clause FOR XML EXPLICIT just produces the XML from this intermediate table, which is quite simple to do. For example, this is much simpler than in the AUTO mode, which must figure out for itself the XML structure to be returned. In the EXPLICIT mode, the responsibility of specifying the XML structure is left to the client application, so the database system has actually less work to do.

Suppose that we would like to perform the query "SELECT * FROM Products WHERE Price <= 500" and obtain the results in the form of Listing 5.12. This output is different from what either the RAW mode or the AUTO mode would be able to produce. The Ref value is included as an attribute (line 1), while the remaining column values are inserted are sub-elements of a <Product> element (lines 2–3). The exact structure of this XML output can be obtained with the EXPLICIT mode by writing a query that can generate the intermediate table in Fig. 5.11.

Before we delve into the SQL query, for the moment we will focus on the structure of the table in Fig. 5.11. The table has five columns, each with a particular purpose. The Tag and Parent columns refer to the XML elements and their nesting in one other. Each element is identified by a tag (in the Tag column), and has a parent which is also identified by tag (in the Parent column). For example, the tags 1, 2, and 3 represent three different XML elements, and the elements with tags 2 and 3 both have element 1 as the parent; therefore, elements 2 and 3 are nested in element 1. The root element, which has no parent, has NULL in the Parent column.

Each row in this table refers to a different XML element. The tag numbers may repeat along the table if the same structure is intended to be repeated in the XML. Comparing Fig. 5.11 with Listing 5.12 it is possible to recognize the correspondence between each block with tags 1, 2, and 3 in the table and a <Product> element together with its sub-elements in the XML, respectively.

As with regular XML, each element may have a number of attributes and some text (or other elements) between the start and closing tags. The values for the attributes or text are specified in the remaining columns of the intermediate table in Fig. 5.11. The column Product!1!Ref refers to the elements with tag 1; similarly, the columns Description!2 and Price!3 refer to the elements with tags 2 and 3, respectively. Now it becomes clear why the table in Fig. 5.11 has so many NULL values in the last two columns: it is because these columns only apply to elements with the given tag (in the column header). Filling in these columns for rows with a different tag is irrelevant, since they will not be considered when creating the corresponding XML element. However, the attentive reader may have noticed that the column Product!1!Ref has values for all rows; this was done in order to sort rows by Ref value, as will be explained ahead.

The column headers have also the interesting function of setting the names for the XML elements. For example, the column header Product!1!Ref means that the element with tag 1 will be called Product, the header Description!2 means that the element with tag 2 will be called Description, and Price!3 means that the element with tag 3 will be called Price. In addition, Product!1!Ref (with Ref after the tag number) means that the value provided under this column will be used as the value for an attribute called Ref. On the other hand, the values under Description!2 and Price!3 (with no attribute after the tag) are to be used as text content within those elements. This fits the overall structure of the <Product> elements in Listing 5.12.

With this background information, we are now in a position to understand the query that must be written to generate the XML in Listing 5.12. Basically, the query will have to generate the intermediate table shown in Fig. 5.11, and it will have to include the FOR XML EXPLICIT clause in order to translate the intermediate table into the output XML. The query is shown in Listing 5.13.

By looking at Fig. 5.11 it becomes clear that the query has to generate different kinds of rows, and these correspond to the three different SELECT statements in Listing 5.13. In essence, the first SELECT statement in lines 1–8 retrieves the elements with tag 1 (the <Product> elements with a Ref attribute); the second SELECT statement in lines 10–16 retrieves the elements with tag 2 (the product descriptions); and the third SELECT statement in lines 18–24 retrieves the elements with tag 3 (the prices). Everything is brought together by the union operators in lines

Listing 5.13 Example of using EXPLICIT mode

```
1    SELECT
2             1 AS Tag,
3             NULL AS Parent,
4             Ref AS [Product!1!Ref],
5             NULL AS [Description!2],
6             NULL AS [Price!3]
7    FROM Products
8    WHERE Price <= 500
9    UNION ALL
10   SELECT
11            2 AS Tag,
12            1 AS Parent,
13            Ref AS [Product!1!Ref],
14            Description AS [Description!2],
15            NULL AS [Price!3]
16   FROM Products
17   UNION ALL
18   SELECT
19            3 AS Tag,
20            1 AS Parent,
21            Ref AS [Product!1!Ref],
22            NULL AS [Description!2],
23            Price AS [Price!3]
24   FROM Products
25   ORDER BY Ref, Tag
26   FOR XML EXPLICIT
```

9 and 17. Note that for this union to work, all records must have the same number of columns and compatible data types between corresponding data fields.

The reason for using the UNION ALL rather than simply UNION is to guarantee that all records will be included in the result even in case there are duplicate records (i.e., records with the same values in all fields). These duplicates would be eliminated if the UNION operator was used. In this particular example, there are no duplicates, but in a general scenario that may occur if the query does not select a key or discriminator column such as Ref in this example.

Once the results are collected by the UNION ALL operator, the ORDER BY operator in line 25 sorts the rows by Ref, and then by Tag within Ref. This sorting is absolutely necessary, since it ensures that the XML elements will be nested correctly when the table is processed sequentially in one pass. As the database system goes through the table, the current value for Parent refers to the last row with such tag number (except when it is NULL). For example, with the order of rows shown in Fig. 5.11, the rows with description "Bicycle Triban 5" and price "400.00" will be nested in the <Product> element with Ref no. 67038. This reveals how important the final ordering is, and also why the value for Ref had to be included in every row, so that the data for each product can be brought together by sorting.

5.5.4   Using the PATH Mode

The PATH mode provides a much simpler way of achieving the same sort of thing as with the EXPLICIT mode. Rather than requiring the construction of an intermediate

Listing 5.14 Example of using PATH mode

```
1   SELECT
2           Ref AS "@Ref",
3           Description AS "Description",
4           Price AS "Price"
5   FROM Products
6   FOR XML PATH ('Product')
7
8   <Product Ref="68454">
9     <Description>Bicycle Rockrider 6.0</Description>
10    <Price>250.00</Price>
11  </Product>
12  <Product Ref="67038">
13    <Description>Bicycle Triban 5</Description>
14    <Price>400.00</Price>
15  </Product>
16  <Product Ref="63885">
17    <Description>Bicycle Elops City</Description>
18    <Price>170.00</Price>
19  </Product>
20  <Product Ref="69778">
21    <Description>Bicycle Subsin Klassik</Description>
22    <Price>320.00</Price>
23  </Product>
```

table, in PATH mode the columns can be mapped directly to XML attributes or elements through the use of XPath expressions. Listing 5.14 shows an example that produces the same kind of XML structure as in Listing 5.12 (the only difference being in the ordering of products). Line 2 in Listing 5.14 selects the Ref column as an attribute, whereas lines 3–4 select the Description and Price as elements. In line 6, the FOR XML clause specifies the name for row elements (similar to what happened in Listing 5.8); therefore the selected attributes and elements will be nested into a row element called Product. The result is in lines 8–23.

5.5.5   How to Obtain the XML Schema

In RAW and AUTO modes, where the XML structure is decided by the database system, it may be useful to obtain a description (in the form of an XML schema) of the XML structure that is being used by the system to present the results. For practical purposes, such description may be necessary so that other applications are able to understand the results that are coming out from the database.

There are actually two ways to obtain the XML schema: either by the use of XMLDATA or by the use of XMLSCHEMA. Either one of these keywords can be appended to the FOR XML RAW and FOR XML AUTO commands (e.g., FOR XML AUTO, XMLDATA or FOR XML AUTO, XMLSCHEMA). The XMLDATA command generates the schema in XDR (XML Data Reduced) format, which is an older format for specifying the structure of XML documents. The newer and more widely used standard for specifying the structure of XML documents is known as XSD and

Listing 5.15 Example of using XMLDATA

```
1    SELECT *
2    FROM Products
3    WHERE Price <= 500
4    FOR XML AUTO, XMLDATA
5
6    <Schema name="Schema1" xmlns="urn:schemas-microsoft-com:xml-data"
7          xmlns:dt="urn:schemas-microsoft-com:datatypes">
8      <ElementType name="Products" content="empty" model="closed">
9        <AttributeType name="Ref" dt:type="i4" />
10       <AttributeType name="Description" dt:type="string" />
11       <AttributeType name="Price" dt:type="number" />
12       <attribute type="Ref" />
13       <attribute type="Description" />
14       <attribute type="Price" />
15     </ElementType>
16   </Schema>
17   <Products xmlns="x-schema:#Schema1" Ref="68454" Description="Bicycle Rockrider 6.0"
18         Price="250.00" />
19   <Products xmlns="x-schema:#Schema1" Ref="67038" Description="Bicycle Triban 5"
20         Price="400.00" />
21   <Products xmlns="x-schema:#Schema1" Ref="63885" Description="Bicycle Elops City"
22         Price="170.00" />
23   <Products xmlns="x-schema:#Schema1" Ref="69778" Description="Bicycle Subsin Klassik"
24         Price="320.00" />
```

has already been introduced in Sect. 5.3.2. The XSD description can be obtained with the XMLSCHEMA command. An example of each will help clarify both options.

Listing 5.15 illustrates the results obtained with XMLDATA. Lines 1–4 contain the query, where the command XMLDATA has been included in line 4. Lines 6–24 display the results, where two separate segments can be identified: the first segment in lines 6–16 describes the XML schema in XDR format, and the second segment in lines 17–24 contains the results. These are the same results which have been obtained earlier in Listing 5.9 on page 123. In Listing 5.15 each element in the results (lines 17–24) refers to XML namespace called Schema1 which is defined in line 6. Lines 8–15 define the element type Products with the three attributes in lines 12–14; the types for these attributes are defined in lines 9–11.

Listing 5.16 illustrates the results obtained with XMLSCHEMA. The query is in lines 1–4 with the command XMLSCHEMA in line 4. The results are in lines 6–41 where again two segments can be identified: the first segment in lines 6–33 contains the XML Schema specification and the second segment in lines 34–41 include the results, which are the same as before except from the XML namespace being used. The XML Schema specification in Listing 5.16 appears to be significantly longer and more complicated than the XDR definition in Listing 5.15. However, this is mostly due to the use of several namespaces, including a namespace that defines SQL data types (lines 9, 11, 12 in Listing 5.16). Line 13 begins the definition of the Products element as a *complex type* which includes three attributes: Ref (line 15), Description (line 16), and Price (line 23). The lines in between these attribute definitions specify the data types. Therefore, Ref is an integer, Description is a string with a maximum length of 255 characters, and Price is a numeric data value with 2 fractional digits. These data types correspond to the data types that have been used

Listing 5.16 Example of using XMLSCHEMA

```
1    SELECT *
2    FROM Products
3    WHERE Price <= 500
4    FOR XML AUTO, XMLSCHEMA
5
6    <xsd:schema targetNamespace="urn:schemas−microsoft−com:sql:SqlRowSet1"
7              xmlns:schema="urn:schemas−microsoft−com:sql:SqlRowSet1"
8              xmlns:xsd="http://www.w3.org/2001/XMLSchema"
9              xmlns:sqltypes="http://schemas.microsoft.com/sqlserver/2004/sqltypes"
10             elementFormDefault="qualified">
11       <xsd:import namespace="http://schemas.microsoft.com/sqlserver/2004/sqltypes"
12             schemaLocation="http://schemas.microsoft.com/sqlserver/2004/sqltypes/sqltypes.xsd" />
13       <xsd:element name="Products">
14         <xsd:complexType>
15           <xsd:attribute name="Ref" type="sqltypes:int" />
16           <xsd:attribute name="Description">
17             <xsd:simpleType>
18               <xsd:restriction base="sqltypes:varchar">
19                 <xsd:maxLength value="255" />
20               </xsd:restriction>
21             </xsd:simpleType>
22           </xsd:attribute>
23           <xsd:attribute name="Price">
24             <xsd:simpleType>
25               <xsd:restriction base="sqltypes:numeric">
26                 <xsd:totalDigits value="12" />
27                 <xsd:fractionDigits value="2" />
28               </xsd:restriction>
29             </xsd:simpleType>
30           </xsd:attribute>
31         </xsd:complexType>
32       </xsd:element>
33     </xsd:schema>
34     <Products xmlns="urn:schemas−microsoft−com:sql:SqlRowSet1" Ref="68454"
35           Description="Bicycle Rockrider 6.0" Price="250.00" />
36     <Products xmlns="urn:schemas−microsoft−com:sql:SqlRowSet1" Ref="67038"
37           Description="Bicycle Triban 5" Price="400.00" />
38     <Products xmlns="urn:schemas−microsoft−com:sql:SqlRowSet1" Ref="63885"
39           Description="Bicycle Elops City" Price="170.00" />
40     <Products xmlns="urn:schemas−microsoft−com:sql:SqlRowSet1" Ref="69778"
41           Description="Bicycle Subsin Klassik" Price="320.00" />
```

for the columns of the table in the database; hence the need to include a proper namespace that defines these data types.

In both Listing 5.15 and Listing 5.16, the query returns the results in an XML structure together with the definition of that structure, be it in XDR or XSD, respectively. Naturally, there is no need to provide the XML structure definition every time a query is run. If the query being executed is always the same (possibly with different input parameters), then the XML schema is already known from previous runs. Actually, for a given query with FOR XML RAW or FOR XML AUTO it is possible to run the query with XMLDATA (or XMLSCHEMA) only once in order to get to know the XML schema. In subsequent runs, there is no need to include XMLDATA (or XMLSCHEMA) since the XML schema is already known.

In the next section, we will see that this point plays an important role when integrating with a database system through the exchange of XML messages.

5.6 Using the SQL Adapter

In Chap. 2 we have introduced an integration platform (BizTalk Server) which, in a similar way to other integration platforms available today, is based on the concept of having orchestrations to coordinate the exchange of messages between applications. To facilitate processing and message transformation, messages are usually represented in XML. Basically, an orchestration specifies the integration logic by means of a sequence of steps (called *shapes* in the BizTalk platform). These steps represent activities such as sending, receiving, and transforming messages.

In a practical scenario, the integration logic may require, for example, that some data is retrieved from an external database. In this case, the orchestration must have at least one activity to send the request to the database and another activity to receive the results. In addition, the request to be sent to the database must be somehow *constructed*, i.e., if the request is to carry some input data, then these input data must be included when the request is created. This suggests that before sending the request to the database system, the orchestration will probably have a transformation activity in order to create the request. But having this transformation means that there will be some preexisting message from which the database request will be created. Indeed, the request will be created from the initial message that triggers the orchestration and brings the input data to be sent to the database.

This behavior is illustrated in Fig. 5.12. The orchestration begins with a receive shape to receive an initial message that triggers (i.e., instantiates) the whole orchestration. After that comes a transform shape inside a construct shape to create the request message. The transform shape creates the request message through a transformation map that uses the initial message as input. The construct shape around the transform indicates that a new message is being created at this point. The orchestration then sends the request message to the database system and waits for a response. Once the response is received, if needed it can be transformed to another schema and returned as an output message from the orchestration.

Figure 5.12 is conceptually important because it depicts the main steps in an orchestration that invokes an external application. In this case it interacts with a database system, but if it would be another kind of application, such as a Web service or a message queuing system, the steps in the orchestration would be the same.

In Chap. 2 we have seen that orchestrations communicate with external applications through ports. Each port includes an appropriate adapter to communicate with the external application. There are several adapters available (e.g., e-mail, HTTP, FTP, etc.) and there is also a special-purpose SQL adapter. The SQL adapter is a software layer that manages the interaction between the orchestration and the external database which is being accessed. From the orchestration, the SQL adapter receives a request in the form of an XML message. It reacts to this request by executing a command over the database system and then retrieving the results. In this context, the SQL adapter acts as a client which communicates with the database through a database API, in a similar way to the example programs that we have seen throughout Sect. 5.4. After collecting the results, the SQL adapter assembles an

Fig. 5.12 Basic orchestration
to query a database

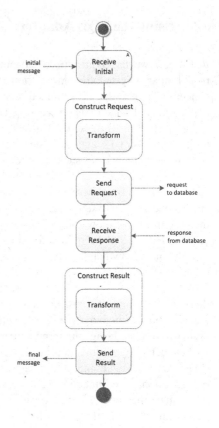

XML message with the output data and returns it to the orchestration. This behavior
is illustrated in Fig. 5.13.

5.6.1   Creating the Stored Procedure

The request that the SQL adapter receives from the orchestration, in the form of an
XML message, contains the input data that is necessary in order to run a query over
the database. It should be emphasized that this request does not contain the query
itself, but only the parameters that are necessary to complete the query. So, for the
example query,

        SELECT Description, Price FROM Products WHERE Ref <= ? FOR XML AUTO

the XML message that is sent from the orchestration to the SQL adapter contains
only the product reference number to be filled in as a parameter. The query itself
must have been previously created and stored in the database, and for that purpose
the SQL adapter relies on a *stored procedure*. Using a stored procedure means that
all that the SQL adapter has to do is to invoke the stored procedure by passing

Fig. 5.13 The SQL adapter as a mediator between the integration logic and the external database

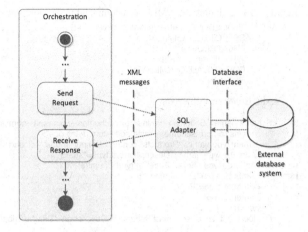

Listing 5.17 Example of a stored procedure to be used with the SQL adapter

```
1    CREATE PROCEDURE GetProductInfo(@Ref int) AS
2            SELECT Description, Price
3            FROM Products
4            WHERE Ref = @Ref
5            FOR XML AUTO
6            RETURN
7
8    EXEC GetProductInfo 67038
9
10   <Products Description="Bicycle Triban 5" Price="400.00" />
```

the input parameters. Such stored procedure, along with an example of its use, is illustrated in Listing 5.17.

In lines 1–6 the command CREATE PROCEDURE creates a stored procedure called GetProductInfo with one input parameter of type integer named @Ref. The stored procedure contains a single SELECT statement that corresponds to the example query shown earlier. In this query, the WHERE clause selects only those rows whose product reference number matches the value of the input parameter. Line 8 shows an example of how this stored procedure can be invoked manually, and line 10 shows the result of such execution. However, such invocation is shown here for illustrative purposes only, since the stored procedure will be invoked automatically by the SQL adapter, when this adapter is properly configured.

5.6.2 Defining the Message Schemas

In order to configure the SQL adapter to be used in an orchestration, it is necessary to define two XML schemas: (1) the schema for the message to be sent to the SQL adapter, which we will call the *request* schema, and (2) the schema for the message that will be returned by the SQL adapter, which we will call the *response* schema. The request schema will carry the input parameter values for the stored procedure,

Listing 5.18   Including the XMLDATA command in the stored procedure

```
1    ALTER PROCEDURE GetProductInfo(@Ref int) AS
2            SELECT Description, Price
3            FROM Products
4            WHERE Ref = @Ref
5            FOR XML AUTO, XMLDATA
6            RETURN
7
8    EXEC GetProductInfo 67038
9
10   <Schema name="Schema1" xmlns="urn:schemas−microsoft−com:xml−data"
11          xmlns:dt="urn:schemas−microsoft−com:datatypes">
12     <ElementType name="Products" content="empty" model="closed">
13       <AttributeType name="Description" dt:type="string" />
14       <AttributeType name="Price" dt:type="number" />
15       <attribute type="Description" />
16       <attribute type="Price" />
17     </ElementType>
18   </Schema>
19   <Products xmlns="x−schema:#Schema1" Description="Bicycle Triban 5" Price="400.00" />
```

so it will have a set of elements that correspond to those parameters. For the stored procedure shown in Listing 5.17, the request schema will have a single element in order to supply the value to the input parameter @Ref.

With regard to the response schema, this can be obtained by running the stored procedure so as to retrieve the XML schema along with the query results. As explained in Sect. 5.5.5, the XML schema can be obtained by including either the XMLDATA or the XMLSCHEMA command in the query. The XMLDATA command generates the XML schema in XDR format, and XMLSCHEMA generates the schema in XSD format. The current version of the SQL adapter included in BizTalk Server works with the XDR format, so it is necessary to include the XMLDATA command in the stored procedure. This can be done as shown in Listing 5.18.

In lines 1–6 the procedure is changed by the command ALTER PROCEDURE in order to include the XMLDATA keyword in line 5. Executing now the stored procedure, as in line 8, returns the output shown in lines 10–19, where the response schema is in lines 10–18 and the query result is in line 19. In line 12 it is possible to see that the each row element in the results will be called Products, and this element will have two attributes called Description and Price (lines 15–16) of type string and number, respectively (lines 13–14). This can be confirmed in line 19.

Listing 5.19 shows an example of the XML messages that will flow between the orchestration and the SQL adapter. In the request message (lines 1–3) the root element contains a single child element called GetProductInfo with an attribute Ref that provides the value for the input parameter of the stored procedure. In the response message (lines 5–7) the Products element contains the Description and Price elements as explained above. It should be noted that the response message does not carry the product reference number (Ref) of the original request. If needed, these data can be brought together in a third message by means of a transformation map. This is precisely the purpose of having the second transform shape in Fig. 5.12.

Listing 5.19 Example of request and response messages exchanged with the SQL adapter

```
1    <InProduct>
2            <GetProductInfo Ref="67038" />
3    </InProduct>
4
5    <OutProduct>
6            <Products Description="Bicycle Triban 5" Price="400.00" />
7    </OutProduct>
```

5.6.3 Defining the Transformation Maps

In addition to the request and response messages exchanged with the SQL adapter, the orchestration in Fig. 5.12 receives an initial message with the product reference number and returns a final message with the product info (Ref, Description, and Price). For simplicity, we will assume that the initial message and the final message have the same schema. In particular, they both have an element for Ref, Description, and Price. However, in the initial message only the Ref element will be filled in, while the other elements will be empty (if they are not empty, their values will be ignored anyway). In the final message, all elements will be filled in.

Figure 5.14 illustrates the two transformation maps for the orchestration shown earlier in Fig. 5.12. The first map has one source schema and one target schema; it collects the product reference number from the initial message and copies its value to the Ref attribute in the request message to be sent to the SQL adapter. The second transformation map, which is used after the SQL adapter returns the response, has actually two source schemas: one for the initial message in order to get the product reference number, and another for the response message in order to get the product description and price that came from the database. The three elements are loaded into the final message to be sent in the last step of the orchestration.

5.6.4 Configuring the Ports in the Orchestration

Now that the schemas, the transformation maps, and the orchestration logic have been defined, it is time to complete the orchestration in Fig. 5.12 by including the send and receive and ports. The orchestration will have three different ports: one receive port for the initial message, one bidirectional port to send the request and receive the response from the SQL adapter, and one send port to return the final message. We will refer to these ports simply as the *receive port*, the *SQL adapter port*, and the *send port*, respectively. The ports are illustrated in Fig. 5.15.

For simplicity, we assume that the receive port fetches the initial message from some folder in the file system. In a similar way, we assume that the send port places the final message in some other folder in the file system. (The folders for the receive port and for the send port must be different, otherwise as soon as the send port would place the final message in the folder, the message would be immediately consumed

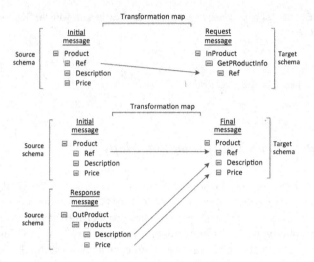

Fig. 5.14 The two transformation maps used in the orchestration

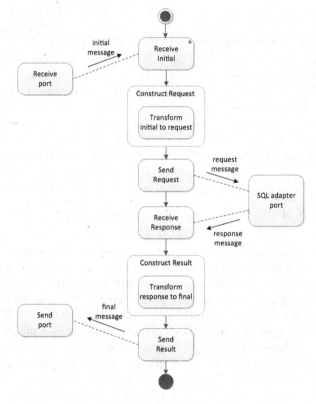

Fig. 5.15 Orchestration and ports to invoke the SQL adapter

by the receive port and this would trigger a new instance of the orchestration.) Therefore, both the send port and the receive port will use file adapters, and it is necessary to configure the folders to be used with those ports.

On the other hand, the SQL adapter port will be used to interact with the SQL adapter. This special-purpose component will receive the request message, extract the Ref value, execute the stored procedure with that parameter value, and return the result back to the orchestration in a response message.

As explained in Sect. 2.3, besides an adapter each port also has an associated pipeline. However, in this scenario there is no need for special processing as the messages enter or leave the orchestration, so the default pipelines (XMLReceive and XMLTransmit) will suffice. Also, since the messages are being transformed in the orchestration through the use of transform shapes, there is no need to include transformation maps in any port.

Although configuring the ports is relatively straightforward, it should be noted that the SQL adapter port is of a different type than the receive ports and sends ports that are commonly used in orchestrations. The simple receive ports and send ports (such as those in this orchestration) can be created and configured manually by specifying the port direction (inwards or outwards) and the message that will be received or transmitted. However, in the case of the SQL adapter port the configuration is more complicated because the actual messages that will be sent and received through that port (it is a bidirectional port) must be determined by inspecting the stored procedure and running it at least once in order to obtain the response schema. To facilitate this task, in the BizTalk platform the port type for the SQL adapter port is generated automatically by a wizard available in the development environment. This wizard inspects and invokes the stored procedure in order to generate several artifacts, namely the XML schemas for the request and response messages, and the port type to be used in the SQL adapter port. Therefore, when creating the SQL adapter port it is necessary to specify that this port is of an existing type, i.e., the port type that has been generated automatically by the wizard.

5.6.5 Removing the XMLDATA Command

One thing that should not be forgotten before deploying and starting the orchestration is to remove the XMLDATA command from the stored procedure. As shown in Listing 5.18, including the XMLDATA command results in the stored procedure returning the response schema together with the results. When running the orchestration, the presence of the XML schema in the response is undesirable since it interferes with message processing and prevents the orchestration from handling the message correctly. Therefore, only the actual results (as in line 10 of Listing 5.17) should be returned.

Removing the XMLDATA command from the stored procedure can be done by running ALTER PROCEDURE once more, as shown in Listing 5.20, where line 5 was changed back to FOR XML AUTO rather than FOR XML AUTO, XMLDATA as before.

Listing 5.20 Removing the XMLDATA command from the stored procedure

```
 1    ALTER PROCEDURE GetProductInfo(@Ref int) AS
 2              SELECT Description, Price
 3              FROM Products
 4              WHERE Ref = @Ref
 5              FOR XML AUTO
 6              RETURN
 7
 8    EXEC GetProductInfo 67038
 9
10    <Products Description="Bicycle Triban 5" Price="400.00" />
```

Testing the stored procedure as in line 8 produces the result in line 10, which can be directly inserted into the response message shown in lines 5–7 of Listing 5.19.

5.6.6 Deploying and Running the Orchestration

As explained in Sect. 2.5, a set of schemas, transformation maps, orchestrations and possibly other artifacts as well, such as pipelines, can be brought together to create a complete integration solution. In such solution, each artifact has its own purpose: the schemas define the structure of messages to be exchanged, the transformation maps define how messages from one schema can be transformed into messages of another schema, and the orchestration specifies the integration logic as a sequence of messages exchanges between ports connected to external applications. In the BizTalk platform, such solution is referred to as a BizTalk application.

The solution must be compiled and deployed to the run-time infrastructure. In some cases, the solution may have to be configured after deployment. At this stage, configuration typically involves creating a physical port for each logical port defined in the orchestration. (The concepts of logical port and physical port have been introduced in Sect. 2.5.) This distinction is necessary because the logical ports in an orchestration, such as those shown in Fig. 5.15, define the direction and type of message that will be exchanged, but the actual addresses and other parameters that are needed to connect to the external applications are defined in physical ports.

For example, the receive port in Fig. 5.15 reads the initial message from a folder in the local file system. However, the specific folder being used is defined in the physical port rather than in the logical port in the orchestration. This way, it is possible to take the entire solution to another machine or environment and deploy it there with different configurations for the physical ports, but with exactly the same behavior in terms of integration logic. For the SQL adapter port, the actual machine where the database system resides is also configured in the physical port.

Once the solution is deployed and all physical ports have been configured, it is possible to start the orchestration. The orchestration is then ready to receive messages. As soon as a new message is placed at the location of the physical receive port, the message is consumed and a new instance of the orchestration is created and triggered. (For this to work, the first receive shape in the orchestration must be

Listing 5.21 Example of initial and final messages for the orchestration

```
1    <ns0:Product xmlns:ns0="http://BikeStore.ProductInfo">
2       <Ref>67038</Ref>
3       <Description></Description>
4       <Price></Price>
5    </ns0:Product>
6
7    <ns0:Product xmlns:ns0="http://BikeStore.ProductInfo">
8       <Ref>67038</Ref>
9       <Description>Bicycle Triban 5</Description>
10      <Price>400.00</Price>
11   </ns0:Product>
```

configured as an activating receive, as explained in Sect. 2.4.) The initial message should have a similar structure to what is shown in lines 1–5 of Listing 5.21.

According to the behavior shown in Fig. 5.15, the orchestration will transform the initial message into the request message to be sent to the SQL adapter. For this purpose, it uses the transformation map shown at the top of Fig. 5.14. The SQL adapter will receive the request message and invoke the stored procedure, and a response message will be returned to the orchestration. The response will be used in the second transformation map of Fig. 5.14 to build the final message, which will then be sent to the folder specified in the physical send port. The final message will be similar to what is shown in lines 7–11 of Listing 5.21.

5.7   Conclusion

In this chapter we have introduced the idea of performing integration at different application layers. When the application architecture is completely closed, then the only option is to integrate at the user interface layer, but this requires the use of ad-hoc techniques to capture the user interface and send commands to the application. Things get easier if the data layer is accessible, particularly if the application relies on a standard database system. If the application relies on files then it may be possible to handle these files as plain text, or preferably as XML. When using a database, there are several technologies and APIs to connect to the database system. In general, all of these APIs are based on the concept of opening a connection, executing the query, iterating through the results, and closing the connection.

Since current integration platforms favor the use of XML messages and of XML schemas to define the structure of messages, it becomes very convenient to retrieve data from a database system in XML form. Several database systems provide this possibility, although the mechanisms associated with retrieving XML are not yet standardized. Here we have seen how to produce XML from a SQL Server database. This can be done in several different ways, but for the purpose of integration it is often enough to use the AUTO mode, provided that it is possible to retrieve a description of the XML schema used by the database system.

The XML coming from the database can then be used directly as an XML message in an orchestration. In particular, it can be easily transformed to another schema, in order to send part or all of the data to another application. Integration, after all, is all about exchanging data between applications. The current approach to integration is to implement this exchange with XML schemas, transformation maps, and orchestrations. However, in addition to these artifacts it is necessary to solve the problem of how to actually connect to an application in order to be able to exchange data with it. In this chapter we have seen how this can be done at the user interface layer and at the data layer as well. The next chapter is devoted to the technologies that allow integration to be performed at the application layer.

Chapter 6
Application Adapters

In the previous chapter we have introduced the approaches that can be used to integrate with an application either at the user interface layer or at the data persistence layer. When the application is completely closed and there is no way to interact with it other than through its user interface, then it is possible to create an adapter that mimics the behavior of a user in order to automate the exchanges with that application. However, this is perhaps the most unfavorable scenario, since integration through the user-interface is highly application-dependent, i.e., it requires a solution that is highly customized for the application at hand. Also, the technology that is used to integrate with the user interface may be different for each application.

A more favorable scenario is to integrate at the data layer, especially if the application relies on a relational database system. Here, it is possible to make use of more standard and mature database technologies, as described in the previous chapter. Still, this provides no direct access to the application functionality; instead, it relies on the assumption that the application will seamlessly handle the data that is read from or written to its database. Integrating at the data layer provides a more convenient mechanism for data exchange but still does not allow to invoke particular functions of the application, as would be desirable in order to make the application perform some action within the scope of an orchestration, for example.

The most favorable scenario for integration is when the application logic layer (the middle tier in Fig. 5.1) is accessible and it is possible to interact directly with it. This scenario is definitely more advantageous than integrating at the data layer since it does not require knowing how the application manages its own data. By being able to invoke functionality at the level of the application code, it is possible to build more efficient and sophisticated integration solutions by composing the functionality of different applications into an overall integration logic. In its simplest form, this composition can be done with additional application code that "glues" together the applications to be integrated. However, this is not the most flexible solution; better is to integrate through an orchestration that can be easily configured and reconfigured to address new requirements.

If integration at the data layer can be done with well-known, mature, and often standardized technologies, then one would expect the same to be true about

D.R. Ferreira, *Enterprise Systems Integration*, DOI 10.1007/978-3-642-40796-3_6,
© Springer-Verlag Berlin Heidelberg 2013

integration at the application layer. In a certain way, it is true: if we look at the Web services technology available today, then it is a standard, vendor-neutral, and platform-independent way of exposing and invoking application functionality. On the other hand, the Web services technology that exists today is the result of years of evolution over a wide range of technologies (such as RPC, RMI, and CORBA) that have tried to achieve similar goals in slightly different ways. In general, every time a new technology came along, it combined a small set of new features with a large set of existing concepts from previous technologies. Therefore, while each new technology was introduced as something entirely new and revolutionary, in reality it was more of an incremental improvement over previous technologies. These stepwise improvements eventually led to the Web services technology, which can be regarded as a distillation of the essential features of previous technologies, influenced by the general use of XML and HTTP as the preferred transport protocol.

Therefore, in order to understand how and why Web services came about, it is useful to have a look at its predecessors and some alternative technologies. It is only after having a look at other technologies that one can fully appreciate the advantages of using the level of abstraction and the run-time infrastructure of Web services. These provide the ideal way to build application adapters today, since the concept of orchestration itself has arisen out of the need to orchestrate the invocation of Web services. If everything can be exposed as a service, then indeed an orchestration becomes simply an orchestration of services. However, not every application is amenable to being exposed as a service or set of services (although it is possible to build adapters that expose themselves as services), so it will still be necessary to invoke different kinds of systems from an orchestration.

In the next sections we will focus on integration at the application layer, and particularly on technologies that allow different applications to interoperate with each other. Knowing about the inner workings of these technologies is important in order to be able to assess the merits of different technological solutions. We will start by the crudest approach, which is to integrate application code directly, and then move on to integration over the network, RPC, CORBA, and finally Web services. But before that, we will start by reviewing some software engineering concepts that are present in all of these technologies.

6.1   Methods and Interfaces

In its simplest form, a program can be a sequence of instructions that runs linearly from begin to end. However, this does not support any kind of reuse; if the same task must be carried out twice or more within the program, the code must be repeated in the sequence. An easy way to avoid such repetition is to have the possibility of jumping back in order to repeat a segment of code. That segment of code is now being reused, but it executes every time in the same way. Since it may be necessary to parameterize each execution, it is useful not only to jump but also to provide some input parameters for the next execution. Hence the concept of *function* is born as a delimited segment of code that can be invoked multiple times with different parameters. Functions provide modularity since they encapsulate units of application logic that can be reused multiple times. A function may also call other functions, meaning that it is possible to use functions as building blocks to develop other functions, leading to the paradigm of *structured programming*.

However, functions operate over data, and the data being used depends on the problem at hand. For example, scientific problems use quantities that are represented as numbers with a certain precision, while business problems manipulate objects with a set of attributes of different types. For different problems (or sub-problems) there are different data structures, and functions can be grouped according to the data structures that they use. In fact, some data structures have an associated set of functions so that the program can manipulate the data structure through the use of those functions, rather than accessing the data directly. In this case, both the data structure and associated functions can be encapsulated into an *object*, with the functions serving as *methods* to change the state of the object, while the inner data structure inside the object is not directly accessible in order to avoid unintended modifications by other parts of the program. Indeed, the encapsulation of data within objects and the use of methods to control data access and modification are considered to be much better practices than just allowing the data to be modified in any (and possibly inconsistent) way by all parts of the program. The idea of developing applications with data encapsulated in objects with callable methods led to the paradigm of *object-oriented programming*.

In the object-oriented paradigm, modularity is provided by the fact that objects can themselves be used in the inner data structures of other objects, and the interaction with that inner data structure is also attained through method invocation. The paradigm is then pervasive across the program, since everything is turned into an object and the program logic becomes a sequence of method invocations.

The concept of having data encapsulated in objects and having to call methods to interact with those objects introduced an unprecedented level of *decoupling* between the different parts of a program. In particular, the inner data structure and the implementation of the methods in an object can be changed without affecting the callers of those methods, as long as the methods keep the same function prototype and the object appears to provide the same functionality to the outside world. In other words, one can change the object implementation as long as its *interface* (i.e., the set of methods) to the outside world remains the same. The interface of an object serves as a *contract* that cannot be broken, but its implementation is a different story since it can be changed, for example, to improve efficiency.

6.1.1 Interfaces and Adapters

In many technologies, such as RPC, CORBA, and Web services, the decoupling between interface and implementation is an essential feature in order to have objects or components that are developed independently and are still able to interoperate

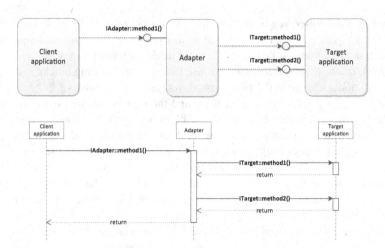

Fig. 6.1 An adapter providing a simplified API to interact with a target application

with one another when brought together. Interoperability is ensured by the fact
that both the caller and the object being called adhere to the published interface.
This interface then has a life of its own: it becomes independent of the object that
implements it or of the object that invokes it. The interface is the cornerstone of
interoperability, and a whole system can be specified in terms of a set of interfaces.

Naturally, the use of interfaces is extremely important in the context of integration. The interface, as a set of methods that are exposed by an application or
component, is what allows it to be invoked by other applications. The notion of API
(Application Programming Interface) is based precisely on the idea of having an
application expose a callable interface to the outside world. It may be the case that
other applications are able to invoke this interface directly; in this case, integration
is greatly facilitated. Otherwise, in case other applications are unable to call the API
directly, or in case they use only a subset of that API, or in case the original API
is unnecessarily complicated and could be simplified, then it is more convenient to
create and use an adapter to translate the original API into another API that can be
more easily invoked by the potential callers.

This corresponds directly to the concept of *application adapter*. An adapter is
a layer of software that sits between the caller and the application that is being
invoked. On the side of the caller, the adapter provides an interface that the caller
can easily understand; on the other side, the adapter is able to speak to the invoked
application using its original API. In the context of integration, the caller may be
an orchestration; we have already seen a similar scenario in Fig. 5.13 on page 133,
where the SQL adapter sits between the orchestration and the external database
system in order to translate the request coming from the orchestration into the
execution of a stored procedure in the database. Here we are dealing with method
calls, and the idea is to translate a method call on the adapter into one or more
method calls in the target application, as illustrated in Fig. 6.1.

In Fig. 6.1 the target application provides an interface ITarget and the adapter provides a simplified interface IAdapter for the same target application. When the client application calls method method1() of IAdapter, the adapter in turn calls method1() and method2() of ITarget. The adapter returns the result to the client application only after the necessary calls to ITarget have completed. In this scenario, the client application is able to achieve with a single call to the adapter what would otherwise require two calls to the original API of the target application.

For simplicity, Fig. 6.1 does not depict any input parameters or return values for these method calls. However, it is possible to imagine that the adapter will receive some input parameters from the call to method1() of IAdapter, and will use these parameters to derive the input parameters for method1() and method2() of ITarget. In a similar way, the adapter will use the output parameters or return values from those methods of ITarget to create the return value or output parameters to be sent back to the client application as a result of the invocation of method1() on IAdapter.

6.1.2   Forward and Callback Interfaces

In Fig. 6.1 the interaction between the client application and the adapter, as well as the interaction between the adapter and the target application, are being done using blocking calls. In particular, the client application does not receive the result of calling method1() on IAdapter until the adapter completes its multiple-call interaction with the target application. (Similarly, the calls on method1() and method2() on ITarget are assumed to be blocking.) It would be interesting to make the call to method1() on IAdapter asynchronous, so that the client application is not blocked while waiting for a response from the adapter.

This can be done through the use of an asynchronous call together with a *callback interface*, which is implemented by the client application, so that the adapter can invoke it whenever the result is ready to be returned. Figure 6.2 illustrates the use of such callback interface. Here, the call to method1() on IAdapter is asynchronous, so the client application is free while the adapter is busy interacting with the target application. When the result is ready, the adapter will call the receive() method on ICallback in order to return it to the client application.

It should be noted that the call to receive() is now a synchronous method call, but it should be rather short-lived since its sole purpose is to make sure that the client application receives the result. The client application is not supposed to do any lengthy processing here, and should rather do such processing in another thread, since otherwise it will be blocking the adapter (for this reason, calls to callback methods are usually carried out in a separate thread on the caller itself). In addition, the callback method does not have to return anything back to the adapter, so in languages such as C/C++ or Java the return type is usually void.

It is interesting to note that, usually, an interface is implemented by the object that defines it. For example, the IAdapter interface is defined by the adapter, it is implemented by the adapter, and it is invoked by the client application. On the

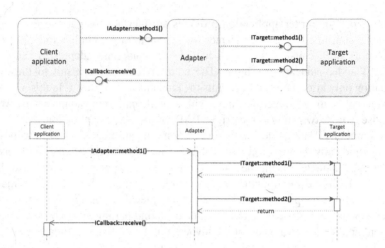

Fig. 6.2 Use of callback interface for asynchronous calls to the adapter

other hand, the ICallback interface is defined by the adapter, it is implemented by
the client application, and it is invoked by the adapter. Here it becomes apparent
what we meant earlier with an interface having a life of its own and serving as a
contract between parties. Indeed, an interface defined by an object does not have
to be implemented by that same object; that is usually the case, but it may also be
the case that the interface is intended to be implemented by other objects so that it
becomes callable by the first object. To distinguish between the two cases, we refer
to *forward interface* or *callback interface* depending on whether the interface is to be
implemented by the object that defined it or is to be implemented by other objects.

Before we conclude this section, it should be noted that the use of callback
interfaces has already been illustrated in Sect. 3.1.6, particularly in Fig. 3.8 on
page 44, where a callback interface is used by the messaging system to deliver the
message to the receiving application. In this case, the callback interface is defined
by the messaging system, it is implemented by the receiving application, and it
is invoked by the messaging system. In this scenario, the messaging system must
have been developed (or at least specified) *before* the receiving application, so that
the callback interface to be implemented by the receiving application was already
defined.

Therefore, a component that defines a callback interface—be it the adapter in
Fig. 6.2 or the messaging system in Fig. 3.8—is prepared to communicate with
any application, provided that the application implements the callback interface that
has been defined by the component. This is an interesting and powerful concept,
since the callback interface serves as an advanced preparation of the component
to be able to interact with future applications. On one hand, the forward interfaces
implemented by the component allow other applications to invoke the component;
on the other hand, the callback interfaces enable the component to invoke other
applications. Using both mechanisms, the component is ready to communicate with
other applications in a bidirectional way.

6.2   Integration of Application Code

When integrating at the application logic layer, we assume that either the source code or a set of interfaces for the target application are available. If the source code is available and can be changed, then the problem becomes more of a software engineering nature than a systems integration one. On the other hand, if only the interfaces are available, which is usually the case, then it is necessary for other applications to communicate directly through the API or use an adapter. If both the source code and an API are available, it may be preferable not to change the code (which could introduce unexpected bugs) but to use the provided API, again either directly or through an adapter. The conclusion is that in most cases using an API is the preferred method to integrate at the application layer.

However, in some cases there may be no API available, while it may be possible to work with the source code directly. Then the problem arises of whether the applications to be integrated run on the same platform and are written in the same programming language. For the moment, let us assume that they are.

In general, all programming languages provide some mechanism to make use of code developed by third parties. For example, in C/C++ there is a distinction between source files, header files, and library files. Library files contain code that has already been compiled and that can be linked with other code to build a new application. But in order to invoke the code in the library, the new application must have access to the data structures and function prototypes that are implemented in the library file. For this purpose, in addition to the library file there must be one or more header files that describe those data structures and function prototypes. These header files are to be included in the source files for the new application. When the new application is compiled, the function calls will be linked to the code in the library file. This is illustrated in Fig. 6.3.

The situation is slightly different in Java. Here, there is no separation between library, header and source files, there are only source files and compiled source files (referred to as class files). Java code can be organized in *packages*, and these packages can be imported in other applications. Whether the packages are available in source files or class files does not matter, because everything will be compiled into class files, if it has not been compiled already. Java packages follow a naming convention which translates into a folder structure where the code is located. For example, the package javax.xml.transform refers to a set of class files that are located somewhere in a directory structure in the form ..\javax\xml\transform\ (or ../javax/xml/transform/ depending on the operating system). In order to use these classes in a new application, it is necessary to import the package (with, e.g., import javax.xml.transform) and to make sure that their root folder is included in the *classpath* variable. Figure 6.4 illustrates this scenario.

Things get more complicated when the applications to be integrated are written in different programming languages. In this case it may still be possible to integrate their code through some mechanism provided by one of those programming

Fig. 6.3 Use of header files
and library files to integrate
code in C/C++

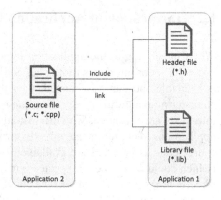

Fig. 6.4 Use of Java
packages to integrate code in
Java

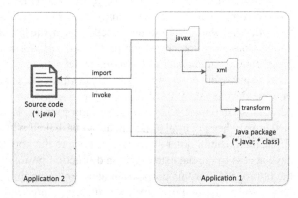

Listing 6.1 Function to convert temperature from Fahrenheit to Celsius

```
1    double ConvertTemperature(double fahrenheit)
2    {
3            return ((fahrenheit − 32) * 5) / 9;
4    }
```

languages. For example, Java provides a mechanism known as Java Native Interface
(JNI) that allows Java programs to call native code written in C/C++ and also allows
native code in C/C++ to call Java code. Such possibilities can be used to create an
adapter in Java for a C/C++ application (when Java calls C/C++) or to create an
adapter in C/C++ for an existing Java application (when C/C++ calls Java). The
following sections explain these possibilities in more detail.

6.2.1   Calling C/C++ Code from Java

Suppose that there is a C/C++ application with a function to convert a temperature
value in Fahrenheit to Celsius. The function could look like the one in Listing 6.1.

Listing 6.2 Creating an exported function in C to be called from Java

```
1    #include <jni.h>
2    #include "Convert.h"
3
4    JNIEXPORT jdouble JNICALL Java_Convert_convertTemperature(JNIEnv* env, jobject obj,
5            jdouble fahrenheit)
6    {
7            return ConvertTemperature(fahrenheit);
8    }
```

To invoke this function from Java, one needs to wrap this code into an exported function that can be invoked by the Java Virtual Machine (JVM). For this purpose, the function can be wrapped as shown in Listing 6.2.

In lines 4–8 of Listing 6.2 a new function is being implemented. The prototype for this function is shown in lines 4–5 and it contains the JNIEXPORT and JNICALL macros required by JNI. The return type for the function is specified between those two macros. Note that the function makes use of JNI data types (e.g., jdouble rather than double, although there is a direct mapping between these data types). In addition, the exported function has three parameters rather than a single one. The first two parameters are required for any function to be called by the JVM. The first parameter (of type JNIEnv*) provides a pointer to a data structure that gives access to several JNI functions, but these are not used in this simple example (they will be used, though, when calling Java code from C/C++). The second parameter is a reference to the Java method or class that calls this exported function. Finally, the third parameter carries the temperature value to be converted.

It should be noted that there is no need to write the function prototype in Listing 6.2 manually. In fact, it has been generated automatically (as we will see ahead) and the name of the function itself was also generated automatically. The function prototype is contained in Convert.h and that is the reason why this header file is being included in line 2. Basically, Listing 6.2 is a source file that implements the exported functions declared in that header file. In line 1, the header file jni.h is being included to account for the JNI data types that are being used in this code.

Now, the code in Listing 6.2 must be loaded by the JVM when the Java application is about to invoke the exported function. Therefore, it must be compiled into a shared library such as Dynamic-Link Library (DLL) or Shared Object (SO) file, depending on the system being used. In this example, we assume that the shared library is called Convert.dll (or Convert.so). At run-time, the Java application will request the virtual machine to load this shared library and then invoke the exported function. The code to achieve this is illustrated in Listing 6.3.

In line 3 of Listing 6.3 the program declares a native method. This method is not implemented in Java; rather, the keyword native indicates that the method is mapped to an external function. The JNI conventions are such that this method will be mapped to an external function called Java_Convert_convertTemperature(), which is obtained by concatenating the prefix Java_ with the class name and the method name. Hence the function name in line 4 of Listing 6.2 now becomes clear.

Listing 6.3 Calling a native method from Java

```
1    public class Convert
2    {
3             public native double convertTemperature(double fahrenheit);
4
5             public static void main(String args[])
6             {
7                     System.loadLibrary("Convert");
8
9                     Convert conv = new Convert();
10                    celsius = conv.convertTemperature(100);
11                    System.out.println(celsius);
12             }
13   }
```

When the program in Listing 6.3 runs, it will start with the static function main() in line 5. Line 7 loads the shared library where the external function is implemented. In line 9 the program instantiates the class, and in line 10 it invokes the convertTemperature() method by passing an input value of 100 °F. This will result in the external function being called. Line 11 prints the result, which is around 37.8 °C.

In practice, since the prototype for the function in Listing 6.2 is generated from the code in Listing 6.3 (line 3), things are done in a slightly different order from what we have presented here. To start with, we assume that there is an existing C/C++ application whose source code is available (in the example above, this role is played by Listing 6.1). Then the following sequence of steps apply:

1. The first step is to write the Java code (equivalent to Listing 6.3) where all the required native methods are included (as in line 3). Note that this involves an early decision of how the shared library where those methods are implemented will be called (e.g., Convert.dll or Convert.so in this example).
2. The next step is to compile the Java program (with, e.g., javac Convert.java) to generate the corresponding class file (i.e., Convert.class).
3. The third step is to run the javah command on the class file in order to generate a C header file with all the function prototypes for the native methods to be invoked. Every call to a native method (e.g., convertTemperature()) will be mapped to a call to the corresponding external function (e.g., Java_Convert_convertTemperature()). For the example above, running javah -jni Convert will generate the Convert.h header file that is included in Listing 6.2 (line 2) and that contains the prototype for the Java_Convert_convertTemperature() function.
4. Finally, what is left to do is to implement the external functions (as in lines 4–8 of Listing 6.2) using the available source code from the legacy C/C++ application. The implementation must be compiled into a shared library with the same name as the one used in step 1.

After these steps, running the Java code will make the JVM load the shared library and invoke the native methods as external functions implemented in C/C++.

Listing 6.4 Java method to convert temperature from Fahrenheit to Celsius

```
1    public class Convert
2    {
3          public static double convertTemperature(double fahrenheit)
4          {
5                return ((fahrenheit − 32) * 5) / 9;
6          }
7    }
```

6.2.2   Calling Java Code from C/C++

Invoking Java code from C/C++ is more straightforward. We assume that there is a
legacy Java application for which the class files (or source code that can be compiled
into class files) are available. The goal is to invoke methods of these classes in a
C/C++ program. For that purpose, it is necessary to write C/C++ code to instantiate
the Java Virtual Machine (JVM), find the desired class and method to be called, and
invoke the method by passing a set of input parameters. Finally, it is necessary to
release resources by unloading the JVM.

Listing 6.4 shows perhaps the simplest possible example of a Java class that
contains a single static method to convert a temperature in Fahrenheit to Celsius.
The goal is to invoke this method from a C/C++ program. The fact that the method
is static facilitates the task even further, since it is not necessary to instantiate the
class in order to invoke that method.

Listing 6.5 contains the full source code that is necessary to invoke the Java
method. The program begins by including the jni.h header file in order to have access
to the complete set of JNI functions and data structures which, among other things,
allow instantiating the JVM, finding Java classes, and invoking their methods. Lines
5–8 declare a set of variables that will be used to initialize the JVM. In particular,
these include options and arguments such as the classpath and the JNI version to be
used, which are specified in lines 15–19. In this example, the classpath points to the
local directory (line 15) and the JNI version is set to 1.2 (line 17).

The env and jvm variables in lines 7–8 will hold pointers to the JNI execution
environment and to the JVM, respectively (we will see these pointers in action
ahead in the program). The env and jvm pointers will be valid only if the
JNI_CreateJavaVM() function (line 21) returns successfully; this can be checked
through the returned value that is stored in the status variable (line 22).

With the env pointer to the JNI execution environment, the program retrieves
the Java class by name in line 24 (note that for this to work, the class must be in
the classpath, hence the need to set the classpath when initializing the JVM). As a
result, the cls variable will hold a handle to that class. Next, in line 27 the program
obtains a handle to the method. The fact that the method is static requires the use
of GetStaticMethodID() rather than the more general GetMethodID() function; anyway,
both functions are very similar. The function receives a pointer to the environment,
a handle to the Java class, and the name of the desired method. However, due to
the possibility of overloading there may be several methods with the same name

Listing 6.5 Calling a Java method from C

```
1    #include <jni.h>
2
3    int main()
4    {
5            JavaVMOption options[1];
6            JavaVMInitArgs vm_args;
7            JNIEnv* env;
8            JavaVM* jvm;
9
10           long status;
11           jclass cls;
12           jmethodID mid;
13           jdouble celsius;
14
15           options[0].optionString = "−Djava.class.path=.";
16           memset(&vm_args, 0, sizeof(vm_args));
17           vm_args.version = JNI_VERSION_1_2;
18           vm_args.nOptions = 1;
19           vm_args.options = options;
20
21           status = JNI_CreateJavaVM(&jvm, (void**)&env, &vm_args);
22           if (status != JNI_ERR)
23           {
24                   cls = (*env)−>FindClass(env, "Convert");
25                   if (cls != 0)
26                   {
27                           mid = (*env)−>GetStaticMethodID(env, cls, "convertTemperature", "(D)D");
28                           if (mid !=0)
29                           {
30                                   celsius= (*env)−>CallStaticDoubleMethod(env, cls, mid, 100);
31                                   printf("Result: %f\n", celsius);
32                           }
33                   }
34                   (*jvm)−>DestroyJavaVM(jvm);
35                   return 0;
36           }
37           else return −1;
38   }
```

but with different parameter types. For this reason it is necessary to specify the desired method more precisely, by indicating the data types for the parameters and for the return value. In line 27, the fourth parameter that is being passed to GetStaticMethodID() is "(D)D". This is called the *method signature* and it specifies that there is a single parameter of type double and a return value of type double as well.

Using the method identifier (mid) obtained in line 27, the program invokes the method through the use of a special-purpose function named CallStaticDoubleMethod() in line 30. There are other similar functions for calling methods that return different data types, but their use is very similar: basically, the function receives the pointer to the environment, the handle to the class, the handle to the method, and finally a set of parameters to be forwarded to the method. The return value is stored in the celsius variable and printed to standard output in line 31. In line 34, the program terminates by unloading the JVM.

It should be noted that the three methods FindClass(), GetStaticMethodID(), and CallStaticDoubleMethod() have been made available through the env pointer, while

Fig. 6.5 Integration through
network communication

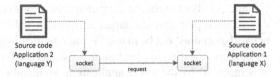

the jvm pointer has been used solely to release the JVM at the end of the program. This illustrates how JNI has its own API, and how this API is far from trivial. On the other hand, the API that we used as an example for integration was very simple, since it comprised a single method to convert between two temperature values. In practice, it may be possible that the API of the application to be integrated is of comparable or even greater complexity than JNI or other standard APIs. For the systems integrator, it is important to be exposed to several different APIs, as this will improve the ability to address difficult integration problems in practice.

6.2.3   Integrating Across the Network

In this section we have seen how it is possible to invoke code from applications written in different programming languages, using C and Java as an example. This required the use of a special mechanism, which in this case was JNI, to create a bridge between two different execution environments, namely the native environment of the C application and the JVM environment of the Java application. In some cases, it may be possible to rely on common mechanisms provided by the operating system in order to create such bridge, provided that such mechanisms are accessible from both programming languages.

An example is the use of network communication. Suppose that there is an application written in a programming language X whose source code can be changed so that the application opens a network socket in order to listen for requests on some port on the local machine. Now, suppose that there is another application written in a programming language Y which opens its own network socket (on the same or on a different machine) in order to send requests to application X. This scenario is illustrated in Fig. 6.5. Naturally, such approach will work regardless of the programming languages of both applications, but provided that it is possible to do this sort of network programming in both languages.

Even though such approach can be quite generic, it creates some problems from a practical point of view. First, assuming that the network connection is established between both applications, there is the problem of defining the syntax for the requests or commands to be sent to the target application. If something similar to a method call is intended, then it is necessary to transmit at least the method and its parameters. Conversely, it is necessary to send the result back to the requesting application. For these purposes, one needs to define some wire format for the data to be transmitted in both directions between these applications.

Other kinds of problems may also arise. For example, it is necessary to specify the network port that the target application will use to listen for requests. This network port must not be in use by other applications running on the same machine. Also, the requesting application must somehow know or learn about the port that is being used by the target application. Hardcoding this port in both applications will reduce flexibility and possibly generate conflicts with future applications. Most likely, it would make sense to define a standard port to be used for this purpose, in a similar way to what is done for a variety of network protocols. This need for standardization also applies to the wire format mentioned above.

Clearly, although the approach in Fig. 6.5 looks feasible, one should avoid developing this kind of solution in an ad-hoc way. On one hand, there are technical issues associated with this approach that should be given proper attention and should be addressed in a systematic way. On the other hand, the proliferation of ad-hoc connections between applications can easily lead to a scenario similar to the one discussed in Sect. 1.3, particularly Fig. 1.3 on page 10. If the connections between applications are developed in an ad-hoc way, then the resulting scenario will be very hard to manage and to change in the future.

Nevertheless, network communication does provide an interesting mechanism for integrating applications written in different programming languages or running in different platforms, machines, or environments. What is need is a convenient and standard way of performing method invocation across the network. Unsurprisingly, there are technologies to perform just that, such as RPC, CORBA, and Web services. What is surprising is that some of these technologies—especially CORBA—which were once seen as the most advanced middleware platforms for distributed systems and were used to build large-scale and mission-critical enterprise systems, have been completely abandoned and are today virtually unheard of.

This was, most of all, due to a change in direction. As the CORBA platform and its associated services grew and increased in sophistication and complexity, a much simpler alternative was in the making, one which relied on widely used Web standards such as XML and HTTP rather than on special-purpose protocols as CORBA did. That alternative is called Web services, and it completely replaced RPC and CORBA. This is not to say, however, that Web services is a better technology than CORBA. In fact, by the time Web services appeared, CORBA was much more sophisticated, with a wide range of associated services and functionality. In part, Web services drew on some of the same concepts, but implement them in a simpler and more widely accessible run-time platform.

6.3   Revisiting RPC and CORBA

To understand where CORBA came from, one can go back to the original ideas of RPC (Remote Procedure Call). The goal of RPC was to facilitate the invocation of functions on a remote application, called *server*, as opposed to the invoking application which is referred to as *client*. The idea was that the function call would

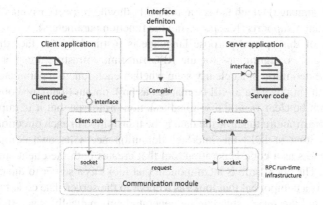

Fig. 6.6 Communication between RPC client and server

be issued by having the client send a request over the network to the server, in a similar way to Fig. 6.5. However, rather than having the client and server agree on the communication protocol and wire format, this is taken care of by the RPC run-time infrastructure. A server needs only to specify the procedure to be exposed, in the form of a function prototype, and the RPC infrastructure will provide the mechanisms that allow such procedure to be invoked by remote clients.

Figure 6.6 illustrates those mechanisms. The RPC run-time infrastructure includes a communication module to transmit the request between the client and the server. However, neither the client nor the server needs to be aware that such communication is taking place. Instead, they both interact with local modules, so the function call appears to be made locally in either case. For the client, the RPC infrastructure provides a *client stub*, which works as a surrogate for the actual server. The client stub provides the same interface as the server, and the client performs the invocation locally on that stub. The invocation is done in the same programming language and in the memory space of the client application.

The client stub is implemented in such a way that, when it is invoked, it passes on the request to the communication module. The communication module transmits the request over the network to the server application. On the server application, there is a *server stub*, which acts as a surrogate for the client. Upon receiving the request from the network, the server stub performs the invocation of the server code. Again, this invocation takes place locally, using the same programming language and memory space of the server application. The RPC run-time infrastructure therefore achieves the interesting feat of transforming one remote invocation into two local invocations, with network communication in between.

However, for this to work the client stub and the server stub need to have some common knowledge about the procedure to be invoked. This knowledge is provided by an interface definition, also depicted in Fig. 6.6, which is essentially a piece of code that contains the function prototypes for the available remote procedures. This interface definition is written in a special-purpose language called IDL (Interface

Definition Language) which is very akin to C both with respect to syntax and to the data types that it supports (for specifying the function parameters).

The use of this special-purpose language is justified by the fact that it may include special configurations for the RPC run-time infrastructure. For example, the interface definition must clearly state whether each function parameter is being used as input (in this case it will be marked as [in]), output ([out]), or both ([in,out]). This may not be clear from the original function prototype, but it is important for the RPC infrastructure to know the data to be transmitted in each direction.

Being written in IDL, the interface definition needs its own compiler. This compiler works as a code-generation tool that creates both the client stub and the server stub. The client stub is a component that looks as a server to the client. The server stub is a component that looks as a client to the server. The code for both the client stub and the server stub can be generated automatically, since the interface definition specifies the function parameters, their data types, and their direction. The RPC infrastructure will therefore have all the information that it needs in order to handle the procedure call between client and server.

The process of packaging the function parameters for transmission over the network is referred to as *marshalling* in the RPC terminology. Marshalling is the process of transforming a data structure that exists in application memory into a format that is suitable for transmission. When sending the procedure call, marshalling is done by the client stub. At the receiving end, the parameters are transformed back to their original form by the server stub, through a process known as *unmarshalling*. Through the use of marshalling, transmission, and unmarshalling, it is possible to replicate the data from the client at the server end. When the server executes the procedure and produces the output parameters or result, the same process takes place in the opposite direction, with marshalling being done by the server stub and unmarshalling being done by the client stub. In this case, the transmission takes place from server to client.

6.3.1   *From RPC to CORBA*

With the advances in object-oriented methodologies in software engineering and the adoption of object-oriented programming languages such as C++ and Java, there was a natural need to extend RPC into the object-oriented paradigm. Rather than simply calling remote functions, there was a need to instantiate remote objects, invoke their methods, pass them references to other remote objects, etc., all of this taking place in a distributed environment. Moreover, such environment should be open to multiple platforms and to different programming languages.

The result was the development of CORBA (Common Object Request Broker Architecture) where the name comes from the fact that the main component in the CORBA run-time infrastructure is the ORB (Object Request Broker) which connects applications in a similar way to the RPC run-time infrastructure discussed above. In CORBA, the server stub is called *skeleton*, while the client stub is simply referred to as *stub*. The skeleton and stub are conceptually similar to their RPC counterparts, and they fulfill the same role, respectively.

As in RPC, there is a compiler to generate the skeleton and stub automatically from an interface definition, and this interface definition is also written in a language called IDL, albeit a slightly different one from RPC. In particular, the CORBA IDL allows specifying interfaces with both attributes (data members) and operations (methods). Also, the language supports method parameters with the usual data types as well as object references. In addition, there is interface inheritance, exceptions, and other advanced features.

In CORBA, there is an additional reason to have a special-purpose interface definition language, and that is the fact that the interface is defined independently of the programming language that will be used for implementation. In fact, there are IDL mappings for different programming languages, including C++ and Java as well as several others. In general, for each programming language there is an IDL compiler in order to generate the skeleton and stub in that language.

It should be noted, however, that the fact that the IDL compiler can generate both skeleton and stub does not mean that they will both be used. It could be that an IDL compiler in C++ is used to generate the skeleton for the server implementation in C++, while an IDL compiler in Java is used to generate the stub for a client in Java. The multi-language support in CORBA comes from the fact that the mapping of IDL to each programming language is subject to standardization. Application developers can therefore work with their preferred programming language, while the CORBA run-time infrastructure will ensure interoperability with objects implemented in other programming languages.

Figure 6.7 illustrates the possibilities introduced with CORBA. A language-specific IDL compiler is able to generate the skeleton or stub as needed for each application. There may be multiple implementations of the same server object in different applications, and there may be different clients for each server object. The interaction between client and server objects takes place across one or more ORBs. It is possible for the client and server objects to use the same ORB, if they belong to the same application. In general, however, client and server objects will be distributed across applications, so a client object from one application will invoke a server object from another application. In this case, each application uses its own ORB, and the ORBs communicate through a standard inter-ORB protocol.

One of the original goals of CORBA was to provide a mechanism through which applications can invoke local and remote objects in the same way. Such goal is achieved by having all invocations—both remote and local invocations—go through the ORB. At first sight, this would seem to be an unnecessary requirement and could even be thought to degrade application performance. However, this is not much of a problem since local interactions will be handled by the local ORB alone, whereas for remote invocations the local ORB will communicate with the remote ORB without the need to perform any additional work by either the client or server. This way, CORBA promotes the development of truly distributed applications by completely abstracting from the location of the object being invoked.

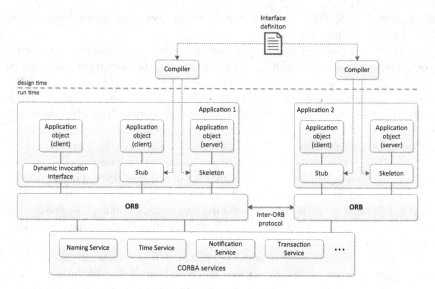

Fig. 6.7 Distributed application objects and services with CORBA

This means that the CORBA mechanisms can be used not only for interacting with remote objects but also to support the interaction between objects within the same application. For this to happen, it is necessary to define the interfaces for all objects—both remote and local—using IDL. Then by compiling the IDL, one obtains the skeletons and stubs for all interfaces. By making sure that all calls are done through client stubs (rather than, say, calling a local server object directly), every call will go through the ORB, and therefore it becomes irrelevant whether the server object is implemented in the same or in another application.

In the example of Fig. 6.7, we assume that there is a single interface defined in IDL, and that there are two applications written in two different programming languages. One compiler is used to generate the stub and skeleton for Application 1, and another IDL compiler is used to generate the stub and skeleton for application 2. Now, in general one application acts as server and another acts as client, but in this example both applications implement a client and a server. This means that the client object from Application 1 can invoke either the local server object available in Application 1 or the remote server object available in Application 2 (the same applies to the client object from Application 2). For the client, the two server objects look exactly the same. It is only at the level of the ORB that the requests are processed differently; in particular, in the remote invocation the ORB of the client interacts with the ORB of the server using the standard inter-ORB protocol.

6.3.2   The CORBA Services

A distinctive feature of CORBA in comparison with other similar technologies is the fact that CORBA includes a rich set of associated services, as depicted at the bottom of Fig. 6.7. These services can be used for multiple purposes, such as discovering objects by name, synchronizing time between objects, subscribing to events from other objects, and managing transactions across objects. These correspond, respectively, to the *Naming Service*, the *Time Service*, the *Notification Service* (which, in turn, is based on the *Event Service*), and the *Transaction Service* depicted in Fig. 6.7. Other services exist, and these are meant just as an example of some of the services that are most commonly used.

In itself, CORBA is a set of standards that can be implemented by different vendors. The CORBA services are also part of these standards, but not all CORBA implementations may provide these services. Anyway, it is possible for an ORB implemented by one vendor to interact with CORBA services implemented by another vendor, since each service is accessible through the same mechanisms that are used to invoke remote objects. A vendor may also specialize in the implementation of CORBA services alone, where these services are intended to interoperate with ORBs from other vendors. However, the most common scenario is to have a CORBA implementation that includes the ORB and at least a few basic services, such as the Naming Service.

The role of the CORBA Naming Service is especially important since it is often the only means for an object to obtain a reference to another object. For example, a client must somehow obtain a reference to the server object to be invoked. The preferred way to do this is to have the server object register itself in the Naming Service as soon as it is instantiated. Registering means providing an object reference and a convenient name which clients can use to lookup the object reference in the Naming Service. The clients need to know only the name which the server uses to register itself in order to retrieve the object reference from the Naming Service. Naturally, such name must not be used by other objects, and the Naming Service ensures this by not allowing other objects to register with the same name.

It is interesting to note the conceptual similarity between the CORBA Naming Service and centralized facilities used in other technological platforms as well. For example, in Sect. 3.5.2 on page 54 we have seen how a JMS (Java Message Service) client application must use JNDI (Java Naming and Directory Interface) to retrieve references to different kinds of objects, namely in order to create a connection to JMS and to send a message to a destination. In this context, JNDI plays the same role as the CORBA Naming Service by allowing objects to be registered and clients to lookup those objects by their registered name.

Also, in the Web services technology to be introduced ahead in Sect. 6.4, a similar role is played by UDDI (Universal Description Discovery and Integration). A UDDI registry is used to publish and discover Web services. Here, the published information may go well beyond the address to invoke the Web service and may include a complete specification of the Web service interface for potential clients. Still, it is possible to recognize a parallel between the way Web services can be registered and discovered through an UDDI registry, and the way object references can be registered and retrieved from the CORBA Naming Service.

The CORBA Naming Service in particular has been devised in such a way that there is an IDL definition that clients can use to invoke the service like they would invoke any other CORBA object, i.e., by compiling the IDL, generating the stub, and invoking the service through that stub. Vendors intending to implement the Naming Service have to compile the IDL, generating the skeleton, and use that skeleton in their implementation. In fact, the standard that defines the Naming Service is essentially a specification of the IDL interfaces that the service provides. The same applies to the remaining CORBA services. For example, the CORBA Notification Service is a specification of the IDL interfaces for a publish–subscribe service where objects can subscribe to particular types of events produced by other objects.

6.3.3 Dynamic Invocations in CORBA

CORBA includes an advanced mechanism called the Dynamic Invocation Interface (DII), which is illustrated at the left-hand side in Fig. 6.7. Using DII, it is possible for a client to invoke any server object without having a stub for that object. Given that the stub is usually generated from an IDL file, the Dynamic Invocation Interface becomes especially useful to invoke an object for which an IDL definition of its interface is not available at design-time. Through the use of DII, a client can learn about the interface of a server object at run-time.

However, the use of DII alone does not completely remove the need to use IDL. In fact, the IDL specification for the server object must exist at some point, and it has to be imported into a special service called the *Interface Repository* (abbreviated as IFR). Only then can other objects learn about the interface from the IFR and invoke those objects through DII. Basically, from the IFR, the client learns about the methods and parameters to be supplied. The client then creates a special Request object which contains the method name and the parameters to be passed. This Request object has a special method called invoke() which performs the invocation on the remote object. The Request object defined by DII therefore works as a dynamic stub that can be adapted for calling any CORBA interface.

Another mechanism that is closely related to DII is the Dynamic Skeleton Interface (DSI). Using DSI, it is possible to build a server object with a dynamic skeleton, which can respond to any call issued by a client. To illustrate how DSI might be useful, suppose that a client has been programmed to invoke a certain server object, through a stub that has been properly generated from the IDL. However, suppose that when the server object is being developed, the IDL is not available (e.g., because the server is being developed *before* the IDL interface is actually defined). Then using DSI it is possible to implement a server that can learn about the method name and the parameters being passed at run-time, as it is being invoked. Such server is called a DSI *servant* and it receives a special ServerRequest object that brings all the call info, including the expected return type. The servant can then return a result in a way that is compatible with what the client is expecting.

Dynamic invocations in CORBA, either through the use of DII or DSI, are usually (and perhaps mistakenly) considered to be a complicated topic and are often avoided in practice. However, they can be extremely useful for the purpose of integration. Given a legacy application developed with CORBA, and for which no documentation or IDL specifications are available, it may be possible to write an adapter to invoke the application functionality through DII, or to write an adapter to receive calls from the application through DSI.

Such dynamic binding between client and server is so important nowadays that even Web services, which superseded CORBA, provide the possibility for clients to learn about the interface of a Web service at run-time, and to interact with the Web service without having to know its interface at design-time. That is in fact one of the main purposes of using UDDI registries, i.e., to have a repository of interface definitions where clients can discover Web services according to their needs. The dynamic invocation of Web services is further facilitated by the fact that this technology makes extensive use of XML, both for the purpose of defining the Web service interface and for the purpose of serializing and transmitting method calls between client and service, as we will see in the next section.

6.4 Web Services

As described in the previous section, CORBA is an advanced and comprehensive platform for distributed applications. In the CORBA platform, each application uses an ORB to handle the method calls between objects, both local and remote. In the case of a remote method call, and in a similar way to RPC, the ORB performs marshalling of the method parameters and sends the request to the destination ORB, where unmarshalling takes place and the server object is invoked. The return result and possibly output parameters as well are transferred back to the client in another marshalling–transmission–unmarshalling sequence. A special-purpose inter-ORB protocol is used for communication between ORBs.

The fact that such an advanced and comprehensive platform as CORBA has lost popularity and has virtually disappeared today has been attributed to multiple factors [14], of which the complexity of use, and the lack of vendor support for the full range of CORBA standards, are often the most cited. However, a careful analysis of the technology that came to replace CORBA (i.e., Web services) suggests that while there was nothing wrong with the CORBA platform itself, the attention shifted to different standards and protocols. Indeed, the essential concepts underlying RPC and CORBA can still be recognized in the Web services technology; however, these concepts have been implemented using a different and more widely accepted set of standards for the supporting infrastructure.

The first factor to shift attention away from CORBA was the disseminated use of XML. At a time when RPC had already been improved to make use of XML to serialize the data going back and forth during a procedure call (resulting in a technology known as XML-RPC), CORBA was still making use of proprietary marshalling mechanisms that led to a binary and opaque representation of data. Naturally, the ease with which XML can be created and processed at the receiving end made it an attractive alternative to conventional marshalling and unmarshalling mechanisms. Any primitive data type, as well as more elaborate structures such as sequences or arrays, can be easily represented in an XML structure.

The second factor that contributed to the development of an alternative to CORBA was the widely disseminated use of HTTP as a transport protocol. In particular, HTTP can be used to carry an XML payload, making it an ideal transport protocol for data serialized in XML. In contrast, CORBA required the implementation and use of a special-purpose inter-ORB protocol. Given the widespread use of HTTP in the World Wide Web, and the fact that it was a perfect fit for the problem at hand, the development of inter-ORB protocols lost pace and together with it the use of ORBs also started to be looked upon as an inconvenience.

The third factor that sentenced the use of CORBA was the development of an alternative to IDL. In CORBA, IDL was devised as a neutral language for interface definitions that could be mapped to several programming languages, especially C++ and Java, but others as well. However, using IDL had the inconvenience of requiring a special syntax and a dedicated compiler to generate the stubs and skeletons. Then the idea arose that it would be much easier to handle interface definitions if these were defined in XML and processed through an XML parser rather than a special-purpose compiler, as in IDL. This would also enable client applications to retrieve and use the interface definition at run-time in order to perform dynamic invocations, similar to those described in Sect. 6.3.3 but using much simpler mechanisms.

The result was the development of WSDL (Web Services Description Language),[1] an XML-based language to define the interface of a Web service. Together with SOAP (Simple Object Access Protocol), which defines how a service invocation can be serialized in XML and transmitted over HTTP, these standards are at the core of the Web services technology.

A third element known as UDDI (Universal Description Discovery and Integration) was part of the original set of standards for Web services, but it is not as widely used as the other two (SOAP and WSDL). Basically, UDDI specifies a repository for storing information and metadata about Web services that enables client applications to discover and interact with Web services at run-time. However, a UDDI repository was originally intended to store much more info than just the service interface, and practice has shown that there was not much use for that extended info. In most cases, Web services have a limited or private scope, which makes them inappropriate for being published in a wider or even public repository.

The most common way to locate a Web service is to provide a URL where the Web service is available. This makes sense since Web services are usually *hosted* in a Web server. Most Web service platforms (i.e., implementations from different vendors or for different programming languages) include the possibility of generating the WSDL interface definition on-the-fly (i.e., at run-time) by querying the Web service URL. This provides an additional level of flexibility since the interface definition can be generated *after* the Web service has been implemented. For a client, this also provides a convenient way to retrieve the service interface

---

[1] WSDL is usually pronounced informally as "wisdle."

Listing 6.6   A C# Web service

```
1    using System.Web.Services;
2
3    [WebService(Namespace="http://example.org/")]
4    public class TempConvert : WebService
5    {
6        [WebMethod]
7        public double ConvertTemperature(double dFahrenheit)
8        {
9            return ((dFahrenheit − 32) * 5) / 9;
10       }
11   }
```

from the Web service itself rather than from an external repository. The client can then parse the WSDL file to learn about all the operations that can be invoked on the Web service. Each operation requires the exchange of one or more SOAP messages, whose XML content and structure are also specified in the WSDL file.

6.4.1   A Simple Example

Listing 6.6 shows a simple example of a Web service written in C# to convert a temperature in Fahrenheit to Celsius. The Web service is implemented as a subclass of System.Web.Services.WebService available in the .NET framework (line 4) and that is why the System.Web.Services namespace is being included (line 1). The class has a single method called ConvertTemperature() that accepts a Fahrenheit value and converts it to Celsius using the same formula as in Listing 6.1.

Besides the fact that the TempConvert class in Listing 6.6 is a subclass of System.Web.Services.WebService, what makes this code behave as a Web service are the code attributes in lines 3 and 6. In line 3, the [WebService] attribute is used to indicate that this class provides a Web service to the outside world. Since there may be other services out there on the Web with the same name, a namespace can be used to distinguish this Web service from others. In line 6, the [WebMethod] attribute specifies that the method that comes afterward is exposed as an operation of the Web service. Together, the attributes [WebService] and [WebMethod] allow the system where the Web service is hosted (usually, a Web server) to automatically generate the interface definition by introspection. In this case, it will expose one Web service (TempConvert) with a single operation (ConvertTemperature()).

When hosted in a Web server, the Web service will be accessible through a Web page, which will execute the code in Listing 6.6. Since this Web service is implemented in C#, it can be hosted in the Web server of the Windows platform, which is known as IIS (Internet Information Services). In addition, the Web page that exposes the Web service can be written in a server-side scripting language known as ASP.NET. Fortunately, the ASP.NET code required to expose the Web service in IIS is quite simple and is shown in Listing 6.7. The actual code is between

Listing 6.7 Contents of the TempConvert.asmx file

```
1    <%@ WebService Language="C#" CodeBehind="TempConvert.asmx.cs" Class="TempConvert" %>
```

Listing 6.8 SOAP request to Web service

```
1    POST /TempConvert/TempConvert.asmx HTTP/1.1
2    Host: localhost
3    Content–Type: text/xml; charset=utf–8
4    Content–Length: nn
5    SOAPAction: "http://example.org/ConvertTemperature"
6
7    <?xml version="1.0" encoding="utf–8"?>
8    <soap:Envelope xmlns:soap="http://schemas.xmlsoap.org/soap/envelope/">
9      <soap:Body>
10       <ConvertTemperature>
11         <dFahrenheit>100</dFahrenheit>
12       </ConvertTemperature>
13     </soap:Body>
14   </soap:Envelope>
```

the delimiters `<%@` and `%>` and it contains a single directive called WebService to specify that this page is a front-end to a Web service.

The Web service can be found in the TempConvert.asmx.cs file that is specified in the CodeBehind parameter. The remaining parameters specify that the Web service is written in C# (Language parameter) and that its implementation can be found in the class TempConvert (as indicated by the Class parameter). The TempConvert.asmx.cs file simply contains the C# code in Listing 6.6. The ASP.NET code in Listing 6.7 is saved in a file called TempConvert.asmx. According to ASP.NET conventions, the supporting code for an .asmx file should be in a .asmx.cs file, where the .cs extension denotes the fact that the code is written in C#. The Web service can then be invoked by accessing the TempConvert.asmx page. In the following, we assume that the page is available on the URL: http://localhost/TempConvert/TempConvert.asmx.

6.4.2 Invoking Operations with SOAP Messages

A Web service hosted in a Web server will wait for a client to invoke one of its operations by sending a request in the form of a SOAP message. On its turn, the Web service will produce a response also in the form of an SOAP message. Basically, an SOAP message is an HTTP message with an XML payload, where the content of the XML payload depends on the operation being invoked and its parameters. As an example, Listing 6.8 shows a SOAP request that could be sent to the Web service defined earlier. The request contains two main parts: the HTTP command together with a set of headers in lines 1–5, and the XML payload in lines 7–14.

In line 1 it can be seen that the SOAP request is being transmitted with an HTTP request using the POST method. The HTTP request is for the TempConvert.asmx page which, as explained before, is hosting the Web service. Line 2 indicates that the request is being sent to a Web server running on the local machine. Line 3

Listing 6.9 SOAP response from Web service

```
 1   HTTP/1.1 200 OK
 2   Content—Type: text/xml; charset=utf—8
 3   Content—Length: nn
 4
 5   <?xml version="1.0" encoding="utf—8"?>
 6   <soap:Envelope xmlns:soap="http://schemas.xmlsoap.org/soap/envelope/">
 7     <soap:Body>
 8       <ConvertTemperatureResponse>
 9         <ConvertTemperatureResult>37.7777777777778</ConvertTemperatureResult>
10       </ConvertTemperatureResponse>
11     </soap:Body>
12   </soap:Envelope>
```

specifies the media type of the payload contained in this HTTP request, as well as
the character encoding. Line 4 specifies the length of the payload, where nn will be
replaced by the number of bytes using the current character encoding. Finally, line
5 contains a special-purpose header field (SOAPAction) to indicate that this HTTP
request is actually a SOAP request. This header is used in case the Web server
wants to handle SOAP requests in some special way. The value in this header field
is simply an identifier (not necessarily a URL) that may or may not be used; the
important thing is that this header is present in all SOAP requests.

Line 7 begins the XML content of the SOAP request. The request comprises an
Envelope (line 8) and a Body (line 9). The Envelope element serves as root node
for the document, while the Body contains the actual request to be forwarded to
the Web service. The body of the SOAP request contains an element that relates
to the operation being invoked (ConvertTemperature in line 10) and one or more
parameters as required by that operation (dFahrenheit in line 11). These names come
from the WSDL interface of the Web service; since the WSDL interface definition
is usually generated by introspection from the Web service code, the operations and
parameters in the WSDL usually end up having the same names as the methods and
parameters in that code. In the particular example of Listing 6.8, the request is to
convert a temperature value of 100 °F to Celsius.

Listing 6.9 shows the SOAP response. It is basically an HTTP response (as can
be seen from line 1) with an XML payload (lines 5–12). Lines 2–3 contain similar
HTTP headers to the request message described above. The SOAP response has an
Envelope (line 6) and a Body (line 7) as before. The body contains the response
from the Web service operation. The response is being returned as a message
called ConvertTemperatureResponse (line 8). In turn, this message contains the
return value in the ConvertTemperatureResult element (line 9). Again, these names
come from the WSDL interface definition for the Web service. The return value
for the ConvertTemperature() method is actually anonymous (as can be seen in
Listing 6.6) so the names for the ConvertTemperatureResponse message and the
ConvertTemperatureResult element have been generated based on the method name.
The next section will help clarify where these names come from.

Listing 6.10 Overview of the WSDL interface definition

```
1    <?xml version="1.0" encoding="utf—8"?>
2    <wsdl:definitions xmlns:wsdl="http://schemas.xmlsoap.org/wsdl/" ... >
3
4            <wsdl:types> ... </wsdl:types>
5
6            <wsdl:message name="..."> ... </wsdl:message>
7            ...
8
9            <wsdl:portType name="..."> ... </wsdl:portType>
10           ...
11
12           <wsdl:binding name="..." type="..."> ... </wsdl:binding>
13           ...
14
15           <wsdl:service name="..."> ... </wsdl:service>
16
17   </wsdl:definitions>
```

6.4.3 The WSDL Interface Definition

For a Web service that is hosted in IIS, it is possible to obtain the WSDL interface definition by appending the suffix "?WSDL" to the Web service URL. For the Web service we have been working with, the WSDL can be obtained by accessing the following URL: http://localhost/TempConvert/TempConvert.asmx?WSDL. As explained above, the resulting WSDL is generated on-the-fly by introspection of the Web service code (this is the main reason for using the declarative attributes [WebService] and [WebMethod] in the code of Listing 6.6). Rather than presenting the WSDL definition all at once, here we will look at it in several parts. Listing 6.10 shows the overall structure of the WSDL definition.

The WSDL has five main parts, whose purpose can be described as follows:

- The <types> element defines the data structures to be used when interacting with the Web service. In particular, there will be a request and a response when invoking the ConvertTemperature() method, and since these messages are transmitted using SOAP, they will have an XML structure. In general, the <types> element defines the XML structures that will be used when interacting with the Web service through any of its operations. Each data structure is defined as an XML schema element in XSD (XML Schema Definition) format.

- The <message> elements specify the set of messages that can be exchanged with the Web service, either from the client to the service or from the service to the client. Messages are closely related to the operations that the Web service provides. For example, the ConvertTemperature() method involves two messages: the request message and the response message. Each of these messages has a certain type, which corresponds to one of the XML structures defined in <types>. There may be multiple <message> elements, and there may be more than one message using the same XML structure, hence the need to define these XML structures separately in <types>.

- The <portType> element is used to define the operations that the Web service provides. Each port type may comprise multiple operations (i.e., <operation> elements), and together these operations can be regarded as an interface (in the same sense of an IDL interface with multiple methods). In general, there may be several <portType> elements, representing the different interfaces that the Web service implements. Within a port type, each operation usually consists in a pair of messages that are exchanged between the client and the Web service. The message being sent from the client to the Web service is referred to as the input message (and takes the form of an <input> element), while the message being sent from the Web service to the client is referred to as the output message (<output> element). An interesting feature of WSDL is that it allows for several possibilities regarding the input and output message:

  - if the operation consists in an input message followed by an output message then the interaction is referred to as *request–response*;
  - if the operation consists in an input message alone then the interaction is referred to as a *one-way* request;
  - if the operation consists in an output message followed by an input message then the interaction is referred to as *solicit-response*; in this case it is the Web service who initiates the interaction with the client;
  - if the operation consists in an output message alone then the interaction is referred to as a *notification*.

- The <binding> elements specify how the Web service operations are mapped to a particular transport protocol. Each <binding> element associates one port type with one transport protocol. The same port type can be associated with other (alternative) transport protocols through the use of multiple <binding> elements. If the Web service has multiple port types, then there will be at least one <binding> element for each port type. In our example, the binding specifies that the ConvertTemperature operation uses SOAP as the transport protocol and is mapped to a particular SOAP action, and also that the input and output messages are transmitted "literally," without any special kind of encoding.
- The <service> element is used simply to specify the address (URL) where the Web service can be found. There may be multiple addresses in case there are multiple bindings. In general, each binding has its own address, so that a client can choose between one of the available transport protocols.

In more detail, the WSDL definition begins with a series of namespace declarations as in Listing 6.11. The namespace "wsdl" in line 2 is used to distinguish between the original WSDL elements and possibly other elements with the same name but unrelated to WSDL. The namespace "s" in line 3 is used due to the XML schema definitions to be introduced in the <types> section. The namespaces "soap" and "soap12" are used to define bindings for two different versions of SOAP.

In line 6, a *target namespace* is being specified. The purpose of having this target namespace is to enable the WSDL definition to refer to elements that have been introduced in this WSDL document itself. For example, the WSDL defines

Listing 6.11 Beginning of the WSDL interface definition

```
1   <?xml version="1.0" encoding="utf–8"?>
2   <wsdl:definitions xmlns:wsdl="http://schemas.xmlsoap.org/wsdl/"
3                     xmlns:s="http://www.w3.org/2001/XMLSchema"
4                     xmlns:soap="http://schemas.xmlsoap.org/wsdl/soap/"
5                     xmlns:soap12="http://schemas.xmlsoap.org/wsdl/soap12/"
6                     targetNamespace="http://example.org/"
7                     xmlns:tns="http://example.org/">
8       ...
9   </wsdl:definitions>
```

Listing 6.12 WSDL types element

```
1    <wsdl:types>
2      <s:schema elementFormDefault="qualified"
3                  targetNamespace="http://example.org/">
4        <s:element name="ConvertTemperature">
5         <s:complexType>
6          <s:sequence>
7           <s:element minOccurs="1"
8                        maxOccurs="1"
9                        name="dFahrenheit"
10                       type="s:double" />
11          </s:sequence>
12         </s:complexType>
13        </s:element>
14        <s:element name="ConvertTemperatureResponse">
15         <s:complexType>
16          <s:sequence>
17           <s:element minOccurs="1"
18                        maxOccurs="1"
19                        name="ConvertTemperatureResult"
20                        type="s:double" />
21          </s:sequence>
22         </s:complexType>
23        </s:element>
24      </s:schema>
25    </wsdl:types>
```

two messages called ConvertTemperatureSoapIn and ConvertTemperatureSoapOut, respectively, for the request and the response from the ConvertTemperature operation. These messages are defined within the specified target namespace. Line 7 introduces a prefix "tns" for the target namespace, so that the two messages can be referred to as tns:ConvertTemperatureSoapIn and tns:ConvertTemperatureSoapOut.

Listing 6.12 presents the data types to be used in those messages. There is actually a single schema being defined in lines 2–24. This schema has two elements named ConvertTemperature and ConvertTemperatureResponse. The ConvertTemperature element (line 4) has a single child element called dFahrenheit (line 9) of type double (line 10). The ConvertTemperatureResponse element (line 14) has also a single child element called ConvertTemperatureResult (line 19) of type double (line 20). These definitions are consistent with the SOAP request and response shown earlier in Listings 6.8 and 6.9, respectively.

Listing 6.12 defines the data types to be used in messages, but it does not define the actual messages. The messages are defined in Listing 6.13. As previously mentioned, there are two messages: one is called ConvertTemperatureSoapIn (line 1)

Listing 6.13 WSDL message elements

```
1    <wsdl:message name="ConvertTemperatureSoapIn">
2      <wsdl:part name="parameters"
3                  element="tns:ConvertTemperature" />
4    </wsdl:message>
5    <wsdl:message name="ConvertTemperatureSoapOut">
6      <wsdl:part name="parameters"
7                  element="tns:ConvertTemperatureResponse" />
8    </wsdl:message>
```

Listing 6.14 WSDL port type element

```
1    <wsdl:portType name="TempConvertSoap">
2      <wsdl:operation name="ConvertTemperature">
3        <wsdl:input message="tns:ConvertTemperatureSoapIn" />
4        <wsdl:output message="tns:ConvertTemperatureSoapOut" />
5      </wsdl:operation>
6    </wsdl:portType>
```

and represents the request from the client to the Web service; the other is called
ConvertTemperatureSoapOut (line 5) and represents the response from the Web
service to the client. The message ConvertTemperatureSoapIn has a single part which
corresponds to an element of type ConvertTemperature defined in Listing 6.12.
The message ConvertTemperatureSoapOut has also a single part which corresponds
to an element of type ConvertTemperatureResponse.

Now comes the port type (i.e., interface) implemented by the Web service in
Listing 6.14. This port type is called TempConvertSoap (line 1) and has a single
operation named ConvertTemperature (line 2). Note that there is a collision between
this operation name and a schema element defined in Listing 6.12. This is just the
way the WSDL has been generated automatically, and fortunately this collision is
harmless since there is no place in the definition where the operation and the schema
element can both be used, which would cause ambiguity. Back to Listing 6.14, the
operation ConvertTemperature uses the message ConvertTemperatureSoapIn as input
(line 3) and the message ConvertTemperatureSoapOut as output (line 4). These are
the messages that have been previously defined in Listing 6.13.

Listing 6.15 shows the bindings of the port type to transport protocols. The first
binding in lines 1–14 specifies that the HTTP protocol will be used (line 3) and
that the operation ConvertTemperature will be mapped to a SOAP action (line 5).
This SOAP action has the same identifier (http://example.org/ConvertTemperature)
that we have seen earlier in Listing 6.8. Lines 7–12 in Listing 6.15 specify that the
input and output messages can be included directly in the SOAP body without any
special encoding. The same applies to the second binding defined in lines 15–28.
This is actually a binding for version 1.2 of the SOAP standard.

Finally, Listing 6.16 shows the <service> element. This contains the addresses
for each binding defined in Listing 6.15. Lines 2–5 in Listing 6.16 define a first
port which refers to the binding TempConvertSoap defined earlier in Listing 6.15.
This means that the Web service is accessible via the SOAP protocol at the URL
specified in line 4. In the same way, lines 6–9 in Listing 6.16 define a second port

Listing 6.15 WSDL binding elements

```
1   <wsdl:binding name="TempConvertSoap"
2                   type="tns:TempConvertSoap">
3     <soap:binding transport="http://schemas.xmlsoap.org/soap/http" />
4     <wsdl:operation name="ConvertTemperature">
5       <soap:operation soapAction="http://example.org/ConvertTemperature"
6                         style="document" />
7       <wsdl:input>
8         <soap:body use="literal" />
9       </wsdl:input>
10      <wsdl:output>
11        <soap:body use="literal" />
12      </wsdl:output>
13    </wsdl:operation>
14  </wsdl:binding>
15  <wsdl:binding name="TempConvertSoap12"
16                  type="tns:TempConvertSoap">
17    <soap12:binding transport="http://schemas.xmlsoap.org/soap/http" />
18    <wsdl:operation name="ConvertTemperature">
19      <soap12:operation soapAction="http://example.org/ConvertTemperature"
20                          style="document" />
21      <wsdl:input>
22        <soap12:body use="literal" />
23      </wsdl:input>
24      <wsdl:output>
25        <soap12:body use="literal" />
26      </wsdl:output>
27    </wsdl:operation>
28  </wsdl:binding>
```

Listing 6.16 WSDL service element

```
1   <wsdl:service name="TempConvert">
2     <wsdl:port name="TempConvertSoap"
3                 binding="tns:TempConvertSoap">
4       <soap:address location="http://localhost/TempConvert/TempConvert.asmx" />
5     </wsdl:port>
6     <wsdl:port name="TempConvertSoap12"
7                 binding="tns:TempConvertSoap12">
8       <soap12:address location="http://localhost/TempConvert/TempConvert.asmx" />
9     </wsdl:port>
10  </wsdl:service>
```

for the SOAP 1.2 protocol. As can be seen from lines 4 and 8, the URL is the same in both ports; this means that the Web service is able to respond via any of those protocols at the same address. The URL points to the page where the Web service is hosted, here assumed to be in a Web server on the local machine.

6.4.4   Creating a Client for the Web Service

The WSDL interface definition above provides all the details about the Web service: it specifies the address where the Web service is located (<service> element), the transport protocols that can be used to communicate with the service (<binding> elements), the operations that the Web service provides (<portType> elements), the messages that are to be exchanged during the invocation of those operations

Listing 6.17 Excerpt of proxy code

```
1   public partial class TempConvert : System.Web.Services.Protocols.SoapHttpClientProtocol {
2
3       ...
4
5       public double ConvertTemperature(double dFahrenheit) {
6           object[] results = this.Invoke("ConvertTemperature", new object[] {dFahrenheit});
7           return ((double)(results[0]));
8       }
9
10      ...
11
12      public void ConvertTemperatureAsync(double dFahrenheit, object userState) {
13          this.InvokeAsync("ConvertTemperature", new object[] {dFahrenheit},
14                              this.ConvertTemperatureOperationCompleted, userState);
15      }
16
17      ...
18
19  }
```

(<message> elements), and the data types that are used in those messages (<types> element). Therefore, for a client that wants to invoke the Web service, having access to its WSDL is the first step, since it contains all the information that is necessary in order to be able to interact with the Web service.

In a similar way to what happened in CORBA, where a client had to compile the IDL interface definition in order to generate a stub that could be used to invoke the server object, a Web service client will compile the WSDL interface definition in order to generate a *proxy* to communicate with the Web service. And just like there were different IDL compilers for different programming languages, there are also different WSDL compilers for each platform and programming language. In C#, for example, the WSDL is compiled using a command-line utility which, for our Web service, can be invoked as follows:

> wsdl /language:cs /protocol:soap /out:TempConvertProxy.cs
> http://localhost/TempConvert/TempConvert.asmx?WSDL

In the first line, wsdl is the command and the remaining parameters are compiler options: /language:cs specifies C# as the language to be used when generating the service proxy; /protocol:soap specifies the protocol to be used when communicating with the Web service; and /out:TempConvertProxy.cs tells the compiler to write the proxy code to a file named TempConvertProxy.cs. The second line contains simply the path or URL where the WSDL can be found.

Running the command above instructs the compiler to fetch the WSDL definition and generates a C# proxy to interact with the Web service via the SOAP protocol. Most users will not care about looking at the generated code and will start implementing the client immediately. However, a brief inspection of the generated proxy provides some insight on how things work under the hood. Listing 6.17 shows an excerpt of the generated code, where one can find a class called TempConvert that inherits from SoapHttpClientProtocol (line 1). This superclass has a method Invoke() that is able to invoke any Web service operation through SOAP.

In lines 5–8 there is a method that works as a *wrapper* for the ConvertTemperature operation. This is called a wrapper because it is not the actual Web service operation, but it has the same signature and its sole purpose is to serve as a proxy to invoke that operation. Note that the function prototype for the ConvertTemperature() method has been generated automatically and exclusively from the information available in the WSDL, namely the <portType>, the <message>, and the <types> elements. This eventually resulted in a method that has the same signature as the original Web service method in Listing 6.6. This is not entirely surprising if one considers the fact that the WSDL has been generated automatically from the Web service code.

Inside the ConvertTemperature() method in Listing 6.17, line 6 calls the Invoke() method of the superclass SoapHttpClientProtocol, which implements the required functionality to invoke a Web service operation through SOAP. The first parameter is the operation name, and the second is an array of objects to be passed as input arguments. In this case, there is just one argument, which is the temperature to be converted. In a similar way, the result of the invocation is an array of objects (line 6). Since there is a single output (the result of the temperature conversion), the proxy method returns the first element in the array to the client (line 7).

In lines 12–15 there is a second wrapper, called ConvertTemperatureAsync(), for the Web service operation. This second wrapper is intended to allow the client to call the operation asynchronously. Note that the Web service itself does not include any asynchronous version of the ConvertTemperature() method. This possibility is introduced by the proxy alone. If the client so desires, it may call ConvertTemperatureAsync() rather than ConvertTemperature(). The first is an asynchronous (i.e., non-blocking) method, while the second is a synchronous (i.e., blocking) method.

The ConvertTemperatureAsync() method relies on the InvokeAsync() method of the SoapHttpClientProtocol superclass to create and submit the SOAP request to the Web service. The proxy then waits for the response from the Web service, while the client is free to proceed. As soon as the response arrives, the proxy delivers it to the client through a callback method. This method is called ConvertTemperatureOperationCompleted() and it can be seen in line 14. This callback method must be implemented by the client if the client wants to use ConvertTemperatureAsync().

Basically, the client may call ConvertTemperatureAsync() in line 12, passing the temperature value and also an arbitrary object as input. This object will be passed again to the client when the proxy invokes the callback method, so it can be used for the purpose of correlating the response with the previous request. Inside ConvertTemperatureAsync(), the proxy calls InvokeAsync() in lines 13–14 by passing the method name, the parameters as an array of objects, a reference to the callback method in order to deliver the response, and the correlating object (userState). For simplicity, we will use the synchronous ConvertTemperature() method instead.

Listing 6.18 shows the code required to implement the client, once the proxy code has been generated by the WSDL compiler. The client is surprisingly simple, and in essence it is implemented in just two lines (lines 7–8 in Listing 6.18). Basically, line 7 creates an instance of the TempConvert class, which is the proxy class generated by the WSDL compiler (introduced in line 1 of Listing 6.17). Then line 8 invokes the synchronous ConvertTemperature() method (declared in line 5 of Listing 6.17).

Listing 6.18 A C# Web service client

```
1   using System;
2
3   class TempConvertClient
4   {
5       static void Main(string[] args)
6       {
7           TempConvert tc = new TempConvert();
8           double celsius = tc.ConvertTemperature(100);
9           Console.WriteLine(celsius);
10      }
11  }
```

The result returned by the Web service is stored in the celsius variable. In line 9, the program just prints the result to standard output.

In summary, creating a client for a Web service can be done in three steps. First, one must retrieve or obtain the WSDL definition by some means, be it from a repository, from the Web service itself, or from a third-party in some other way. Then the second step is to compile the WSDL in order to generate a proxy for the Web service. Finally, the third step is to write the client code that uses the proxy in order to invoke the Web service operations.

Strictly speaking, the second step (using the WSDL compiler to generate a proxy) is not absolutely mandatory since it is possible to generate SOAP requests by other means. One can imagine, for example, an application that creates a SOAP request, sends it through HTTP to the Web server where the Web service is located, and then listens for the response. However, the main purpose of using Web services is to have the WSDL serve as a contract between client and service, so, although possible, it would not be a good practice to bypass the WSDL altogether and to implement the interaction with a Web service using low-level mechanisms alone.

Some authors have actually argued in favor of simplifying the Web services technology in order to take full advantage of low-level HTTP mechanisms, as an alternative to the combination of SOAP and WSDL. Such view has led to the development of REST and "RESTful" Web services [25]. According to the REST philosophy, Web services are replaced by online data resources (equivalent to distributed objects) which can be queried or modified through the use of standard HTTP methods, such as PUT for creating, GET for reading, POST for updating, and DELETE for deleting. Every REST resource has then the same interface, which corresponds to the set of available HTTP methods, and each resource gives its own meaning to those methods. For example, for a resource that manages customers, the POST method may be used to change customer data such as the customer address; while for a resource that manages products, the POST method may be used to change the price.

In typical REST applications, the result of invoking an operation (through an HTTP request) is to receive a plain (i.e., non-SOAP) XML document in the HTTP response. Other kinds of payload are also possible; in general, any HTTP content type is supported. Basically, REST dispenses with the need to define Web service interfaces and the need to serialize messages in a special format. Therefore, rather than a simplification of the Web services, REST should be regarded as an alternative to the technology branch that includes RPC, CORBA, and Web services.

6.5 Invoking a Web Service from an Orchestration

In integration scenarios, Web services can be used as adapters for existing
applications. This may occur either because the applications to be integrated
have been originally developed as a set of Web services, or because the existing
applications (or a subset of their functionality) have been exposed as Web services.
For example, using a similar code to Listing 5.5 on page 118, it would be possible
to write a Web service in C# that connects to the database and retrieves the price for
a given product. Additional methods, for example to update the product info in the
database, could be implemented as well. Then other applications could invoke this
Web service instead of having to query the database directly. In this scenario, the
Web service would work as an adapter for the database.

In Sect. 5.6 we have used a special-purpose adapter—the SQL adapter—to
query the database through a stored procedure. This adapter was invoked in an
orchestration and served as a mediator between the orchestration and the external
database, as illustrated in Fig. 5.13 on page 133. A Web service can also be invoked
from within an orchestration and it can serve as a mediator between the orchestration
and an external application, if the Web service is an adapter for that application.
Alternatively, the Web service may represent the application itself, if the application
exposes one or more Web service interfaces. In any case, invoking the Web service
in an orchestration allows the application to participate in the flow of message
exchanges in a complex integration scenario.

In this section, we develop an orchestration to invoke the simple Web service
for temperature conversion that was used as a running example in the last section.
The orchestration to invoke the Web service is very similar to the one that was
used to invoke the SQL adapter, and it is shown in Fig. 6.8. Basically, the orchestration receives an initial message that brings a temperature value in Fahrenheit.
The orchestration then uses this temperature value to construct the request message
to be sent to the Web service. However, rather than using a transformation map as
in the case of the SQL adapter, here the request to the Web service is constructed
through the use of a different shape called *message assignment.*

The use of a message assignment rather than a transformation map is explained
by the fact that this Web service, in contrast to the SQL adapter in Chap. 5, works
with simple data types (double) as input and output, instead of more elaborate input
and output XML as the SQL adapter does. Of course, the actual request and response
from the Web service will both be transmitted as SOAP messages, but this takes
place at the transport layer. At the application (or rather, orchestration) layer, the
Web service is seen as having a method that takes a double value as input and returns
another double value as output. Therefore, in order to construct the request to be sent
to the Web service, the orchestration needs to set the value of the double parameter to
be provided as input to the Web service method. This can be done using a message
assignment shape, which is basically a placeholder for C# code.

By using C# in a message assignment shape, it is possible to write code to set
the content of a message while it is being constructed. In particular, here we would

Fig. 6.8 Basic orchestration
to invoke a Web service

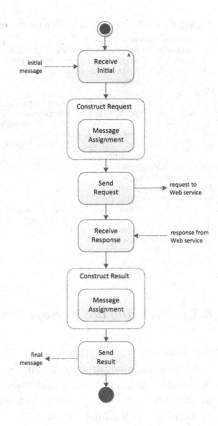

like to set the Fahrenheit value to be provided as input to the Web service. For this
to happen, the element whose value is to be set must be a *distinguished property*
in the message schema. As explained in Sect. 4.5, a distinguished property is a
message element that can be explicitly used in an orchestration, for example to
make decisions that change the flow of the orchestration.

Here we use the Fahrenheit value that comes in the initial message as a
distinguished property, so that it can be copied to the request to be sent to the Web
service. In the same way, the Celsius value in the Web service response is to be
copied to the Celsius element in the final message, which is also a distinguished
property. Therefore, in this scenario there are two distinguished properties: the
Fahrenheit element is a distinguished property in the initial message that arrives
(and triggers) the orchestration, and the Celsius element is a distinguished property
in the final message produced as an output from the orchestration. The Fahrenheit
property value is copied from the initial message to the Web service request in the
first message assignment, and the Celsius property value is copied from the Web
service response to the final message in the second message assignment.

Listing 6.19 XML schema definition for the initial and final messages of the orchestration

```
1    <?xml version="1.0"?>
2    <xs:schema xmlns:xs="http://www.w3.org/2001/XMLSchema"
3                    targetNamespace="http://DemoWS.Temperature">
4      <xs:element name="Temperature">
5        <xs:annotation>
6          <xs:appinfo>
7            <b:properties xmlns:b="http://schemas.microsoft.com/BizTalk/2003">
8              <b:property distinguished="true"
9                          xpath="/*[local−name()='Temperature']/*[local−name()='Fahrenheit']" />
10             <b:property distinguished="true"
11                         xpath="/*[local−name()='Temperature']/*[local−name()='Celsius']" />
12           </b:properties>
13         </xs:appinfo>
14       </xs:annotation>
15       <xs:complexType>
16         <xs:sequence>
17           <xs:element name="Fahrenheit" type="xs:double" />
18           <xs:element name="Celsius" type="xs:double" />
19         </xs:sequence>
20       </xs:complexType>
21     </xs:element>
22   </xs:schema>
```

6.5.1   Defining the Message Schema

For simplicity, we will use the same schema for the initial message and for the final message in the orchestration. This means that the schema will have to accommodate both the temperature value in Fahrenheit (that comes as input to the orchestration in the initial message) and the value in Celsius (that is sent as output from the orchestration in the final message). The schema definition is shown in Listing 6.19. It begins by declaring the xs prefix in line 2 that refers to the namespace where the XML Schema syntax is defined. In line 3, a target namespace is used to specify that the new elements to be defined in this schema will belong to that namespace. That is the case, for example, of the Temperature element in line 4, which will serve as root node in messages that are instances of this schema.

In general, each message flowing in or out of an orchestration can be regarded as having a certain *type* (i.e., schema). In the Biztalk system, the message type is defined as a combination of the target namespace and the root node, separated by the symbol '#'. For example, a message that is an instance of the schema in Listing 6.19 has the target namespace http://DemoWS.Temperature (line 3) and the root node Temperature (line 4), and therefore can be said to have the following type:

http://DemoWS.Temperature#Temperature

After the definition of the root element in line 4, there are two different parts, one in lines 5–14 and another in lines 15–20, which can be better explained in reverse order. Lines 15–20 specify what comes within the root element. Basically, there is an element of type double to store the temperature in Fahrenheit (line 17) and there is another element of type double to store the temperature in Celsius (line 18). Now, these two elements have been *distinguished*, as can be seen in lines 5–14. In line 8, the schema defines a distinguished property which can be retrieved through the XPath expression in line 9. This XPath expression points to the Fahrenheit element inside the Temperature node. In a similar way, line 10 defines a distinguished property which can be retrieved through the XPath expression in line 11. This expression points to the Celsius element inside the Temperature node.

The schema definition in Listing 6.19 would be a regular schema if it were not for the special annotations in lines 5–14. These are used to define the distinguished properties in this schema. Since the concept of distinguished property is specific to the BizTalk system, line 7 introduces the namespace (through prefix b) to be used when defining these properties. When using C# code to access the Fahrenheit and Celsius elements, BizTalk will know, from the XPath expressions, where to find those properties in the XML message.

6.5.2 Adding a Reference to the Web Service

The schema for the initial and final messages of the orchestration has been defined above in the way that seemed most convenient for the scenario at hand. However, the schema for the messages that are to be exchanged with the Web service cannot be defined arbitrarily in the same way, because they are fully determined by the WSDL interface definition for the Web service (see Sect. 6.4.3). In particular, the WSDL specifies that the ConvertTemperature operation takes a message with a double element named dFahrenheit as input, and produces a message with a double element named ConvertTemperatureResult as output (Listing 6.12).

Therefore, the messages to be exchanged with the Web service must be defined according to the requirements that are specified in the WSDL. At first sight, this would appear to complicate matters, but it actually simplifies them. Having the message details completely defined in the WSDL allows a platform such as BizTalk to automatically generate the required artifacts to communicate with the Web service, much in the same way that the WSDL compiler automatically generates a proxy for a client from the WSDL definition. In fact, BizTalk invokes a WSDL compiler to generate two kinds of artifacts:

- it creates the message types (as *multi-part message types*) for each message defined in the WSDL; in contrast with regular XML messages, these multi-part messages are capable of carrying arbitrary objects in addition to XML; in the present scenario, there will be one ConvertTemperature_request message type, and one ConvertTemperature_response message type; both of these message types carry an object of type System.Double;
- it also creates a *port type* to communicate with the Web service; this port type is automatically configured with the SOAP binding specified in the WSDL.

Invoking the Web service in the orchestration is then a matter of creating a pair of messages and adding a new port. The messages should be of the same type as the multi-part message types that have been automatically generated from the WSDL. In the BizTalk platform, these multi-part message types are sometimes referred to as *Web message types*. Regarding the new port to be created, this should have the same port type as the one that has been generated from the WSDL.

6.5.3 Configuring the Message Assignments

The first message assignment in Fig. 6.8 is inside a *construct message* shape. This is used to indicate that a new message is being created at that point of the orchestration, and not before. The message that is being created is the request to be sent to the Web service. This request must carry the Fahrenheit value that comes in the initial message. Therefore, the value must be copied from the initial message into the request message. This can be achieved by inserting the following C# expression in the message assignment shape:

```
msgRequest.dFahrenheit = msgInitial.Fahrenheit;
```

In the expression above, msgInitial refers to the initial message that triggers the orchestration, and msgInitial.Fahrenheit refers to a distinguished property in that message (the Fahrenheit element). On the left-hand side, msgRequest refers to the request to be sent to the Web service. This message is of type ConvertTemperature_request; it is a multi-part message that carries an object of type System.Double that is identified as dFahrenheit. Therefore, the expression above is setting the dFahrenheit object to be equal in value to the distinguished property Fahrenheit.

The second message assignment in Fig. 6.8 takes care of transferring the result coming from the Web service, i.e., the temperature value in Celsius, to the final message produced by the orchestration. This message assignment is also inside a construct message shape. The message being constructed is the final message; this message does not exist in the orchestration before the construct message shape, and after this point it cannot be modified anymore. It can be modified only during construction. In this case, the message is being constructed through a message assignment shape, and this message assignment has the following C# instructions:

```
msgFinal = msgInitial;
msgFinal.Celsius = msgResponse.ConvertTemperatureResult;
```

The first instruction sets the content of the final message (msgFinal) to be equal to that of the initial message (msgInitial). As explained in Sect. 6.5.1, these two messages have the same schema, so there is no problem in making them have the same content. By equating one to the other, the final message will carry the original Fahrenheit value that came in the initial message. Regarding the Celsius value, this is being overwritten in the second instruction; here, msgFinal.Celsius refers to a distinguished property in the final message (i.e., the Celsius element). The value for this property is being obtained from the response of the Web service (msgResponse). This response is a message of type ConvertTemperature_response, which carries

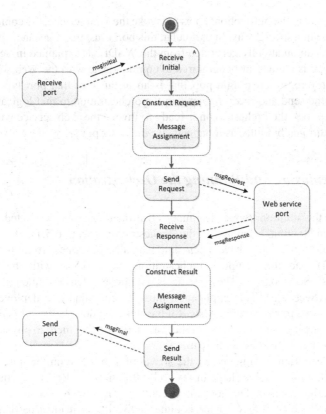

Fig. 6.9 Orchestration, ports, and messages to invoke the Web service

an object of type System.Double that is identified as ConvertTemperatureResult. The value of this object is being copied to the distinguished property Celsius.

6.5.4 Configuring the Ports in the Orchestration

The orchestration that invokes the Web service will have three ports: one port to receive the initial message, one port to send the final message, and one bidirectional port to invoke the Web service in between. These ports are shown in Fig. 6.9 and they must be configured separately. The receive port and the send port can be bound to any kind of physical receive port and physical send port, respectively. The simplest option is to bind these logical ports to physical ports using the file adapter. In this case, the receive port fetches the initial message from some folder in the file system, and the send port writes the final message to some other folder.

With respect to the bidirectional port to invoke the Web service, the configuration must be done in a special way. In particular, this port must be an instance of the port type that was automatically generated from the WSDL, as explained in Sect. 6.5.2. That port type is already pre-configured to communicate with the Web service via SOAP. Therefore, by creating a port that is an instance of that port type, and by connecting the send and receive shapes in the orchestration to that logical port, as shown in Fig. 6.9, the orchestration is ready to invoke the Web service without the need for additional bindings as it happens for the other ports.

6.5.5   Deploying and Running the Orchestration

To develop the solution above, a number of artifacts have been created, namely: the input and output schema for the orchestration (Sect. 6.5.1), the message types and port type that have been automatically generated from the WSDL (Sect. 6.5.2), and the complete orchestration (Sect. 6.5.4) with the message assignments (Sect. 6.5.3). These artifacts comprise what is called a BizTalk application (Sect. 2.5). This application must be compiled and deployed to the BizTalk run-time infrastructure. Also, if it has not been done before, it is necessary to configure the logical ports in the orchestration by binding them to physical ports. Only then is the orchestration ready to start.

The orchestration is triggered by the arrival of a message on the initial receive port, hence the first receive shape in the orchestration (i.e., "Receive Initial") must be an activating receive. The concept of activating receive has been discussed in Sects. 2.5 and 4.6. A receive shape is either activating or it must participate in a correlation. In the orchestration in Fig. 6.9, there is second receive shape to receive the response from the Web service, and this receive is non-activating (i.e., it does not start a new orchestration instance). However, there is no need for an explicit correlation in the orchestration since the request and response from the Web service are implicitly correlated through the use of a bidirectional port.

Listing 6.20 shows an example of an initial message that can be used to trigger the orchestration (lines 1–4). This message conforms to the schema shown earlier in Listing 6.19. Note that the root element in Listing 6.20 (line 1) includes a namespace so that the message type can be determined as explained in Sect. 6.5.1. In the initial message (lines 1–4) only the Fahrenheit value is filled in, while the Celsius value has been left empty. In the final message produced by the orchestration (lines 6–9), both elements are filled in. The Fahrenheit value comes from the initial message, and the Celsius value comes from the Web service response. These values are set during the second message assignment. After constructing the final message, the orchestration sends it through the send port and terminates.

Termination means the end of the current process instance. In practice, there may be multiple orchestration instances running concurrently, and the same Web service will be invoked by all of them. For this reason, special care must be taken in scenarios where the Web services being invoked make use of limited resources, such as memory, network bandwidth, or database connections.

Listing 6.20 Example of initial and final messages for the orchestration

```
1   <ns0:Temperature xmlns:ns0="http://DemoWS.Temperature">
2     <Fahrenheit>100</Fahrenheit>
3     <Celsius></Celsius>
4   </ns0:Temperature>
5
6   <ns0:Temperature xmlns:ns0="http://DemoWS.Temperature">
7     <Fahrenheit>100</Fahrenheit>
8     <Celsius>37.7777777777778</Celsius>
9   </ns0:Temperature>
```

6.6 Conclusion

In this chapter we have discussed a number of technologies that are relevant for integration at the application logic layer. Such kind of integration usually involves having to change or to extend application code in order to develop mechanisms that allow applications to interoperate with each other. For applications that have been developed in different programming languages, it might be possible to integrate their code directly by resorting to special mechanisms (e.g., JNI) available in one of those programming languages. A more generic approach is to integrate through network communication, since in general every programming language allows for some form of network programming (e.g., sockets). However, this is impractical without the ability to specify the remote interface and to define the way in which method calls and parameters must be transmitted between both ends. This explains why technologies such as RPC and CORBA have been developed: these technologies raise the level of abstraction and allow applications to invoke functions and objects across different platforms and programming languages.

The problem of RPC and CORBA was that they relied on special mechanisms and dedicated protocols when some of the same features could be achieved through open standards based on XML and widely used protocols such as HTTP. Eventually, this led to the development of Web services, which completely replaced CORBA as the preferred technology to develop distributed applications. Web services are also especially convenient to build application adapters. The fact that their interfaces are defined in an XML-based language (WSDL) facilitates interoperability. Also, the fact that communication with Web services is based on the exchange of XML messages reduces the overhead and complexity of the underlying infrastructure.

The Web services technology was so successful that the concept of *service* (rather than *object*) has become central in modern application architectures, hence all the emphasis on *service-oriented architectures*. Having such a profound impact on the way applications are designed, the concept of service would also have a profound impact on systems integration, as we will see in the next chapter.

Part IV
Orchestrations

Chapter 7
Services and SOA

As we have seen in the previous chapter, a Web service is a software component with a well-defined interface that can be invoked in an automated way. The fact that Web services make extensive use of XML-based technologies—namely SOAP for message exchange and WSDL for interface definitions—is one of the main reasons for their large success and wide adoption.

In fact, Web services opened up new possibilities for interoperability across different systems, platforms, and languages. The fact that interfaces are defined in XML finally removed the bias that existed towards certain languages, namely the proximity of IDL to C/C++ both in RPC and CORBA. Nowadays, any program written in any programming language and running in any platform can interpret the interface definition of a Web service, provided that it has some minimal XML-processing capabilities. Also, the fact that a Web service can be hosted in a Web server makes it easier for clients to communicate and interact with the service using a network infrastructure and network protocols that are widely available, rather than special-purpose run-time platforms as in the case of RPC or CORBA.

In addition, Web services facilitate reuse while maintaining a high degree of decoupling between their outside interface and their inner implementation. The interface that a Web service exposes to the outside world is like a contract. Everything runs well when both client and service adhere to the interface contract. Breaking the contract is not impossible, but it may have serious consequences such as broken code, malfunctions, application errors, and other undesired situations that render the interaction useless. A Web service adheres to the contract by having an implementation that conforms to the specified operations in the WSDL. The client adheres to the contract by invoking the operations correctly as specified in the contract. In general, every Web service operation involves a set of message exchanges, and both the service and the client are expected to perform their role in those exchanges, by producing or consuming messages as determined by the contract.

Now, the concept of contract and the decoupling between interface and implementation can be discussed independently of the supporting technologies, such as WSDL or SOAP. From a conceptual point of view, it is unnecessary to keep referring

D.R. Ferreira, *Enterprise Systems Integration*, DOI 10.1007/978-3-642-40796-3_7,   185
© Springer-Verlag Berlin Heidelberg 2013

to *Web services*; instead, one can simply refer to *services*, where a service has a contract and an implementation, and there is some technological infrastructure through which clients can communicate with services. Present day technology mandates WSDL and SOAP, but one can imagine that the same concepts could be achieved with other technologies as well. What is important here is to focus on the possibilities introduced by such conceptual (rather than technological) framework. Services, whether implemented as Web services or as something else, have the potential to change the way applications can be developed and integrated.

Even more importantly, and as we will see in this chapter, services have the potential to change the whole IT landscape in an organization by providing, for the first time, an approach that can be systematically applied to bridge the gap between low-level systems and high-level business processes and related requirements.

7.1   Services and Applications

The fact that a service exposes an interface to the outside world while its actual implementation is hidden allows for a service to become a gateway for a wide variety of systems. In Sect. 6.5 we have mentioned the possibility of developing a service that connects to a database system and serves as an adapter for a database. This would replace the need for a client to interact with the database directly, and instead would make it possible to query or modify data by invoking service operations. The advantage of doing this is that the service can provide a simpler interface than what would be the case if the client would have to interact with the database system through a database API as explained in Sect. 5.4. As an alternative to this scenario, the service can hide the details of creating and using a database connection, while exposing an interface that focuses on data operations alone.

In general, when integrating with a legacy application the same approach can be employed to create a service-based adapter that hides the integration mechanisms that are being used to exchange data with the application. At the same time, the adapter can expose a set of methods that appear to the client as if it is invoking the application logic directly. For example, some applications are completely closed and integration can only be done at the user interface layer, as discussed in Sect. 5.2. In this case, it becomes very convenient to have an adapter that hides the details of how the integration is being performed, while at the same time providing access to the application functionality. This is possible to achieve with a service whose internal implementation can be rather complicated, but whose external interface may be quite simple to invoke from the client perspective.

A service may also provide an interface to access not one, but multiple applications simultaneously. A typical scenario is when there is a service that must invoke multiple systems (in a parallel or serial fashion) before returning a result to the client. In this case, the client simply invokes an operation from the service interface, and the service is implemented in such a way that it interacts with multiple applications in order to achieve the desired goal or generate the desired result.

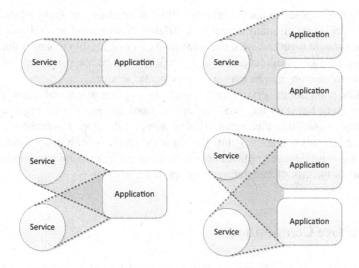

Fig. 7.1 Possible relationships between services and applications

Such operation is effectively at a higher level of abstraction than the underlying systems that are being invoked. A service or set of services comprising such kind of operations may be developed in order to create a layer of abstract functionality on top of an infrastructure comprising several heterogeneous applications.

If it is true that a service can become a point of access to multiple applications, it is also true that a single application can provide several services to the outside world, depending on how its functionality has been structured and exposed. Today, applications can be designed from the beginning while having in mind the set of services to be provided. However, in the context of integration a more common scenario is to have legacy applications that were not developed in a service-oriented way but have to be integrated using a service-based approach. In this case, and especially if the application code is available, it may be possible to extend those applications in order to expose their functionality, or the required subset of their functionality, as a set of services. Even if the application code is not available, in general it is possible to develop adapters that expose a service interface, or a set of service interfaces, to the outside world.

The relationship between applications and services can therefore take many forms, and Fig. 7.1 illustrates the main possibilities. In the upper-left corner, an application is exposed as a single service interface, and this corresponds to a one-to-one mapping between service and application. This scenario takes place, for example, when the service is serving as an adapter for the application. In the upper-right corner, a service exposes functionality that can only be obtained by invoking multiple applications; this corresponds to a one-to-many relationship. In the lower-left corner, an application exposes its functionality through multiple services (many-to-one). Finally, in the lower-right corner, the combined functionality of multiple applications is exposed as a set of services, illustrating a many-to-many relationship. Note that this many-to-many scenario is different from having several one-to-one scenarios brought together; what the many-to-many relationship means is that there are several possible combinations of functionality from both applications, and each of these combinations can be exposed as a separate service.

The key point about services and applications is that in general there is not a direct mapping between the two. The applications are just there, they represent preexisting systems that the organization acquired or developed over time and that need to be integrated at some point. The services, on the other hand, are developed in order to reshape these applications into a set of easily callable components that can facilitate the task of integrating those applications.

7.2   Service Composition

An important issue that is not illustrated in Fig. 7.1 is the possibility of having services invoking other services. In the same way that services can be used to create a layer of abstraction over the functionality of one or more applications, new services can also be developed to create a layer of abstraction over the functionality of existing services. In this context, every box that represents an application in Fig. 7.1 can be replaced by a circle representing a service, and the same relationships would still hold. For example, a one-to-one relationship between two services would mean that a new service is created to encapsulate an existing service. Although at first sight such one-to-one encapsulation would appear to be of hardly any use, it can actually serve useful purposes, such as providing the same service functionality through a different interface, or extending the functionality of an existing service while keeping its interface unchanged.

For example, a new service with logging capabilities could be used as a wrapper for an existing service without logging capabilities. In this case, the new service would have the same interface as the old one and would forward all calls to the old one. However, in every method call the new service would log some data (e.g., by writing to a file) before invoking the same method on the old service. This could be useful, for example, for debugging purposes.

Of special interest is the one-to-many relationship depicted in the upper-right corner of Fig. 7.1. If the applications are to be replaced by services, then this one-to-many relationship essentially means that a new service will provide a combination of functionality from other services. In practice, this means that when a client invokes an operation from the new service, this operation will consist in invoking several operations from other services. The new service is effectively an abstraction over the functionality provided by other services and such scenario can be regarded as being a form of *service composition*.

Service composition is a concept with far-reaching implications that adds an additional degree of flexibility when developing integration solutions over a landscape of legacy applications. Figure 7.2 illustrates how a new layer of services

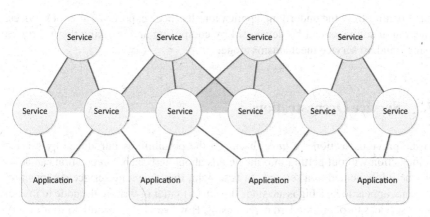

Fig. 7.2 Service composition

can be built on top of a layer of existing services through composition. The bottom layer of services represents a set of low-level services whose main purpose is to expose application functionality. In general, the interfaces of these low-level services will be very much related to the specific application logic that needs to be exposed, and most likely the methods provided by these services will correspond to specific operations that can be performed by those applications.

On the other hand, the top layer of services consists in a set of higher-level services which are obtained by composition of the low-level ones. Composition means that these high-level services rely on low-level services in order to provide operations with a higher level of abstraction. For example, if a low-level service manages product information (e.g., by providing access to the product database) and another service manages customer information (e.g., by providing access to a CRM system), then a third, higher-level service might need to use both of those services in order to place an order for a given customer.

This means that while low-level services are very much connected to the underlying application infrastructure, high-level services built through composition can achieve a level of abstraction that is closer to the actual business tasks that must be performed in an organization. Figure 7.2 shows just two layers of services, but more services could be built on top of these in order to support business tasks of increasing complexity. In terms of integration, what is especially challenging is to build the first layer of services that expose the functionality of the underlying applications. From that point onward, it is a matter of developing as many layers of services as necessary in order to address the business requirements.

This is not to say that the integration problems cease to exist above the first layer of services; rather, there will always be integration problems to solve across the whole infrastructure, with services included. What happens above the first layer of services is that the integration problems can be addressed in a systematic way through the use of service technology. There is no longer the need to create application adapters or having to deal with native APIs. Once all of the required functionality from the underlying applications has been exposed as a set of services, integration solutions can be developed by composing and invoking these services using standard service mechanisms alone.

7.3   Service Orchestrations

In the previous section we have discussed the possibilities introduced by service composition without getting into the details about how such composition can actually be implemented in a service. At first sight, implementing service composition does not appear to be a big issue since it is just a matter of writing the code to invoke other services through standard mechanisms. However, if one would do so for every new service to be created, the integration logic would end up being embedded in service code, and this would significantly reduce the flexibility to reconfigure the integration solution to meet changing business requirements.

Therefore, while implementing service composition through code is certainly possible within the realm of software engineering, it is definitely not the approach that should be systematically employed to create new layers of services in an integration scenario. Sooner or later such services would suffer from some of the same problems of legacy applications, namely the fact that they would become closed and rigid, and new services would have to be developed to address new business requirements. Over time, this would contribute to a proliferation of services without an overall strategy, and it would make it very difficult to maintain and develop new solutions over that infrastructure. In the context of integration, a more systematic and flexible way of implementing service compositions is required, and that is precisely the purpose of having *service orchestrations.*

In general, a service composition involves multiple operations from other services, and these operations must be invoked according to some logic. In most cases, the composition is such that the output from one service operation is processed and forwarded as input to another service operation, so a composition involves a structured sequence of steps. It may also involve data transformation between steps, since the output data from previous operations may not be in an appropriate format to be directly forwarded as input to subsequent operations. Furthermore, invoking service operations means exchanging messages with services, so a composition can be described as a sequence of message exchanges. All of these characteristics point to the fact that a service composition can be implemented as an orchestration.

Figure 7.3 illustrates the use of service orchestrations to implement service compositions. As before, at the bottom layer there is a set of services that expose the functionality of the underlying systems and applications. On top of these, there is a new layer of services built as service compositions. Each of these compositions is implemented as a service orchestration, i.e., a sequence of steps where, in general, each step consists in the invocation of some service. The orchestrations themselves are exposed as services, and therefore they can be used in further compositions as well. This allows the development of services with an increasing level of abstraction,

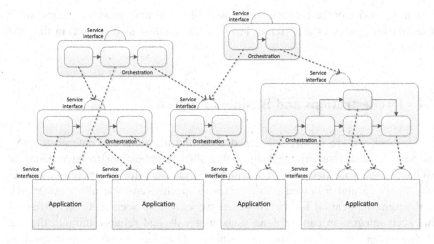

Fig. 7.3 Service composition through orchestrations

while at the same time retaining the flexibility to modify or reconfigure these services by changing the corresponding orchestrations.

Figure 7.3 highlights one of the most important concepts in service-oriented approaches, which is the mutually reciprocal and recursive relationship that exists between services and orchestrations. The relationship is *reciprocal* in the sense that a service is an orchestration and an orchestration is a service. More precisely, a service can be implemented as an orchestration, and an orchestration can be exposed as a service. This means that often one can use the terms "service" and "orchestration" interchangeably, depending on whether one is referring to the outer interface ("service") or to the inner implementation ("orchestration").

The relationship between services and orchestrations is *recursive* in the sense that a service may be implemented as an orchestration of services, which in turn may be implemented as orchestrations of yet other services, and so on, until one finally reaches the bottom layer of the underlying applications. In the limit, one could consider the theoretically interesting case of a service whose implementation is an orchestration that invokes itself. Although this may seem unrealistic, the problem that it creates may occur in practice, if there is a loop in service invocations, for example due to an orchestration that invokes a service from an upper layer, rather than from a lower layer as is usually the case.

This recursive relationship can be seen from the point of view of orchestrations as well. Each orchestration invokes services that are possibly implemented as orchestrations themselves. Therefore, a service interface provides a mechanism through which one orchestration can invoke another orchestration. If the invocation is synchronous, then the child (i.e., the invoked) orchestration will run within the life cycle of the parent (i.e., the invoking) orchestration. This makes it possible to devise integration solutions where one orchestration comprises one or more sub-orchestrations. Besides the aesthetic appeal that this concept may have when designing service orchestrations, such possibility is of much practical interest since it allows for processes at different levels of abstraction, as discussed in the next section.

7.4   Orchestrations and Business Processes

In this book we are mostly concerned about the integration of enterprise applications, and therefore any mechanism that allows applications to interoperate or exchange data with one another might be of relevance for this purpose. That is why Chaps. 5 and 6 delved into a series of mechanisms that allow integration at different application layers. However, we have also seen in Chaps. 3 and 4 that such integration can be done asynchronously and reliably through the use of messaging systems and message brokers. Therefore, rather than integrating applications directly, one can use the technologies in Chaps. 5 and 6 to build application adapters, and then use the platforms described in Chaps. 3 and 4 to implement the integration logic through message exchanges and orchestrations.

In this context, orchestrations are seen mainly as a special kind of artifact that allows implementing the integration logic in a flexible way. Instead of hardcoding and therefore hiding this logic into a program, an orchestration is an explicit description of the sequence of steps, including the message exchanges and message processing that must take place in order to glue applications together and implement a desired business process over a heterogeneous application infrastructure. Compared to a program, an orchestration can be easily modified by reconfiguring the sequence of message exchanges between applications without, in general, having to deal with application code. This is because an orchestration represents the integration logic as a process, and this brings the process to the forefront and allows it to be changed and configured according to business requirements.

In this sense an orchestration is a process, or better, an executable implementation of a process. If an orchestration is used simply as a means to integrate applications, then the process is rather low level since it is very much connected to the way in which applications are structured and to the specific application functionality that must be invoked at each step. However, in this chapter we have seen that the concept of orchestration has also its roots in the need to coordinate a sequence of service invocations, together with the possibility of creating new, higher-level services as compositions of existing ones. This means that orchestrations can be regarded as a general mechanism to automate the invocation of services, regardless of the level of abstraction of those services. If the services to be orchestrated are the service interfaces exposed by the application infrastructure at the bottom layer, then the orchestration will be at a low-level of abstraction. If, on the other hand, the services to be orchestrated are compositions on top of layers of other services, then the orchestration will be at a higher level of abstraction.

Eventually, if one is to keep developing layers of services and orchestrations with an increasing level of abstraction, as suggested in Fig. 7.3, at some point these services will be far away from the underlying application infrastructure and will be closer to the actual business tasks that are performed in an organization. It is possible to imagine, for example, that at the lowest level a service may be opening a database connection and fetching some rows from a table, while at the highest level another service is invoking that functionality to check a customer's credit status and then approve a new shipment to that customer. However, not every task can be carried out automatically by services, and this becomes one of the main differences between orchestrations and business processes.

A business process, like an orchestration, can be defined in terms of a sequence of activities, where each activity is performed by some resource. However, unlike an orchestration, where these resources are mainly services and applications, in a business process the resources may also include people, teams, organizational units, as well as different kinds of systems and machines. Regardless of the type of resource being invoked, each activity in the process can be regarded as transforming a set of inputs into a set of outputs. At any time during process execution, the outputs produced by previous activities can be provided as inputs to subsequent activities. As a whole, the process can be seen as producing some desired result, so it is usual to define a business process in terms of the goal that it achieves or in terms of the product or service that it provides to some customer, be it external (e.g., the end customer) or internal to the organization (e.g., a department).

Figure 7.4 tries to convey the multiple views that it is possible to have over a business process. At the top of the diagram, the process is represented as a single box with inputs and outputs, which is used to indicate that the main goal of the process is to perform such transformation. Below that, the process is divided into a set of stages, where each stage comprises a subset of the activities in the process, hence a stage can be also referred to as a *subprocess*. Dividing the process into stages is useful to facilitate understanding, and it is also a common practice during process design, when the actual sequence or flow of activities is not yet fully determined but there is a already notion that the process should achieve some set of intermediate results, or *milestones*. Then each stage encapsulates the process logic that is necessary to achieve a certain milestone in the process.

At the third layer from top in Fig. 7.4, one gets to the point where the process is described in terms of executable tasks or activities. In general, each of these activities is assigned to some resource or group of resources. If the activity is to be performed automatically, then it can be further refined into a sequence of steps or instructions to be executed by some kind of system. In Fig. 7.4 this is illustrated by having a sequence of steps similar to an orchestration over multiple systems. On the other hand, if the activity is to be performed manually, it is assigned to a user. The assignment can be done in one of several different ways (called assignment rules or policies), such as assigning the task to a predefined user or assigning it to a group of users, from which one of them will pick the task according to availability, expertise, or current work load, for example.

Now, the hierarchical structure of a business process that is illustrated in Fig. 7.4 bears a resemblance to the way in which orchestrations can be stacked on top of each other as suggested in Fig. 7.3. In fact, each block in Fig. 7.4—be it a step, an

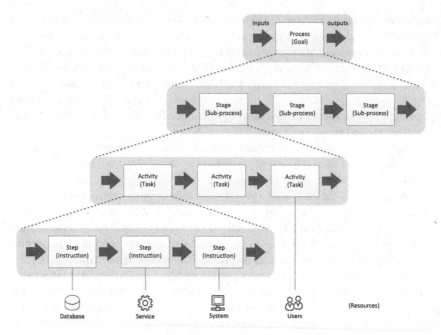

Fig. 7.4 Hierarchical structure of a business process

activity, a stage, or even the whole process—can be represented as a service that takes some input and produces some output, and the sequencing of blocks within each layer can be implemented as an orchestration.

At the bottom layer, there is an orchestration to automate a sequence of steps over an application infrastructure. This orchestration is exposed as a service and invoked in another orchestration that implements a sequence of activities, where each activity invokes a different service (for the moment we assume that the interaction with users can be managed through a service). The orchestration of activities is exposed as a service that represents a stage in the process; other stages have their own orchestrations as well. Finally, the sequence of stages can also be represented as orchestration and exposed as a service. The topmost service represents the whole process and provides an interface through which the process can be invoked.

Services and orchestrations therefore provide a general mechanism for the implementation of business processes. If the interaction with every resource can be abstracted as a service, then it is possible to use one or more layers of services and orchestrations to automate the process logic at any level of abstraction. In practice, what happens is that not every resource is captured as a service, and therefore other mechanisms are needed in order to involve those resources in the process. Also, it is often the case that a business process is not structured to the point that it can be described by orchestrations. In some scenarios, users can simply interact in any possible way to get the job done. This means that the above vision of having a fully automated business process may not apply to every business scenario, but it certainly provides a systematic way of looking at business processes.

7.5   SOA and Service Design Principles

The term Service-Oriented Architecture (SOA) is commonly used to refer to a paradigm which advocates a set of principles for service design [11]. These principles can be used both for systems development and for systems integration based on services. Although there are different views regarding what exactly these principles should comprise, the following ideas are commonly associated with SOA:

- A service is defined by a *contract* (i.e., an interface definition and possibly additional information regarding the use of the service). Knowing the service contract must be enough for a client to be able to interact with the service.
- The service is defined in a way that is independent of its implementation. The same contract can be implemented in different languages or platforms without having an effect on the interaction with clients. A client does not need to know how a service is implemented in order to be able to use it. This is referred to as the principle of *decoupling* between the service contract and implementation.
- A service is an *abstraction* of some functionality. Ideally, the service contract should be defined before the functionality is actually implemented. This principle is meant to ensure that services are designed according to a purpose and that potential dependencies from a concrete implementation are minimized.
- The principle of abstraction applies to legacy applications as well. When a legacy application is being exposed as a service (or as a set of services), the service contract should be an abstraction of the desired functionality. The contract does not have to adhere to the logic of the underlying application and may expose a different interface in order to focus on its essential purpose.
- Services should be sufficiently *generic* in order to be *reusable* in multiple scenarios. Any dependencies on time, state, context, or environment in which the service is being invoked should be avoided in order to maximize the usefulness and potential reuse of the service in different compositions, for example.
- Somewhat related to reusability is the principle that services should not maintain an inner state. This principle is known as *statelessness*. A service that maintains an inner state may have to be instantiated multiple times in order to keep a separate state for each client or even for each call. Such service would require an indefinite amount of resources for its own state management and could possibly become a performance bottleneck as well. Instead, services are intended to be as light as possible and be as ready as possible for each new invocation. For services that cannot avoid some kind of inner state, the state management can be delegated to other components, such as a database, so that the service itself remains as stateless as possible.

- Services should be *autonomous*, i.e., they should not have dependencies between each other, and they should avoid relying on shared resources to the furthest extent possible. In some cases, it may be difficult to comply with this principle. For example, several services may need to query the same database, and depending on the workload, number of connections, or transactions running on the system, some services may be prevented from doing that until other services complete their job. Such behavior is undesirable since it introduces a level of uncertainty and even a possible lack of availability or reliability.
- Services should be *composable*, i.e., it should be possible to design new services on top of existing ones, meaning that the functionality of existing services should be reused as much as possible to build more abstract or more complex services, rather than developing these new services from scratch. The design of services with a view towards composition also contributes to having a more coherent service infrastructure, and more potential to facilitate the development of new services with higher levels of abstraction. Composition can be implemented through orchestrations to automate invocation and data exchange between services.
- Services should be *discoverable* both at design-time and at run-time. At design-time, service discovery facilitates reuse, prevents duplication, and provides an overall view of the current service infrastructure. At run-time, service discovery allows for clients to find and perform dynamic invocations over existing services. Service discovery is typically supported through the use of a service registry, which can be used to store not only the service contracts but also information about the parties who provide the services (i.e., the service providers).

These and other principles are advocated in order to build a scenario similar to Fig. 7.5. In this scenario, there are business processes, services, and applications, and services play a central role in bridging the gap between the business processes coming from business requirements at the top layer, and the underlying application infrastructure at the bottom layer. At first sight, one could think that business processes could be directly connected to applications and there would be no need for the middle layer. This, in fact, has been tried over and over again for many years, even decades, with mixed results. Organizations that succeeded in doing this can be divided into two main groups:

- Organizations that are able to adapt their processes to their application infrastructure, sometimes resulting in suboptimal processes and even awkward activities that have to be done just because of the way systems are structured. In these organizations, flexibility to change the business processes is reduced due to the fact that processes are tied to the application infrastructure.
- Organizations that are able to completely revise or to devise an entirely new application infrastructure to support their business processes. This results in extraordinary large and costly IT projects. If successful, in the end the organization is left with an optimal implementation of its business processes, but only for a short period of time, until new business requirements arise. In these

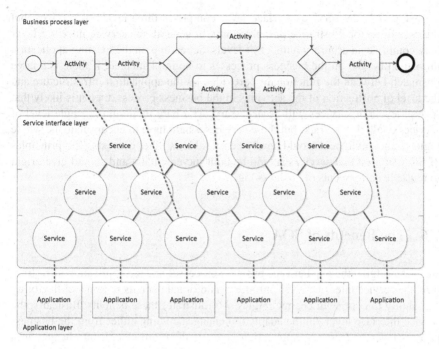

Fig. 7.5 The three main layers of SOA

organizations, flexibility to change the business processes is reduced due to the fact that it implies new changes to the application infrastructure.

Clearly, the middle layer of services in Fig. 7.5 serves to decouple the business process layer from the application layer, while at the same time providing the mechanisms to implement one on top of the other. Within the service interface layer, there may be several levels of services. As explained in the previous sections, at the lowest level there are services whose purpose is to expose the functionality of the underlying applications as a set of service interfaces. The next level of services, to be built by composition on top of the previous ones, creates abstractions to represent meaningful operations on business entities. For example, if a first-level service encapsulates access to an ERP system, then a second-level service may provide an abstraction to manage customer orders stored in that system.

The third level of services comprises further abstractions that can be directly invoked within the scope of an activity in a business process. For example, if a second-level service is able to retrieve the pending orders for a given customer, and another second-level service is able to determine the shipping costs for a given item, then a third-level service may use both of these second-level services in order to generate an invoice and send it to the customer. This step could be represented as an "invoicing" activity in an order-fulfillment process.

In Fig. 7.5, the service interface layer comprises three levels of services, but this was done for illustrative purposes only. In general, the service interface layer may comprise an arbitrary number of levels, depending on the existing application infrastructure and on the business processes to be implemented. If there is a large mismatch between the functionality provided by the application infrastructure and the level of abstraction of the activities in the business process, then it is likely that several levels of services will be necessary. At a bare minimum, a single level of services could do the trick, but these services would have to encapsulate the whole logic of an activity and would hardly be reusable in other contexts. The principles of SOA suggest that services should be built incrementally and should give origin to reusable components of business logic.

7.6 The Benefits of SOA

Besides bridging the gap between business processes and the application infrastructure, the service interface layer introduces additional benefits in terms of flexibility and ability to cope with change. Figure 7.6 illustrates these benefits. Basically, the service interface layer can be adapted to changes coming either from the business process layer or from the application layer. If there are significant changes in a business process, then rather than having to embark on a major overhaul of the application infrastructure, those changes can be absorbed by the service interface layer. In this case, the first services to be changed are the top-level ones, and if necessary the changes propagate to lower levels but with a decreasing impact at each subsequent level. Eventually, no change will be required at the lowest level of services, and definitely no change will be required to the underlying applications either. This means that services and SOA provide a means to cope with changes in business processes without affecting the underlying application infrastructure.

The converse is also true. If there are changes in one or more of the supporting applications, these do not necessarily affect the business processes. Changes in an application may affect, first of all, the service interfaces through which the application exposes its functionality. In turn, changes in these low-level services may propagate to higher levels but, again, with a decreasing impact at each subsequent level. Eventually, no change will be required at the highest level of services, and no change will be required at the business process layer.

At this stage, we already know that higher-level services are compositions of lower-level ones, and that compositions are implemented through orchestrations, as illustrated in Fig. 7.3. If a business process can be described as a series of service invocations, as in Fig. 7.5, then it too can be implemented through an orchestration. This means that there is not a clear-cut separation between the service interface layer and the business process layer, as suggested in Figs. 7.5 and 7.6. Rather, the service interface layer and the business process layer are a continuum of services and orchestrations built on top of each other. While going across this hierarchy of services and orchestrations, the point at which one starts regarding these

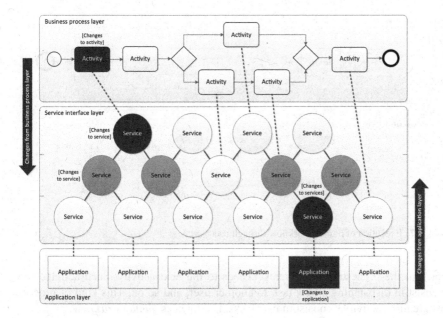

Fig. 7.6 The effect of changes on the service infrastructure

orchestrations as business processes becomes a matter of subjectivity. Also, since every process that is implemented as an orchestration can be exposed as a service, the top-most business process can be exposed as *business service* both within the organization and to external customers or business partners.

7.7 Support for Human Workflows

As discussed in Sect. 7.4, in practice not every resource can be represented as a service and therefore not every business process can be implemented as a service orchestration. However, in the context of integration it may be the case that some system is not exposed as a service, and yet it is possible to develop an orchestration to coordinate the exchange of messages through the use of adapters. This means that orchestrations can be used not only to compose services, but also to implement an integration logic that spans across different kinds of systems. Whether these systems include the required functionality to support human participation in the process, it depends on the particular scenario at hand.

In scenarios that involve human participation, typically one of the available systems is a user portal through which users can retrieve tasks assigned to them, through a mechanism that is similar to a mailbox. An orchestration can communicate with such system through an adapter in order to deliver a task to a certain user. Then, as soon as the user completes the task, the portal sends a message

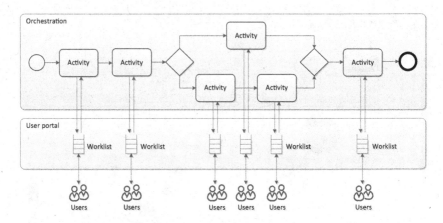

Fig. 7.7 Execution of human workflow through user portal

back to the orchestration, which proceeds to the next activity. Such activity may consist in dispatching a new task to another user, and so on. This kind of process, where most activities consist in user tasks, is known as *human workflow*.

Figure 7.7 illustrates the execution of a human workflow through a user portal. Here, every activity has been depicted as requiring user participation, but some of these activities may consist in invoking services, applications, or other kinds of systems, and the process can still be referred to as a *workflow*. By definition, a workflow is "the automation of a business process, in whole or in part, during which documents, information or tasks are passed from one participant to another" [16]. According to the workflow terminology, the list of tasks that are currently assigned to a user (or group of users) is referred to as the *worklist* or *to-do list*. The worklist is managed by a special-purpose *workflow client application* which receives tasks (also referred to as *work items*) from the *workflow engine*. In Fig. 7.7, the workflow engine is the integration platform where the orchestration is running, and the user portal is playing the role of workflow client application.

One aspect that should not go unmentioned is that even though each activity in Fig. 7.7 is assigned to a different worklist, each worklist may end up having multiple tasks, since the orchestration itself can be instantiated multiple times. For each new instance of the orchestration, a new instance of the each task will be dispatched to the corresponding worklist. In the meantime, the user (or group of users) may not have had enough time to complete the previous task instances, so tasks can stack up in a worklist to the point that the user becomes overloaded with work items. To deal with this problem, some systems that are purposely built for human workflows have dynamic assignment rules, such as dispatching tasks according to workload.

Another important aspect is that when a user completes a task and the portal returns the result to the orchestration, it must be possible to route this result to the correct orchestration instance. This can be done through the use of correlations, as explained in Sect. 4.6 (see in particular Fig. 4.5 on page 86). In any case, the mechanisms that are employed to interact with services and applications from within orchestrations can also be employed to interact with workflow clients that manage the worklists of users. Therefore, in this book we will keep focusing on the integration of services and applications, knowing that user participation in a process can be supported as an extension of the same mechanisms.

To provide an idea of how the mechanisms described in previous chapters can be extended to support human participation, the portal and worklists in Fig. 7.7 could be replaced by a set of message queues (as in Fig. 3.5 on page 41), where each worklist would be stored in a queue, and users (or their workflow clients) would fetch tasks from their respective queues. The use of asynchronous messaging is an especially interesting solution to support human participation, and it would also provide the possibility of setting message priorities in order to prioritize tasks.

Alternatively, the portal could be implemented as a publish–subscribe system (as in Fig. 4.2 on page 78) where the target applications would be workflow clients that manage the worklist for each user. In the orchestration, one could also use ports with e-mail adapters in order to interact with users directly, and in this case the worklists would be stored in their mailboxes. Still, the most common solution is to have a user portal, possibly with service interfaces so that it can be easily invoked from an orchestration, while at the same time providing sophisticated capabilities to manage worklists and support users in performing their tasks.

7.8 Conclusion

The concept of service, rather than the technology itself, has the potential to change the way enterprise systems are developed and integrated. While previous technologies focused mainly on how distributed objects can interoperate with each other, services introduced the idea and possibility of using composition to create new services out of existing ones. This means that, through composition, it is possible to create services with an increasing level of abstraction, to the point that some of these services can implement the logic of business tasks to be invoked within the scope of a business process. While previous generations of technologies addressed "horizontal" concerns, i.e., interoperability at the application layer, services and SOA address "vertical" concerns by providing a methodical approach to bridge the gap between the application layer and the business process layer.

A key enabling concept for service compositions is that of service orchestrations. A composition may involve several services, and orchestrations provide the means to coordinate the exchanges with those services. In fact, an orchestration allows automating a series of service invocations as a sequence of steps, much in the same way that a workflow automates a sequence of tasks. And like workflows, orchestrations can implement sophisticated behavior such as branching, parallelism, and loops, as we will see in the next chapter.

Orchestrations can also invoke systems and applications other than services, as we have seen in previous chapters. For example, in Sect. 4.7 we have discussed how an orchestration can interact with a messaging system; in Sect. 5.6 we have seen how an orchestration can interact with a database system; and in Sect. 6.5 we have seen how an orchestration can invoke a Web service.

The orchestration itself can be exposed as a service, which in turn can be invoked from higher-level orchestrations. This allows an orchestration to be used as a subprocess in another orchestration. Eventually, as it happens with services too, orchestrations can reach a level of abstraction where they can be regarded as direct implementations of business processes. This means that orchestrations are a pervasive concept that finds application across all layers of SOA, from the application layer where they can be used to integrate application functionality, to the business process layer where they can be used to automate business processes.

In the following chapters, we will go through the main constructs that can be used to build orchestrations in different integration platforms.

Chapter 8
Orchestration Flow

An orchestration is both an abstraction and an executable implementation of a certain process logic. It is an abstraction because it captures the essential behavior of a process as a sequence of steps. It is also executable because it includes the mechanisms to invoke the required run-time components at each step in the process. In the context of integration, the process logic can be something as low-level as a series of method calls over the application infrastructure, or something as high-level as a series of business tasks, where each task is handed over to some resource for remote execution. The advantage of approaching integration with a service-oriented paradigm is that everything—be it a low-level application, a high-level resource, or even the orchestration itself—can be regarded as a service. For this reason, orchestrations are often referred to as *service orchestrations*, although in practice they can interact with different kinds of systems.

In general, the interaction between an orchestration and an external system is achieved through message exchanges. The most typical scenario is to have an orchestration sending a request to an external system and then waiting for the response. Usually, both the request and the response take the form of XML messages, since the use of XML facilitates the definition of different message schemas according to the particular requirements of each system to be invoked. The request–response interaction is the most typical, but in general any sequence of message exchanges may take place between the orchestration and an external system. For example, the orchestration may send out one request and receive two responses, or it may send out three requests and only wait for a single response. Any combination of outgoing and incoming messages is possible, in any order. In particular, an orchestration may itself be the recipient of an incoming request and produce an outgoing response; this pattern is referred to as solicit–response [30].

Sending and receiving messages from within an orchestration is achieved through the use of special constructs. In fact, every step within an orchestration is achieved by means of some special-purpose construct. There are constructs to create messages and to transform them, and there are also constructs to control the sequence of steps in the orchestration, such as decisions between alternative paths, parallel branches, loops, and even the possibility of invoking other orchestrations

D.R. Ferreira, *Enterprise Systems Integration*, DOI 10.1007/978-3-642-40796-3_8,
© Springer-Verlag Berlin Heidelberg 2013

as subprocesses. These constructs enable the development of orchestrations which can implement virtually any process logic that one may find in practice. There are also advanced constructs to support exception handling and transactions, but these will be discussed in the next chapter. For the moment, we will focus on the basic elements to define the control flow. However, before we begin it is useful to introduce some general remarks about the structure of orchestrations.

8.1   Block Structure

Every orchestration is built as a sequence of blocks. In its simplest form, a block may stand for a specific activity, such as sending or receiving a message. A block may also represent a more elaborate construct, such as a set of alternative or parallel branches. In any case, each branch is in itself a sequence of blocks where, again, each block may be either a simple activity or a more elaborate construct comprising other blocks. Blocks can therefore be nested into other blocks, and orchestrations are said to follow a *nested block structure*. Figure 8.1 illustrates such block structure.

In Fig. 8.1 the orchestration is defined as a sequence of two blocks between the leftmost Begin element and the rightmost End element. The first block in the sequence is an activity (Activity 1) and the second block is an elaborate construct (Decide 1) that is used here to specify that there are two alternative branches. Either the top branch or the bottom branch will be executed depending on some condition (the condition is not shown in Fig. 8.1). Both branches contain a sequence: the top branch is a sequence of an activity (Activity 2), a decision construct (Decide 2), and another activity (Activity 4), while the bottom branch is a sequence comprising a single block (Parallel) which introduces two parallel branches. Again, each of these parallel branches is a sequence by itself. The upper branch is a sequence of an activity (Activity 5) and a loop construct, where the loop executes a sequence of two activities (Activity 6 and Activity 7). The loop block is nested into the parallel block, which in turn is nested into a decision block (Decide 1).

The second decision block in Fig. 8.1 (Decide 2) deserves a further explanation. This is a decision between two alternative branches where the upper branch in particular will result in the orchestration terminating at that point (after Activity 3). If not, then the orchestration will proceed to Activity 4. Apparently, the decision block Decide 2 does not seem to fit perfectly in the philosophy of nested block structure, since the orchestration flow may never come out of that block (if terminates inside the block). However, it is worth noting that whatever happens inside the Decide 2 block, there is only one way in and one way out, and therefore this block can certainly be used in combination (i.e., sequence) with other blocks.

The Decide 2 block can also be redesign to avoid the use of the End element inside it. Since another End element follows Activity 4, it is possible to bring Activity 4 into the decision block and have the two branches come out as a single connection to the final End element, as illustrated in Fig. 8.2.

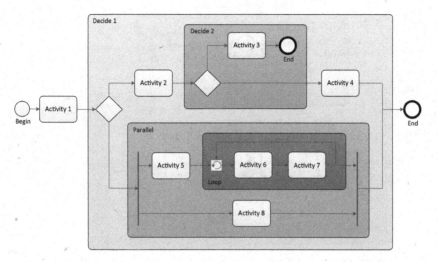

Fig. 8.1 The nested block structure of an orchestration

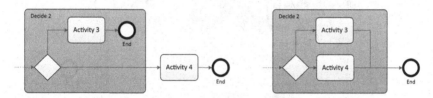

Fig. 8.2 Two alternative designs for the Decide 2 block in Fig. 8.1

Note, however, that this strategy would be more complicated to employ if there would be an additional activity, say Activity 9, between the Decide 1 block and the rightmost End element in Fig. 8.1. As shown in Fig. 8.3, it would still be possible to avoid the use of an End element in Decide 2, but only at the expense of duplicating Activity 9 in each branch of Decide 1. (This duplication must be done in order to ensure that Activity 9 is executed also in case the orchestration follows the lower branch in Decide 1.) In general, given the possibility of using such tricks, one can always redesign an orchestration in order to check that the desired behavior actually fits into a nested block structure.

The original Decide 2 block in Fig. 8.1 also illustrates the fact that it is possible to have a branch with no activities at all (Activity 4 appears later on that branch, but is already outside the block). Besides duplicating activities, having empty branches is another trick that can be used to fit behavior into a nested block structure. It is often used when there is a path in the flow that can be skipped in certain conditions.

Another common behavior that often appears in practice is the need to "jump back" to a previous step in the orchestration. Although the first idea that comes to mind is the use of a decision with a branch that goes back to some earlier step the sequence, this solution does not fit into a nested block structure, since the branch

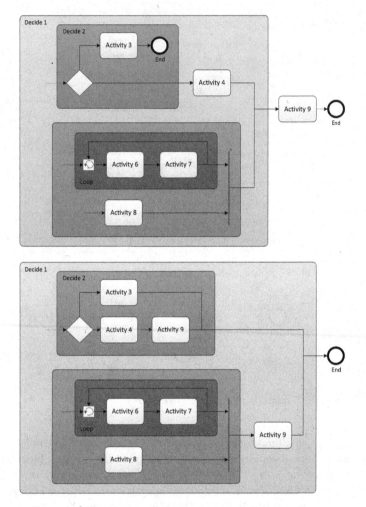

Fig. 8.3 Duplication of Activity 9 in order to avoid End element in Decide 2

going backwards would have to come out of the block that has just been initiated by the decision. Figure 8.4 illustrates the problem, along with a possible solution. The solution is to use a loop construct and to insert, in that loop, all the activities which may have to be repeated during execution. The loop has a condition (not shown in the Fig. 8.4) that is to be evaluated at each new iteration. The loop executes for as long as the condition remains true; as soon as the condition evaluates to false, the loop block is exited and execution proceeds to Activity 4.

In some scenarios, such as when the execution flow may have to jump back but this is allowed to occur only once, it may be simpler to actually duplicate the required activities in a decision block, rather than using a loop block. The decision block will have one branch with the duplicated sequence (in this case, Activity 2

Fig. 8.4 Jumping back
implemented using a loop

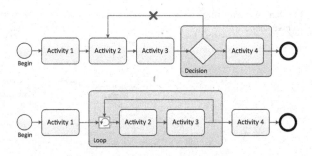

followed by Activity 3), and another branch which is completely empty. This way it
is possible either to run those activities once more or to skip them entirely. Then
Activity 4 may follow the decision block (but already outside the block).

The problem of duplicating elements in an orchestration is that, up to this point,
we have been assuming that they are simple activities. However, if the blocks
to be duplicated contain an intricate logic with other nested blocks, then all of
this logic will have to be duplicated in the orchestration. This is not much of a
problem to do (most likely it can be done with some copying and pasting) but it
can become a troublesome solution to maintain, because a change in one block may
have to be replicated in all duplicates of that block. This is prone to error, either
by forgetting to do the change in all duplicates or by introducing mistakes when
doing the same change in multiple blocks. This can be recognized as the general
problem of introducing redundancy, which can lead to inconsistencies. As a general
principle, redundancy should be avoided in orchestrations, unless there is no other
way to fit the desired behavior into a nested block structure.

8.2 Beginning the Flow

In the previous section we have seen that an orchestration is made up of building
blocks, where each building block may be a specific activity or a more elaborate
construct that contains other blocks within. For the moment we will focus on
blocks that represent simple activities such as sending or receiving a message. To
distinguish between different types of activities, it is common to refer to blocks
as of *shapes*, so there is a *send shape*, a *receive shape*, and so on. In general, every
orchestration begins with a receive shape, and it should not be difficult to understand
why: an orchestration must be triggered somehow, and since most of what it does
is to send and receive messages from applications, the easiest way is to have the
orchestration waiting to receive a message before it starts.

What is missing in this equation is that orchestrations send and receive messages
through ports, so in order to receive a message there must be a *receive port*. We
therefore need a receive shape and a receive port in order to deliver a message to
an orchestration. Figure 8.5 illustrates these constructs. There is an orchestration

Fig. 8.5 An activating
receive shape

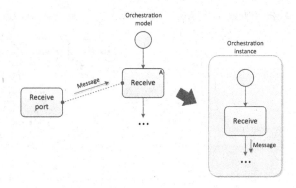

model where the first activity takes the form of a receive shape; this receive shape is connected to a receive port, so that once a new message arrives to that port, the message is handed over to the receive shape, where it enters the flow.

Up to this point, we have described the standard behavior of a receive shape, and this could be any receive shape in the orchestration (an orchestration may have multiple receive shapes along the flow). However, the receive shape that is represented in Fig. 8.5 must be of a special kind, which is different from any other receive shape possibly contained in the same orchestration. The first receive shape in an orchestration must be an *activating receive*, i.e., it is a receive shape that creates a new *instance* of the orchestration every time a new message arrives on its port. Each new orchestration instance will have a separate life and will be executed independently from every other orchestration instance.

To understand why there must be separate orchestration instances, we draw an analogy with an online bookstore. Every time a customer places an order for some books, a new instance of an order handling process is triggered. The process is the same for every customer and for every order, but each order corresponds to a different instance of the order handling process. In fact, each order is usually given a unique number, which allows the store to identify the corresponding process instance. For inquiries about the status of an order, the customer must provide the order number; the bookstore then retrieves the process instance and checks its current status. Each order is processed independently, and therefore there must be separate process instances to keep track of the status of each order.

This is precisely what the initial receive shape in an orchestration must do: it must create a separate instance of the orchestration, to be run and managed independently from other instances. In Fig. 8.5, this is illustrated by having an *orchestration model* from which several *orchestration instances* can be created. The model begins with an activating receive, meaning that whenever a new message is received at that point in the orchestration, a new instance is created. Naturally, this can apply only to the first receive shape in an orchestration; any subsequent receive shapes are assumed to be running within a previously created instance.

In other words, in an orchestration there must be at most one activating receive, and this must be the first shape in the orchestration, before anything else happens.

On the other hand, everything that happens after the activating receive is already taking place within the scope of a separate orchestration instance. We say that an orchestration has *at most* one activating receive because in some rare cases it may have none. For example, an orchestration could begin immediately by constructing a message and sending it to an external application through a send shape. However, such orchestration cannot be triggered by a message; instead, it can only be invoked from within another orchestration. Invoking a *child* orchestration from a *parent* orchestration results in the creation of a new instance of the child orchestration. This instance will run within the scope of the parent orchestration.

Every orchestration instance is an identical copy of its original model. However, instances are executed separately and their behavior may be different depending on particular conditions that are found at run-time, or depending on the input data (i.e., the message) that was used to trigger the orchestration. In any case, the set of allowed behaviors must have been fully specified in the original model. For example, using a decision shape it is possible to specify alternative branches depending on conditions to be evaluated at run-time (as in Fig. 2.5 on page 23). A given instance may follow one path, while another instance may follow another path; the orchestration model specifies what happens in every possible path.

8.3 Message Construction

In Fig. 8.5 the orchestration is instantiated by the arrival of a new message to the initial receive shape. After the orchestration instance is created, it starts executing the flow from that point onward. The message that was used to trigger the orchestration now becomes part of that instance (and of that instance alone) and it is accessible to every shape in the orchestration. (In general, a message is accessible to every shape that comes *after* the point at which the message has been received or created.) However, the initial message may be only a means to bring some input data to the orchestration, while the applications that the orchestration will interact with may require the use of a different format and content as well.

Now, in some integration platforms, notably BizTalk, messages are treated as immutable objects, i.e., once they are created or received they cannot be changed anymore throughout the orchestration. They can certainly be used as input to external applications, but they cannot be changed in any way, so messages will always keep their original form. This means that if a message with a different format or content is required to communicate with a certain application, that message will have to be created from scratch as a brand new message. Fortunately, there are ways to reuse data from existing messages in order to create new message, but this can be done only at the point where the new message is being created and not afterwards, since after that the message becomes an immutable object.

As a result of this behavior, as an orchestration is being executed more and more messages are available to the next shapes. These are the messages that the orchestration either received or created along the flow up to the present point. Every one of these messages is available for reuse in forthcoming shapes, but none of them can be changed. The minimum change requires the creation of a new message, and this message will be available to any subsequent step.

At first sight one could think that this behavior could lead to a lot of messages being created for a single use at some point in time, and that the orchestration would be increasingly populated with extraneous messages along the way. However, in practice this is not the case, as the number of messages is, typically, significantly less than the number of shapes in the orchestration. Having a large number of messages would mean that the orchestration itself would be very large and/or complex, and then the real problem would be the size of the orchestration and not the number of messages that are created along the way.

On the other hand, having immutable messages is actually an advantage when developing orchestrations, since it is always possible to access the data that has been previously used at some point during the flow. For example, at the end of the orchestration it is still possible to reuse data from any previous message, up to the initial message that triggered the orchestration. That is precisely what happens in the orchestration shown in Fig. 6.9 on page 179, where the second message assignment picks the temperature value in °F from the initial message and the temperature value in °C form the Web service response, and brings them together to create a final message to be sent out as the output from the orchestration.

The immutable nature of messages also plays an important role in avoiding errors and unexpected bugs during execution. If messages could be changed freely, then this could lead to their content being overwritten in unpredictable ways, depending on the flow of the orchestration. At the point where the message is being needed, it could be the case that it no longer contains the data that it was expected to contain, and this might lead to run-time errors and malfunctions of the entire orchestration. These arguments in favor of immutable messages also seem to agree with the common perception that functional programming (where variables cannot be changed) tends to be less error-prone than imperative programming (where variables can be changed at will, if they have not been declared as constants).

8.3.1 Constructing Messages Through Transformation

Messages can be created through the use a special shape called *construct message*. This shape can be placed at any point within the flow of an orchestration. As with other shapes, the construct message shape has access to all messages that have been previously received or created during the flow. For messages that have been previously received, these must have been received through the use of a receive shape; similarly, for messages that have been previously created, these must have been created through the use of a construct message shape.

The construct shape allows the creation of a single message; for multiple messages, multiple construct shapes must be used. However, if several construct shapes are used in alternative or parallel branches, they will not be aware of the messages that are being created by each other. In general, a construct shape (like any

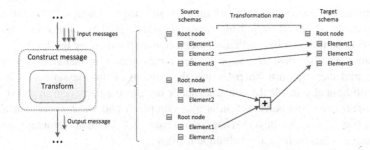

Fig. 8.6 The transform shape as a placeholder for a transformation map

other shape) has access to the messages that have been created along the execution path that precedes it. Other messages are simply not available as input.

On its own, the construct shape does little more than specifying the type of message being created (here, the message type corresponds to a certain schema). However, the construct shape is a placeholder for other shapes, and it is these other shapes that fill in the content for the output message. In other words, the construct shape just *instantiates* the message (from a given schema), and then relies on other shapes to write the actual content. Typically, the content for a new message is a combination of data from previous messages. Such combination can be obtained, for example, through the use of transformation maps.

Figure 8.6 illustrates the use of a transform shape within a construct shape. The purpose of this transform shape is to perform a transformation based on a map depicted at the right-hand side of the figure. Since there are multiple input messages available, the transformation can make use of some or all of these messages in order to retrieve the data to be written to the output message. This example shows the transformation map using all three input messages, but it is not uncommon to have a transformation map that uses a single input message, if the purpose is simply to convert one message from one schema to another.

As explained in Sect. 2.2, the transformation map is defined based on an XSLT transformation between XML schemas. The schema or schemas on the left are called the *source schemas* and they represent the schema of each input message, respectively. On the other hand, the schema on the right is called the *target schema* and it represents the schema of the output message. The transformation map is defined in terms of schemas rather than messages, because it can be defined in a way that is independent of the actual message content. In simple terms, the transformation map specifies that the content of a certain element in a source schema is to be copied to another element in target schema, so this operation can be performed on any pair of messages that adhere to those schemas.

In addition to simply copying values from a source schema to a target schema, a transformation map may contain special mechanisms (called functoids) to perform more sophisticated operations, such as combining multiple source elements in order to derive a result to be written to some target element. Figure 8.6 illustrates the use of a sum functoid to add the values of two elements from the source schemas and transfer the result to a third element in the target schema. Other functoids for mathematical operations, string manipulation, logical functions, etc. may be available, depending on the particular integration platform being used.

In summary, the construct shape creates a message as an instance of a certain schema, and the transform shape writes the content of the message. In Fig. 8.6, there is nothing else inside the construct shape besides the transform shape, so after the transformation the construction is also complete, and we can say that a new message (i.e., the output message) has been *constructed*. From that moment onward, the message is available to any subsequent shape.

In Fig. 8.6 the content of the output message is written in one step, i.e., through one transformation, but it could be constructed in several steps, such as having several transform shapes with different transformation maps, where each map would fill in a different part of the message. These transform shapes would be executed as a sequence inside the construct shape. As long as the flow is inside the construct shape, the output message is still being constructed and therefore can be changed as many times as necessary. However, once the construct shape completes, the message is considered to be in its final state and cannot be changed anymore.

8.3.2 Constructing Through Message Assignment

In Sect. 5.6 we developed an orchestration to invoke the SQL adapter, and this orchestration used transform shapes to construct messages (see Fig. 5.15 on page 136). However, in Sect. 6.5 we built another orchestration to invoke a Web service, and this orchestration used message assignment shapes instead (see Fig. 6.9 on page 179). These are, in fact, the two options available for constructing messages: either through the use of transformation maps, as described in the previous section, or through the use of message assignments.

Both options can be used interchangeably, but it may be easier to use one instead of the other, depending on the particular message being constructed. Typically, transformation maps are used when the output message has a schema that is either relatively large or significantly different from those of the input messages. In this case, each element in the output message has to be filled in by applying a specific operation over a set of input elements. The transformation map then becomes a convenient tool to visualize and configure all the operations that are required to fill in the different elements in the output message.

On the other hand, when the output message has only a few elements or when it is to a large extent similar to an existing message, it may be easier to use a message assignment shape instead. Basically, a message assignment is a placeholder for expressions written in some programming language (C# in the case of BizTalk). These expressions specify how the content of the output message is to be filled in. In other words, the message assignment allows the output message to be constructed through actual code, rather than through the use of a transformation map. Figure 8.7 shows an example, based on the same logic of Fig. 8.6.

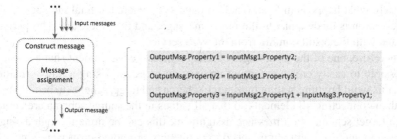

Fig. 8.7 The message assignment shape as a placeholder for expressions

Here, the output message has three elements which have been defined as distinguished properties (the concept of distinguished property has been introduced in Sect. 4.5). The elements from input messages that are required for the purpose of constructing the output message have also been defined as distinguished properties. Hence, the expressions in Fig. 8.7 refer to properties, rather than elements as in Fig. 8.6. The purpose of defining a certain element of a schema as distinguished property is precisely to be able to access it (i.e., both read and write it) in expressions throughout the orchestration. Such expressions appear in message assignment shapes and may appear in a few other kinds of shape as well.

The first expression in Fig. 8.7 specifies that Property1 in the output message is to be filled in with the value of Property2 from InputMsg1. A similar assignment in the second expression involves OutputMsg.Property2 and InputMsg.Property3. In the third expression, Property1 in InputMsg2 and Property1 in InputMsg3 may refer to similar elements (if InputMsg2 and InputMsg3 are instances of the same schema) or they may refer to different elements (if InputMsg2 and InputMsg3 have different schemas). This illustrates the fact that the name of a distinguished property is valid only within the scope of a given schema. Back to the third expression, the value of both properties is being added and given to Property3 in the output message.

Overall, the three expressions in Fig. 8.7 implement a similar logic to the transformation map in Fig. 8.6. This has been done deliberately, in order to illustrate that the same logic can be implemented either through a transformation map (possibly with functoids) or through a message assignment shape. In general, since virtually any code can be included in a message assignment, it is possible to implement operations as sophisticated as certain advanced functoids, and even more. However, in practice this is not usually done, since the logic will be embedded in code, defeating the whole purpose of having an orchestration in the first place.

For this reason, the message assignment shape is used only when it leads to an implementation that is simpler than what would be obtained through the use of a transformation map. In particular, if the output message has only a few elements (or properties) to be set, then it is possible to do this easily through a couple of expressions. An especially important use for the message assignment shape is when the output message has the same schema as one of the input messages and can therefore be created (or at least initialized) as a copy of an input message. This is precisely what happens in Sect. 6.5.3 on page 178, where the final message of the orchestration is made equal to the initial message, and then the Celsius property is updated with the result coming from the Web service.

Therefore, one of the advantages of using a message assignment shape is that it is possible to easily create a copy of an existing message. Using a transformation map, this would require setting the source schema and target schema to be the same, and then connecting all elements so that all values in the source schema are copied to the target schema. In a message assignment, this can be done through a single expression and even without the need to define any promoted properties, since the message content will be copied as is, and all at once. In general, however, the input and output schemas will be different, and the transform shape provides a more explicit way to specify the mapping between the input and output messages.

8.4   Controlling the Flow

The concept of having an orchestration driving the message exchange between applications is especially interesting due to the fact that orchestrations can support different kinds of behavior through special constructs. Among these constructs, one can find the possibility to decide between alternative branches, to run parallel branches, and even to execute loops. These behavioral patterns are intimately associated with the nature of process logic, and they often appear in depictions of business processes such as flowcharts, UML activity diagrams [7], and process models created with modeling languages such as BPMN [34].

An orchestration is in itself an implementation of some process logic. At higher levels of abstraction, an orchestration can even be regarded as an implementation of some business process. Therefore, it makes sense to have the behavioral patterns that are used during process modeling also available for the development of orchestrations. In the literature, the common behavioral patterns that can be found in process models are known as *workflow patterns* [2]. The ability to decide between alternative branches, run parallel branches, and execute loops are among some of the most well-known and recurrent patterns in practice.

As explained in Sect. 8.1, orchestrations are built according to a nested block structure. Basically, this means that any given construct must be used in a sequence with other constructs or inside other constructs. For example, it is possible to nest parallel paths into a decision (as in the lower branch of Decide 1 in Fig. 8.1), it is possible to nest a decision inside another decision (as in the upper branch of Decide 1 in Fig. 8.1), it is possible to nest a loop in a parallel path (as in the upper path of the Parallel shape in Fig. 8.1), etc. In general, any combination is possible, and this is what provides the flexibility to implement any desired process behavior in an orchestration. What is not allowed is to create paths in the flow that go across the boundaries of any given block, as illustrated in Fig. 8.4.

In the following presentation and discussion of decisions, parallel paths, and loops, one should bear in mind these principles:

- Any of those flow constructs can appear anywhere in an orchestration, either in the main (i.e., top-level) flow of the orchestration, or as a nested block somewhere inside other constructs in the orchestration.
- All of those flow constructs involve one or more possible paths, where each path contains a sequence of activities (such sequence may contain zero, one, or more activities). Each activity in a path may be a simple activity (such as sending or receiving a message), but it may also represent a placeholder for nesting other blocks at that point in the orchestration.

So even though we will discuss each construct based on examples with simple activities, the reader should be aware that these constructs can be nested into each other to build much more complex structures.

8.4.1 The Decide Shape

The decide shape is what allows the orchestration to have multiple possible paths built in, and to be able to select one of those paths based on conditions that are to be evaluated at run-time. In terms of workflow patterns, it corresponds to a combination of an OR-split (at the point where the decision of which path to take is made) and an OR-join (at the point where the alternative paths merge back to the main flow in the orchestration). Figure 8.8 illustrates the use of a decide shape. Here, some message (called MsgOrder) is received and then follows a decision.

The left branch has a condition specifying that, if the order quantity is above 500, then this path should be taken. This condition is being evaluated as a code expression, much like in the way the expressions in a message assignment shape are evaluated (see Fig. 8.7). The difference is that while the expressions in Fig. 8.7 represent assignments between message properties, in Fig. 8.8 the expression takes the form of a boolean condition yielding a value of either True or False. If the condition is true, then the orchestration flow proceeds along this branch, and other branches are simply ignored as if they would not be there. On the other hand, if the condition is false, then this branch will be disregarded, and the engine executing the orchestration will look for another branch whose condition will yield True.

In the condition associated with the left branch in Fig. 8.8, the expression refers to Quantity, which must be a distinguished property in the message schema. The value of this property is being compared to a constant, in order to determine whether the condition is True or False. In contrast, the condition in the branch on the right-hand side of Fig. 8.8 has no expression at all. It simply says "Else," which means that this branch will be executed if no other branch has a condition which yields True. In this example, the "Else" branch will be executed if the promoted property Quantity has a value of 500 or lower.

From this example, it should be clear that there is some order for evaluating the conditions associated with branches in a decision shape. Naturally, it would not make sense to consider executing the "Else" branch before the conditions for

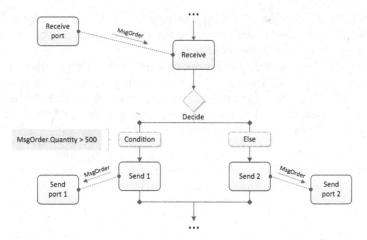

Fig. 8.8 The decide shape

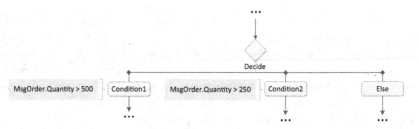

Fig. 8.9 Multiple conditions in a decide shape

all other branches have been evaluated. Therefore, in Fig. 8.8 the condition in left branch must be evaluated before the condition in the right branch.

In general, in a decide shape the conditions of the several possible branches are evaluated in a left-to-right fashion and, as a consequence, the "Else" must be the rightmost branch. At first sight, such convention might seem strange, since it imposes a left-to-right priority between branches. However, this structure corresponds to the programming construct if ... else if ... else ... available in most programming languages, and such prioritization actually helps avoiding conflicts when the conditions of different branches are not mutually exclusive.

Figure 8.9 illustrates the logic of a decide shape with non-exclusive conditions. In this case, the Quantity property is being used in two conditions associated with different branches. According to the left-to-right evaluation rule, the first condition to be evaluated is Condition1, then Condition2 if Condition1 does not hold, and finally the "Else" branch will be considered if none of the previous conditions holds true.

Now, any Quantity value that obeys Condition1 will also obey Condition2. Therefore, both conditions will be true for any Quantity value above 500. The fact that conditions are evaluated in a left-to-right fashion serves to disambiguate the problem of which branch should be followed: the branch to be followed is the leftmost branch with a condition yielding True, so the orchestration will follow at most one branch. For quantity values above 250 but not above 500, the second branch will be followed. For quantity values up to 250, the "Else" branch will be followed. An important fact about the "Else" branch is that it guarantees that execution will proceed in any case (i.e., even if no other condition is true) so the orchestration will never be stuck, even if the conditions for branches have been badly designed.

8.4.2 The Parallel Shape

The parallel shape is a construct that allows multiple branches to run in parallel. This is the logic counterpart of the decide shape: if the decide shape corresponds to an OR-split, then the parallel shape corresponds to an AND-split. In addition, while the branches in a decide shape come together in the form of an OR-join, the branches in parallel shape come together as an AND-join, which becomes a synchronizing merge. This means that all branches in a parallel shape must complete their execution before the orchestration can move on to the next shape in the flow. Even if some branches run much faster than others (because they have fewer activities), the orchestration still has to wait for all branches to complete.

Figure 8.10 illustrates the use of a parallel shape by means of an example. After receiving a customer order (MsgOrder), the orchestration starts two branches in parallel. The left branch sends the order (as is) to the sales department, while the right branch transforms the order into a new message to be sent to the shipping department. The transformation is needed because the shipping department has its own system that requires shipping orders to arrive in a certain format. The two branches run in parallel and each message is sent to the corresponding department, independently of what is happening in the other branch. The left branch will probably complete first, since it has less to do. However, the orchestration will not proceed beyond the parallel shape until both branches complete.

Although there are only two branches in the example of Fig. 8.10, in general a parallel shape can have any number of branches, all of which will be executed in parallel and synchronized at the end. One could imagine that each branch corresponds to a separate thread, and that a multi-threaded orchestration engine would manage the execution of these threads concurrently. However, in practice the execution engine is usually single-threaded and it only appears to be running things in parallel, when in reality it is not executing more than one step at a time.

What happens is that the execution engine picks one branch at a time and checks whether it can execute anything in that branch. If the branch has actions that can be immediately executed (such as send shapes, construct shapes, and other shapes that do not require any waiting time), then they are executed immediately. But as soon as the branch reaches a point where it has to wait for something to happen (typically, receiving a message through a receive shape), then execution moves to another branch, where it follows the same behavior. So, in essence, the execution

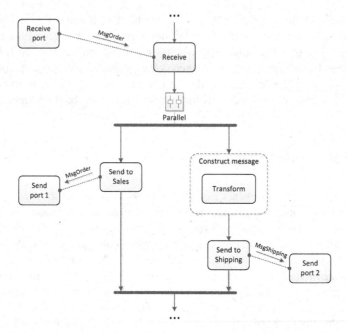

Fig. 8.10 The parallel shape

engine proceeds in a round-robin fashion over all branches (e.g., left-to-right and then back to the beginning) until every action in every branch is completed.

Therefore, the parallel shape, rather than specifying true parallelism, specifies that a set of tasks can be executed in any order, but subject to the ordering constraints established in each branch. Going back to the example of Fig. 8.10, the parallel shape specifies that the three shapes "Send to Sales," "Construct message," and "Send to Shipping" can be executed in any order, as long as "Send to Shipping" takes place after "Construct message." This means that "Send to Sales" can take place either before, after, or in between "Construct message" and "Send to Shipping," and no other ordering is allowed. As the number of branches or the number of shapes in each branch increases, there will be an increasing number of possible orderings; these represent the different ways in which a single-threaded execution engine can emulate the behavior of a parallel shape.

8.5 Using the Loop Shape

Conceptually, the behavior of the decide shape and of the parallel shape are quite simple to understand and these shapes are also relatively simple to use. The parallel shape is perhaps the simplest to include in an orchestration, since it is just a matter of specifying a number of parallel branches. The decide shape is only slightly more complicated since it requires specifying the alternative branches as well as the condition associated with each branch. Typically, these conditions are specified in terms of boolean expressions involving some message elements. These elements need to be distinguished in the message schema (hence becoming distinguished properties) in order to be accessible in expressions within the orchestration.

Besides having alternative and parallel branches, there is also the possibility of running loops through the use of the loop shape. The loop shape, as a means to control the flow of an orchestration, could have been presented in Sect. 8.4 together with the decide shape and the parallel shape. However, in comparison with those shapes, the use of a loop shape can be rather complicated, because the typical scenarios where the loop shape finds application almost invariably involve iterating through message elements or assembling a new message out of several parts. As explained in Sect. 8.3, messages are immutable objects and there are special mechanisms to construct them. These mechanisms do not fit very well with the logic of the loop shape, and therefore it becomes necessary to use some tricks in order to be able to carry out some forms of message processing inside a loop.

In Sect. 6.5 we developed an orchestration to invoke a Web service that converted a temperature value in Fahrenheit to degrees Celsius. Here we will use the same Web service to build a complete example of an orchestration that uses a loop shape in order to convert several temperature values. This will allow us to illustrate not only the iteration over message elements but also the assembly of all results into a new message. Besides illustrating the typical uses of the loop shape, this example will also serve to introduce additional shapes and mechanisms that can be used in BizTalk orchestrations. Despite the present focus on BizTalk, these mechanisms find their equivalents in other integration platforms as well.

8.5.1 Overview of the Solution

The main purpose of the orchestration to be developed here is to receive an initial message comprising several temperature values in Fahrenheit and to provide a final message containing those Fahrenheit values together with their conversion to Celsius scale. Figure 8.11 illustrates the idea. The initial message contains one or more Temperature elements, each with its own Fahrenheit and Celsius fields. On input, the Celsius field is empty, while the Fahrenheit field provides the temperature value to be converted. On output, a final message brings both fields filled in, for a set of Temperature elements in the same order as in the input message.

Inside the orchestration, the Fahrenheit values are converted to Celsius using the same Web service that was used as an example in Chap. 6. However, this Web service can take only one input at a time, and therefore the orchestration has a loop to iterate over all Fahrenheit values provided in the initial message. (Alternatively, one could have another Web service to implement the loop itself, but this would not allow us to illustrate the use of the loop shape; besides, that would require the

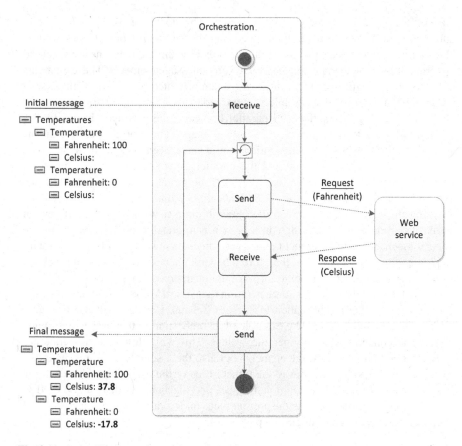

Fig. 8.11 A simplified overview of the orchestration

Web service to receive and process the XML with the list of temperatures.) After invoking the Web service, each Fahrenheit value together with its conversion to Celsius is written to a final message that is sent as output from the orchestration.

Listing 8.1 shows the XML schema to be used for the initial and final messages in the orchestration. Basically, after some headers and namespaces, line 6 specifies that the message has a root element called Temperatures and inside it there is a sequence (line 8) of child elements called Temperature (line 9). An arbitrary number of Temperature elements may be present, as specified by the minOccurs and maxOccurs attributes in line 9. Each Temperature element has two subsequent child nodes: one Fahrenheit element and one Celsius element, both of type double (lines 12–13).

Before we go on, we should note that there is no need to write such XML schema definitions by hand, since most integration platforms provide tools to define XML schemas graphically in a user-friendly way. In particular, the schema in Listing 8.1 was automatically generated using a tool of such kind. In general, the user needs only to specify a hierarchical structure similar to the ones depicted in the left-hand

Listing 8.1 Message schema for the initial and final messages

```
 1    <?xml version="1.0" encoding="utf−16"?>
 2    <xs:schema xmlns="http://DemoLoop.Temperatures"
 3                    xmlns:b="http://schemas.microsoft.com/BizTalk/2003"
 4                    targetNamespace="http://DemoLoop.Temperatures"
 5                    xmlns:xs="http://www.w3.org/2001/XMLSchema">
 6      <xs:element name="Temperatures">
 7        <xs:complexType>
 8          <xs:sequence>
 9            <xs:element minOccurs="1" maxOccurs="unbounded" name="Temperature">
10              <xs:complexType mixed="true">
11                <xs:sequence>
12                  <xs:element name="Fahrenheit" type="xs:double" />
13                  <xs:element name="Celsius" type="xs:double" />
14                </xs:sequence>
15              </xs:complexType>
16            </xs:element>
17          </xs:sequence>
18        </xs:complexType>
19      </xs:element>
20    </xs:schema>
```

side of Fig. 8.11, possibly together with some additional details such as the type of elements (in this case, double). The tool can then automatically generate the XML schema in some format, usually XSD as explained in Sect. 5.3.2.

We are now in a position to have a look at the complete orchestration that is required to implement this solution. The orchestration is depicted in Fig. 8.12, together with all expressions that are embedded in its shapes. These constructs will be explained in more detail in the next sections. For the moment, it suffices to say that the orchestration has a set of send shapes and receive shapes to interact with external applications through its ports. It also has a couple of construct message shapes: one to create the request for the Web service, and another to create the final message to be sent out in the last step. The main novelty here is the use of the loop shape, and for this purpose a couple of *expression shapes* are needed as well.

8.5.2   The Use of Expression Shapes

The loop shape has a condition to specify when it should stop iterating. More precisely, this condition is usually specified in terms of a boolean expression which, being true, keeps the loop iterating. When the condition becomes false, this prevents further iterations and makes the orchestration proceed to the next shape after the loop block. In the orchestration of Fig. 8.12, the loop must iterate over all Fahrenheit values provided in the initial message. Let us suppose that the number of Temperature elements in the initial message is stored in a variable called tempCount. Also, let us suppose that there is another variable called counter to count the number of times that the loop has been executed. Then the condition that keeps the loop running is expressed in code: counter < tempCount.

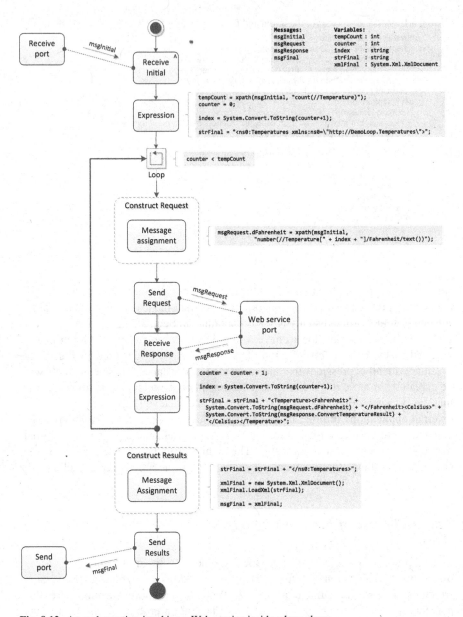

Fig. 8.12 An orchestration invoking a Web service inside a loop shape

This is precisely the condition that is associated with the loop shape in Fig. 8.12: while the number of times that the loop has been run is less than the number of Temperature elements, the loop is kept running in order to process the next element. Otherwise, when the counter variable indicates that all elements have been processed, the loop is exited. In this context, counter and tempCount are auxiliary variables, i.e., they are variables in the sense of *programming variables* and they have a different behavior from messages in an orchestration. Whereas messages must be created through the use of special constructs and cannot be modified later on, variables can be read and written anywhere, wherever there is an opportunity for inserting an expression in the orchestration.

In Sect. 8.3.2 we have already seen that the message assignment shape provides a means to construct messages through expressions. If necessary, such expressions may involve the manipulation of some variables. In addition to message assignments, it is possible to insert expressions anywhere in an orchestration through the use of the *expression shape*. Figure 8.12 illustrates the use of two expression shapes: one just before the loop, and another as the last step inside the loop. Given that the loop condition is counter < tempCount, it should not be too difficult to understand what these expression shapes are doing: the first expression shape is initializing the tempCount and counter variables, and the second expression shape is incrementing the value of the counter variable. (The other tasks that are also being performed in each expression shape will be explained in the next section.)

The tempCount variable is being initialized by means of the XPath expression: count(//Temperature). This expression begins with the count() function, which returns the number of nodes that match the given template. The template //Temperature matches every Temperature node in an XML document, no matter where it is in the XML structure. In the first expression shape in Fig. 8.12, the XPath expression is being applied over msgInitial, which effectively counts the number of temperature values in the initial message. In the same expression shape, the counter variable is being initialized with zero. This variable is incremented in the second expression shape, which can be found inside the loop.

Therefore, the counter variable begins with a value of zero and is incremented in every loop iteration, as intended. Once the value of counter reaches the same value as tempCount, the loop stops. Note that the counter variable is being used both outside and inside the loop, which means that this variable has a global scope, i.e., it can be used anywhere in the orchestration. The same happens with other variables. Also, note that these variables need to be declared somewhere. In Biztalk, they are declared as "orchestration variables." These orchestration variables are shown in the top right corner of Fig. 8.12. Each variable has a certain name and type; in particular, both counter and tempCount have been declared as integers.

8.5.3 Constructing the Request Message

There are actually two messages being constructed inside the loop: one is the request message to be sent to the Web service; the other is the final message to be produced as output from the orchestration and which collects all the results coming from the Web service. The request message to be sent to the Web service can be constructed using a single construct shape. Basically, one needs to fetch a Fahrenheit value from the initial message and copy it to the request message. The problem is that in each loop iteration one must fetch a different value from the initial message. This is achieved through an XPath expression in the form:

number(//Temperature[index]/Fahrenheit/text())

The number() function is intended just to convert the result to a number, since the Fahrenheit value must be passed on to the Web service as a double parameter. Inside the number() function, there is a template that matches a Temperature element that contains a Fahrenheit element with some content. The text() function retrieves that content and the number() function converts it. Now, we want to retrieve not just any Temperature element, but a new Temperature element in every loop iteration. For that purpose, we use an index in the expression above ([index]) to indicate which Temperature element should be retrieved.

Naturally, index is a variable that must be somehow initialized and updated in every loop iteration. According to XPath conventions, the index starts at 1. For this reason, the index variable is always one unit ahead of the counter variable, which starts at 0. Therefore, it makes sense to have: index = counter + 1. On the other hand, it is necessary to replace the index variable in the XPath expression above with its actual value. Since the XPath expression is provided as a string, we must do some string concatenations, and therefore it is convenient to have the index value available as a string, hence: index = System.Convert.ToString(counter+1) (in C#). This expression can be found in the first expression shape in Fig. 8.12 to initialize the index variable. It can also be found in the second expression shape in Fig. 8.12 where it increments the value of the index variable at every loop iteration.

Now it becomes clear what the first message assignment in Fig. 8.12 is doing: it inserts the index variable (as a string) in the XPath expression, and it applies the XPath expression to the initial message in order to retrieve a Fahrenheit value that will be assigned to the request message. This request message is used as input to the Web service, which then returns a response with the Celsius value.

8.5.4 Constructing the Final Message

At the end of the orchestration, it is necessary to provide a final message with all temperatures both in Fahrenheit and in Celsius. This message must be created at some point during the orchestration and, like any other message, it must be created inside a construct shape. In the particular scenario of Fig. 8.12, with every loop iteration there is a new result to be included in the final message, and therefore it would be useful to construct the message incrementally, but this is not possible. Instead, the final message is constructed all at once in a construct shape after the loop block. In the meantime, the results must be stored in some variable.

One could store the results in a list or some other kind of data structure, but it becomes more convenient to store them in a way that can be loaded directly into the final message. For that purpose, we store the intermediate results in an XML string that is built along with each loop iteration. The idea is to have the content ready

Listing 8.2   Example of initial and final messages for the orchestration

```
1    <ns0:Temperatures xmlns:ns0="http://DemoLoop.Temperatures">
2      <Temperature>
3        <Fahrenheit>100</Fahrenheit>
4        <Celsius></Celsius>
5      </Temperature>
6      <Temperature>
7        <Fahrenheit>0</Fahrenheit>
8        <Celsius></Celsius>
9      </Temperature>
10   </ns0:Temperatures>
11
12   <ns0:Temperatures xmlns:ns0="http://DemoLoop.Temperatures">
13     <Temperature>
14       <Fahrenheit>100</Fahrenheit>
15       <Celsius>37.7777777777778</Celsius>
16     </Temperature>  ,
17     <Temperature>
18       <Fahrenheit>0</Fahrenheit>
19       <Celsius>−17.7777777777778</Celsius>
20     </Temperature>
21   </ns0:Temperatures>
```

to load into the final message as soon as the loop is over. Listing 8.2 provides an example of an initial and a final message for the orchestration. For an initial message as in Listing 8.2, lines 1–10, one should expect the final message in Listing 8.2, lines 12–21. We therefore build the message in lines 12–21 as a string, as we go along the loop. The string is stored in a variable called strFinal.

The first expression shape in Fig. 8.12 initializes the strFinal variable with line 12 in Listing 8.2. Then the second expression shape in Fig. 8.12 does most of the work, by adding the chunks in lines 13–16 and 17–20 in the two passes through the loop, respectively. The expression for strFinal in the second expression shape adds a Temperature element with two sub-elements: one to contain the Fahrenheit value and another to contain the Celsius value. The Fahrenheit value is obtained from the request message (msgRequest.dFahrenheit) and the Celsius value is obtained from the response (msgResponse.ConvertTemperatureResult). Both values are converted to strings in order to be concatenated with the rest of the XML content.

Finally, the message assignment shape after the loop finishes the XML by closing the root element of strFinal, and then performs a trick that finds application in many practical scenarios. This trick consists in several steps, namely: creating an XML object (xmlFinal in Fig. 8.12); loading the XML string (strFinal) to the XML object; and initializing the message (msgFinal) with that XML object. This is an artificial way to construct the final message, but it is a useful workaround that often solves the problem of constructing a message whose content must be assembled from several parts and across several steps in the orchestration.

In this discussion, we will skip the issue of configuring the ports in the orchestration. This can be done exactly in the same way as explained in Sect. 6.5.4. Basically, the initial receive port and the final send port can be bound to physical ports using the file adapter, and the Web service port must be an instance of the port type that was automatically created when the Web service was added to the solution. After configuring and deploying the orchestration, it is possible to trigger it by placing a message similar to lines 1–10 in Listing 8.2 in the folder associated with the receive port. The orchestration will run and produce the final message (as in lines 12–21 of Listing 8.2) in the folder associated with the send port.

8.6 Orchestrations as Subprocesses

Suppose that we want to hide the part where the orchestration in Fig. 8.12 interacts with the Web service. In particular, we want to hide those details in a separate orchestration that can be embedded as a subprocess in a main orchestration. Such embedding is possible if we publish the orchestration in Fig. 6.9 on page 179 as a Web service, and then invoke this new Web service in another orchestration. That would be certainly useful if the two orchestrations were developed by different people or at different points in time. It could also be done for the purpose of service composition in a service-oriented architecture, as explained in Chap. 7.

However, here we are interested in hiding those details just for the purpose of organizing the orchestration logic in two orchestrations, where one can be nested into the other. Such simple nesting is possible and can be achieved through the use of a *call orchestration* shape. Figure 8.13 illustrates the use of a call orchestration shape to invoke another orchestration, also referred to as the *sub-orchestration*. Before going into the details of the orchestration in Fig. 8.13, one should compare this orchestration with the one shown earlier in Fig. 8.12. Basically, the logic inside the loop has been somewhat simplified, as the first construct shape and the interaction with the Web service in Fig. 8.12 have been replaced by an expression shape and a call orchestration shape to invoke the sub-orchestration.

8.6.1 The Main Orchestration

A comparison of Fig. 8.12 with Fig.8.13 reveals that there have been some changes in the messages and variables associated with the orchestration. The msgRequest and msgResponse messages have disappeared in Fig. 8.13, and two new variables (dFahrenheit and dCelsius of type double) have been created. The reason for using these variables will become apparent if we look at the sub-orchestration that is being invoked in the call orchestration shape. For the moment, we will focus on what is common in both orchestrations of Figs. 8.13 and 8.12.

Both orchestrations have an expression block before the loop shape to determine the number of iterations and initialize counter and index variables. This first expression shape also serves to initialize a string (strFinal) that is used to assemble the final message that will be sent out at the end of the orchestration. Just before the end of the loop, both orchestrations have another expression shape to increment the

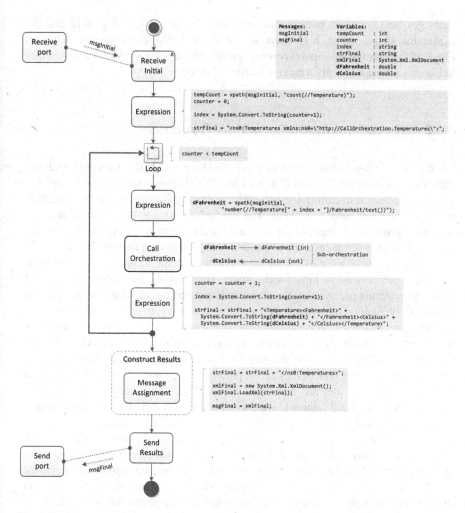

Fig. 8.13 An orchestration using a call orchestration shape

counter and index variables and to load the next chunk of temperature values into the strFinal variable. Whereas in Fig. 8.12 the Fahrenheit value was obtained from the request message and the Celsius value was obtained from the response from the Web service, in Fig. 8.13 these values are being obtained from the dFahrenheit and dCelsius variables. After the loop, there is a construct message shape that does exactly the same thing in both orchestrations.

So, as expected, the main difference between both orchestrations is inside the loop. Where the orchestration in Fig. 8.12 constructs the request message through a message assignment shape, the orchestration in Fig. 8.13 sets the value of the dFahrenheit variable in an expression shape. It is interesting to note that the Fahrenheit value comes from the same place (i.e., from an element in the initial message), and therefore both the message assignment shape in Fig. 8.12 and the expression shape in Fig. 8.13 make use of the same XPath expression. Then in Fig. 8.12 follows the send and receive shapes to interact with the Web service, while in Fig. 8.13 there is simply a call orchestration shape.

8.6.2   The Sub-orchestration and Its Parameters

Clearly, if the sub-orchestration is to be invoked from within the main orchestration, there must be some way to pass data back and forth between them. In particular, the main orchestration is calling the sub-orchestration with the purpose of converting a given Fahrenheit value to Celsius. The Fahrenheit value to be converted must be somehow provided as input to the sub-orchestration, and the output value that the sub-orchestration produces must be handed back to the main orchestration.

From the point of view of the calling orchestration, the sub-orchestration is seen as a black box with some inputs and outputs. These inputs and outputs are referred to as *orchestration parameters*. An orchestration parameter can have many different forms, but typically it represents either a message with a certain schema or a variable of some type. However, orchestration parameters work in a different way from either messages or variables. First, an orchestration parameter can be defined either as "in" or "out," depending on whether the parameter is being used as input or output in the sub-orchestration. Second, orchestration parameters are not meant to be exchanged through ports; rather, they are exchanged when the sub-orchestration is being called, and when it finishes and returns to the calling orchestration. In the call orchestration shape, it is possible to define what happens at these two key moments.

In our scenario, all there is to be exchanged between the two orchestrations can be reduced to a couple of double values. Therefore, in order to simplify the solution we develop a sub-orchestration with two orchestration parameters that represent variables rather than messages (since messages would need to have a certain schema shared between both orchestrations). One orchestration parameter is a variable of type double called dFahrenheit, and the other is a variable of type double called dCelsius. The dFahrenheit parameter will be used as input and therefore will be defined as "in," while the dCelsius parameter will be used as output and therefore will be defined as "out." The two orchestration parameters dFahrenheit and dCelsius, to be defined in the sub-orchestration, are meant to have a direct relationship with the two variables dFahrenheit and dCelsius in the calling orchestration.

In particular, and as shown next to the call orchestration shape in Fig. 8.13, the dFahrenheit variable in the main orchestration is mapped to the dFahrenheit parameter in the sub-orchestration, and the dCelsius variable is mapped to the dCelsius parameter accordingly. However, the dFahrenheit parameter is an "in" parameter, meaning that it gets its value from the dFahrenheit variable, while the dCelsius parameter is an "out" parameter, meaning that it sets the value of the dCelsius variable in the main orchestration. Furthermore, the dFahrenheit parameter

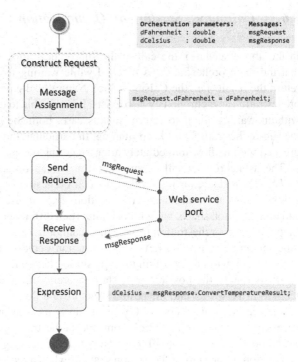

Fig. 8.14 An orchestration to be invoked in a call orchestration shape

is set before the sub-orchestration starts, while the dCelsius variable is set after the sub-orchestration finishes its execution. In general, "in" parameters are written before the orchestration starts, and "out" parameters are read after the orchestration finishes.

Figure 8.14 shows the actual flow of the sub-orchestration. When the orchestration starts, its input parameters (in this case, dFahrenheit) have already been set, so the orchestration can immediately proceed with what it has to do. The first thing to do is to construct the request to be sent to the Web service. This is done using a message assignment shape with a simple expression that copies the value of the dFahrenheit parameter to the dFahrenheit property in the request. The orchestration then sends request to the Web service and waits for the response. As a fourth and final step, it sets the value of the dCelsius parameter based on the response from the Web service. Then it just ends, as everything is done. The call orchestration shape in the orchestration of Fig. 8.13 will make sure that the value of the dCelsius parameter is copied to the dCelsius variable in the main orchestration.

Figure 8.14 illustrates the rare case of an orchestration which does not begin with an activating receive. This is possible in this case because the orchestration is meant to be called from another orchestration. As it stands, the orchestration in Fig. 8.14 cannot run on its own. Instead, it should be regarded as a piece of orchestration logic that is to be called within the flow of other orchestrations.

8.6.3 Calling vs. Starting an Orchestration

In the above scenario, the call to the sub-orchestration is synchronous, meaning that the main orchestration is blocked while waiting for the sub-orchestration to return the result (i.e., the Celsius value). Naturally, the possibility of calling a sub-orchestration asynchronously also exists. It is possible to trigger a sub-orchestration without waiting for it to return. In this case, both the calling orchestration and the sub-orchestration will keep running. In particular, the calling orchestration will proceed with its flow immediately after triggering the sub-orchestration.

The asynchronous call of an orchestration can be achieved through the *start orchestration* shape (as opposed to the call orchestration shape, which is used for synchronous calls). The start orchestration shape is used in a similar way to the call orchestration shape, but with one important difference: in the start orchestration shape, the sub-orchestration to be called cannot have any output parameters; only input parameters are allowed. This restriction comes naturally, since the calling orchestration will not be waiting for the sub-orchestration to finish its execution.

At first sight the possibility of starting orchestration asynchronously does not seem to fit very well into the nested structure and flow of orchestrations. However, this possibility can become very useful in some scenarios, such as when it is necessary to hand over control from one orchestration that is about to finish to another orchestration that will proceed with a further stage of processing. A typical application of the start orchestration shape is when a message has several items that can be processed independently. Figure 8.15 illustrates one such example.

Here, the orchestration receives an order comprising several items (i.e., a repetition of XML elements as in the case of multiple temperatures). The first expression shape determines the number of items and initializes a counter and an index variable, as in the examples of the previous sections. The loop iterates through all items and each item is represented as a separate message that is constructed through a message assignment. The message for an individual item is passed as a parameter to a sub-orchestration that is called asynchronously through the use of a start orchestration shape. An expression shape at the end of the loop is used to increment the counter and index variables. Once the loop has iterated through all items, the main orchestration terminates while the items are being processed separately and simultaneously in different instances of the sub-orchestration.

In some integration platforms, such as BizTalk, the same behavior can be achieved through other mechanisms, namely pipelines, as explained in Sect. 2.3. As can be seen in Fig. 2.3 on page 21, a receive pipeline may include a disassemble stage, whose purpose is to split an incoming message into multiple messages that are built from different elements in the incoming message. For this purpose, it is necessary to define an *envelope schema* and an XPath expression that specifies where the element to be used for splitting can be found in the incoming message.

Typically, a receive pipeline with a disassemble stage is associated with a receive port which in turn is associated with an activating receive in an orchestration. As a message arrives at the receive port, it goes through the pipeline and is split into

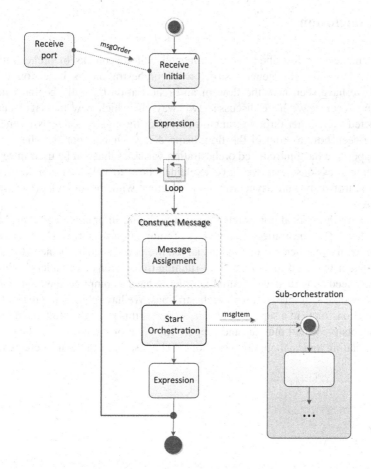

Fig. 8.15 An orchestration using a start orchestration shape

multiple messages; each of these messages will trigger a different instance of the orchestration. Therefore, instead of having a main orchestration with a loop to start multiple instances of the sub-orchestration, as in Fig. 8.15, it would be possible to have the sub-orchestration alone with an activating receive and a receive port that uses such pipeline with a disassemble stage.

On the other hand, the opposite process, i.e., that of assembling a message from multiple items, is difficult (in BizTalk, impossible) to achieve with a pipeline. The reason for this is that, as explained in Sect. 3.1.3, a pipeline works by processing the stream of messages that go through it. Assembling multiple messages into a single aggregated message would require a pipeline to store the messages that come along, and to know how many messages it should wait for before aggregating all of them in a single message. In general, this is impossible to do with a pipeline. However, in this chapter we have seen how to do that within an orchestration, through the use of a loop shape and several expressions, as in Fig. 8.12.

8.7 Conclusion

In this chapter we described the fundamental building blocks of orchestrations: we have seen how the general structure of orchestrations is based on nested blocks; we have seen how the flow of an orchestration typically begins with an activating receive; we have discussed two ways in which new messages can be constructed (i.e., either through transformations or through message assignments); we have seen how to control the flow using decide shapes, parallel shapes, and loop shapes; we have introduced orchestration variables that can be used in several kinds of expressions; and we have explained how to call a sub-orchestration, both synchronously and asynchronously, together with the use of orchestration parameters.

These are the typical constructs than can be found in practice and that can be used to develop orchestrations in a variety of integration scenarios. However, there are additional constructs to address special requirements, such as the need to handle exceptions or the need to support long-running transactions. An understanding of these advanced constructs is essential in order to have a complete knowledge about what is possible to implement with orchestrations. We have chosen to present those advanced constructs in a separate chapter, so that at this point the reader can review the concepts presented thus far and prepare for some of the most complicated but also fascinating topics about orchestrations, to be discussed in the next chapter.

Chapter 9
Advanced Constructs

Some integration scenarios involve special features or requirements which are not supported by the basic constructs described in the previous chapter, or at least can be very difficult to implement with those constructs. These special requirements may have several origins. First, they may come from the need to implement a certain business behavior. For example, in business scenarios there are usually deadlines that must be met, after which the process may take different paths depending on whether something happened before the deadline, as it was supposed to, or not. For this purpose, one can use the *delay shape* together with a *listen shape* in order to wait for events within a certain time frame, as explained in Sect. 9.1.

A second source of special requirements may come from the technical characteristics of the applications to be integrated, or from the technical characteristics of the integration platform itself. For example, up to this point we have seen request–response interactions with external systems being implemented with bidirectional ports, e.g., the SQL adapter port in Fig. 5.15 on page 136, or the Web service port in Fig. 6.9 on page 179. In both cases, such bidirectional ports were created by introspection of the external system to be invoked. For example, from a Web service interface it is possible to figure out which methods are available together with their input and output parameters, and therefore it is possible to automatically create a bidirectional port to invoke any of those methods; the same can be done for a stored procedure in a database. However, in practice not everything is as transparent as a Web service or a stored procedure, and there will be legacy systems which are not amenable to introspection. For these systems, it will be necessary to specify each message to be exchanged, and to create a unidirectional port to send or to receive that message. This means that the interaction with such systems will have to be attained through separate unidirectional ports. In such scenario, the use of *correlations* will be mandatory, for the reasons that have been already explained in Sect. 4.6 and that will be further developed in Sect. 9.2.

A third source of special requirements often comes from the need to improve the reliability and fault-tolerance of integration solutions. Unfortunately, in complex scenarios involving large application infrastructures, many things can go wrong when trying to execute even a simple orchestration. In a real-world environment,

D.R. Ferreira, *Enterprise Systems Integration*, DOI 10.1007/978-3-642-40796-3_9,
© Springer-Verlag Berlin Heidelberg 2013

such faults may have undesirable consequences in terms of extra costs or even damages to corporate image. Therefore, it is worthwhile to spend a significant amount of effort in anticipating those faults and being able to cope with them at run-time. That is where the topic of *exception handling* (Sect. 9.3) comes in, but that is not all. In some scenarios it is not enough to be prepared to catch an error (if it occurs) and handle it; in addition, it must be ensured that the whole process is in a consistent state at all times. If the process cannot proceed due to some error, then it may have to recede to a previous state that is known to be consistent. However, for practical reasons, it may not be possible to undo a previous action (e.g., if a variable was written, then it cannot be unwritten; instead, it must be written again with an old value), so it may be necessary to carry out additional activities to bring the process back to a consistent state. This is referred to as *compensation* and it is carried out in the scope of a *transaction*. If an error occurs during a transaction, then the transaction fails and it may be necessary to compensate what has been done in order to bring the process to a consistent state. This is explained in Sect. 9.4.

Overall, the constructs described in this chapter are meant to deal with events—either foreseen or unforeseen events. Being able to capture and respond to events requires a slightly different paradigm from what we have seen in the previous chapter, where orchestrations were developed essentially as a flow of activities. Here we will look at a set of new shapes that can also be used in the orchestration flow in order to deal with events. At first sight, some of these artifacts may seem strange and even hard to understand due to their inherent complexity. However, one should bear in mind the inner workings of an integration platform such as BizTalk; namely, the fact that it comprises an orchestration engine on top of a messaging platform. This creates the need to route messages to the correct orchestration instance, and the need to fit exception handling and transaction mechanisms into the nested block structure of orchestrations. With these ideas in mind, it should be easier to understand why these advanced constructs have been devised in a certain way.

9.1 Listening for Events

Suppose that, in a given business scenario, an orchestration sends out a request and waits for a response. If the response does not arrive, then the orchestration will wait indefinitely. (This does not necessarily mean a waste of resources since, after some time, the orchestration instance will be dehydrated, as explained at the end of Sect. 3.1.4.) Now suppose that, due to business requirements, the response is expected to arrive within 3 days after the request has been sent. If the response does not arrive within that time frame, then the orchestration should proceed, either in the same way or in a different way than what would happen if the response had been received, but it should proceed nevertheless.

It is hard, if not impossible at all, to implement this behavior using the flow constructs described in the previous chapter. For example, one could think of using a decision shape with two branches, one for the case when the message is received

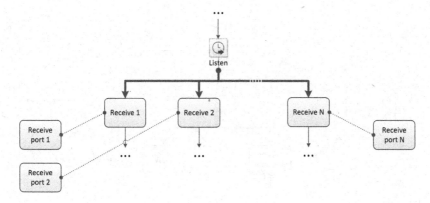

Fig. 9.1   The listen shape

within 3 days, and another (the "Else" branch) if it happens otherwise. Even if it would be possible to specify such condition (which is not) then one would still have the problem that, as soon as the orchestration flow enters a receive shape, it will be stuck there indefinitely until some message arrives. There is no mechanism to skip or abandon a task once it has been initiated.

The *listen* shape provides a solution to this problem. The listen shape is similar to the decide shape, but with an important difference: rather than a condition, each branch has an event associated with it (typically, a receive shape). Among the set of events that may occur, the event that occurs first determines the branch that is chosen for execution. For example, in a listen shape with two branches (there may be more), where each branch starts with receive shape, the branch to be followed depends on which receive shape gets its message first; the other branch will be skipped, much like a branch in a decide shape whose condition is false.

Figure 9.1 illustrates this behavior. There are several branches for the listen shape, and all of these branches start with a receive shape. Naturally, each receive shape is associated with its own receive port. The first receive shape to get a message will trigger the corresponding branch, and the listen shape will ensure that the other branches are skipped. Such behavior can be extended to an arbitrary number of branches N, and only one out of N branches will be executed.

Besides the receive shape, a branch in a listen shape can also be triggered by a timer. For this purpose, it is necessary to use the *delay* shape. Basically, the delay shape is a means to insert a delay during the execution of an orchestration instance. The delay pauses execution for a given amount of time, or until a specified date and time is reached. As with other shapes, the condition that specifies the delay is given as an expression in code (C# in the case of BizTalk). Essentially, the delay shape can be seen as a special kind of expression shape, where the expression must specify either a date and time (using System.DateTime) or a time span (using System.TimeSpan) which can be measured in days, hours, minutes, or seconds. Execution will proceed beyond the delay shape only when that time has passed.

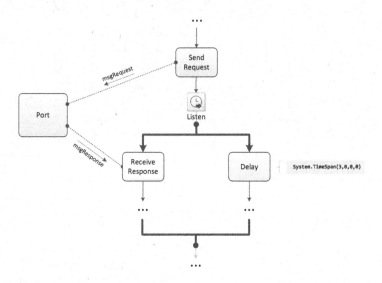

Fig. 9.2 A listen shape with a delay shape

Now we can go back to the business scenario described at the beginning of this section and devise a solution to the problem based on the listen and delay shapes. The solution is depicted in Fig. 9.2. Basically, it comprises a listen shape with two branches. The branch on the left-hand side is intended to receive a response after a previously sent request. However, if the response does not arrive within 3 days then the branch on the right-hand side will be executed instead. This branch contains a delay shape with an expression that specifies a time span of 3 days (and zero hours, zero minutes, and zero seconds). As a result, either a response is received within that time frame, or execution will proceed through the right branch and in this case the left branch is skipped (the orchestration stops waiting for a message). One and only one of these branches will be executed. After the branch completes, the orchestration resumes the main flow, which will be executed in either case.

In the above examples we have seen several receive shapes, but none of them were activating receives, i.e., none of these receive shapes were being used to trigger the orchestration; instead, they were being used somewhere along the flow. It is possible to use activating receives in a listen shape, but in this case there are some constraints that must be obeyed to. First, the listen shape must be the first shape in the orchestration. Second, all branches must contain activating receives, and the use of the delay shape is not allowed. Figure 9.3 illustrates an example.

Here, the orchestration is triggered by receiving either a message of type *A* or a message of type *B*, whichever comes first. The receive shapes are activating receives, meaning that both of them are capable of creating a new orchestration instance. This solution finds application in scenarios where a business process can be triggered by different types of message. For example, in an airline reservation

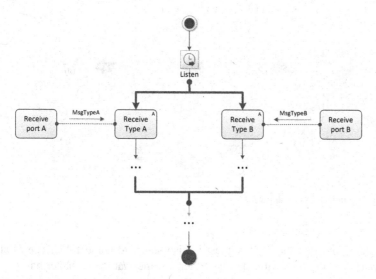

Fig. 9.3 A listen shape with activating receives

scenario it may be possible to handle new flight bookings as well as changes to existing bookings in the same orchestration (because both of them involve setting up a new flight reservation). Therefore, message type A could represent a new booking request, whereas message type B could represent a request for change, which carries different data and may require some additional processing.

It should be noted that there is no need to use the solution in Fig. 9.3 if the only difference between the triggering messages is where they come from. If both messages have the same type, but one arrives through e-mail while the other comes in a HTTP request, then it is possible to use the same receive port (and therefore the same receive shape) for both. As explained in Sect. 2.3 (see in particular Fig. 2.4 on page 22), a receive port may have several receive locations with different adapters, so there would be no need to have different receive ports. The solution in Fig. 9.3 applies only if there is a noticeable difference at the orchestration level, namely in terms of message schemas and the processing they require.

9.2 Correlations

Suppose that in some business organization there is a mandatory procedure for approving purchase requests. The procedure consists in forwarding the request to a manager, who will decide whether the request is to be approved or not. Once a decision has been made, a final request is produced with all the data from the original request plus the approval result. Figure 9.4 illustrates this process. For simplicity, we assume that the initial purchase request can be fetched from some folder in a

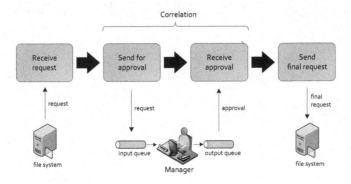

Fig. 9.4 A purchase approval process

file system, and that the final request is also saved to some folder (i.e., both of these ports use the file adapter). We further assume that the manager has a simple application for decision making that displays the request and records the approval result. Communication with this application is attained through message queues (i.e., through ports using the MSMQ adapter). Now that the physical send ports and receive ports have been specified, we can bring our main focus to the process itself.

Each new purchase request will create a new instance of the process, and all the requests will go through the manager for approval. In other words, there will be multiple process instances sending requests to the manager and waiting for an approval result. Ideally, the manager would dispatch work as quickly as possible, so that as a new request comes along, the approval decision would be made immediately. However, at some point in time the manager may have several requests pending for approval, especially if the rate at which new requests are submitted is higher than the rate at which the manager is able to dispatch them.

For example, suppose that three new purchase requests are submitted in a short period of time. Each of these requests will be subject to separate analysis and approval by the manager. Suppose that the manager picks one of these purchase requests and approves it. Then the response must be returned to the correct process instance. (The situation is similar to Fig. 4.5 on page 86, where three requests have been sent out and one response is coming back in.) Now the problem is: which process instance does the approval belong to?

To answer this question, there must be some way to *correlate* the response that is now being produced with a previous request. If each request can be identified by a unique number, for example, then the response should carry that same number, so that it becomes clear which request the response belongs to. Such number effectively works as a *correlation id*. In practice, a correlation id does not need to be a single field, but it can be any set of message properties. All messages exchanged within a given correlation must carry the same values in that set of properties. For simplicity, here we will use a unique request number to serve as correlation id.

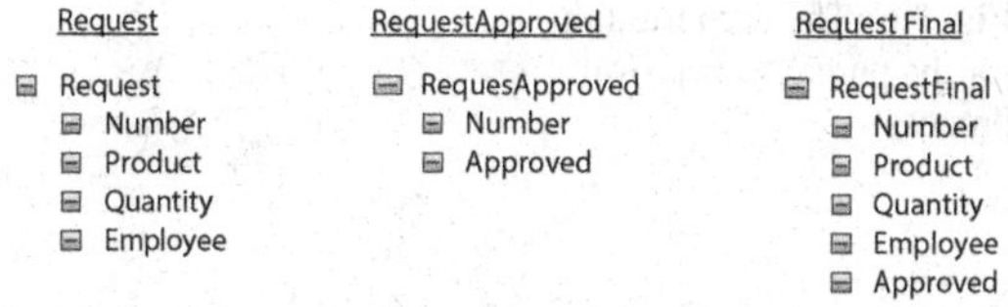

Fig. 9.5 Schemas for the
purchase process

Request	RequestApproved	Request Final
⊟ Request	⊟ RequesApproved	⊟ RequestFinal
▤ Number	▤ Number	▤ Number
▤ Product	▤ Approved	▤ Product
▤ Quantity		▤ Quantity
▤ Employee		▤ Employee
		▤ Approved

9.2.1 Defining the Schemas and the Orchestration

Figure 9.5 illustrates the schemas that will be used to develop a solution for the process above. There are three main schemas, namely: the Request schema, the RequestApproved schema, and the RequestFinal schema. The Request schema contains the details of the purchase request, namely the product and quantity to be ordered as well as the employee who submitted the request. The RequestApproved schema contains the approval result in the Approved field, which may contain either "Yes" or "No." The RequestFinal schema contains the details of the purchase request together with the approval result. All three schemas contain the request number.

The process in Fig. 9.4 is to be implemented as an orchestration, and it can be implemented as shown in Fig. 9.6. This orchestration begins by receiving the purchase request (hence the activating receive) and then sends this message, without change, to the manager for approval; it then waits for the approval and, once the approval message is received, it constructs the final request, sends it, and terminates. In this orchestration, each message is represented by its own message variable. As such, msgRequest is a message of type Request, msgApproval is a message of type RequestApproved, and msgFinal is a message of type RequestFinal.

In this orchestration, there is one send port to send the purchase request to the manager's input queue, and there is a receive port to fetch the approval from the manager's output queue. If the manager's application would expose a Web service interface, then it would have been possible to use a bidirectional port instead of two unidirectional ports. However, since the orchestration is interacting with the application through message queues, there needs to be a separate port for each queue. Here we are interested precisely in having these ports separated, in order to create the need for a correlation, and to illustrate the use of correlations in general.

In each instance of the orchestration in Fig. 9.6, the "Send for Approval" shape sends the purchase request to the manager's input queue, and the "Receive Approval" shape listens for messages on the manager's output queue. Now, there will be multiple orchestration instances (one for each purchase request), but here is only one input queue and one output queue. This means that all orchestration instances will send the request to the same input queue, and all orchestration instances will be listening for the response on the same output queue. Clearly, there must be a way to ensure that each orchestration instance will receive the approval message that corresponds to its purchase request. In addition, it must be ensured that each orchestration instance receives *only* the correct response; otherwise, the responses for other instances will be inadvertently removed from the queue.

Fig. 9.6 The orchestration for the purchase approval process

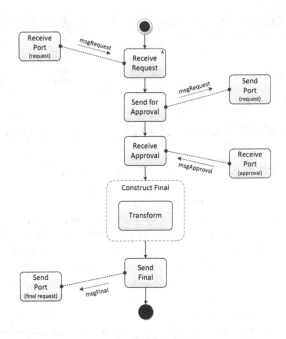

The solution to this problem is to use a correlation. This correlation will work by having a unique number assigned to each purchase request and by requiring each approval message to include that number, so that it can be correlated with its original request. In other words, the request number in both messages will serve as the correlation id. For an incoming approval, it is necessary to establish this correlation in order to identify the correct process instance which the approval should be dispatched to. Therefore, the correlation must take place *before* the approval message reaches the orchestration instance, and for this purpose it is necessary to promote the request number in both messages, as explained in the next section.

9.2.2 Defining the Property Schema

As shown in Fig. 4.4 on page 82, an orchestration runs on top of a messaging platform which sends messages through physical send ports and receives messages through physical receive ports. It is the duty of this messaging platform to determine, for a given incoming message, which orchestration instance should receive that message. In our present scenario, we have an incoming approval, and the orchestration instance which is to receive that message must be determined based on the request number in that approval message. Therefore, the request number must be accessible at the level of the messaging platform, and the way to do this is to *promote* that property, as described in Sect. 4.3.

Fig. 9.7 Schemas and
property schema for the
purchase process

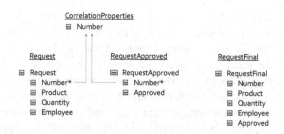

To promote a message property (i.e., in order to make it accessible to the
messaging platform), it is necessary to create a *property schema*. This concept has
been briefly discussed in Sect. 4.3 and its use is illustrated in Fig. 4.3 on page 80,
where the goal is to route an incoming message to a number of possible send ports.
The property schema is basically a list of properties whose values can be retrieved
from the incoming message. As illustrated in Fig. 4.3, these values can then be used
to evaluate the filter expression associated with each send port in order to decide
whether the message should be forwarded to each of those send ports.

In our present scenario, the incoming message is the approval result, which is a
message of type RequestApproved. This message is to be forwarded not to a send
port, but to an existing orchestration instance. This orchestration instance must be
determined based on the request number that is present in the message. Therefore,
the request number must be promoted in the RequestApproved schema. However,
this request number in the approval message must match the request number in
the purchase request that was previously sent for approval. Therefore, the request
number in the Request schema must also be promoted, so that the messaging
platform has access to both in order to determine the correct orchestration instance.

Figure 9.7 shows the message schemas and also the property schema Correlation-
Properties which holds a property called Number. This property could have been
given a different name; what is important is to define where the value for this
property comes from. Figure 9.7 shows that the value for the Number property can
be obtained either from a Request message or from a RequestApproved message. In
both schemas there is a Number element that is mapped to the Number property in the
property schema. For illustrative purposes only, the star next to each Number element
indicates that it has been promoted, i.e., its value can be retrieved by the messaging
platform as the message is being routed to its destination. For the outgoing Request
message, the destination is a send port, whereas for the incoming RequestApproved
message the destination will be an orchestration instance.

9.2.3 Defining the Correlation Type

In the previous section we promoted the Number property both in the Request
schema and in the RequestApproved schema. This makes the property available
to the messaging platform, but now we must specify what we are going to do

with it. In Sect. 4.3 we used promoted properties to specify the message filters associated with multiple send ports. Here we want to use promoted properties to specify a correlation between a message that goes out of the orchestration (i.e., the purchase request) and another message that comes back into the orchestration (i.e., the approval result). In other words, we say that the outgoing purchase request *initiates* the correlation, and the incoming approval result *follows* the correlation.

Even though message filters and correlations are different mechanisms, it helps thinking about a correlation as a kind of message filter. When an orchestration instance reaches a point in its execution where it initiates a correlation, it is as if a filter is being created in the messaging platform for that orchestration instance. This "filter" specifies that this particular orchestration instance is associated with a certain value for the correlation properties (e.g., a certain value for the Number property, as in our example above). Other instances of the same orchestration will be associated with different values for the correlation properties. So, when a particular orchestration instance wants to receive a message that follows a previously initialized correlation, only a message which has matching values for the correlation properties will be delivered to that orchestration instance.

Now, we know from Sect. 4.3 that a message filter is specified as an expression in terms of promoted properties. Therefore, it is not surprising that a correlation is also defined in terms of promoted properties. In Fig. 9.7 we created a property schema called CorrelationProperties. Of course, the name we have chosen for this property schema is an indication that we intend to use those properties in a correlation, but the property schema might as well have been given another name; what is important is to define a correlation based on those properties (in this case, based on the Number property). This is done in two steps: first we define a *correlation type*, and then we define a *correlation set* based on that correlation type.

For the moment, we focus on the correlation type. In essence, a correlation type specifies which properties will be used in the correlation. In our scenario, we define a correlation type that uses a single property—the Number property.

In general, a correlation type may have multiple properties. Usually, these properties are promoted properties that can be found in the content of a message, just like the Number property above. However, the properties to be used for correlation may also include *context properties* that can be found in the message envelope. For example, if the message arrives from a message queue, then it is possible to retrieve any of the properties that are usually associated with a MSMQ message, such as Label, Priority, and DestinationQueue. (A description of MSMQ message properties can be found in Sect. 3.6.4.) If needed, these context properties can also be used for the purpose of correlating messages.

However, it is important to note that, for the purpose of correlation, one must choose properties that can be found in all messages to be exchanged within the correlation. For example, the correlation may include one message to be sent to a system folder and another message to be received from a message queue. In this case it is impossible to use MSMQ properties for the correlation because the first message does not include those properties. For this reason, in practice it is usually the case that correlations are defined based on promoted properties. In our present scenario, the correlation is defined based on the Number property that can be found both in the Request message and in the RequestApproved message.

9.2.4 Defining and Using a Correlation Set

Now that a correlation type has been defined, it is possible to define a *correlation set* to be used in the orchestration. Basically, a correlation set can be regarded as an instance of a given correlation type. Whereas the correlation type specifies only the properties to be used in the correlation, the correlation set defines which message exchanges will be part of the correlation. In our scenario, we want the correlation to include the purchase request that is sent to the manager and the approval result that comes back as a response. The purchase request (msgRequest) is sent by the "Send for Approval" shape in the orchestration of Fig. 9.6, while the approval result (msgApproval) is received by the "Receive Approval" shape. These are the two message exchanges that will be part of the correlation set.

Figure 9.8 shows the same orchestration as in Fig. 9.6 but now the orchestration has been updated to make use of a correlation set. In particular, the shape "Send for Approval" *initializes* the correlation set, while the shape "Receive Approval" *follows* the correlation set. There may be several shapes following a correlation set, but there must be one (and only one) shape initializing the correlation set. "Initializing" the correlation set means setting the property values that all messages belonging to the same correlation should have; "following" the correlation set means subscribing to messages which have those same property values.

The practical effect of having the correlation set in Fig. 9.8 is that the "Receive Approval" shape will wait for a message that has the same Number as the request that has been sent by the "Send for Approval" shape. The "Send for Approval" initialized the property value and the "Receive Approval" shape, by following the correlation set, will subscribe to messages having that same property value. As a result, the messaging platform will route to each orchestration instance only the approval message which matches the same value for the correlation property.

The correlation set ends with the "Receive Approval" shape, but it would be possible to have other shapes (i.e., other send and receive shapes) following the same correlation set throughout the orchestration. In general, a correlation set may include an arbitrary number of message exchanges. In addition, it is possible to have multiple correlation sets as well. Since a correlation set is an instance of a correlation type, there may be several such instances, for use at different points in the orchestration. For example, one could think of a scenario where several interactions with different applications would require the use of a specific correlation set for each, using either the same or different correlation types.

In the present scenario, the possibility of using multiple correlation sets does not apply, because there is a single interaction that requires the use of a correlation, so this can be addressed with a single correlation type and a single correlation set based on that correlation type. Furthermore, suppose that there would be another interaction requiring the use of a correlation; for example, suppose that the purchase

Fig. 9.8 An orchestration
using a correlation set

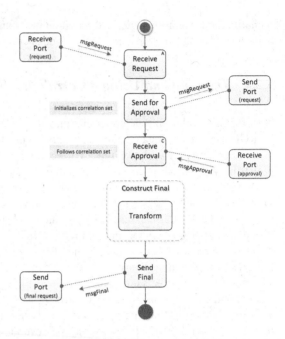

request would need to go through a second approval, similar to the first one. Even
in this case there would be no need to create a second correlation set because this
second approval could "follow" the same correlation set that has been initialized
before. The reason for this is that the correlation type is based on the Number
property and there is only one value for this property in each orchestration instance,
so there would be no need to create multiple correlation sets from this correlation
type, since these correlation sets would use the same property value.

9.2.5 Running the Orchestration

Now that the "Receive Approval" shape in Fig. 9.8 has already been configured
with a correlation set, the orchestration can actually be run. Without this correlation
set, it would be impossible to run multiple instances of this orchestration, since the
approval messages could end up being mixed up. Now, with the correlation set, it is
ensured that each approval will be routed to the correct process instance. In general,
the receive shapes that are used along the flow of an orchestration must be following
some correlation set, with the only exceptions being the first (i.e., activating) receive
in an orchestration and any receive shapes using bidirectional (i.e., *self-correlating*)
ports, as in Fig. 6.9 on page 179, or Fig. 5.15 on page 136.

We can therefore state the following general rule about receive shapes:

> *Any receive shape that is non-activating and that is not connected
> to a self-correlating port must follow some correlation set.*

Fig. 9.9 Transformation map for the purchase process

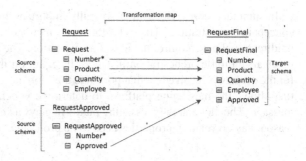

Listing 9.1 Examples of each message

```
 1   <ns0:Request xmlns:ns0="http://DemoCorrelations.Request">
 2     <Number>123</Number>
 3     <Product>Printer Cartridge</Product>
 4     <Quantity>2</Quantity>
 5     <Employee>P45</Employee>
 6   </ns0:Request>
 7
 8   <ns0:RequestApproved xmlns:ns0="http://DemoCorrelations.RequestApproved">
 9     <Number>123</Number>
10     <Approved>Yes</Approved>
11   </ns0:RequestApproved>
12
13   <ns0:RequestFinal xmlns:ns0="http://DemoCorrelations.RequestFinal">
14     <Number>123</Number>
15     <Product>Printer Cartridge</Product>
16     <Quantity>2</Quantity>
17     <Employee>P45</Employee>
18     <Approved>Yes</Approved>
19   </ns0:RequestFinal>
```

Before we are able to run the orchestration, there is one additional component that needs to be defined, and that is the transformation map associated with the transform shape in Fig. 9.8. This transformation map is shown in Fig. 9.9. Basically, it gathers all data from the purchase request and additionally it brings in the approval result to create a RequestFinal message. In particular, the value for the Number element is being taken from the Request message, but it could as well be taken from the RequestApproved message since, by force of the correlation, the Number element has the same value in both messages.

We are now ready to deploy and run the orchestration. Listing 9.1 shows an example of the three types of messages used in this orchestration. Lines 1–6 contain an example of the initial message that can be used to trigger the orchestration. This purchase request has been numbered "123," and it is forwarded as-is to the manager's input queue. From the manager's output queue, the orchestration retrieves the approval message shown in lines 8–11, where the Number element matches the previous request. In this case, the purchase has been approved, as indicated by the "Yes" value in the Approved field. The orchestration then applies the transformation map in Fig. 9.9 to construct the final request shown in lines 13–19.

In summary, correlations are a critically important, but often poorly understood concept in orchestrations. The fact is that every non-activating receive connected to a unidirectional port requires the use of a correlation. The reason for this should now be clear: multiple orchestration instances listening on the same port will compete for the messages received on that port; it is therefore necessary to have a correlation that allows the messaging platform to determine which instance should get each message. The fact that the messaging platform plays a key role in this process is the reason why correlation properties need to be promoted.

9.3 Exception Handling

In orchestrations, as in many other kinds of processes, there is always the possibility that things do not run exactly as they would be expected to. At run-time, there may be particular circumstances, operating conditions, or external events which interfere with the execution of an orchestration instance. For example, a typical problem encountered in practice is that of an orchestration which gets stuck waiting for a response that will never arrive; this may be because there is something wrong with the way the response is being received, but most often it has to do with some previous error that occurred in the orchestration and that prevented an earlier request from reaching its destination.

The occurrence of errors in orchestrations is, unfortunately, more frequent than it would be desirable. Especially for large and complex orchestrations involving interactions with several external systems, it may become hard to ensure that everything is correctly configured and that all systems will be available and will respond to the orchestration when needed. As with traditional programming, where it is hard to debug large programs, it is hard to avoid the occurrence of faults in large orchestrations which implement complex behavior. Fortunately, as in traditional programming, there are ways to prepare an orchestration to deal with the occurrence of errors at run-time. This is referred to as *exception handling*.

An exception may represent a particular kind of *system error* raised during execution. For example, if an orchestration is trying to invoke a Web service and the invocation fails because the Web service is unreachable, or because the Web service raised an exception during execution, then it is possible to catch this exception in the orchestration and process it accordingly, rather than just letting the error abort the execution of the current process instance.

Alternatively, an exception may represent a condition or *logical error* that points to a problem in the process rather than in the applications. For example, during execution the orchestration may find that a given customer does not exist in a database, or that an employee issued a purchase order for a larger quantity than it is allowed. In these cases the problem is not technical, but logical, and it is possible to deal with these run-time problems using exception handling as well.

Fig. 9.10 The scope shape

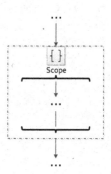

9.3.1 The Scope Shape

The key to using exception handling in orchestrations is to include a special kind of shape, called the *scope* shape. This shape is illustrated in Fig. 9.10. Basically, the scope shape is a block of orchestration logic enclosed within curly braces. This block is meant to represent a *local scope* within the *global scope* of the orchestration. The idea is to have the possibility of declaring and using local messages, variables, and correlations sets that are not accessible outside of this block. Therefore the scope shape is similar to the concept of having local scopes delimited by curly braces in traditional programming languages such as C or Java.

An interesting feature of the scope shape is that it can also be used as a *try-catch* construct for exception handling. In this case, the main block within the curly braces works as a try block, and it contains the orchestration logic that may raise one or more exceptions. Below the main block, and as illustrated in Fig. 9.11, it is possible to have an arbitrary number of *exception handlers*, or catch blocks. The idea is that each exception handler catches a different type of exception, and may contain just about any orchestration logic to treat that exception. In general, it is possible to implement rather sophisticated ways of handling an exception, including interacting with external systems if necessary.

For example, if the main block in the scope shape invokes a Web service, then it may raise exceptions such as SoapException or SoapHeaderException. There could be one catch block to deal with exceptions of type SoapException and another catch block to deal with exceptions of type SoapHeaderException. However, in C# the class SoapHeaderException is a *subclass* of SoapException, so the catch block for SoapHeaderException should be placed *before* the catch block for SoapException. Otherwise, if the catch block for SoapException appears first, then both SoapException and SoapHeaderException will be caught by that exception handler.

This means that when an exception occurs in the scope block, the orchestration engine goes through the available exceptions handlers, in the order they appear after the scope block. The first exception handler that is able to catch the exception is the one to be invoked. Therefore, the first exception handlers to appear after the main block should be the ones which catch the most specific (i.e., subclass) exceptions,

Fig. 9.11 Catch blocks in a
scope shape

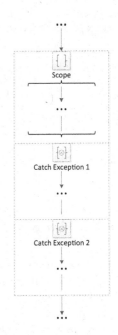

while the ones which catch the most general (i.e., superclass) exceptions should be
the last ones to appear. In particular, it is possible to include an exception handler
for System.Exception. Since System.Exception is the base class for all exceptions,
such exception handler is able to catch *any* kind of exception. This is equivalent to
catch(System.Exception ex){...} in C#, where ex is an arbitrary argument name.

9.3.2 Nested Scopes

As mentioned above, a scope block may contain just about any orchestration logic,
including send shapes, receive shapes, construct message shapes, etc. In particular,
a scope block may contain other scope shapes. This opens up the possibility of
devising an orchestration as a structure of nested scopes, which is in accordance with
the nested structure of orchestrations as explained in Sect. 8.1. Naturally, an inner
scope may have its own exception handlers, independently of the outer scope. If an
exception is raised in an inner scope and there is no appropriate exception handler
to catch it, then the exception goes out to the outer scope, where there may be some
catch block for it. If not, then the exception escalates to the main orchestration,
causing the orchestration instance to suspend execution.

Figure 9.12 illustrates this behavior. The inner scope throws an exception which,
in principle, should be caught by one of its exception handlers. However, if that
does not happen, then the exception goes to the outer scope which has its own
exception handlers as well. In case the exception is not caught by any of these

Fig. 9.12 Flow of an
unhandled exception

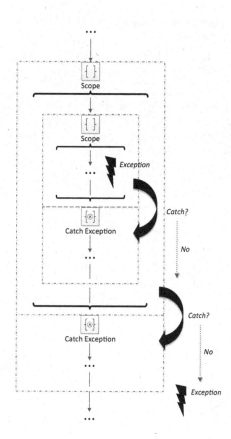

exception handlers, then it goes out to the main orchestration where it will result
in a run-time error that suspends the execution of the orchestration instance.

If the exception is caught by an exception handler, then the catch block is
executed and the orchestration flow continues after the scope shape. For example, if
the exception in Fig. 9.12 is caught by the exception handler in the inner scope, then
after executing the catch block the orchestration continues the flow after that inner
scope (and still within the outer scope). On the other hand, if the exception is caught
by the exception handler in the outer scope, then after executing the catch block the
orchestration resumes the main flow after the outer scope.

Naturally, if there is no exception, then the orchestration just skips all catch
blocks. The catch blocks will come into play only if an exception is raised.

9.3.3 The Throw Exception Shape

When an exception is caught by an exception handler, the catch block executes and
after that the orchestration carries on with its flow. However, in some cases the flow

Fig. 9.13 Re-throwing an
exception

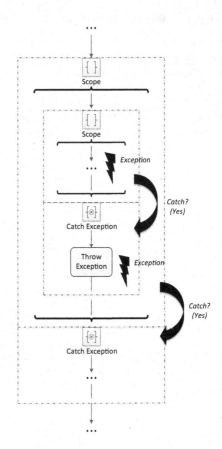

should not be allowed to continue, and instead the exception should be handled and
then *re-thrown* to an outer scope for further treatment. Figure 9.13 illustrates the re-
throw of an exception inside a catch block. Basically the exception is raised inside
the inner scope and is caught by an exception handler within that scope. Then the
catch block re-throws the exception by means of a *throw exception* shape, so now
the exception can be caught by the outer scope.

In this example, the throw exception shape in the inner catch block of Fig. 9.13
was used to re-throw the same exception that was caught to the outer scope.
However, the throw exception shape could have been used to throw a different
exception from the one that was caught. In fact, a catch block may involuntarily
raise an exception if something goes wrong when handling a previous exception.

For example, suppose that there is a scope with shapes to invoke a Web service in
order to book a hotel reservation. Also, suppose that after the reservation was booked
successfully, something went wrong—an exception was raised—and the reservation
has to be canceled. A catch block can be used to cancel the hotel reservation by
invoking another method of the same Web service. However, suppose that when the
catch block is about to cancel the reservation, the Web service is no longer available,

and a new exception is raised. In this case, this second exception has been raised involuntarily, rather than explicitly through the use of a throw exception shape. In principle, there should be an outer scope with an appropriate catch block to deal with this exception. If there is not, then the exception will escalate to the main flow and it will suspend the execution of the orchestration instance.

In most cases, an exception will be raised when there is some unexpected, low-level technical problem, such as a system error. However, it is also possible to make use of exception handling to deal with situations that arise during the execution of a business process, which do not involve any system malfunction but may represent scenarios that were not supposed to happen from a logical or business point of view. That is when the throw exception shape becomes most useful, because it can be used to interrupt the current flow and deal with the problem in some way.

In Fig. 9.13 we used the throw exception shape in a catch block, but of course this shape can be used anywhere in an orchestration. Typically, it will be used inside the main block (i.e., curly braces) of a scope shape that includes one or more exception handlers, as in Fig. 9.11. Under certain conditions, and not necessarily because those conditions are infrequent but simply because their occurrence might be undesirable, the orchestration logic within the scope block will raise an exception to be handled by one of the catch blocks. The catch block may be able to handle the exception and let the orchestration flow resume after that, or it may terminate the orchestration instance if it is impossible to continue.

9.3.4   Exception Objects

When a throw exception shape throws an exception, this exception is an instance of some exception class. The base class for all exceptions is System.Exception, so the exception being thrown may be an instance of System.Exception, but more often it is an instance of some subclass of System.Exception. The more specific the exception is, the more descriptive it is and, in general, the use of specific (i.e., subclass) exceptions allows a more fine-grained control of the errors that may occur at run-time. Still, by way of System.Exception, all exceptions share some common features. Namely, all exception classes have a data member of type string called Message. This field is intended to carry a user-friendly description of the error and, despite its name, should not be confused with an orchestration message.

So, in order to use the throw exception shape, one needs to create an object of type System.Exception or one of its subclasses. This is the object which will be "thrown" when the throw exception shape is executed. On the other hand, this is also the object which will be "caught" by an exception handler, if there is an exception handler for such exception class. For example, suppose that one wants to throw an exception with the error message "quantity is above limit." Then one could create an object as an instance of the System.Exception class and set the desired error message in that object. The object would be thrown by a throw exception shape and subsequently caught by an exception handler. Inside the catch block, the orchestration logic will have access to the exception object that was caught and will be able to retrieve the error message contained in that object.

Usually, an exception handler retrieves the error message from the exception object and records it in an event log or log file so that it is possible to keep track of run-time errors, find their causes, and eventually eliminate them. However, if a catch block is configured to record the error message in an event log, then all instances from that orchestration will record their errors in the same event log. This creates a problem if the error message to be recorded is something as simple as "quantity is above limit." In this case, it will be impossible to know in which particular orchestration instance the error occurred.

Therefore, it is often necessary to include additional data in an error message to allow a system administrator to investigate the cause of the exception. These data should make it possible to identify the orchestration instance where the error occurred. For example, if the error is "quantity is above limit" then at least the actual quantity value should be included, in order to look for the orchestration instance (or the set of orchestration instances) which had that quantity value. If possible, all data pertaining to an orchestration instance should be logged when an exception occurs. However, this may also create some privacy concerns if the data being logged are sensitive for the business point of view.

In the next section we present a simple example where we do not consider such privacy issues. In practice, one may choose to record only those data that are useful to "debug" an orchestration, without getting into sensitive business details. On the other hand, most integration platforms provide their own tracking and tracing tools, so in the event of an exception—and especially for those exceptions which are not caught by the orchestration and therefore result in an execution failure—it will be possible to use those monitoring tools to check which orchestrations instances failed and, if needed, what went wrong in each of them.

9.3.5 An Example

Suppose that there is an orchestration to check if the quantity being specified in a purchase request is within a certain limit. If the quantity is up to 500 units, then the purchase request will be forwarded to an ERP system via a send port. Otherwise, if the quantity is above 500, then an exception will be thrown and caught by an exception handler. This exception handler will record an error message in a system event log. Figure 9.14 illustrates this orchestration.

The orchestration begins as usual with an activating receive that receives a purchase request. The schema for this message contains three elements: the first element identifies the employee submitting the request, the second element describes the product to be purchased, and the third element contains the requested quantity. Once the purchase request is received, the orchestration enters a scope shape which has a main block and one catch block as well.

Inside the main block, there is a decide shape to check the quantity in the request. The left branch contains a condition with an logical expression to test whether the

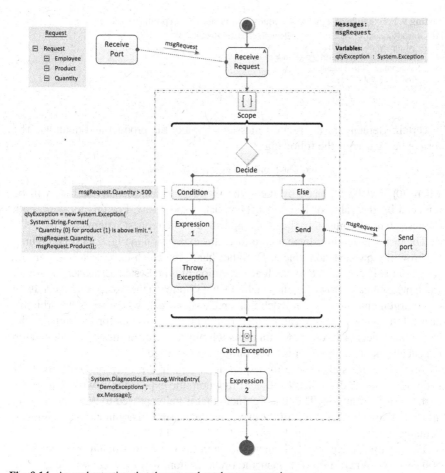

Fig. 9.14 An orchestration that throws and catches an exception

quantity is above 500. (For this condition to work, the Quantity element in the request schema must have been *distinguished*, as we did, for example, with the Fahrenheit and Celsius elements in Sect. 6.5.1.) If the condition is true, then the orchestration follows the left branch; otherwise, it follows the right branch.

On the left branch, there is an expression shape and a throw exception shape. The main goal of this branch is to throw an exception but, as explained in the previous section, a throw exception shape will throw an exception object, and this object needs to be created first. The purpose of having the expression shape is precisely to create the exception object. In the example of Fig. 9.14, the exception object is kept in an orchestration variable of type System.Exception called qtyException.

The exception object qtyException is being created in the expression shape by means of a constructor which takes a string as input. This string is used to initialize the error message in the exception. In this case, the string will contain the values

Listing 9.2 Example of a purchase request that raises an exception

```
1    <ns0:Request xmlns:ns0="http://DemoExceptions.Request">
2      <Employee>P45</Employee>
3      <Product>Printer Cartridge</Product>
4      <Quantity>600</Quantity>
5    </ns0:Request>
```

of certain elements in the request message, namely the product and quantity. The format being used is the following:

"Quantity {0} for product {1} is above limit."

where {0} will be replaced by the value of msgRequest.Quantity, and {1} will be replaced by the value of msgRequest.Product, respectively. For this to work, both of these elements must have been distinguished in the request schema.

The throw exception shape that follows this expression in Fig. 9.14 is configured to throw the qtyException object. On other hand, the catch exception block in the scope shape is configured to catch an exception of type System.Exception, so it will catch qtyException. However, the catch block will refer to the exception object using some argument name, as in catch(System.Exception ex), where ex is an arbitrary name. In this example, the catch block is configured to use ex for the name of the exception object. Therefore, within the catch block, the error message contained in the exception object can be retrieved through ex.Message.

Now it becomes clear what the expression shape in the catch block of Fig. 9.14 is doing. With a call to the WriteEntry() function, the expression is writing an entry to the system event log. The first argument that is being passed to WriteEntry() is an arbitrary name for the source of the event, while the second argument is a string that contains the error message to be written to the event log.

For example, the purchase request shown in Listing 9.2 has quantity value above 500 (line 4). When used to trigger the orchestration, this message will lead to an exception being thrown. The exception will be caught by the catch block, and the following event will be written to the event log: "Quantity 600 for product Printer Cartridge is above limit.". In the Windows environment, this event can be seen using the *Event Viewer* administrative tool, specifically in the "Application" log.

9.4   Transactions

In Sect. 3.2 we have seen that the concept of transaction, which has its origin in database systems, can be extended to messaging systems. In this case, the transaction may include a number of messages to be consumed and/or produced, as long as the messages to be consumed do not depend on the messages to be produced, as in a request–response interaction (as explained in Sect. 3.2, a request–response interaction cannot be enclosed in a single transaction because the request will not be sent until the transaction commits, and therefore the response cannot be received within the same transaction). Typically, message transactions are used in solicit–response interactions, where the client application receives a request and produces a response. In this scenario, the use of a message transaction ensures that no request is left without a response because, if the transaction fails, a *rollback* will take place. This rollback consists in returning all consumed messages to their original queues and destroying any messages produced within the transaction. After the rollback, the client application will have the opportunity to execute the transaction again from the beginning, as if nothing had happened.

The concept of transaction can also be extended to orchestrations, but in this case the mechanisms for executing transactions and for recovering from failed transactions are completely different. Usually, an orchestration is an implementation of some business process, and since a business process may take days, weeks, or even months to complete, so too an orchestration may take long to finish. Consider the example of the business process depicted in Fig. 9.4 on page 238. This is a purchase approval process, where the manager may take several days to approve a given purchase request. The process is implemented by the orchestration shown in Fig. 9.8 on page 244. If the manager takes several days to approve a purchase request, then this means that there will be an instance of the orchestration which will be running for several days. Running this orchestration instance as a transaction is impractical, because it would mean having a transaction that is active for several days.

In database systems, a transaction will lock certain resources (e.g., a row or a table) during a period of time, and those resources are released when the transaction commits (or rolls back). In the meantime, other transactions are unable to access the same resources, and they must wait for the running transaction to complete its execution. It is easy to see that such behavior would not work well with *long-running transactions* in orchestrations, because it would mean that an orchestration could lock resources over a long period of time, preventing other running orchestrations from carrying out their work. Instead, an orchestration should commit its actions as it goes along, in order to release the resources that it is using for other running orchestrations. In practice, this means that a long-running transaction may have to be partitioned into a set of short-lived transactions.

However, if a long-running transaction is substituted by a set of short-lived transactions, then the long-running transaction is not atomic anymore (in the sense of executing all or nothing), because parts of this long-running transaction are being executed and committed by shorter transactions. This creates a problem, because a long-running transaction, as a whole, is meant to be atomic (otherwise, it cannot be called a transaction). But how can a long-running transaction be atomic if parts of it are being committed separately? For example, if a long-running transaction is partitioned into three short transactions, and after the first two transactions complete successfully the third transaction fails, then what should happen to the two transactions that have already committed? The answer is that they need to be *compensated*, i.e., their effects need to be logically undone, even though they have already committed. This is referred to as *compensation*, and it is different from rollback in the sense that rollback takes place *before* a transaction commits, while

Fig. 9.15 A compensation
block in a scope shape

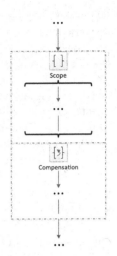

compensation takes place *after* a transaction commits. Compensation refers to the
possibility of undoing the effects of actions that have been already committed.

9.4.1   Revisiting the Scope Shape

In Sect. 9.3.1, particularly in Fig. 9.11 on page 248, we have seen that a scope shape
can have one or more catch blocks that work as exception handlers. The scope shape
also plays a key role with respect to transactions, since it can be used to delimit a
long-running transaction within an orchestration. It can also be used as a container
for other transactions. Figure 9.15 shows that a scope shape, when used to delimit
a transaction, can have a special-purpose compensation block. This compensation
block is intended to be invoked in case the actions that have been executed within
the scope need to be compensated. This could only happen when this scope has
already been completely and successfully executed, but an error or exception at a
later stage create the need to undo the actions of this scope.

9.4.2   The Compensate Shape

Typically, the use of a compensation block in a scope shape makes sense if the scope
is part of a long-running transaction. Then, should the long-running transaction fail,
its internal scopes (i.e., the short-lived transactions) will need to be compensated.
Figure 9.16 illustrates such scenario. Here, there is a scope labeled "outer scope" to
represent a long-running transaction, and there is a scope labeled "inner scope" to
represent a short-lived transaction. Executing the outer scope means executing the

Fig. 9.16 Use of compensate shape to invoke compensation block

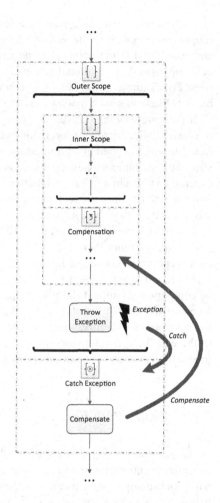

shapes within the curly braces of the outer scope; in a similar way, executing the inner scope consists in executing the shapes inside its curly braces.

Assuming that the inner scope has executed successfully, execution will proceed to the next shape in the outer scope which, in this case, is a throw exception shape. An exception is thrown and caught by the catch block of the outer scope, which works as an exception handler. Inside the exception handler, there is a *compensate shape*. This means that any inner transactions will be compensated in order to retract to a consistent state. In this specific example, only a single inner scope is to be compensated. The compensation block in the inner scope may contain any orchestration logic; for example, it may communicate with external systems in order to nullify the effects of the actions that have been performed within that scope.

The goal of compensation is to undo the effects of all committed actions in order to bring the orchestration back to an execution state that is equivalent to the state of the orchestration that was in place before the long-running transaction (i.e., the outer scope) had begun. Since the actions of the inner scope have already been performed and committed at the point when an exception was raised, those actions need to be compensated by additional actions in order to nullify the effects of the previous ones. For example, if the inner scope booked a flight ticket, then its compensation block is likely to send a message in order to cancel that flight booking.

If the long-running transaction includes multiple inner scopes, then compensation takes place in reverse order of execution. Figure 9.17 extends the previous example with a second inner transaction inside the outer scope. An exception occurs after the two inner scopes have completed execution. This means that when the exception is caught and handled, both of these scopes will have to be compensated. However, since inner scope 1 has been executed before inner scope 2, then inner scope 2 is the first to be compensated, followed by inner scope 1.

It should be noted that in Fig. 9.17 the exception occurs after inner scope 2. Therefore, both inner scope 2 and inner scope 1 will be compensated. However, if the exception occurs within inner scope 2, then this scope does not run to the end. Its execution is interrupted by the exception, and therefore inner scope 2 cannot be compensated, since it did not complete. In this case, only inner scope 1 would be compensated. On the other hand, if the exception occurs in inner scope 1, then there is nothing to compensate, since none of the inner scopes have been performed to the end. In general, compensation can only be invoked for those scopes (i.e., transactions) which have run successfully till the end (i.e., committed).

9.4.3   Using Both Exception and Compensation Handlers

In the example of Fig. 9.17 there are three scope shapes. The outer scope has an exception handler but no compensation handler. On the other hand, each inner scope has its own compensation handler, but has no exception handlers. In practice, it often happens that a scope has either a set of exception handlers (there may be multiple ones, as explained in Sect. 9.3.1) or a compensation handler (there is at most one, since only one form of compensation can be defined for a given transaction). However, nothing prevents a scope from having both types of handlers. Figure 9.18 illustrates the general structure of a scope shape.

The catch blocks are meant to handle any exception that occurs within the scope itself, and there may be multiple catch blocks for different exceptions. On the other hand, the compensation block is meant as a recovery plan, should the need arise to compensate the actions of this scope. Such need can only arise after this scope has been executed, and the compensation block can only be invoked from some larger transaction that includes this scope, as in the example of Fig. 9.17. If everything runs well, it may be the case that none of these blocks is actually invoked during the execution of an orchestration instance. If no exceptions occur within the scope, then no exception handler will be invoked; and if no errors occur after the scope, then the compensation handler will not be invoked.

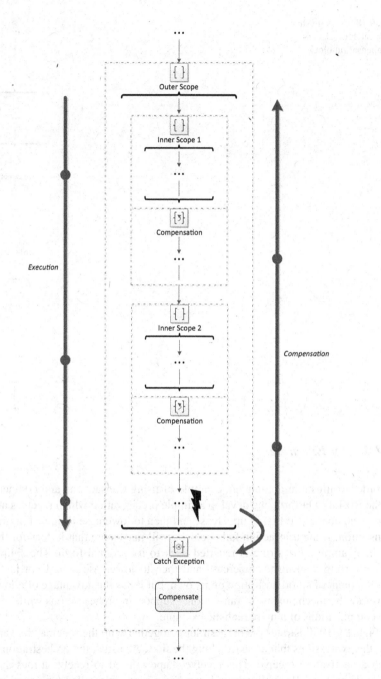

Fig. 9.17 Compensation in reverse order of execution

Fig. 9.18 A scope shape
with catch blocks and a
compensation block

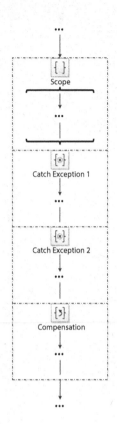

9.4.4 An Example

In order to illustrate a complete example of using transactions and compensation in the BizTalk platform, we develop a simple orchestration which receives an input string and converts it first to uppercase and then to lowercase inside a long-running transaction. If the transaction fails (and we will make sure that it does for the sake of the example), the string is reverted back to its original form. The simple task of converting a string to uppercase and then to lowercase would not justify the development of an orchestration on its own, but it has the advantage of allowing to illustrate the mechanisms of transactional support in orchestrations while avoiding the complications of a more realistic example.

Figure 9.19 illustrates the orchestration, together with the schema, the variables, and the expressions that are used along the flow. As usual, the orchestration begins with an activating receive. This receive shape is used to receive a message with a simple schema. Basically, the schema has a root node called Input, and a single element called Text, which contains the string to be converted to uppercase and then to lowercase. In this schema, the Text element is defined as a distinguished property, so that it becomes accessible to all expressions in the orchestration.

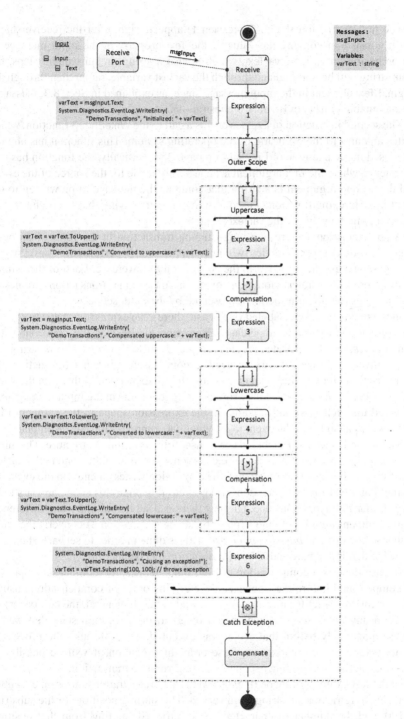

Fig. 9.19 An orchestration with compensation

The first expression shape (Expression 1) appears right after the receive shape, and it consists in copying the value of the Text property in the input message to the orchestration variable varText, which is also a string. In subsequent steps, the input string will be manipulated through the varText variable, rather than through the original Text element in the input message since, as explained in Sect. 8.3, messages are immutable objects in BizTalk orchestrations.

The second instruction in Expression 1 is a call to the WriteEntry() function, which writes an entry to the event log of the operating system. This function has already been used in the example of Fig. 9.14 on page 253. Basically, the function has two arguments, where the first argument is an arbitrary name for the source of the event, and the second argument is a string that contains the message to be written to the event log. Here, the function is used to write an entry saying that the orchestration is initializing the value of the varText variable.

After Expression 1 there is a long-running transaction in the form of an outer scope. This outer scope includes two inner scopes: one to perform the conversion to uppercase and another to perform the conversion to lowercase. Each of these inner scopes represents a transaction on its own. These two inner transactions are nested into the long-running transaction represented by the outer scope.

In the first inner scope, labeled Uppercase, there is an expression shape to convert the contents of varText to uppercase (Expression 2). Besides the conversion, the same expression shape writes an entry to the event log saying that the string has been converted. In case there is a need to compensate this inner transaction, the compensation block includes an expression shape (Expression 3) that sets the value of the varText variable back to the original string that came in the input message that triggered the orchestration. In addition, the expression shape in the compensation block writes an entry to the event log saying that compensation has taken place.

The second inner scope, labeled Lowercase, follows a similar structure. This inner scope contains an expression shape (Expression 4) to convert the contents of varText to lowercase. Besides the conversion, the expression writes an entry to the event log saying that the string has been converted. Up to this point this scope appears to be very similar to the previous one, but now there is a subtle but important difference: in the compensation block, the expression shape (Expression 5) converts the value of the varText variable *back to uppercase*. This is done in order to set varText back to the value that it had before this inner transaction had begun.

In case there is a compensation of both inner scopes, the Lowercase scope will be compensated before the Uppercase scope. This order of compensation ensures that the varText variable ends up with its initial value. In general, the compensation block in any given scope shape should revert to the execution state that was in place immediately before that scope was executed. Then, through the process of compensation, which works in reverse order of execution, it will be possible to backtrack across several inner scopes of a long-running transaction.

In the last expression shape (Expression 6), the orchestration causes an exception by trying to retrieve a substring from varText. The starting position for the substring is 100, and the number of characters to be retrieved, starting from that position, is 100. This means that if varText holds a string of less than 200 characters, such

Listing 9.3 Example of input message

```
1  <ns0:Input xmlns:ns0="http://DemoTransactions.Input">
2    <Text>Printer Cartridge</Text>
3  </ns0:Input>
```

Listing 9.4 Events recorded in the system log

```
1  Initialized: Printer Cartridge
2  Converted to uppercase: PRINTER CARTRIDGE
3  Converted to lowercase: printer cartridge
4  Causing an exception!
5  Compensated lowercase: PRINTER CARTRIDGE
6  Compensated uppercase: Printer Cartridge
```

substring cannot be retrieved and an exception will be raised. This exception is of type ArgumentOutOfRangeException, but the type is not important since the catch block of the outer scope is configured to catch a general exception.

Before Expression 6 attempts to retrieve the substring, there is an instruction to write an entry to the event log saying that the orchestration is causing an exception (even though such exception will only be raised if the text string in msgInput contains less than 200 characters). When the exception is thrown, execution of the outer scope is interrupted and the exception is caught by the exception handler of that scope (but only because this exception handler is able to catch that kind of exception; otherwise, the exception would escalate to the global scope of the orchestration, which would cause the orchestration instance to become suspended).

The exception handler at the bottom of Fig. 9.19 could have included any orchestration logic, but in this case it contains a single shape—a compensate shape—to specify that all nested transactions that have been previously executed should be compensated. If the orchestration flow enters this catch block, it is a sign that the outer transaction has failed, and therefore the nested transactions should be compensated. In this example, the exception occurs after both inner scopes have been executed, and therefore both of them will need to be compensated.

Since compensation is carried out in reverse order of execution, the value of the varText variable will be converted back to uppercase (during compensation of the Lowercase scope) and then set to its initial value (during compensation of the Uppercase scope). Listing 9.3 shows an example of an input message that can be provided as input to the orchestration of Fig. 9.19. The string to be converted is "Printer Cartridge." This string is less than 200 characters long, so it will raise an exception in Expression 6. Such exception will trigger compensation.

For the input message shown in Listing 9.3, the orchestration will leave a trace in the system log with the events shown in Listing 9.4. Line 1 is the result of Expression 1 and shows the initial value for the varText variable. Lines 2 and 3 are the result of executing the inner scopes Uppercase and Lowercase, respectively. Line 4 contains the event that is recorded by Expression 6, just before the exception is raised. After that, lines 5 and 6 show the result of compensation: the first to be compensated is the Lowercase scope, followed by the Uppercase scope; the compensation handlers for these scopes are invoked in this order. The last value of the varText variable in line 6 is equal to the initial one, in line 1.

9.4.5 A Note About the Previous Example

In the previous example, the compensation handlers of both inner scopes change the value of a global orchestration variable (varText). Due to a limitation of the BizTalk platform, these changes are not visible outside the compensation blocks. This means that after compensation, the value of the varText variable will still be in lowercase. This happens because, at the beginning of each compensation block, the variable is temporarily initialized with the value that it had at the time when the scope finished (i.e., committed). During compensation, this value can be changed as desired, but these changes are not visible after the compensation block has run.

Therefore, if one would read the value of the varText variable after the outer scope, this value would be the same as before the compensation has started (i.e., varText would be in lowercase). This behavior only applies to orchestration variables (or variables that exist in an outer scope with respect to the scope that is being compensated). If instead of an orchestration variable or outer-scope variable we would be changing an external resource (such as a database record, for example), then the changes in the compensation block would modify the external resource, and these changes would be certainly visible from outside the compensation block.

9.4.6 Long-Running vs. Atomic Transactions

In this section, we have referred to every transaction as a long-running transaction. For example, the outer scope in Fig. 9.19 is a long-running transaction, and the inner scopes that are nested inside that outer scope are long-running transactions as well. In general, a long-running transaction is a construct that allows the specification of custom orchestration logic for exception handling and compensation. A long-running transaction also allows nesting of other long-running transactions inside it, as in Fig. 9.19, and this provides a means to partition a long transaction into several steps to be committed separately. However, such long-running transaction is no longer atomic, and the fact that it may fail when certain steps have already been committed is the reason why compensation is needed.

In orchestrations it is possible to use also *atomic transactions*, which work in a way that is more similar to traditional transactions. They have a single commit phase at the end, and it is not possible to have any nested transactions. They are "atomic" in the sense that all or nothing is executed, and they are also "isolated" from other transactions, meaning that no transaction that may interfere with the same resources can be executed at the same time. This is in contrast with long-running transactions, which are neither atomic nor isolated. However, with respect to the remaining ACID properties [27], both long-running transactions and atomic transactions ensure consistency and durability. In long-running transactions, consistency is ensured by compensation mechanisms; in atomic transactions, consistency is ensured by automatic rollback to a previous execution state.

In practice, integration platforms such as BizTalk record the state of an orchestration at several points during execution. These are called *persistence points*. If something goes wrong during execution, it is possible to recover a previous state of the orchestration by reloading one of those persistence points. This possibility is the basis for automatic rollback in atomic transactions. If a scope is configured as an atomic transaction, and if it fails during execution (e.g., because an exception is thrown), then the execution engine will automatically reload the state of the orchestration that was in place before the scope was executed. In atomic transactions, rollback takes place automatically if an exception occurs.

This is in contrast with long-running transactions, where there needs to be a catch block with some orchestration logic in order to handle the exception and clean up whatever has been done before (as in the outer scope in Fig. 9.19). In an atomic transaction there are no catch blocks, because the behavior in case of failure is already defined: it rolls back automatically to a previous execution state. However, an atomic transaction may have a compensation block, if it is nested inside a long-running transaction; in this case, if the outer transaction fails, then it may be necessary to compensate the inner transactions, regardless of whether they are long-running or atomic. In general, a long-running transaction may contain other long-running transactions and atomic transactions as well; in contrast, an atomic transaction cannot have any nested transactions, since it is atomic.

In the example of Fig. 9.19, the Uppercase scope and the Lowercase scope could be configured either as long-running transactions or as atomic transactions. In this example it does not make much of a difference since none of these scopes includes nested transactions, nor do they include any special form of error handling. When the exception occurs in Expression 6, both of these inner scopes will be compensated regardless of whether they are long-running transactions or atomic transactions. However, if these scopes would be configured as atomic transactions, and an exception would occur in Expression 2 or Expression 4, then the corresponding scope would be rolled back automatically by the execution engine.

In particular, assuming that the Uppercase scope and the Lowercase scope have been configured as atomic transactions, if the exception occurs in Expression 2 then the Uppercase scope is rolled back and nothing happens to the Lowercase scope, since it did not even start. On the other hand, if the exception occurs in Expression 4 then the Lowercase scope is rolled back and the Uppercase scope will be compensated. If the exception happens in Expression 6, both inner scopes will be compensated in reverse order of execution, as before.

Another reason why the Uppercase and Lowercase scopes could be atomic transactions is that they do not interact with external resources. So, in case failure, it is possible to roll back just by reloading a previous state of the orchestration. However, if a scope interacts with external applications, then the automatic rollback performed by the execution engine may not be enough to ensure consistency. The execution state of the orchestration will be recovered, but the effects on external applications may still remain. In this case, it may be necessary to use an exception handler with a set of appropriate actions in order to reset the state of the external applications as well. But then the scope should be a long-running transaction, since atomic transactions do not allow for custom exception handling.

A scenario where atomic transactions are of much use is in distributed transactions involving transactional components. In Sect. 3.6.3 we mentioned the possibility of having a Distributed Transaction Coordinator (DTC) to manage transactions across several kinds of systems, such as messaging systems, databases, and file systems that support transactions. In this case, an atomic transaction can be used to implement a distributed transaction, and the rollback of the atomic transaction will trigger a rollback in all components associated with that distributed transaction.

However, as in the case of message transactions, an atomic scope cannot include request–response interactions (in the form of send and receive shapes) where the response is an answer to a request that has been issued within the same transaction. As explained in Sect. 3.2, and the same principle applies here, the request will not be sent until the transaction commits, so the response cannot possibly be received within the same transaction. It is somewhat surprising that, even though transactions in orchestrations are so different from transactions in messaging systems, the same principle would apply here, but one must recall that an orchestration is, after all, a way of specifying the logic of messages exchanges between applications.

9.5 Conclusion

In this chapter we have discussed the most sophisticated mechanisms associated with orchestration flow, namely correlations, exception handling, and transactions. The concept of correlations is often poorly understood, but it is an absolutely essential mechanism to build orchestrations that are able to carry out message exchanges across multiple send and receive ports. Basically, the need for correlations has to do with the fact that an orchestration can be instantiated multiple times, and therefore it becomes necessary to determine which instance should receive a given incoming message. There is no need to specify a correlation for an activating receive since, by definition, an activating receive creates a new orchestration instance. However, for other receive shapes along the flow, these are either coupled with send shapes through self-correlating ports (such as bidirectional ports) or they must use (i.e., "follow") a correlation that has been initialized by some previous shape, usually a send shape. In some practical scenarios, a correlation is initialized as early as the activating receive, and then used in all subsequent receive shapes.

While correlations are used in almost every scenario, the use of exception handling and transactions is optional, but they bring a new degree of robustness and reliability to orchestrations. In particular, exception handling (in the form of scopes with catch blocks) provides a convenient and familiar way to build fault-tolerance into an orchestration, and in some cases it can be used simply as a mechanism to control the orchestration flow, as in the example of Sect. 9.3.5. On the other hand, transactions improve reliability by ensuring that, whatever happens, the orchestration, and the external applications it interacts with, will be left in a consistent state. For practical reasons, orchestrations use a special form of transactions, known as long-running transactions. These are neither atomic nor isolated, since they allow work to proceed and be committed in chunks, which take the form of nested transactions. In case of failure, some chunks may have to be undone if they have been already committed, and hence the need for compensation mechanisms.

In this chapter we have discussed these mechanisms in detail, and we have seen their use in some practical examples with the BizTalk platform. A natural question that may arise at this point is whether knowledge about how these mechanisms work in the BizTalk platform translates into knowledge about how to use the same mechanisms in other platforms. As a matter of fact, it does, and in the next chapters we will see how the same concepts are present in other platforms and languages for modeling and executing business processes as orchestrations.

Chapter 10
Orchestrations with BPEL

In previous chapters, particularly in Chaps. 8 and 9, we have studied a wide range of constructs that can be used to design the flow of an orchestration. These constructs have been represented graphically by means of certain shapes, but more important than being able to represent them, it is fundamental to understand the concepts that underlie those constructs. For example, the use of an activating receive shape means that a new orchestration instance will be created when a certain message is received. As another example, the use of a correlation presumes that there is a set of messages which share some common data with exactly the same values (the correlation id). The use of certain shapes in an orchestration therefore requires a good understanding of the concepts that are embedded in those constructs. For example, a good knowledge of what compensation is and how it works is essential in order to use transactions in orchestrations, as explained in Sect. 9.4.

At some point one may ask: where did these concepts come from? Who invented them? Are they specific to a particular integration platform, or can they be found in all integration platforms? The answer to these questions is that the set of constructs that are currently available to design the orchestration flow are the result of several years of development, maturing, and refinement of ideas. This effort has been made by both industry and academia, but eventually it was only when a group of major IT vendors joined forces that it was possible to arrive at a commonly agreed set of constructs. The result of these efforts has materialized into a new standard known as the Business Process Execution Language (BPEL) [19]. Most, if not all, of the constructs that we have described in Chaps. 8 and 9 are based either directly on BPEL or on ideas that preceded and eventually led to BPEL.

In Chap. 7 we have described how business processes can be implemented on top of a heterogeneous application infrastructure through several layers of services (see for example Fig. 7.6 on page 199). These services are built on top of one another, i.e., a higher-level service can be built as a composition of lower-level ones. As we have seen in Chap. 7, particularly in Fig. 7.3 on page 191, a service composition can be implemented as an orchestration, which in turn exposes itself as a new service. We have also seen that, at the topmost layer, the business process itself can be implemented as an orchestration of services. Therefore, there is a close

D.R. Ferreira, *Enterprise Systems Integration*, DOI 10.1007/978-3-642-40796-3_10,   269
© Springer-Verlag Berlin Heidelberg 2013

interplay between orchestrations and services: an orchestration is a series of service invocations, and an orchestration can also be exposed as a service.

It was with these ideas in mind that several IT vendors saw a need to have a language to specify orchestrations as a series of service invocations. In addition, at a time when Web services and their interface definition language WSDL (see Sect. 6.4.3) were so popular, it was clear that the new language to define orchestrations should bear some relationship to WSDL. In particular, the new language should make it easy to invoke service interfaces described with WSDL, and it should also allow exposing an orchestration as a Web service through a WSDL interface. Now, the fact that WSDL is an interface definition language based on XML suggests that the new orchestration definition language, which is to have a close relationship to WSDL, should also be based on XML.

Around 2001, both IBM and Microsoft had their own XML-based languages for orchestrating Web services, and other players were pushing their own languages too. There was not yet a consensus, and each vendor was defining its own constructs and mechanisms for designing service orchestrations. However, it became apparent that these different initiatives were trying to address basically the same needs. Eventually, the two initiatives from IBM and Microsoft merged into the BPEL language in 2003, which succeeded in gathering the support of several other vendors as well. After being submitted to OASIS[1] for standardization, BPEL kept being developed and improved. The BPEL standard was issued in April 2007 with the name "WS-BPEL 2.0," where the "WS-" prefix highlights the focus on orchestrations which comprise mainly the invocation of Web services. Since then, BPEL has been implemented by several vendors, as well as in some open-source tools.

10.1   An Example

The BPEL language does not have a graphical representation of its constructs, since it is based solely on XML. This makes it rather difficult to describe BPEL in detail without resorting to code listings in order to explain the purpose of each XML element in a BPEL orchestration. Here we adopt a more "hands-on" approach, and instead of delving into the BPEL language directly, we first introduce an example that will guide us through the main parts and elements in a BPEL orchestration. As previously mentioned, BPEL is in essence a language for specifying orchestrations which comprise mainly the invocation of Web services. Therefore, in the following example we make use of three Web services that are to be invoked sequentially. This is perhaps the simplest possible example, but it will provide useful insight into how an orchestration is typically defined with BPEL. The more intricate elements of BPEL can then be explained through adaptations of this example.

---

[1]Organization for the Advancement of Structured Information Standards (OASIS)

Suppose that we would like to have a Web service to find the current weather conditions (to simplify, we will use only the current temperature) in any given US city. For that purpose, we assume that there is already a Web service available, called Weather. However, this Weather service has some restrictions:

- As input, it must be given the ZIP code for the city.
- As output, it returns the current temperature value in Fahrenheit.

Our goal is to have a Web service that receives the city name as input and returns the current temperature in Celsius. To achieve this, we have to find the ZIP code for the given city, call the Weather service, and then convert the result from Fahrenheit to Celsius. In Sect. 6.4 we have seen an example of a Web service that converts a temperature value in Fahrenheit to Celsius, so we will assume that such service is available. On the other hand, we need another Web service to get the ZIP code for a given city, and there are several such services available on the Web,[2] so we assume that such Web service will be available as well.

Our solution will therefore consist in an orchestration that does the following:

1. The orchestration begins by receiving a message with the name of the city whose temperature is to be obtained.
2. The orchestration invokes a Web service called USZipCode in order to get a ZIP code for the given city.
3. The orchestration invokes the Weather service in order to get the current temperature for the location that corresponds to the given ZIP code.
4. The orchestration invokes the TempConvert service in order to convert the temperature value in Fahrenheit to Celsius.
5. The orchestration returns the temperature in Celsius as the final result.

Figure 10.1 illustrates the orchestration in a graphical notation that tries to highlight the main elements in any BPEL definition. It should be noted that such graphical notation is not part of BPEL, since BPEL is purely XML. However, this graphical depiction is useful to provide an initial idea of the structure and flow of the orchestration which is to be defined using BPEL.

First of all, the outermost block in Fig. 10.1, which is called <process>, is always the root node in any BPEL definition. Inside this root node, one can find several types of other elements. Some of these elements represent *partner links*, others represent variables to be used within the flow, and yet others represent the flow itself, which in this case has been defined as a <sequence> containing a series of <invoke> elements to invoke the required Web services. These different types of elements will be explained in more detail in the next sections. Here, we would like to highlight the essential features of a BPEL definition.

The flow itself is conceptually very similar to what we have seen in Chaps. 8 and 9. Basically, it follows a nested block structure as explained in Sect. 8.1, with each block corresponding to a specific BPEL tag that may contain other elements.

---

[2] An example is the USZip Web service available at: http://www.webservicex.net/uszip.asmx.

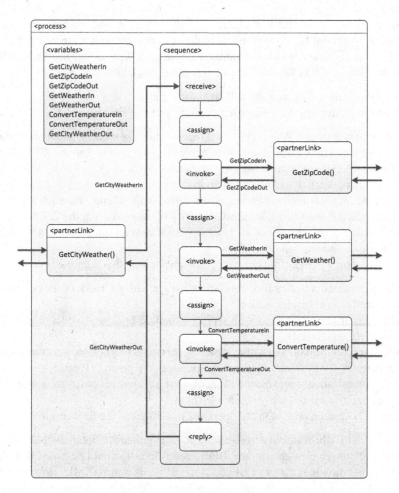

Fig. 10.1 Graphical depiction of an orchestration to be defined using BPEL

Some of the basic activities that can be included in a BPEL orchestration are: <receive> to receive a message; <invoke>, which may work either as a send or as a send and receive; and <reply> which is used as a send that is correlated to the initial <receive> in a BPEL orchestration. Messages are represented as <variables> (each defined in its own <variable> element), and therefore all activities that have to do with message exchange (namely <receive>, <invoke>, and <reply>) must refer to variables that hold the messages to be sent or received.

In Fig. 10.1, the initial <receive> activity uses GetCityWeatherIn as input variable, meaning that this variable will hold the incoming message. The first <invoke> activity uses GetZipCodeIn as input variable (the message to be sent) and GetZipCodeOut as output variable (the message to be received) when invoking the USZipCode Web service. Here, the suffix -In and -Out are always used from the perspective of the service being invoked, so GetZipCodeIn carries the input to the service and GetZipCodeOut carries the output from the service. The same logic applies to the input and output messages for the orchestration: once the orchestration is exposed as a Web service, GetCityWeatherIn is the input message and GetCityWeatherOut is the output message. The remaining <invoke> activities work in a similar way. For example, GetWeatherIn is used as input variable and GetWeatherOut is used as output variable for the Weather service. The same applies to the TempConvert service.

In contrast with BizTalk, in BPEL there is no distinction between orchestration messages and orchestration variables; both of them are represented as variables, and variables can be changed at any point in the orchestration, so there is no need for special shapes such as the construct message shape described in Sect. 8.3. There is also no explicit distinction between changing a message through a transformation map or through message assignment. In BPEL, both kinds of message manipulation can be carried out inside the <assign> activity.

In Fig. 10.1 there are four <assign> activities, with the following purposes:

- The first <assign> copies the city name from GetCityWeatherIn to GetZipCodeIn.
- The second <assign> copies the ZIP code from GetZipCodeOut to GetWeatherIn.
- The third <assign> copies the temperature value (in Fahrenheit) from GetWeatherOut to ConvertTemperatureIn.
- Finally, the fourth <assign> copies the temperature value (in Celsius) from ConvertTemperatureOut to GetCityWeatherOut.

At the end of the <sequence>, the variable GetCityWeatherOut is sent as the output message from the orchestration, through the use of a <reply> activity. This activity is a very special kind of element, which can only be used for this purpose. Despite the fact that the <reply> activity sends a message, it cannot be used to send an input message to a Web service. It can only be used as a means to return an output message to the caller of orchestration. A BPEL orchestration exposes a WSDL interface of its own, and this interface is represented on the left-hand side in Fig. 10.1. It is through this interface that a client can invoke the orchestration.

To the outside world, the orchestration appears to be a simple Web service. In this example, it has a single operation called GetCityWeather(). The client who invokes this operation provides a city name as input and obtains the current temperature in that city (assuming that everything runs as expected and without error). For the client, it does not matter what the orchestration does, or even if this Web service is implemented as a orchestration or in code. Once the orchestration is exposed as a Web service, it can be invoked just like any other Web service.

In particular, this Web service can be invoked from other orchestrations, which in turn expose themselves as Web services. The BPEL language therefore provides a convenient way to implement orchestrations that expose themselves as services, and that can be easily invoked from other BPEL orchestrations. This recursive relationship between BPEL orchestrations and Web services means that BPEL is able to realize the vision depicted in Fig. 7.3 on page 191, and therefore BPEL is a key enabler for service-oriented architectures, as described in Chap. 7.

10.1.1   Understanding Partner Links

From the previous discussion it becomes apparent that a BPEL orchestration can play two different roles with respect to a given WSDL interface:

- Either the orchestration invokes the WSDL interface somewhere along the flow, and in this case the orchestration plays the role of a client;
- Or the orchestration implements the WSDL interface, and in this case the orchestration plays the role of a service.

Therefore, when a WSDL definition is imported into a BPEL orchestration, the two options should remain available. This is why a WSDL interface is represented as a *partner link* inside a BPEL orchestration. The partner link retains the two possible roles and offers the choice of either invoking or implementing the interface.

In Fig. 10.1 there are four partner links: one for each Web service to be invoked, and one for the interface that the BPEL orchestration exposes to the outside world. For the partner links on the right-hand side, the orchestration plays the role of client, while for the partner link on the left-hand side, the orchestration plays the role of service. In general, it is up to the BPEL orchestration to define what it will do with each partner link, by selecting the desired role.

Listing 10.1 contains an excerpt of the BPEL orchestration showing how the partner links are defined. This is actually the first part of the BPEL definition for the orchestration in Fig. 10.1. In line 2 there is a root node called <process>, as depicted earlier in Fig. 10.1. Inside this root node, one finds a series of <import> elements in lines 7–27, followed by the partner links in lines 29–45.

The purpose of the <import> elements is to bring in all the WSDL interfaces that are required for the BPEL orchestration. The first <import> element in lines 7–9 actually imports a WSDL file that defines the interface that the orchestration will expose to the outside world. The remaining <import> elements concern the Web services that are to be invoked within the orchestration.

For each Web service to be invoked, there are actually two WSDL files being imported, as can be seen in lines 10–27:

- One is the main service interface. It comes from the Web service itself and is fetched from the location where the Web service is available. It is imported using a location attribute that contains the HTTP address for the Web service together with the suffix "?WSDL" (lines 11, 17, 23).
- In addition, there should be a *partner link type* defined for each Web service. Since the WSDL interface for a Web service does not usually define the corresponding partner link type, this has to be done somewhere else. Here we assume that the partner link type is defined in a separate WSDL file, which is often called a *wrapper WSDL file*. For convenience, this auxiliary WSDL file has a name ending with the suffix "-Wrapper.wsdl" (lines 14, 20, 26).

Listing 10.2 shows an example of how the wrapper looks like for the USZipCode Web service. Basically, in lines 7–8 the wrapper imports the WSDL interface

Listing 10.1   Partner links in the BPEL orchestration

```
1    <?xml version="1.0" encoding="UTF−8"?>
2    <process name="cityWeatherProc"
3              targetNamespace="http://example.org/"
4              xmlns:tns="http://example.org/"
5              xmlns="http://docs.oasis−open.org/wsbpel/2.0/process/executable">
6
7    <import namespace="http://example.org/"
8              location="CityWeatherProc.wsdl"
9              importType="http://schemas.xmlsoap.org/wsdl/"/>
10   <import namespace="http://example.org/"
11             location="http://localhost:8080/WebServices/USZipCodeService?WSDL"
12             importType="http://schemas.xmlsoap.org/wsdl/"/>
13   <import namespace="http://example.org/"
14             location="USZipCodeServiceWrapper.wsdl"
15             importType="http://schemas.xmlsoap.org/wsdl/"/>
16   <import namespace="http://example.org/"
17             location="http://localhost:8080/WebServices/WeatherService?WSDL"
18             importType="http://schemas.xmlsoap.org/wsdl/"/>
19   <import namespace="http://example.org/"
20             location="WeatherServiceWrapper.wsdl"
21             importType="http://schemas.xmlsoap.org/wsdl/"/>
22   <import namespace="http://example.org/"
23             location="http://localhost:8080/WebServices/TempConvertService?WSDL"
24             importType="http://schemas.xmlsoap.org/wsdl/"/>
25   <import namespace="http://example.org/"
26             location="TempConvertServiceWrapper.wsdl"
27             importType="http://schemas.xmlsoap.org/wsdl/"/>
28
29   <partnerLinks>
30      <partnerLink name="USZipCodePL"
31                xmlns:tns="http://example.org/"
32                partnerLinkType="tns:USZipCodeLinkType"
33                partnerRole="USZipCodeRole"/>
34      <partnerLink name="WeatherPL"
35                xmlns:tns="http://example.org/"
36                partnerLinkType="tns:WeatherLinkType"
37                partnerRole="WeatherRole"/>
38      <partnerLink name="TempConvertPL"
39                xmlns:tns="http://example.org/"
40                partnerLinkType="tns:TempConvertLinkType"
41                partnerRole="TempConvertRole"/>
42      <partnerLink name="ClientPL"
43                partnerLinkType="tns:CityWeatherProc"
44                myRole="CityWeatherProcPortTypeRole"/>
45   </partnerLinks>
46   ...
```

in order to have access to the available port types. Then in lines 9–12 the
wrapper defines a new partner link type (USZipCodeLinkType) with a single role
(USZipCodeRole) associated with the port type defined in the WSDL interface for the
Web service. The wrappers for the other Web services are similar, and they define
their own partner link types. It is up to the orchestration to create one or more partner
links based on each partner link type, and to choose, for each partner link, whether
to invoke or implement the role defined in the corresponding partner link type.

This is precisely what is being done in lines 30–41 of Listing 10.1. For example,
a new partner link is being defined in line 30 (USZipCodePL). The partner link type
is USZipCodeLinkType (line 32), which is precisely the partner link type defined in

Listing 10.2 Wrapper for the USZipCode Web service

```
 1    <?xml version="1.0" encoding="UTF−8"?>
 2    <definitions name="USZipCodeServiceWrapper"
 3                targetNamespace="http://example.org/"
 4                xmlns="http://schemas.xmlsoap.org/wsdl/"
 5                xmlns:plnk="http://docs.oasis−open.org/wsbpel/2.0/plnktype"
 6                xmlns:ns="http://example.org/">
 7      <import namespace="http://example.org/"
 8              location="http://localhost:8080/WebServices/USZipCodeService?WSDL"/>
 9      <plnk:partnerLinkType name="USZipCodeLinkType">
10        <plnk:role name="USZipCodeRole"
11                portType="ns:USZipCode"/>
12      </plnk:partnerLinkType>
13    </definitions>
```

Listing 10.2, lines 9–12. This partner link type has role, and therefore the BPEL orchestration must specify whether it will invoke or implement this role. In line 33 of Listing 10.1, the BPEL orchestration specifies that the role will be invoked since the partnerRole attribute is being used (line 33).

Had the myRole attribute been used instead, this would mean that the orchestration would implement the role defined in the partner link type. In general, for a partner link type that defines one or more roles, the BPEL orchestration must specify whether each role will be used as partnerRole or myRole. The use of partnerRole means that the orchestration will play the role of client. In contrast, the use of myRole means that the orchestration will play the role of service; this implies that the orchestration will implement the port type associated with that role.

The use of myRole can be seen in the partner link defined in lines 42–44 of Listing 10.1. This represents the WSDL interface to be implemented by the orchestration, and therefore it is not surprising that the orchestration will play the role of service here. The partner link has a partner link type called CityWeatherProc, which is defined in CityWeatherProc.wsdl (imported at line 8). The contents of this file are shown in Listing 10.3. This is a regular WSDL file (see Listing 6.10 on page 166), except for the fact that the <binding> and <service> elements have been omitted for simplicity, and there is a partner link type being defined in lines 25–28.

This partner link type has a role named CityWeatherProcPortTypeRole that is associated with the port type defined earlier in lines 17–24. This port type has a single operation called GetCityWeather, which accepts a message of type GetCityWeather-Request as input, and returns a message of type GetCityWeatherResponse as output. The GetCityWeatherRequest message contains a string (line 11) to hold the city name, and GetCityWeatherResponse has a double (line 15) to hold the temperature (in Celsius). When the BPEL orchestration uses the myRole attribute to refer to the role CityWeatherProcPortTypeRole (line 44 of Listing 10.1), this means that it will implement that port type. Therefore, the GetCityWeatherIn variable in Fig. 10.1 will carry a message of type GetCityWeatherRequest, and the GetCityWeatherOut variable will carry a message of type GetCityWeatherResponse.

Listing 10.3 The WSDL interface for the orchestration

```
 1   <?xml version="1.0" encoding="UTF-8"?>
 2   <definitions name="CityWeatherProc"
 3                   targetNamespace="http://example.org/"
 4                   xmlns="http://schemas.xmlsoap.org/wsdl/"
 5                   xmlns:xsd="http://www.w3.org/2001/XMLSchema"
 6                   xmlns:plnk="http://docs.oasis-open.org/wsbpel/2.0/plnktype"
 7                   xmlns:tns="http://example.org/">
 8       <types/>
 9       <message name="GetCityWeatherRequest">
10          <part name="city"
11                  type="xsd:string"/>
12       </message>
13       <message name="GetCityWeatherResponse">
14          <part name="temperature"
15                  type="xsd:double"/>
16       </message>
17       <portType name="CityWeatherProcPortType">
18          <operation name="GetCityWeather">
19              <input name="input1"
20                      message="tns:GetCityWeatherRequest"/>
21              <output name="output1"
22                      message="tns:GetCityWeatherResponse"/>
23          </operation>
24       </portType>
25       <plnk:partnerLinkType name="CityWeatherProc">
26          <plnk:role name="CityWeatherProcPortTypeRole"
27                  portType="tns:CityWeatherProcPortType"/>
28       </plnk:partnerLinkType>
29   </definitions>
```

10.1.2   Orchestration Variables

The second part of the BPEL definition that began in Listing 10.1 is shown in Listing 10.4. Basically, this excerpt of the BPEL orchestration defines the variables that will be used as messages in the orchestration flow. In lines 3–6 it is possible to confirm that the variables GetCityWeatherIn and GetCityWeatherOut are of types GetCityWeatherRequest and GetCityWeatherResponse, respectively. As for the other variables, these are meant to hold the messages to be exchanged with each Web service. Each variable has a messageType that refers to some message defined in the WSDL interface of a Web service. For example, the variables GetZipCodeIn and GetZipCodeOut refer to the message types GetZipCode and GetZipCodeResponse that are defined in the WSDL interface for the USZipCode Web service.

The place at which each of these messages is used in the orchestration is shown in Fig. 10.1. However, Fig. 10.1 shows only the points at which these messages are being sent or received. In addition to this, each message (i.e., variable) must be initialized somehow, and that initialization is taking place inside each <assign> activity. For example, the message GetCityWeatherIn that serves as input to the orchestration brings the city name, which must be copied to the GetZipCodeIn message to be sent to the USZipCode Web service.

This can be done as shown in Listing 10.5. The <assign> element has a <copy> element inside, which is used to copy data from one variable to another. In this

Listing 10.4 Variables in the BPEL orchestration

```
1      ...
2      <variables>
3        <variable name="GetCityWeatherIn"
4                  messageType="tns:GetCityWeatherRequest"/>
5        <variable name="GetCityWeatherOut"
6                  messageType="tns:GetCityWeatherResponse"/>
7        <variable name="GetZipCodeIn"
8                  messageType="tns:GetZipCode"/>
9        <variable name="GetZipCodeOut"
10                 messageType="tns:GetZipCodeResponse"/>
11       <variable name="GetWeatherIn"
12                 messageType="tns:GetWeather"/>
13       <variable name="GetWeatherOut"
14                 messageType="tns:GetWeatherResponse"/>
15       <variable name="ConvertTemperatureIn"
16                 messageType="tns:ConvertTemperature"/>
17       <variable name="ConvertTemperatureOut"
18                 messageType="tns:ConvertTemperatureResponse"/>
19     </variables>
20     ...
```

Listing 10.5 Example of variable assignment

```
1      <assign name="Assign1">
2        <copy>
3          <from variable="GetCityWeatherIn"
4                part="city"/>
5          <to>$GetZipCodeIn.parameters/city</to>
6        </copy>
7      </assign>
```

case, the <from> and <to> elements use different forms to refer to the source and destination, respectively. The <from> element uses a variant where it indicates the variable name (GetCityWeatherIn) and the part (city) from which the data is obtained. It can be seen in Listing 10.3 (lines 9–12) that indeed GetCityWeatherRequest is a message type that contains a part called city.

As for the <to> element, this uses a different form which is based on an XPath expression. The term $GetZipCodeIn points to the root element of the message. This message contains a part called parameters, so $GetZipCodeIn.parameters refers to that message part. Furthermore, this message part contains a <city> element which carries a string value. Therefore, the expression $GetZipCodeIn.parameters/city refers to the element <city> inside the parameters part in the message.

As a result of the <assign> activity and its <copy> element in Listing 10.5, the city name will be copied from the message in the GetCityWeatherIn variable to the message in the GetZipCodeIn variable. Then GetZipCodeIn will be sent to the USZipCode Web service in the first <invoke> activity in Fig. 10.1.

10.1.3   The Orchestration Flow

Listing 10.6 shows the third and final part of the BPEL orchestration that began with the partner links in Listing 10.1 and the variables in Listing 10.4. This third part

Listing 10.6 Sequence of activities in the BPEL orchestration

```
1      ...
2          <sequence>
3            <receive name="Receive"
4                     createInstance="yes"
5                     partnerLink="ClientPL"
6                     operation="GetCityWeather"
7                     portType="tns:CityWeatherProcPortType"
8                     variable="GetCityWeatherIn"/>
9            <assign name="Assign1">
10             <copy>
11               <from variable="GetCityWeatherIn"
12                     part="city"/>
13               <to>$GetZipCodeIn.parameters/city</to>
14             </copy>
15           </assign>
16           <invoke name="Invoke1"
17                   partnerLink="USZipCodePL"
18                   operation="GetZipCode"
19                   portType="tns:USZipCode"
20                   inputVariable="GetZipCodeIn"
21                   outputVariable="GetZipCodeOut"/>
22           <assign name="Assign2">
23             <copy>
24               <from>$GetZipCodeOut.parameters/return</from>
25               <to>$GetWeatherIn.parameters/zipcode</to>
26             </copy>
27           </assign>
28           <invoke name="Invoke2"
29                   partnerLink="WeatherPL"
30                   operation="GetWeather"
31                   portType="tns:Weather"
32                   inputVariable="GetWeatherIn"
33                   outputVariable="GetWeatherOut"/>
34           <assign name="Assign3">
35             <copy>
36               <from>$GetWeatherOut.parameters/return</from>
37               <to>$ConvertTemperatureIn.parameters/dFahrenheit</to>
38             </copy>
39           </assign>
40           <invoke name="Invoke3"
41                   partnerLink="TempConvertPL"
42                   operation="ConvertTemperature"
43                   portType="tns:TempConvert"
44                   inputVariable="ConvertTemperatureIn"
45                   outputVariable="ConvertTemperatureOut"/>
46           <assign name="Assign4">
47             <copy>
48               <from>$ConvertTemperatureOut.parameters/return</from>
49               <to variable="GetCityWeatherOut"
50                   part="temperature"/>
51             </copy>
52           </assign>
53           <reply name="Reply"
54                  partnerLink="ClientPL"
55                  operation="GetCityWeather"
56                  portType="tns:CityWeatherProcPortType"
57                  variable="GetCityWeatherOut"/>
58         </sequence>
59     </process>
```

refers to the <sequence> element and its inner activities, as depicted in Fig. 10.1.
The fact that the activities are defined within a <sequence> element means that they
will be executed sequentially, in the same order as they appear in Listing 10.6.

The sequence begins with a <receive>, and this is a special kind of receive
since it has the attribute value createInstance="yes" (line 4). This means that a new
instance of the orchestration will be created whenever a message is received, so
it effectively corresponds to the notion of an activating receive, as explained in
Sect. 8.2. This BPEL orchestration has no other <receive> activities, but if it had
then those <receive> elements would have the attribute value createInstance="no".

The <receive> activity uses the partner link ClientPL (line 5). This partner link
represents the WSDL interface that the orchestration exposes to the outside world.
The partner link is defined in Listing 10.1 (lines 42–44), and it is an instance of
the partner link type defined in Listing 10.3 (lines 25–28). Back to Listing 10.6, the
initial <receive> activity with createInstance="yes" specifies that the orchestration
is triggered as a result of some client invoking the ClientPL partner link, which is
equivalent to saying that the client invokes the WSDL interface exposed by the
orchestration. The specific port type and operation that the client must invoke are
specified in lines 6–7. The orchestration has access to the data submitted by the
client through the GetCityWeatherIn variable (line 8).

The <receive> is followed by the first <assign> activity, named Assign1, which
copies the city name from GetCityWeatherIn to the GetZipCodeIn variable. This is
precisely the assignment that has been used as an example in Listing 10.5.

Now, after the assignment comes the first <invoke> activity. This <invoke> uses
the partner link USZipCodePL (which is defined in Listing 10.1). The port type and
operation being invoked are specified in lines 18–19. Then in lines 20–21 comes the
specification of which message will be sent (inputVariable) and which message will
be received (outputVariable) when the partner link is invoked. In this particular case,
the invocation is synchronous and therefore at this point the BPEL orchestration will
block until the USZipCode Web service returns the result.

Once the ZIP code is obtained, a second <assign> activity (Assign2 in line 22)
copies the ZIP code to the GetWeatherIn variable, which contains the message to be
sent to the Weather service. Both GetZipCodeOut and GetWeatherIn have a message
part named parameters. In the GetZipCodeOut message, there is a <return> element
which contains the ZIP code (line 24); this value is copied to the <zipcode> element
in GetWeatherIn (line 25). An XPath expression is used in both cases.

In line 28 there is a second <invoke> activity, which uses a partner link to
interact with the Weather service. (Again, the partner link WeatherPL is defined
in Listing 10.1.) The port type and operation being invoked are specified in lines
30–31. The message to be sent to the service is GetWeatherIn (line 32), and the
orchestration will be waiting to receive GetWeatherOut (line 33).

The GetWeatherOut message brings a temperature value in Fahrenheit. This value
is copied to the ConvertTemperatureIn message in the <assign> in lines 34–39.

The third <invoke> activity in lines 40–45 converts the temperature in Fahrenheit
to Celsius by calling the TempConvert Web service through the TempConvertPL
partner link. After the Web service returns the result in the ConvertTemperatureOut

message, an <assign> activity in lines 46–52 copies the temperature value (now in Celsius) to the GetCityWeatherOut message.

Finally, GetCityWeatherOut must be sent as a response from the orchestration to the client. In lines 53–57 there is a <reply> activity for this purpose. The <reply> uses the same partner link as the initial <receive>, and the port type and operation in lines 55–56 are also the same as in lines 6–7. In essence, <reply> is the mechanism that BPEL provides to return a result to the client who invoked the orchestration in a synchronous way. The client invoked a Web service operation and is waiting for the result. The <reply> activity is the means to return the result. In this case, the result is the message contained in the GetCityWeatherOut variable (line 57).

The sequence of activities ends in line 58 and the BPEL definition, which had started in line 2 of Listing 10.1, closes in line 59.

10.2 Asynchronous Invocations

The BPEL definition in Listings 10.1, 10.4, and 10.6 is an example of a BPEL orchestration which works fully in synchronous mode. On one hand, the orchestration invokes three Web services, and all three invocations are synchronous, i.e., the orchestration is blocked while waiting for a response. On the other hand, the orchestration itself exposes a WSDL interface which is invoked synchronously from clients, i.e., the client will block until the orchestration completes the sequence of activities and returns a response. Naturally, it is possible to make these invocations asynchronous, but this requires some changes to the BPEL orchestration.

In general, a WSDL interface provides a set of operations which, if nothing is specified otherwise, will be synchronous by default. For example, Listing 6.14 on page 169 defines a port type with a single operation called ConvertTemperature. This operation has input message (with the temperature value in Fahrenheit) and an output message (with the temperature in Celsius). When a client invokes the operation, the invocation is synchronous, i.e., the client will block while waiting for the output message to be returned by the Web service.

It is possible to make such operation asynchronous by having the Web service explicitly delivering the output message to the client, without requiring the client to be waiting for it. Typically, this is done by making the Web service *invoke* the client when the output message is ready. For this purpose, the client must implement a port type and operation that the Web service can call to deliver the output message. In this scenario, there will be two different port types:

- One is the port type that is implemented by the Web service and that the client invokes in order to send an input message for the operation. To make the call asynchronous, this operation will have an input message, but no output message. This way the operation returns immediately after being invoked from the client, and the client may proceed with its work.
- The other port type is to be implemented by the client. This is a port type that the Web service will invoke in order to deliver the response to the client. This port

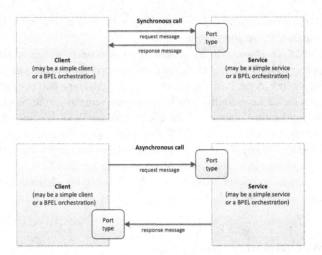

Fig. 10.2 Port types in synchronous and asynchronous calls

type too will have an operation with a single *input* message (from the perspective of the client, the message that is being returned from the Web service is regarded as an incoming message). This operation will be invoked from the Web service when it is ready to return the response.

Figure 10.2 shows the difference between synchronous and asynchronous calls following this approach. While for a synchronous call there is a single port type, for an asynchronous call there are two port types, one to be implemented by the service and another to be implemented by the client. However, both port types must have been defined by the service, so that the service knows beforehand which port type it must invoke on the client to deliver the result. This is similar to the way a messaging system defines a callback interface for clients that wish to receive messages asynchronously (see Fig. 3.8 on page 44).

In fact, the client port type at the bottom of Fig. 10.2 is a kind of callback interface that allows the service to deliver the response asynchronously to the client. This has some implications for BPEL orchestrations as well. In case a BPEL orchestration invokes a Web service asynchronously, then the orchestration must implement the callback interface (i.e., port type) defined by the Web service that is being invoked. On the other hand, if an external client invokes the orchestration asynchronously, then the WSDL interface for the orchestration must define the port type that the client must implement in order to receive the response.

10.2.1   *Invoking a Web Service Asynchronously*

Suppose that the ConvertTemperature operation in the TempConvert Web service is now asynchronous. Then instead of having a single port type with an operation with

Listing 10.7 WSDL port types for asynchronous Web service

```
1    <portType name="TempConvertPT">
2      <operation name="ConvertTemperature">
3        <input message="ConvertTemperatureRequest" />
4      </operation>
5    </portType>
6    <portType name="TempConvertCallbackPT">
7      <operation name="ConvertTemperatureCallback">
8        <input message="ConvertTemperatureResponse" />
9      </operation>
10   </portType>
```

Listing 10.8 Partner link type for asynchronous Web service

```
1    <partnerLinkType name="TempConvertLT">
2      <role name="TempConvertServiceRole"
3            portType="TempConvertPT" />
4      <role name="TempConvertClientRole"
5            portType="TempConvertCallbackPT" />
6    </partnerLinkType>
```

Listing 10.9 Partner link for asynchronous Web service

```
1    <partnerLink name="TempConvertPL"
2                 partnerLinkType="TempConvertLT"
3                 partnerRole="TempConvertServiceRole"
4                 myRole="TempConvertClientRole"/>
```

input and output messages (such as in Listing 6.14 on page 169), the TempConvert Web service would have two port types with one operation for the request and one operation for the response, as in Listing 10.7.

Here, the port type TempConvertPT and the operation ConvertTemperature are used to send the request to the Web service. On the other hand, the port type TempConvertCallbackPT and the operation ConvertTemperatureCallback are implemented by the orchestration in order to receive the response from the Web service.

Such WSDL interface will give origin to a partner link type with two roles, as shown in Listing 10.8. This partner link type will be defined in an auxiliary wrapper for this service, as explained in Sect. 10.1.1. In Listing 10.8 there is a service role (line 2) associated with the TempConvertPT port type (line 3), and a client role (line 4) associated with the TempConvertCallbackPT port type (line 5).

In the BPEL definition for the orchestration, the first change will be in the partner link associated with the (now asynchronous) TempConvert Web service. The new partner link will have a similar form to the one shown in Listing 10.9. Here we can see the simultaneous use of the partnerRole and myRole attributes. This is a strong indication that the interaction with this partner link will be asynchronous, since both the service and the orchestration will have a role to play.

The second important change in the BPEL orchestration is that the <invoke> activity that was used to invoke this partner link (see lines 40–45 in Listing 10.6) needs to be replaced by an <invoke> and a <receive>, as shown in Listing 10.10.

Here we have an <invoke> with an input variable, but without an output variable. The <invoke> returns immediately, and a <receive> follows. This <receive>

Listing 10.10 BPEL invocation of an asynchronous Web service

```
1     <invoke name="Invoke3"
2               partnerLink="TempConvertPL"
3               portType="TempConvertPT"
4               operation="ConvertTemperature"
5               inputVariable="ConvertTemperatureIn"/>
6     <receive name="Receive3"
7               createInstance="no"
8               partnerLink="TempConvertPL"
9               portType="TempConvertCallbackPT"
10              operation="ConvertTemperatureCallback"
11              variable="ConvertTemperatureOut"/>
```

Listing 10.11 WSDL port types for asynchronous BPEL orchestration

```
1     <portType name="CityWeatherProcPT">
2         <operation name="GetCityWeather">
3             <input message="GetCityWeatherRequest"/>
4         </operation>
5     </portType>
6     <portType name="CityWeatherCallbackPT">
7         <operation name="GetCityWeatherCallback">
8             <input message="GetCityWeatherResponse"/>
9         </operation>
10    </portType>
```

Listing 10.12 Partner link type for asynchronous BPEL orchestration

```
1     <partnerLinkType name="CityWeatherProcLT">
2         <role name="CityWeatherProcServiceRole"
3               portType="CityWeatherProcPT"/>
4         <role name="CityWeatherProcClientRole"
5               portType="CityWeatherCallbackPT"/>
6     </partnerLinkType>
```

uses the same partner link, but with a different port type and operation. This ConvertTemperatureCallback (line 10) is the operation that the remote Web service will invoke to deliver the response message. This message will be accessible in the orchestration through the variable ConvertTemperatureOut, as before.

10.2.2   Invoking an Orchestration Asynchronously

Similar steps have to be taken in order to change the BPEL orchestration into an asynchronous Web service. First of all, the WSDL interface for the BPEL orchestration must be changed in order to have a callback operation for the client. This is shown in Listing 10.11. Again, there are two port types with an operation having a single message. The port type CityWeatherProcPT is meant to send the request to the orchestration (which will enter the initial <receive>), and the port type CityWeatherCallbackPT will be used to return the response to the client.

These port types will give origin to a partner link type with two roles, as shown in Listing 10.12. There is a service role associated with the port type CityWeather-ProcPT and a client role associated with the port type CityWeatherCallbackPT.

Listing 10.13 Partner link for asynchronous BPEL orchestration

```
1    <partnerLink name="ClientPL"
2                 partnerLinkType="CityWeatherProcLT"
3                 myRole="CityWeatherProcServiceRole"
4                 partnerRole="CityWeatherProcClientRole"/>
```

Listing 10.14 Sending the response from an asynchronous BPEL orchestration

```
1    <invoke name="Invoke4"
2            partnerLink="ClientPL"
3            portType="CityWeatherCallbackPT"
4            operation="GetCityWeatherCallback"
5            inputVariable="ConvertTemperatureOut"/>
```

This partner link type will be used to define the partner link that allows the BPEL orchestration to interact with external clients. This partner link for clients is shown in Listing 10.13. Again, the fact that the partner link uses both the myRole and the partnerRole attributes is a strong indication that the interaction with client will be asynchronous, since there are two port types involved.

Finally, a subtle but important change must be done in the orchestration flow, where the <reply> must be replaced by an <invoke>. The <reply> activity can only be used to respond synchronously, using the same port type and operation as a previous <receive>. However, here the orchestration will send the response using a different port type and operation from the initial <receive>. Therefore, one must use an <invoke> instead. The <invoke> is shown in Listing 10.14.

This invoke uses the same partner link as the initial <receive>, but the port type and operation being invoked correspond to the callback interface that has been defined for clients in Listing 10.11. The client receives the response as a callback invocation from the orchestration. The response that the client receives is the message contained in the ConvertTemperatureOut variable, as before.

10.3 Controlling the Flow

In the example of Sect. 10.1, the orchestration flow was relatively simple since it comprised a group of activities enclosed in a <sequence> element (see Listing 10.6 on page 279). This means that there is only one possible path in the flow, and that path consists in executing the activities in the same order as they are specified inside the <sequence>. Naturally, BPEL allows for other forms of behavior as well, and the <sequence> element is just one of the available constructs to specify the orchestration flow. In this section we provide a brief overview of the available constructs together with a minimal example. This example may not always be of practical interest in the previous temperature conversion scenario, but it will serve to illustrate how the construct can be used in this and other scenarios.

Listing 10.15 Use of <if> element

```
1       <if>
2           <condition>$ConvertTemperatureOut.parameters/return &lt; 0</condition>
3           ...
4           <elseif>
5               <condition>$ConvertTemperatureOut.parameters/return &lt; 10</condition>
6               ...
7           </elseif>
8           <elseif>
9               <condition>$ConvertTemperatureOut.parameters/return &lt; 20</condition>
10              ...
11          </elseif>
12          <else>
13              ...
14          </else>
15      </if>
```

10.3.1   Decisions

Suppose that after the TempConvert service has been invoked, but before the orchestration returns a response to the client, it is necessary to check the value of the temperature value in Celsius, and decide whether to take some action depending on this value. This can be done with the <if> element, which works in a similar way to the decide shape described in Sect. 8.4.1.

Listing 10.15 shows the basic structure of the <if> element, which may optionally contain any number of <elseif> elements and at most one <else> element. As is the case in many programming languages, the <if> element, as well as any <elseif> elements that it contains, must have an associated condition that evaluates to either true or false, and determines whether a particular block of activities should be executed. In BPEL, the condition is specified by means of a <condition> element, as in lines 2, 5, and 9 of Listing 10.15. In this example, each condition compares the result returned by the TempConvert Web service with some predefined value. The characters "<" are a special entity that represents a "less than" sign (i.e., <) which cannot be inserted directly since it could be confused with the end of an XML tag and therefore interfere with the processing of the BPEL definition.

Below each <condition>, as well as inside the <else> element, there is an ellipsis to represent the fact that any BPEL activity can be inserted in that block. For example, it could be that if the temperature is below 0 °C then it is necessary to invoke some other Web service, and therefore there would be an <invoke> starting on line 3. Other activities, such as <receive> and <assign>, just to mention a few possibilities, could be included as well. However, if more than one activity is to be included in any of those blocks, then the correct way to do it is to include a <sequence> element which, in turn, contains the activities to be executed.

10.3.2   Parallel Activities

As an alternative to <sequence>, it is possible to run activities in parallel. By using <flow> instead of <sequence>, any activities that are specified inside that element

Listing 10.16 Use of <flow> element

```
1    <process ...>
2        <sequence>
3            <receive ... />
4            <flow>
5                <invoke ... />
6                <invoke ... />
7                <invoke ... />
8            </flow>
9            <assign ... />
10           <reply ... />
11       </sequence>
12   </process>
```

Listing 10.17 Use of <flow> with <sequence>

```
1    <process ...>
2        <sequence>
3            <receive ... />
4            <flow>
5                <sequence>
6                    <invoke ... />
7                    <invoke ... />
8                    <invoke ... />
9                </sequence>
10               <sequence>
11                   <invoke ... />
12                   <invoke ... />
13               </sequence>
14           </flow>
15           <assign ... />
16           <reply ... />
17       </sequence>
18   </process>
```

will be executed concurrently. In addition, these activities will be synchronized at
the end, meaning that execution does not proceed beyond the <flow> block until
all activities contained in it are complete. Therefore, the <flow> element works in a
similar way to the parallel shape described in Sect. 8.4.2.

Listing 10.16 illustrates the use of the <flow> element by means of a sketch of a
BPEL orchestration. This orchestration has a main <sequence> with four activities:
a <receive> (line 3), a <flow> (lines 4–8), an <assign> (line 9), and a <reply> (line 10).
Inside the <flow> there are three <invoke> activities that will be executed in parallel.
It is only when all of them are complete that execution proceeds to the <assign>.
This structure could be used, for example, to query three Web services for a certain
quote or price, and then return the best price to the client.

As with other BPEL activities, it is possible to nest <flow> and <sequence> elements in an arbitrary way. Listing 10.17 extends the previous example by inserting
two <sequence> blocks inside the <flow>. This means that the two sequences will be
executed in parallel, but the activities inside each <sequence> block will be executed
sequentially. In other words, inside the <flow> there will be two separate threads of
execution: one with a <sequence> of three <invoke> activities (lines 5–9), and the
other with a <sequence> of two (lines 10–13).

Listing 10.18   Use of links in a <flow>

```
1    <flow>
2        <links>
3            <link name="AtoB" />
4            <link name="BtoC" />
5            <link name="DtoE" />
6        </links>
7        <invoke name="A" ...>
8            <sources>
9                <source linkName="AtoB" />
10           </sources>
11       </invoke>
12       <invoke name="B" ... >
13           <targets>
14               <target linkName="AtoB" />
15           </targets>
16           <sources>
17               <source linkName=BtoC" />
18           </sources>
19       </invoke>
20       <invoke name="C" ... >
21           <targets>
22               <target linkName="BtoC" />
23           </targets>
24       </invoke>
25       <invoke name="D" ...>
26           <sources>
27               <source linkName="DtoE" />
28           </sources>
29       </invoke>
30       <invoke name="E" ... >
31           <targets>
32               <target linkName="DtoE" />
33           </targets>
34       </invoke>
35   </flow>
```

The behavior in the <flow> block of Listing 10.17 can also be obtained through a different mechanism, namely the use of links to specify dependencies between the activities in a <flow>. Listing 10.18 illustrates the use of such links. Here, the five <invoke> activities, now named A through E, have been inserted directly into the <flow> without the use of any <sequence>. If nothing would be said otherwise, then these five activities would run in parallel. However, here there are three links being declared in lines 3–5, and these links are being used to establish some dependencies in the order of execution of these activities.

In line 9 there is a <source> element specifying that activity A (whether it is an <invoke> or something else it does not matter) is a source for the link named AtoB. On the other hand, line 14 specifies that activity B is a target for the same link. This establishes a dependency between the source activity and the target activity, meaning that activity B (the target) can only be executed when activity A (the source) has already completed.

A similar dependency exists between activities B and C. Activity B is at the same time the target for the link AtoB (line 14) and the source for the link BtoC (line 17). Since the target of the link BtoC is activity C (line 22), this means that C can only begin when B is complete. The result of these dependencies is that activities A, B, and C will execute sequentially rather than in parallel.

A similar dependency exists between activities D and E, through the link DtoE, for which D is a source (line 27) and E is a target (line 32). Therefore, activities D and E will be executed sequentially as well. However, it should be noted that there is no dependency between the group of activities A, B, C and the group of activities D, E. Therefore, the sequences A→B→C and D→E will execute in parallel, and the <flow> will complete only when activities C and E have finished.

The use of link dependencies is one of the most complicated features of BPEL, since any activity can have a dependency to any other activity in the same <flow>. Also, an activity may be the target of multiple links and it is necessary to define whether these links work in an AND- or OR-fashion, i.e., whether the target activity must wait for *all* or *any* of the source activities to finish. This can be defined through the use of a *join condition*, which we will leave up to the interested reader to find out more about in the BPEL standard [19].

Also, each activity may be the source of several links, and this does not cause a problem on its own. However, each link may be associated with a *transition condition*, meaning that the target activity will only be executed if the transition condition that is specified at the source of the link is true. (A transition condition takes a similar form to the condition of a <if> element.) If the condition is false, then the target activity is simply skipped, along with any subsequent activities that depend on that target activity. This feature complicates things even further and requires the use of a special mechanism known as *dead-path elimination* [19].

Again, we leave it up to the interested reader to find more about these mechanisms in the literature, for example in [32]. Links provide a flexible way to specify the behavior inside a <flow> element but, in association with join conditions, transition conditions and dead-path elimination, they also introduce the possibility of having conflicts, inconsistencies and deadlocks during execution. In practice, it is easier to ensure the consistency of an orchestration that is built as a nested block structure, as explained in Sect. 8.1. In this sense, the implementation in Listing 10.17 is to be preferred over the implementation in Listing 10.18.

10.3.3   Loops

Another type of construct that BPEL supports are loops, which correspond to the same concept as described in Sect. 8.5. However, BPEL has actually two kinds of loops: <while> and <repeatUntil>. Both of them have a loop condition that evaluates to true or false. The <while> loop will keep executing while the condition is true and will stop executing when the condition becomes false. In contrast, the <repeatUntil> loop will keep executing while the condition is false and will stop executing when the condition becomes true. In addition, in the <while> loop the condition is verified at the beginning of each iteration, whereas in the <repeatUntil> loop the condition is verified at the end of each iteration.

Listing 10.19 Use of a <while> loop

```
 1    <?xml version="1.0" encoding="UTF-8"?>
 2    <process
 3        ...
 4        xmlns:xs="http://www.w3.org/2001/XMLSchema"
 5        ...
 6        >
 7        ...
 8        <variables>
 9          <variable name="counter" type="xs:int"/>
10          ...
11        </variables>
12        <sequence>
13          ...
14          <assign>
15            <copy>
16              <from>0</from>
17              <to variable="counter"/>
18            </copy>
19          </assign>
20          <while>
21            <condition>$counter &lt; 3</condition>
22            <sequence>
23              <invoke ... />
24              <assign>
25                <copy>
26                  <from>$counter + 1</from>
27                  <to variable="counter"/>
28                </copy>
29              </assign>
30            </sequence>
31          </while>
32          ...
33        </sequence>
34    </process>
```

Listing 10.19 illustrates the use of a <while> loop. The actual loop is in lines 20–31, and the loop condition is specified in line 21. This condition tests the value of a variable called counter. Basically, the loop will keep executing for as long as the value of counter is less than 3. As soon as this condition becomes false, execution will proceed to the next activity after the <while> loop.

In this example, the loop is being used to perform a repeated invocation of some Web service, as can be seen by the use of an <invoke> activity in line 23. Also in the body of the loop, we can find an <assign> activity in lines 24–29. Since there is more than one activity to be performed in the body of the loop, the correct way to specify this is to insert a <sequence> element inside the loop and then include the activities to be performed inside the <sequence>, as in lines 22–30.

The loop condition uses a variable (counter) that must be somehow declared and initialized. In addition, the variable must be updated in each loop iteration (otherwise, its value would not change and the loop condition would yield always the same result). In line 9, it is possible to see that the variable is being declared inside a <variables> section. This is the same section that was used in Listing 10.4 on page 278 to declare the variables that will hold the messages to be exchanged through the several partner links in the orchestration.

Listing 10.20 Use of a <while> loop

```
1    <?xml version="1.0" encoding="UTF−8"?>
2    <process
3        ...
4        xmlns:xs="http://www.w3.org/2001/XMLSchema"
5        ...
6        >
7        ...
8        <variables>
9            <variable name="counter" type="xs:int"/>
10           ...
11       </variables>
12       <sequence>
13           ...
14           <assign>
15               <copy>
16                   <from>0</from>
17                   <to variable="counter"/>
18               </copy>
19           </assign>
20           <repeatUntil>
21               <sequence>
22                   <invoke ... />
23                   <assign>
24                       <copy>
25                           <from>$counter + 1</from>
26                           <to variable="counter"/>
27                       </copy>
28                   </assign>
29               </sequence>
30               <condition>$counter = 3</condition>
31           </repeatUntil>
32           ...
33       </sequence>
34   </process>
```

The type of counter is int, which is a built-in data type defined in the XML Schema standard [31]. This standard is included through the namespace defined in line 4. Then in lines 14–19 there is an <assign> activity to initialize the counter. This <assign> simply copies the numeric value 0 to the variable. This is the value that the variable will possess when execution reaches the <while> loop.

In each loop iteration, the counter variable is incremented through the <assign> in lines 24–29. This <assign> overwrites the value of counter with the result of $counter + 1 (where $counter represents "the value" of counter). After the loop has been run three times, the counter variable has been incremented to 3 and the condition in line 21 will evaluate to false. At that point the loop will be exited and execution proceeds to whatever activity is in line 32.

The same behavior can be obtained with <repeatUntil>, as shown in Listing 10.20. The difference is in lines 20–31, where the <while> loop from Listing 10.19 has now been replaced by a <repeatUntil> loop. As before, the purpose of this loop is to invoke some Web service multiple times, by means of the <invoke> activity in line 22. However, besides the <invoke> it is necessary to increment the counter variable, and this is done through an <assign> in lines 24–28. To be inserted into the loop, the two activities—the <invoke> and the <assign>—must be placed inside some container, such as a <sequence> or a <flow>. Here, a <sequence> is being used.

Listing 10.21 Use of a <forEach> loop

```
1    <?xml version="1.0" encoding="UTF−8"?>
2    <process ... >
3       ...
4       <sequence>
5          ...
6          <forEach counterName="counter" parallel="no">
7             <startCounterValue>1</startCounterValue>
8             <finalCounterValue>3</finalCounterValue>
9             <scope>
10               <variables>
11                  ...
12               </variables>
13               <sequence>
14                  <invoke ... />
15                  <receive ... />
16               </sequence>
17            </scope>
18         </forEach>
19         ...
20      </sequence>
21   </process>
```

After the sequence comes the loop condition in line 30. This condition will evaluate to true after the loop has been run three times. Once it is true, the loop is exited and execution proceeds to whatever activity is in line 32.

A third form of loop that is less common, but that can be put to good use in this example, is the <forEach> loop. The <forEach> loop is the ideal solution when the number of iterations is known beforehand, and it has the advantage that it includes its own counter variable, so there is no need to create a separate variable for that purpose. Listing 10.21 illustrates an example.

The <forEach> loop that begins in line 6 has a special attribute called counter-Name. This attribute is used to define an implicit counter variable. The counter starts with the value 1 (line 7) and has a final value of 3 (line 8). This means that the loop will be executed three times, one for each counter value.

An interesting feature of the <forEach> loop is the attribute called parallel (line 6). In this example, this attribute is set to "no", but in other scenarios it might be set to "yes". What this means is that it is possible to choose whether the loop iterations will run in serial mode (i.e., one after the other) or whether they are to be launched in parallel, as concurrent threads. In this example, if parallel would be "yes" then there would be three separate threads (one for each counter value). This parallelism does not exist in other types of loops, but only in the <forEach> loop.

When the loop iterations run in parallel, they should run isolated from each other. For example, shared variables that may cause interference between runs should be avoided. Therefore, the body of the <forEach> loop is placed within a special element called <scope>. A <scope> may declare its own variables, by means of a <variables> section that is similar to the one in the top-level <process> (lines 10–12). However, any variable that is declared inside the <scope> is local, i.e., it is not visible outside that <scope>. When the <scope> ends in line 17, the next iteration (if there are more) will run in its own, separate <scope>.

In particular, in each run of the <forEach> loop in Listing 10.21 there is a variable called counter (line 6) and this variable is local to the <scope>, meaning that it can be changed inside that <scope> without affecting the counter variable for the next iteration. The same principle applies when the iterations run in parallel: each iteration has its own counter variable, and this variable is initialized with a unique value between <startCounterValue> and <finalCounterValue>. Changing this value has no effect on the counter variable of other iterations.

The <scope> is similar to the top-level <process> also in the fact that its activities must be enclosed in one block, such as a <sequence> or a <flow>. Therefore, the activities in this loop have been enclosed in a <sequence> block (lines 13–16). The <scope> element can also be used for other purposes, such as exception handling and compensation, as we will see in Sect. 10.4.

10.3.4   Listening for Events

In Sect. 9.1 we have described a special kind of construct which allows choosing one from several branches based on a set of possible events that may occur at run-time. The construct was referred to as the listen shape (see Fig. 9.1 on page 235), and each branch in the listen shape is associated with a certain event. The event that occurs first will determine the branch to be executed, and all other branches will be skipped. Possible events include the arrival of a certain message or a timer that elapses after a certain length of time or due date.

The BPEL language has a construct, known as <pick>, which is in every respect similar to the listen shape described in Sect. 9.1. The <pick> element contains a set of possible paths for execution, where each path is associated with a certain event that can be the arrival of a message or a timer event.

Listing 10.22 shows the sketch of a <pick> element with three possible paths. Once execution reaches the <pick> element, it will wait for one of the specified events to occur. Lines 6–14 specify that if a message is received on a certain partner link, using a certain port type and operation, then the path to be executed is the sequence in lines 10–13. Similarly, if a message is received on some other partner link, port type or operation (lines 15–18), then the path to be executed is the sequence in lines 19–22. Finally, the third possibility is that a timer elapses before either message is received. The <onAlarm> element is used for this purpose in lines 24–30. In particular, line 25 specifies that the timer will wait for 24 h.

In line 25, the expression 'P0Y0M0DT24H0M0.0S' allows specifying an arbitrary duration in terms of a number of years (Y), months (M), days (D), hours (H), minutes (M) and seconds (S). Everything else being zero, the number 24H means a duration of 24 h, after which the path in lines 26–29 will be selected for execution, and the orchestration will stop waiting for any of the previous messages.

The configuration of the <onMessage> elements is very similar to that of a regular (i.e., non-activating) <receive>. It specifies the partner link, port type, operation, and

Listing 10.22   Use of <pick> construct

```
1     <process ... >
2        ...
3        <sequence>
4           ...
5           <pick>
6              <onMessage partnerLink="..."
7                          portType="..."
8                          operation="..."
9                          variable="...">
10                <sequence>
11                   <invoke ... />
12                   <receive ... />
13                </sequence>
14             </onMessage>
15             <onMessage partnerLink="..."
16                          portType="..."
17                          operation="..."
18                          variable="...">
19                <sequence>
20                   <invoke ... />
21                   <assign ... />
22                </sequence>
23             </onMessage>
24             <onAlarm>
25                <for>'P0Y0M0DT24H0M0.0S'</for>
26                <sequence>
27                   <assign ... />
28                   <reply ... />
29                </sequence>
30             </onAlarm>
31          </pick>
32          ...
33       </sequence>
34    </process>
```

the variable that will hold the incoming message. These are the same attributes as, for example, in the <receive> in Listing 10.10 on page 284.

All possible paths in Listing 10.22 are specified as a <sequence> block, but they could have been specified as another kind of block, such as a <flow> and <while>. In particular, if there would be a single activity in any of these paths, then the activity could have been inserted directly without the use of an enclosing block. This is similar to other BPEL constructs described in this section, namely <if>, <while>, and <repeatUntil>. These constructs have a body where the activities are to be placed. If there is a single activity to be included, then it can be inserted directly into the body of the construct. Otherwise, there needs to be some container to hold multiple activities; this container is typically a <sequence> or a <flow>.

10.4   Using Scopes

In Listing 10.21 we have seen a <forEach> loop that contains <scope> element to encapsulate the activities in the body of the loop. This <scope> element is actually a general construct that can be used anywhere in an orchestration. It appears in the

<forEach> loop because it is mandatory in that kind of loop, but it can also be used on its own as a means to define local variables and behavior.

The <scope> element is actually very similar in purpose to the scope shape introduced in Sect. 9.3.1 and revisited in Sect. 9.4.1. In particular, a scope shape may have exception handlers and possibly a compensation handler as well (see Fig. 9.18 on page 260). In a similar way, a <scope> element in BPEL can include one or more *fault handlers* and at most one compensation handler, as we will see in Sects. 10.4.1 and 10.4.2, respectively. In addition, the <scope> may include a *termination handler*, as explained in Sect. 10.4.3.

These three types of handlers—namely fault handlers, compensation handlers, and termination handlers—are referred to as *FCT-handlers* in the BPEL specification [19]. Although they are used for different purposes, they are all defined in a similar way in BPEL. Also, the <scope> element shares some common features with the top-level <process> element (we have seen, for example, that a <scope> can have its own variables, as a <process> does). This applies to FCT-handlers as well, i.e., a <process> can also have these types of handlers, although here we will be discussing them mainly in connection with the <scope> element.

10.4.1   Fault Handlers

In Sect. 9.3 we have seen that a scope shape can be extended with one or more catch blocks in order to handle any exception that may be raised during execution of the activities in that scope. In a similar way, the <scope> element in BPEL can be extended with one or more *fault handlers* in order to catch any exception raised in the activities contained in the <scope>.

Listing 10.23 shows an example. The <process> (line 1) is specified as a <sequence> of activities (line 3) which, at some point, include a <scope> (line 5). This <scope> has a <variables> section in lines 6–8, a <faultHandlers> section in lines 9–30, and a <sequence> of activities in lines 31–47. The novelty here is the set of fault handlers in lines 9–30. But before delving into these fault handlers, it will be useful to have a look at the sequence of activities first.

In lines 32–37 there is an <assign> activity whose purpose is to copy the result returned by the TempConvert Web service (line 34) to the temp variable (line 35). This variable has been declared earlier in line 7, and it is a local variable in this <scope>. The temp variable is used to specify the conditions of the <if> element in lines 38–46. In line 39 there is a condition (temp < 0) which tests whether the temperature value (in Celsius) is negative, and in line 42 there is another condition (temp > 40) to test whether the temperature is above 40 °C.

In case any of these conditions evaluates to true, then an exception will be thrown. In line 40 there is a special element called <throw>, which is similar in purpose to the throw exception shape described in Sect. 9.3.3. This element is used to throw an exception (i.e., fault) with a certain name. The name of the fault being raised in line 40 is NegativeTemperature.

Listing 10.23 Use of fault handlers

```
1    <process ... >
2        ...
3      <sequence>
4          ...
5        <scope>
6          <variables>
7            <variable name="temp" type="xs:double"/>
8          </variables>
9          <faultHandlers>
10           <catch faultName="tns:NegativeTemperature">
11             <sequence>
12               <invoke ... />
13               <receive ... />
14             </sequence>
15           </catch>
16           <catch faultName="tns:TemperatureTooHigh"
17                   faultVariable="tempResponse"
18                   faultMessageType="tns:ConvertTemperatureResponse">
19             <sequence>
20               <assign ... />
21               <invoke ... />
22             </sequence>
23           </catch>
24           <catchAll>
25             <sequence>
26               <assign ... />
27               <reply ... />
28             </sequence>
29           </catchAll>
30         </faultHandlers>
31         <sequence>
32           <assign>
33             <copy>
34               <from>$ConvertTemperatureOut.parameters/return</from>
35               <to variable="temp"/>
36             </copy>
37           </assign>
38           <if>
39             <condition>temp &lt; 0</condition>
40             <throw faultName="tns:NegativeTemperature"/>
41             <elseif>
42               <condition>temp &gt; 40</condition>
43               <throw faultName="tns:TemperatureTooHigh"
44                       faultVariable="ConvertTemperatureOut"/>
45             </elseif>
46           </if>
47         </sequence>
48       </scope>
49        ...
50      </sequence>
51    </process>
```

On the other hand, there is another <throw> element in lines 43–44. This element throws a fault with the name TemperatureTooHigh, and in this case there is a *fault variable* associated with the fault. Here, the fault variable is the ConvertTemperatureOut variable that is being used in the orchestration to hold the response from the TempConvert Web service. This means that the fault TemperatureTooHigh is being thrown with associated data, the data being the content of the ConvertTemperatureOut variable, which is the response received from the TempConvert Web service.

In the <faultHandlers> section in lines 9–23, it is possible to see that there are three fault handlers (lines 10, 16, and 24):

- The first fault handler in lines 10–15 is for NegativeTemperature faults. If a fault named NegativeTemperature is raised within the <scope>, then this fault handler will catch it by carrying out the sequence of activities in lines 11–14.
- The second fault handler in lines 16–23 is for faults named TemperatureTooHigh and which carry a fault variable of type ConvertTemperatureResponse (line 18). This is a message type defined in the WSDL for the TempConvert Web service. If a TemperatureTooHigh fault is raised but does not carry such data, then it will not be caught by this fault handler; the fault really needs to bring a compatible data type in order to match the definition of this exception handler.

  In this example, the fault that is being thrown in lines 43–44 does match, since ConvertTemperatureOut in line 44 is an orchestration variable that holds a message of type ConvertTemperatureResponse. Therefore, the fault will be handled by performing the sequence of activities in lines 19–22.

  Inside the fault handler, the fault variable is accessible through the name tempResponse (line 17). So, for example, it is possible to use an <assign> (line 20) to read the temperature value contained in the fault variable, and copy it to another message which will be used to invoke some Web service (line 21).
- The third fault handler in lines 24–29 is a <cathAll>, meaning that it will catch any fault that is not handled by the previous fault handlers. In this example it is not clear where such fault could appear from, but anyway a <cathAll> is used precisely as safety measure against unexpected exceptions. In this case, it is not possible to associate any data with the exception, but it is possible to handle it in some way, such as by returning a message to the client, as in line 27.

10.4.2   Compensation Handlers

The use of compensation in BPEL works in a similar way to the compensation mechanisms described in Sect. 9.4. Basically, compensation is a means to undo work that has already been committed. Typically, this requires performing additional actions in order to cancel or revert the effects of activities which have already been performed (e.g., after booking a flight ticket the only way to undo that action is to perform another action to cancel the reservation).

In BPEL, any actions that may have to be compensated need to be enclosed in a <scope> with a compensation handler. In the event of an error (i.e., a fault), the compensation handler will be triggered in order to undo the effects of the actions that were performed within that <scope>. However, it should be noted that, by definition, compensation can only be applied *after* the <scope> has successfully completed. It makes no sense to ask for compensation before the <scope> has been executed, because there is nothing to compensate; and also it does not make sense to ask for compensation during execution of the <scope>, since the outcome of its actions are still unknown (i.e., it may happen that an error occurs and nothing gets done, so there is no need to compensate).

Compensation of a given <scope> can only occur after the <scope> has completed, and therefore the compensating actions can only be invoked from *outside* that <scope>. In other words, a <scope> has a compensation handler so that if an error occurs in the outer element where the <scope> is embedded, that outer element will call the compensation handler. The outer element may be the top-level <process> or a <scope> which contains other nested <scope> elements. The mechanism is similar to the one that is illustrated in Fig. 9.16 on page 257.

Listing 10.24 shows an example in BPEL. Here, there is an outer scope (lines 5–38) which contains two inner scopes (lines 12–23 and lines 24–35). Each of these inner scopes has its own compensation handler (lines 13–18 and lines 25–30). On the other hand, the outer scope has one fault handler (lines 6–10). When a fault is raised within the outer scope (as is the case in line 36), the fault handler (lines 7–9) triggers compensation of the inner scopes.

The outer scope is named OuterScope in line 5, and it has a <faultHandlers> section in lines 6–10, which contains a <catchAll> fault handler. So, whatever fault is thrown inside the OuterScope in line 36, it will be caught by the fault handler in lines 7–9. This fault handler has a special activity, which is called <compensate>. This BPEL activity does exactly the same thing as the compensate shape described in Sect. 9.4.2: it triggers compensation of the inner scopes which have already completed. As always, compensation takes place in reverse order of execution, so the compensation handler for InnerScope2 (lines 25–30) will be run before the compensation handler for InnerScope1 (lines 13–18).

The compensation in this example is very similar to the behavior in the example of Sect. 9.4.4. Also, it should be noted that if an exception occurs within the OuterScope in Listing 10.24, but before line 36, then the exception will still be caught by the fault handler in lines 7–9 (because it is a <catchAll> fault handler) and compensation will be triggered. However, the actual compensating actions that will take place depend on where the exception occurred. If the exception occurred inside InnerScope2, then this scope has not been completed and therefore only the compensation handler for InnerScope1 will be invoked. On the other hand, if the exception occurred inside InnerScope1, then none of the scopes have been completed and therefore there is nothing to compensate.

In addition to <compensate>, BPEL provides another activity known as <compensateScope>. The difference between <compensate> and <compensateScope> is that <compensateScope> includes an attribute called target which is used to indicate which specific inner scope should be compensated. For example, if the <compensate/> activity in line 8 in Listing 10.24 would be replaced by,

```
<compensateScope target="InnerScope1"/>
```

then this would mean that only the compensation handler for InnerScope1 should be invoked (if InnerScope1 completed successfully). Both <compensate> and <compensateScope> can only be used in fault handlers (as in Listing 10.24), in compensation

Listing 10.24 Use of compensation

```
1   <process ... >
2       ...
3       <sequence>
4           ...
5           <scope name="OuterScope">
6               <faultHandlers>
7                   <catchAll>
8                       <compensate/>
9                   </catchAll>
10              </faultHandlers>
11              <sequence>
12                  <scope name="InnerScope1">
13                      <compensationHandler>
14                          <sequence>
15                              <invoke ... />
16                              <receive ... />
17                          </sequence>
18                      </compensationHandler>
19                      <sequence>
20                          <invoke ... />
21                          <receive ... />
22                      </sequence>
23                  </scope>
24                  <scope name="InnerScope2">
25                      <compensationHandler>
26                          <sequence>
27                              <invoke ... />
28                              <receive ... />
29                          </sequence>
30                      </compensationHandler>
31                      <sequence>
32                          <invoke ... />
33                          <receive ... />
34                      </sequence>
35                  </scope>
36                  <throw ... />
37              </sequence>
38          </scope>
39          ...
40      </sequence>
41  </process>
```

handlers (to request compensation of nested scopes), and in termination handlers, which are addressed in the next section.

10.4.3 Termination Handlers

In case an exception occurs inside a <scope>, the orchestration flow is interrupted and control passes over to a fault handler, if there is an appropriate handler for the exception in the current scope. If there is not, then the exception escalates to the parent <scope>, and so on, until an appropriate fault handler is found. If no fault handler is found, then the exception escalates to the top-level <process>, bringing the orchestration to a halt. In any case, regardless of whether the exception is handled or

Listing 10.25 Use of termination handler

```
1    <process ... >
2        ...
3      <sequence>
4          ...
5        <scope name="Scope1">
6           <faultHandlers>
7              <catch ... >
8                 <sequence>
9                    <assign ... />
10                   <reply ... />
11                </sequence>
12             </catch>
13          </faultHandlers>
14          <scope name="Scope2">
15             <terminationHandler>
16                <sequence>
17                   <assign ... />
18                   <invoke ... />
19                </sequence>
20             </terminationHandler>
21             <sequence>
22                <invoke ... />
23                <receive ... />
24             </sequence>
25          </scope>
26       </scope>
27          ...
28      </sequence>
29   </process>
```

not, the original <scope> where the exception occurred does not resume execution, so one can say that it has been forcefully terminated.

Such forced termination may create some problems if, for example, the <scope> was interacting with external resources or manipulating orchestration variables. It may happen that a <scope> should not be interrupted abruptly, even in case of an error, due to the fact that it could leave an inconsistent state in those external resources or internal variables. In this case, and even before control is passed over to a fault handler, some cleanup may be necessary. This is precisely the purpose of a termination handler, i.e., it provides a <scope> (which is being forcefully terminated) with the opportunity to perform some cleanup actions before control is handed over to the fault handling mechanisms.

Listing 10.25 illustrates an example. Here, there is an outer scope called Scope1 (lines 5–26), which contains an inner scope called Scope2 (lines 14–25). The inner scope has no fault handlers, because all the error handling has been left for the outer scope to take care of. For that purpose, Scope1 has a <faultHandlers> section in lines 6–13. Therefore, if an error occurs in Scope2, the error will be caught and handled by the fault handler Scope1. However, if an error occurs in Scope2 (i.e., somewhere in lines 21–24), control cannot be handed over immediately to the fault handler in Scope1, because Scope2 needs to perform some cleanup tasks.

For this reason, Scope2 has a termination handler in lines 15–20 (there can be at most one in any <scope>). This termination handler will come into play only if Scope2 needs to be interrupted. If everything runs without error (or, in the event of an error, the error occurs outside Scope2), there will be no need to run the termination handler. In this example, the termination handler executes a sequence of an <assign> (line 17) and an <invoke> (line 18), but it could run other types of activity as well. In particular, if Scope2 contained other nested scopes with the need for compensation, then the termination handler might include a <compensate> (or <compensateScope>) activity to trigger compensation of those inner scopes.

10.4.4   Event Handlers

Besides the three types of handlers—namely fault handlers, compensation handlers, and termination handlers—described in the previous sections, BPEL provides an interesting feature, which is the possibility of a <scope> (or the top-level <process> element in an orchestration) to respond to external events that occur concurrently during execution. Such events can be either a message that is received from outside the orchestration (through some partner link) or a timer that elapses after a specified interval or deadline. These events are similar to the possible events in a <pick> element, as described in Sect. 10.3.4. However, whereas the <pick> element is used as an activity in the orchestration flow, here we are referring to events that occur in parallel and at any point during the orchestration flow.

The purpose of such events can be better understood by considering a concrete scenario. Suppose, for example, that the order processing of an online bookstore is implemented by means of a BPEL orchestration. Then, as the order is being processed, the customer may at any point inquire about the order status, or may even want to cancel the order if it has not been shipped yet. The order processing orchestration must be prepared to receive and handle these requests at any point in time, in parallel with the main orchestration flow. Such behavior can be implemented in a BPEL orchestration by means of *event handlers*.

Listing 10.26 shows an example of an orchestration with two event handlers. These event handlers are enclosed in an <eventHandlers> section in lines 9–33. The actual orchestration flow is enclosed by the <sequence> block in lines 34–36, so it can be seen that the event handlers are being specified outside of the main orchestration flow. They are intended to run in parallel with the orchestration flow, should any of the specified events occur during execution.

The first event handler in lines 10–23 is intended to handle an incoming message through a given partner link, port type, and operation. These attributes are specified in lines 10–12. In addition, the incoming message will be accessible through a certain variable (line 14) of a certain type (line 13). Together, the messageType and variable attributes are an implicit declaration for a variable that will exist within the <scope> associated with this event handler (lines 15–22). Inside that <scope>, the event handler invokes a Web service (possibly to retrieve the order status as in the scenario above) and replies to the client who invoked the orchestration.

The second event handler in lines 24–32 is a timer that elapses after 48 h, as specified by the expression in line 25. The syntax of <onAlarm> here is similar to the

Listing 10.26 Use of event handlers

```
1    <?xml version="1.0" encoding="UTF-8"?>
2    <process ... >
3        <partnerLinks>
4            ...
5        </partnerLinks>
6        <variables>
7            ...
8        </variables>
9        <eventHandlers>
10           <onEvent partnerLink="..."
11                    portType="..."
12                    operation="..."
13                    messageType="..."
14                    variable="...">
15               <scope>
16                   <sequence>
17                       <assign ... />
18                       <invoke ... />
19                       <assign ... />
20                       <reply ... />
21                   </sequence>
22               </scope>
23           </onEvent>
24           <onAlarm>
25               <for>'P0Y0M0DT48H0M0.0S'</for>
26               <scope>
27                   <sequence>
28                       <assign ... />
29                       <invoke ... />
30                   </sequence>
31               </scope>
32           </onAlarm>
33       </eventHandlers>
34       <sequence>
35           ...
36       </sequence>
37   </process>
```

use of the same element in the <pick> construct of Sect. 10.3.4. After the specified interval, the timer elapses and the event handler executes the <scope> in lines 26–31. All of this happens in parallel and independently of the orchestration flow in the <sequence> block of lines 34–36.

In contrast with the FCT-handlers described in the previous sections, which are invoked only in special circumstances, event handlers are considered to be "normal behavior" of the <process> or <scope> where they are embedded.

Also, event handlers are intended to be triggered by the arrival of certain messages. For this to work, these messages must reach the correct orchestration instance. For example, if a customer inquires about the status of an order, then the request must be routed to the orchestration instance that is handling that order (other orders may be under processing by other orchestration instances at the same time). Therefore, for an event handler to be triggered by an incoming message, it is necessary to use some sort of correlation, so that the message is delivered to the correct orchestration instance, as explained in the next section.

10.5 Correlations

In Sect. 9.2, we addressed the important concept of correlations and why they are needed when a orchestration is instantiated multiple times. When an orchestration includes some form of receive activity (such as a <receive>, <onMessage> or <onEvent> in BPEL), this means that at run-time the orchestration will be waiting for an incoming message at that point in the flow. However, at run-time there will be multiple instances of the same orchestration running at the same time. If all of them are waiting for an incoming message then, as soon as a message arrives, which orchestration instance should get the message?

Correlations are a mechanism that provides an answer to this question. Basically, the message will be delivered to the orchestration instance which has a matching correlation id. Typically, the correlation id is a unique value or some instance-specific data that can be used to identify each orchestration instance and distinguish it from every other. When exchanging messages with an external system, the correlation id should be present in every message, so that every incoming message can be routed to the correct orchestration instance. For example, in a request–response interaction with an external system, the outgoing message carries a correlation id and the external system replicates the correlation id in the response, so that the response can be routed back to the same orchestration instance.

In Sect. 9.2.2 we have seen that a correlation id is defined as a set of properties, and that these properties come from (i.e., they are *promoted* from) the message schemas available to the orchestration (see Fig. 9.7 on page 241). Now, in BPEL, an orchestration is a means to invoke one or more Web services, and the message schemas that are available to the orchestration are the message types defined in the WSDL interfaces for those Web services. Back in Sect. 6.4.3, we have seen that a WSDL interface defines a series of data types and messages to be used when invoking the operations of a Web service. In addition to types and messages, it is possible to define *properties* that correspond to particular elements in those messages. These properties can then be used as a correlation id in BPEL orchestrations.

Once the properties that will serve as correlation id have been promoted, it is possible to define a correlation based on those properties. In Sect. 9.2, we have seen that defining a correlation involves creating a *correlation type* and a *correlation set*. Basically, the correlation type defines the set of properties to be used as correlation id, and the correlation set is an instance of a given correlation type. The correlation set is the actual correlation that will be *initialized* and *followed* by the constructs in the orchestration, as explained in Sect. 9.2.4. In a request–response interaction, for example, the correlation set is "initialized" when the request message is sent out, and it is "followed" when the response comes back in.

The fact that there are two separate concepts—i.e., correlation type and correlation set—makes it possible to create multiple correlation sets based on the same correlation type. This means that there can be several correlation sets of the same type being initialized and followed in an orchestration. This would make sense if these correlation sets would use the same set of properties for the correlation id, but would have different values for those properties. However, usually the properties used for correlation are chosen so that each orchestration instance will have one (and only one) value for the correlation id. Therefore, it is rather uncommon in practice to initialize multiple correlation sets in the same orchestration instance, since a single correlation set will suffice. Once it has been initialized, the correlation set can be followed by other shapes throughout the orchestration.

For this reason, the BPEL language adopts a simplified view of these concepts and considers only the concept of correlation set, but not of correlation type (at least not explicitly). Correlation sets are defined using the <correlationSet> element and, even though it does not appear explicitly, the concept of correlation type can be recognized as being embedded in the definition of a correlation set.

10.5.1   An Example

Suppose that in order to invoke the orchestration in Sect. 10.1 we would need to provide not only the city name (e.g., "San Francisco") but also the state (e.g., "California") so that the input string is in the form "city, state" (e.g., "San Francisco, California"). Suppose that, in order to get such string, we would make use of another orchestration which, given a city and a state, will concatenate the city and state into the form "city, state." We assume that this new orchestration will receive the city name and the state in two separate messages, so it will be necessary to make use of a correlation in the second <receive>.

Figure 10.3 illustrates this new orchestration. It comprises mainly a <sequence> with two <receive> activities, one <assign> and one <reply>. The two <receive> activities are intended to receive the city and state separately, the <assign> concatenates both into one string, and the <reply> returns the result to the client.

The first <receive> is an activating receive, i.e., it contains the attribute value createInstance=yes. The second <receive> is non-activating (i.e., createInstance=no), since it runs within the orchestration instance that was created by the first <receive>. Therefore, this second <receive> needs a correlation, since the second incoming message must be routed to an orchestration instance that already exists.

To implement such correlation, we require that both messages (i.e., SubmitCityIn and SubmitStateIn) include a special field called reqID (for "request id"). When the city name is sent to the orchestration in the first message, this message will carry a certain value for reqID. Afterwards, when the state is sent to the orchestration in the second message, this message will carry the same value for the reqID field. This way it is possible to route the second message to the same orchestration instance.

However, for this to happen, the first <receive> must initialize a correlation set, and the second <receive> must follow that same correlation set. For illustrative purposes, the final <reply> was made to follow the correlation set as well, but this would not be necessary, since the response <SubmitCityOut> is already correlated to the initial request <SubmitCityIn> through the use of the same partner link, port type, and operation. In addition, since the orchestration is synchronous (due to the use of

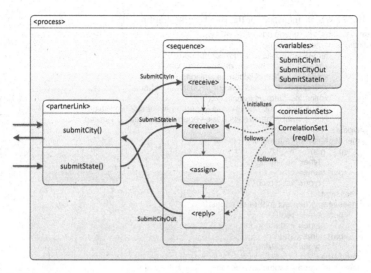

Fig. 10.3 Graphical depiction of an orchestration using a correlation set

<reply>), the client is blocked while waiting for the response, so there is no danger of confusing the responses from multiple requests.

The correlation set relies on the fact that every message has a reqID field. This is the property that will be used for correlation. Therefore, it is necessary to specify how the value for this property can be fetched from each message (this is equivalent to property promotion as described in Sect. 9.2.2). In particular, the value of reqID that comes in SubmitCityIn is used to initialize the correlation set. The second <receive> will follow the correlation set, meaning that SubmitStateIn must have a matching reqID in order to be routed to the same orchestration instance.

10.5.2 Defining Properties and Property Aliases

In BPEL, the properties that are used for correlation are defined in the WSDL interface for the orchestration, using the extensibility mechanisms of WSDL 1.1 [30]. In fact, these mechanisms can be used not only to define each property (with some name and data type), but also to specify how that property can be obtained from each message. In essence, this is how property promotion works in BPEL.

Listing 10.27 shows the WSDL interface for the orchestration in Fig. 10.3. This WSDL interface defines the messages, port type, and operations available to interact with the orchestration. These are standard WSDL elements. Further below, one finds the definition for a partner link type (lines 41–44), one property (lines 45–46), and three property aliases (lines 47–55). These are defined through the extensibility mechanisms of WSDL.

Listing 10.27   WSDL interface for the BPEL orchestration

```
 1    <?xml version="1.0" encoding="UTF-8"?>
 2    <definitions name="corrDemo"
 3                 targetNamespace="http://example.org/"
 4                 xmlns="http://schemas.xmlsoap.org/wsdl/"
 5                 xmlns:wsdl="http://schemas.xmlsoap.org/wsdl/"
 6                 xmlns:xsd="http://www.w3.org/2001/XMLSchema"
 7                 xmlns:tns="http://example.org/"
 8                 xmlns:plnk="http://docs.oasis-open.org/wsbpel/2.0/plnktype"
 9                 xmlns:vprop="http://docs.oasis-open.org/wsbpel/2.0/varprop">
10        <types/>
11        <message name="submitCityRequest">
12            <part name="reqID"
13                  type="xsd:string"/>
14            <part name="city"
15                  type="xsd:string"/>
16        </message>
17        <message name="submitStateRequest">
18            <part name="reqID"
19                  type="xsd:string"/>
20            <part name="state"
21                  type="xsd:string"/>
22        </message>
23        <message name="submitCityResponse">
24            <part name="reqID"
25                  type="xsd:string"/>
26            <part name="result"
27                  type="xsd:string"/>
28        </message>
29        <portType name="corrDemoPortType">
30            <operation name="submitCity">
31                <input name="input1"
32                       message="tns:submitCityRequest"/>
33                <output name="output1"
34                       message="tns:submitCityResponse"/>
35            </operation>
36            <operation name="submitState">
37                <input name="input2"
38                       message="tns:submitStateRequest"/>
39            </operation>
40        </portType>
41        <plnk:partnerLinkType name="corrDemo">
42            <plnk:role name="corrDemoPortTypeRole"
43                       portType="tns:corrDemoPortType"/>
44        </plnk:partnerLinkType>
45        <vprop:property name="reqID"
46                       type="xsd:string"/>
47        <vprop:propertyAlias propertyName="tns:reqID"
48                       messageType="tns:submitCityRequest"
49                       part="reqID"/>
50        <vprop:propertyAlias propertyName="tns:reqID"
51                       messageType="tns:submitStateRequest"
52                       part="reqID"/>
53        <vprop:propertyAlias propertyName="tns:reqID"
54                       messageType="tns:submitCityResponse"
55                       part="reqID"/>
56    </definitions>
```

The partner link type defines the type of partner link that the orchestration exposes to the outside world. It has a single role being defined in lines 42–43, which suggests that the orchestration will be synchronous (asynchronous BPEL orchestrations will define two roles, as explained in Sect. 10.2.2). After that, comes a property definition in lines 45–46. The property is called reqID and is of type string. This defines the property, but does not say where the value for this property comes from. In lines 12, 18, and 24, it is possible to see that every message to be exchanged with the orchestration has a <reqID> element. This is where the value for the reqID property will come from.

It should be noted that in this case, as it often happens in practice, the correlation property reqID has the same name as the message elements <reqID> where the property value comes from. However, this is by no means mandatory, and the property could have a different name from the elements which provide its value. For example, the request id could have a different name in each message, and the property could have yet another name, and it would still be possible to define the relationship between the property and each element where the property value comes from. This relationship is defined by means of a *property alias*.

In lines 47–55 of Listing 10.27 there are three property aliases being defined, one for each message. The first property alias in lines 47–49 defines a relationship between the reqID property and the <reqID> element in the submitCityRequest message (defined above in lines 11–16). The second property alias in lines 50–52 defines a relationship between the reqID property and the <reqID> element in the submitStateRequest message (lines 17–22). Finally, the third property alias in lines 53–55 defines a relationship between the reqID property and the <reqID> element in the submitCityResponse message (lines 17–22). This completes the definition of the correlation property and its property aliases.

10.5.3 Defining the Correlation Set

Now that a property and its property aliases have been defined, it is possible to create a correlation set based on that property. Listing 10.28 illustrates how this can be done. In fact, Listing 10.28 contains the first part of the BPEL orchestration. Here it is possible to recognize a <partnerLinks> section (lines 9–13), a <variables> section (lines 14–21), and a new <correlationSets> section (lines 22–25).

As usual, the BPEL orchestration is enclosed in a <process> element, which opens in lines 2–5 and will close in Listing 10.29 to be shown later. The <import> in lines 8–10 brings in the elements defined in the WSDL interface of Listing 10.27. Among other things, this imports the partner link type defined in lines 41–44 of Listing 10.27. This partner link type is used in lines 10–12 of Listing 10.28 to create a partner link for the orchestration. In this partner link, the orchestration will play the role of service, as indicated by the myRole attribute in line 12.

The <variables> section in lines 14–21 defines three variables that are meant to hold the three messages exchanged between the client and the orchestration, as depicted in Fig. 10.3. The types for these messages—as can be seen in lines 16, 18, 20—correspond to one of the message types defined in the WSDL interface of Listing 10.27. In particular, SubmitCityIn carries the city name, SubmitStateIn carries the state, and SubmitCityOut carries the result of the orchestration in the form "city,

Listing 10.28   Definition of a correlation set

```
1    <?xml version="1.0" encoding="UTF-8"?>
2    <process name="corrDemo"
3              targetNamespace="http://example.org/"
4              xmlns:tns="http://example.org/"
5              xmlns="http://docs.oasis-open.org/wsbpel/2.0/process/executable">
6        <import namespace="http://example.org/"
7                 location="corrDemo.wsdl"
8                 importType="http://schemas.xmlsoap.org/wsdl/"/>
9        <partnerLinks>
10           <partnerLink name="PartnerLink1"
11                        partnerLinkType="tns:corrDemo"
12                        myRole="corrDemoPortTypeRole"/>
13       </partnerLinks>
14       <variables>
15           <variable name="SubmitCityIn"
16                    messageType="tns:submitCityRequest"/>
17           <variable name="SubmitStateIn"
18                    messageType="tns:submitStateRequest"/>
19           <variable name="SubmitCityOut"
20                    messageType="tns:submitCityResponse"/>
21       </variables>
22       <correlationSets>
23           <correlationSet name="CorrelationSet1"
24                           properties="tns:reqID"/>
25       </correlationSets>
26       ...
```

state." It should be noted that SubmitCityOut holds the response to SubmitCityIn. These are the input and output messages for the submitCity operation defined in Listing 10.27. On the other hand, SubmitStateIn holds the input for the submitState operation, which has no output message.

Now, the interesting part comes in lines 22–25, where there is a new section to define the correlation sets that will be used in the orchestration. Here, only one correlation set is being defined: the name is CorrelationSet1 (line 23) and the property to be used in the correlation is reqID (line 24), which has been previously defined in Listing 10.27 and imported through lines 6–8. The attribute in line 24 is actually called properties, meaning that, if several properties would be used for the correlation, these could be all specified in the value for this attribute. In this case, they would be separated by a space (e.g., properties="tns:reqID tns:cityName", if a property called cityName had been defined).

The name of the correlation set (line 23) is important because this is the way the correlation set will be referred to in other constructs.

10.5.4   Using the Correlation Set

Listing 10.29 shows the second part of the BPEL orchestration. Essentially, this is the orchestration flow enclosed in a <sequence> block. This sequence comprises the following activities: a <receive> activity (Receive1 in line 3) to receive the first message with the city name; another <receive> activity (Receive2 in line 14) to receive the second message with the state; an <assign> activity (Assign1 in line 25)

Listing 10.29 Use of a correlation set

```
1     ...
2         <sequence>
3           <receive name="Receive1"
4                    createInstance="yes"
5                    partnerLink="PartnerLink1"
6                    operation="submitCity"
7                    portType="tns:corrDemoPortType"
8                    variable="SubmitCityIn">
9             <correlations>
10                <correlation set="CorrelationSet1"
11                             initiate="yes"/>
12            </correlations>
13          </receive>
14          <receive name="Receive2"
15                   createInstance="no"
16                   partnerLink="PartnerLink1"
17                   operation="submitState"
18                   portType="tns:corrDemoPortType"
19                   variable="SubmitStateIn">
20            <correlations>
21                <correlation set="CorrelationSet1"
22                             initiate="no"/>
23            </correlations>
24          </receive>
25          <assign name="Assign1">
26            <copy>
27                <from>concat($SubmitCityIn.city, ', ', $SubmitStateIn.state)</from>
28                <to variable="SubmitCityOut"
29                    part="result"/>
30            </copy>
31            <copy>
32                <from variable="SubmitStateIn"
33                      part="reqID"/>
34                <to variable="SubmitCityOut"
35                    part="reqID"/>
36            </copy>
37          </assign>
38          <reply name="Reply1"
39                 partnerLink="PartnerLink1"
40                 operation="submitCity"
41                 portType="tns:corrDemoPortType"
42                 variable="SubmitCityOut">
43            <correlations>
44                <correlation set="CorrelationSet1"
45                             initiate="no"/>
46            </correlations>
47          </reply>
48        </sequence>
49    </process>
```

to concatenate the city and state into the form "city, state"; and finally a <reply> activity (Reply1 in line 38) to return the result to the client.

The first <receive> is an activating receive, as can be seen by the createInstance attribute in line 4. This is the <receive> that triggers the orchestration by creating a new orchestration instance. The second <receive> runs within a preexisting orchestration instance, so it must necessarily make use of some correlation. In lines 20–23 there is a nested <correlations> block to specify which correlations (if more than one) are associated with this <receive>. In this case there is only one, and it is the correlation set (CorrelationSet1) defined earlier.

In line 22, the attribute initiate specifies that the correlation set is not being initialized in this <receive>. In fact, this second <receive> must follow some preexisting correlation, because it runs within an existing orchestration instance. In this example, we have chosen to initialize the correlation set right at the beginning of the orchestration, in the first <receive> (in fact, there is no other choice in this orchestration). Therefore, as soon as the first message is received, the reqID property is retrieved (using the property alias defined for that message, see lines 47–49 in Listing 10.27) and the correlation set is initialized.

This initialization takes place in lines 10–11 of Listing 10.29. Here, in the first <receive>, there is also a nested <correlations> block. Inside this block, Correlation-Set1 is being initialized, as indicated by the initiate attribute in line 11.

A third use of the same correlation set can be seen in the <reply> activity in lines 38–47. Here, too, there is a nested <correlations> block to specify that this message exchange follows the same correlation. As in the second <receive>, the initiate attribute in line 45 is set to "no".

Besides "yes" and "no", BPEL provides a third possibility, which is initiate="join". This value means that the activity follows the correlation set, if it has already been initialized; but if it has not, then the activity initializes it. However, the use of this third possibility is relatively less common.

10.5.5   Use of Correlation in Other Activities

In previous sections, we have described some BPEL constructs which actually require the use of a correlation, even though that requirement has not been mentioned at that point, because the use of correlations in BPEL had not been discussed before. The following constructs require the use of an already initialized correlation set (e.g., as in the second <receive> of Listing 10.29):

- When an orchestration invokes a Web service asynchronously, as explained in Sect. 10.2.1, the invocation has two steps: an <invoke> and a <receive>. This <receive> must follow some previously initialized correlation set. If not before, then the correlation set can be initialized in the preceding <invoke>.
- When a orchestration uses a <pick> activity, as described in Sect. 10.3.4, every <onMessage> event must follow some previously initialized correlation set. (This can be done by nesting a <correlations> block, as before.) An exception is when <pick> is the first activity in an orchestration. In this case, the <onMessage> events need not (actually, cannot) follow any correlation, but then the <pick> activity should make use of the createInstance attribute (i.e., as in <pick create-Instance="yes">) in order to instantiate the orchestration.
- In Sect. 10.4.4 we discussed the possibility of an orchestration (or scope) responding to events in parallel with the flow. In particular, we discussed the possibility of receiving a message (through the <onEvent> construct) and performing some tasks while the main flow in the orchestration keeps running

without being interrupted. Naturally, in order for such message to reach a running orchestration instance, the <onEvent> construct must follow some previously initialized correlation set. Again, this can be done by nesting a <correlations> block.

10.6 Conclusion

In this chapter we have discussed the main constructs of the BPEL language, which is a standard, XML-based language for defining orchestrations. Most of the constructs available in BPEL have a direct correspondence to the concepts and constructs that have been presented in previous chapters, namely in Chaps. 8 and 9. For example, the decide shape can be represented by an <if>, the parallel shape by a <flow>, the loop shape by a <while> or <repeatUntil>, and the listen shape by a <pick> activity. Also, exception handlers and compensation handlers can be enclosed in a <scope>, which is equivalent to the scope shape.

There are, however, some distinct and unique features that can only be found in BPEL. The focus on partner links, for example, is one of them. Since BPEL orchestrations have a close relationship with Web services, partner links are a means to define the interface between the two and to specify which part will play the role of client, and which part will play the role of service. In a sense, this is somewhat equivalent to ports in a BizTalk orchestration, but whereas both partner links and ports can be used to specify the interaction between the orchestration and the external services to be invoked, partner links can also be used to specify the interaction between an orchestration and its clients.

Another difference that is worth mentioning is the possibility of using event handlers to respond to events in parallel with the flow. Although this is of much practical interest, this feature is hard to find in integration platforms that are based on languages other than BPEL. In fact, it will be very difficult to develop integration solutions based on platforms that do not have a rich set of constructs with precise semantics, such as the ones provided by BPEL. This shows just how important BPEL is, as an initiative to standardize the constructs that every integration platform should provide. In addition, some BPEL constructs have a certain similarity—at least on a conceptual level—to the graphical constructs that are often used to create business process models, as we will see in the next chapter.

Part V
Processes

Chapter 11
Process Modeling with BPMN

In the previous chapter, we have seen that BPEL provides a set of standard constructs to define the behavior of an orchestration at run-time. These constructs are specified in XML and do not have a graphical representation. However, integration platforms that are based on (or at least inspired in) BPEL often provide development tools where an orchestration can be designed by resorting to graphical elements (or shapes) that represent those constructs. Examples of how flow constructs can be depicted in a graphical way can be found in Chaps. 8 and 9. In fact, this is how we introduced the main concepts associated with orchestration flow, by explaining what a series of shapes actually mean in terms of run-time behavior.

Clearly, BPEL is a standard that is geared towards execution, by defining orchestrations as a series of Web service invocations. Given a BPEL orchestration, which is essentially an XML document, it is possible to have an execution engine that parses the XML and runs each activity according to the behavior of each BPEL element, as defined in the BPEL standard [19]. In this case, we could say that such execution engine is *BPEL-compliant*. However, such engine can work only if a fully specified BPEL orchestration is provided. In other words, the BPEL orchestration is an *executable model* of some business process that has been fully characterized, to the point that it can be run by an execution engine. This is the reason why BPEL stands for *Business Process Execution Language*.

In practice, in order to arrive at such executable model, it is necessary to understand and design the business process. This usually involves a significant amount of effort, as a process model is created and then changed and refined over several iterations. For this purpose, it is necessary to have appropriate tools—namely, a graphical process modeling language—to represent the process in an intuitive way, so that it can be easily understood and manipulated by business analysts. When finished, such *design model* (as opposed to executable model) will serve as the blueprint for system integrators to implement the process as a set of one or more services and orchestrations, according to the view described in Chap. 7.

Just like there is a standard (i.e., BPEL) that defines the constructs that can be used for execution, there is also a standard to define the graphical constructs that can be used for designing business processes. This standard is called BPMN

D.R. Ferreira, *Enterprise Systems Integration*, DOI 10.1007/978-3-642-40796-3_11,
© Springer-Verlag Berlin Heidelberg 2013

(Business Process Model and Notation) [21] and it has succeeded in gathering the support of most IT vendors. There are, of course, other process modeling languages, such as Petri nets [1] and EPCs [26], but here we are interested in the fact that BPMN is not only a standard, but is also a language that shares at least part of its conceptual foundations with BPEL. This makes of BPMN a useful tool to design process models which can be translated into executable orchestrations.

The purpose of this chapter is not to provide an exhaustive presentation of all BPMN features,[1] but to describe the typical structure of BPMN process models and to highlight the similarities between BPMN constructs and BPEL constructs. The correspondence is not one-to-one, but the concepts that underlie some BPMN constructs are very similar to the original purpose of some BPEL constructs. In most cases, it will be possible to figure out a way to implement a given BPMN model with BPEL constructs. This is quite interesting from a practical point of view, since it becomes possible to bridge the gap between the process models developed by business analysts (typically, using BPMN) and the integration solutions that are required to implement those business processes (e.g., using BPEL).

11.1   Elements of a BPMN Process Model

In order to illustrate the basic structure and elements in a BPMN process model, we will use a purchasing scenario as an example. This purchasing scenario can be described as follows:

> In a company, an employee needs a certain commodity (e.g., a printer cartridge). In order to get that product, a requisition form must be filled in and sent to the warehouse. The warehouse will check whether the product is available in stock. If it is available, then the warehouse dispatches the product to the employee. Otherwise, the product must be purchased from an external supplier. In this case, the purchasing department prepares a purchase order and sends it to a supplier. The supplier confirms the order and delivers the product directly to the warehouse. The warehouse receives the product, which includes updating the stock, and dispatches the product to the employee who originally submitted the request.

Figure 11.1 shows how this process could be modeled using BPMN. Basically, there are two different entities here—the company and the supplier—and each of them is represented by its own *pool*. The process in Fig. 11.1 has two pools, one named "Purchase Process" and another named "Supplier." From the description above, we know nothing about what the supplier does internally, other than the fact that it receives the purchase order and returns an order confirmation. Therefore, its pool is left blank, without any details. In contrast, the internal behavior of the company is described in detail. This will be the main focus of this model.

---

[1]For that purpose, the reader may refer to a more thorough introduction, such as [4].

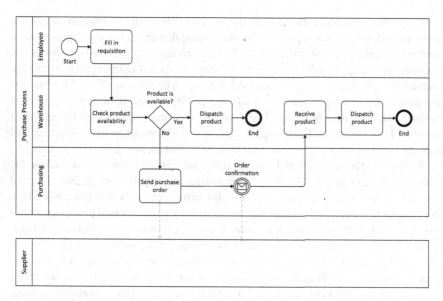

Fig. 11.1 Example of a purchase process represented in BPMN (adapted from [12])

Inside the company, it is possible to identify three different organization units, namely: the employee who requests the product, the warehouse, and the purchasing department. These are represented by so-called *swimlanes* in Fig. 11.1. Each organizational unit that participates in the process has its own swimlane. A swimlane is a placeholder for BPMN flow constructs, such as *activities*, *gateways*, and *events*. Whatever is placed inside a swimlane is assumed to happen within the context of that organizational unit. In other words, the organizational unit is the main responsible for the tasks that are placed within its swimlane. The swimlane is a means to assign responsibility for certain tasks to a given organizational unit.

The process begins in the "Employee" swimlane with a *start event*. The first activity that appears after the start event is "Fill in requisition." This activity is then followed by "Check product availability," which is performed by the warehouse, on a different swimlane. The process description above says that the requisition is "sent" to the warehouse. There is no need to represent this fact explicitly, since the handover of work between organizational units occurs naturally as a result of the task flow across swimlanes. In BPMN, this kind of flow is referred to as *sequence flow* (as opposed to *message flow*, to be discussed later).

The warehouse checks the inventory and determines the quantity available for the requested product. As a result of this step, it may happen that the product is either available (if quantity > 0) or not available (if quantity = 0). Therefore, at this point the process must contain a decision. This decision is represented by a *gateway*, which in this case is an *exclusive-OR gateway* (i.e., either one or the other, but not both options can occur). If the product is available, then the warehouse dispatches it to the employee, and the process ends, as indicated by an *end event*.

If, on the other hand, the product is not available from the warehouse, then it must be ordered from a supplier. The purchasing department is the organizational unit which takes care of such orders. In this process, the purchasing department prepares and sends a purchase order to the supplier. At this point, there is a message exchange between the company and the supplier. The process "flows" beyond the borders of the company (i.e., its pool) and this flow cannot be represented as a normal sequence flow because, outside of the pool, the process is no longer under control of the company. The company can only send a message to the supplier, and it is the supplier who must know what to do with that message.

Therefore, the interaction between the company and the supplier takes the form of *message flows*. These are represented as dashed lines in Fig. 11.1. In general, sequence flows (represented by solid arrows) can only take place within the boundaries of a pool, i.e., sequence flows apply only to the internal processes within an organization. Between organizations, the interaction is represented by message flows. This is because each organization is assumed to be autonomous and capable of defining its own processes. Therefore, it makes no sense to design a continuous process that crosses multiple organizations, when parts of that process are under the control of different organizations, and therefore can be freely modified by those organizations at any point given point in time.

It makes sense to design a business process as a sequence flow only within the scope of an organization, which has the autonomy and authority to enforce that behavior and to change it at any time according to business requirements. This is the reason why the behavior of the supplier has not been specified and has been left blank in this model—because it is up to the supplier to define its own behavior, i.e., its internal processes. With regard to the company who is submitting the purchase order, the supplier is a partner with whom the company exchanges a set of messages. It is assumed that, regardless of the way the supplier designs its own internal processes, these will be *compatible* with those message exchanges.

So, after the company sends the purchase order, the process will wait for the order confirmation to arrive. This is represented as an *intermediate event* in Fig. 11.1 (i.e., "Order confirmation"). Like the start and end event in a process, an intermediate event is also represented by a circle, specifically a double circle with an icon to indicate what kind of event is being awaited for. In this case, the intermediate event is being used to specify that, at this point, the process will wait for a message to arrive. The sequence flow will proceed to the next activity only when the order confirmation has been received.

After that, it is time for the warehouse to receive the product, do whatever it has to do when a product arrives (e.g., update the stock) and then dispatch the product to the employee who submitted the original request.

The activity "Dispatch product" appears twice in the swimlane for the warehouse and it would appear that such activity has been duplicated unnecessarily. For example, by drawing an arrow from "Receive product" to the first "Dispatch product" on the left, it appears that the process would be able to accomplish the same thing without the need for the second "Dispatch product" activity on the right. However, such practice is not to be recommended since it would go against the

Fig. 11.2 Activity types

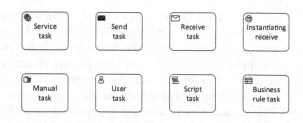

principle of having a nested block structure, as explained in Sect. 8.1. This principle is as important in orchestrations as it is in process models, since it is much easier to ensure the correct behavior of a process which follows a nested block structure, as opposed to one with arbitrary connections between any pair of nodes. As we will see in the next sections, the set of available constructs in BPMN is sufficiently rich to allow any desired behavior to be implemented as a nested block structure.

11.1.1 Activities

In BPMN it is possible to decorate activities with an icon to provide some more information about how the activity is to be performed. Figure 11.2 shows the different types of activities available in BPMN 2.0 [21]. These can be described as follows:

- A *service task* is an automated activity that consists in the invocation of some service or application.
- A *send task* is an activity that consists in sending a message to an external participant. In Fig. 11.1 there was an activity called "Send purchase order" which could have been represented as a send task.
- The *receive task* is the counterpart of the send task. Basically, it represents an activity whose main purpose is to receive a message. The activity is completed only when the message has been received.

  At a certain point in Fig. 11.1, the process waits for an "Order confirmation" message from the supplier. This has been represented as an intermediate event rather than as a receive task. The reason for this is that this step in the process does not represent an actual activity. It is just something that happens and that the process is waiting for; there is no action to be done.

  In contrast, the preceding step (i.e., "Send purchase order") is represented as an activity, because it involves not only the act of "sending" but also the preparation of the purchase order to be sent. Someone must be assigned to carry out this task, and therefore it is represented as an activity.
- In addition to the regular receive task, BPMN 2.0 includes the concept of *instantiating receive*, which is equivalent to the concept of activating receive in orchestrations, as described in Sect. 8.2.

The instantiating receive means that a new process instance will be created upon the arrival of a message. Therefore, BPMN requires that an instantiating receive, if used, must be the first activity in the process and it must have no incoming sequence flows. Its icon (an envelope enclosed in a circle) is intended to resemble a start event which is triggered by a message. In fact, the instantiating receive can be used to replace the start event in a process.

- The *manual task* is intended to represent an activity that is to be performed without IT support. This could be any action in the physical world that is not monitored or supported by an IT system.
- The *user task* represents an activity that is assigned to some user. Typically, this task will be sent as a work item to the user's worklist, and the execution engine will be waiting for an output or completion message before resuming the process. This is what happens in human workflows, as explained in Sect. 7.7.
- The *script task* contains a series of instructions that are to be carried out by the engine that will be executing the process. When the engine reaches the script task, it will execute the code contained therein. For this purpose, the script must be written in a language that the engine is able to interpret and execute.
- Finally, the *business rule task* is used to invoke business rules. This is equivalent to the call rules shape that was briefly mentioned in Sect. 2.6. Basically, business rules can be used to perform calculations or make decisions based on user-defined parameters. The reason why these rules are not embedded in the process is that they can be changed at any time according to business requirements. The business rule task is a means to invoke an external business rules engine that will evaluate the rules and return the results back to process. The process can then use these results to decide how the process should proceed.

11.1.2 Loops and Multi-Instance Activities

The process in Fig. 11.1 represents a sequence of activities where each activity is executed before moving on to the next one. In particular, each activity is executed at most once. However, in practice there may be scenarios where a single activity has to be run multiple times. For example, consider that an employee submits a request for several different items to be purchased. Each of these items may have to be ordered separately from a different supplier. In other words, a single purchase request may originate several purchase orders, and even though they must be handled separately, all of these purchase orders belong to the same process instance.

In BPMN it is possible to specify that an activity is to be executed multiple times. In some cases, the activity will be executed a number of times until a certain condition is true. This is akin to the concept of loop, as described in Sects. 8.5 and 10.3.3. In other cases, the number of times that an activity will run is known in advance, and all those runs can be triggered at once, either sequentially or in parallel. This concept is referred to as *multi-instance* in BPMN, and it is similar to the way a <forEach> loop works in BPEL. As explained in Sect. 10.3.3, by setting

Fig. 11.3 Loop activities

the parallel attribute to "yes" or "no" it is possible to run the loop iterations in parallel or sequentially. In addition, the body of the <forEach> loop is enclosed in a <scope>, meaning that each loop iteration is independent from every other.

Figure 11.3 shows how these concepts can be represented in BPMN. On the left-hand side there is a loop activity, meaning that the activity will run an arbitrary number of times before the process can proceed to the next activity. The number of iterations is determined by some condition that is to be evaluated at run-time. This condition can be included as a attribute of the activity, but it does not have a graphical representation in BPMN.

The next two shapes, in the middle and on the right-hand side of Fig. 11.3, represent the multi-instance concept. Here, the activity is seen as being instantiated multiple times, where each instance is independent from every other. These instances may run in parallel or in sequence, with the sequential multi-instance being a recent addition in BPMN 2.0.

Although it may seem that the loop activity and the sequential multi-instance may be the same, there are some subtle differences between the two. In the loop activity, there is an exit condition that is evaluated after each run. The loop may continue or be exited depending on the particular circumstances that occur when the condition is being evaluated. On the other hand, for the sequential multi-instance the number of instances is known at the start of the activity, and the process can only proceed when all of those instances have been completed.

Usually, the multiple-instance activity, either in parallel or sequential form, is used when there is a collection of objects to be processed independently of each other. In this case, each instance of the activity is intended to handle a different object. The loop activity, on the other hand, is a means to keep an activity running until some condition is true. This may not necessarily involve a different object in each iteration. In fact, the loop may be run over the same object until the state of that object changes, or some other condition becomes true.

11.1.3 Subprocesses

Another interesting possibility is to define an activity as a subprocess. This means that an activity becomes a placeholder for some process logic that one may want to insert at that point in the process. Figure 11.4 illustrates how a subprocess may appear in a BPMN process model. There are two forms: either collapsed or expanded. If collapsed, the subprocess looks like a regular activity except for the plus sign (i.e., "+") indicating that it contains additional process logic. If expanded,

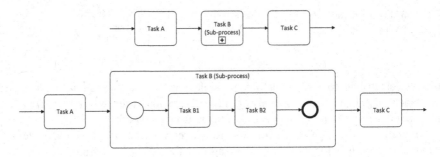

Fig. 11.4 Subprocess in collapsed and expanded forms

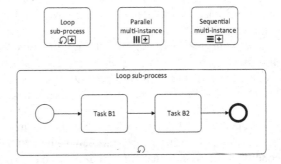

Fig. 11.5 Loop subprocesses

the subprocess shows the logic that is contained inside it. Such logic must follow the same design principles as a top-level process, so usually it contains a start event, a sequence of activities, and an end event. It is only when the subprocess reaches its end event that the parent process can proceed to the next activity.

Just like an ordinary activity, a subprocess may be executed multiple times in the flow of the parent process. In particular, the subprocess can be executed as a loop, as a parallel multi-instance, or as a sequential multi-instance, as shown in Fig. 11.5. In case the subprocess is expanded, it should keep its decoration (i.e., the loop sign), as shown for the expanded loop subprocess in Fig. 11.5.

A particular type of subprocess that has a much different behavior from the rest is the *ad-hoc subprocess*. This is a kind of subprocess that is not bound to the typical, well-structured behavior of a sequence flow. Basically, an ad-hoc subprocess contains a set of activities that can be executed in any order. In particular, there is no restriction on when each activity can begin and end, so the ad-hoc subprocess can be also regarded as a block where everything can run in any order, including in parallel. In this respect, the ad-hoc subprocess is somewhat similar to the <flow> construct in BPEL (see Sect. 10.3.2).

Figure 11.6 shows an example of an ad-hoc subprocess (Ad-hoc subprocess 1) containing 3 tasks X, Y, and Z. These tasks can run in any order, including in parallel. Also, there is no start or end event to specify where the subprocess begins

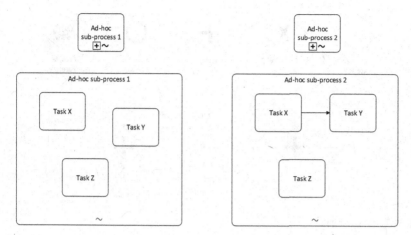

Fig. 11.6 Ad-hoc subprocesses

or ends. It is only when all tasks in the subprocess have been completed that the parent process can proceed to the next activity in the flow.

Also in Fig. 11.6 there is an example of a second subprocess (Ad-hoc subprocess 2) which contains the same tasks but there is a sequence flow between tasks X and Y. This means that task Y can only begin when task X is completed. In this case, the sequence flow inside the ad-hoc subprocess works as a restriction to the execution flow. It means that the sequence X→Y and task Z can run in any order, including in parallel, but Y must follow X in any case.

The sequence flows inside an ad-hoc subprocess work in a similar way to link dependencies inside a <flow> construct in BPEL. These link dependencies have been briefly discussed in Sect. 10.3.2 (there is an example in Listing 10.18 on page 288) and they can generate complicated behavior that is hard to interpret and to verify whether it is really correct according to the desired behavior for the process. As usual, this is easier to do if the process follows a nested block structure. Rather than using an ad-hoc subprocess, the best way to represent parallelism in BPMN is through the use of a parallel gateway, as explained in the next section.

11.1.4 Gateways

At a certain point in the process of Fig. 11.1 there is a decision between two branches. If the product is available, it will be dispatched directly from the warehouse; otherwise, it will be ordered from a supplier. The element that was used to represent this decision is a *gateway*. In this case, it is an *exclusive gateway*, but there are other types of gateways, as illustrated in Fig. 11.7.

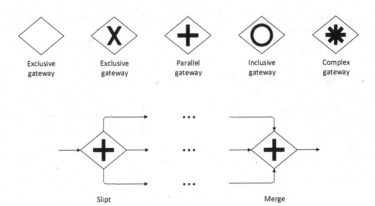

Fig. 11.7 Types of gateways

Each gateway represents a different behavior and has its own symbol. A gateway without a symbol is assumed to be an exclusive gateway. This means that one and only one branch must be chosen. To make things clearer, the exclusive gateway can also be drawn with a symbol (an "X" that stands for XOR, i.e., exclusive-OR). Therefore, the exclusive gateway has two possible representations.

The logical counterpart of the exclusive gateway is the parallel gateway. This means that all branches are to be followed in parallel. Usually, regardless of the type of gateway that is being used, each gateway that splits the flow in multiple paths is matched by another gateway of the same type that merges those paths back into the main flow. This is illustrated in Fig. 11.7 by having 3 paths between a splitting parallel gateway and a merging parallel gateway. Here, parallel gateway has been used, but the same principle applies to other gateways too.

In the case of the parallel gateway, the merging gateway is especially important because it works as a synchronizing merge, i.e., the process will not move on to the next activity until all parallel branches coming into the merging gateway have completed. For the exclusive gateway, this merging works in a different way: as soon as one branch is complete, the process can proceed. Since, in the exclusive gateway, only one branch can be chosen, it does not make sense to wait for the other branches; these are simply skipped.

In Fig. 11.1 there is a splitting exclusive gateway, but there is no matching merge. This is possible because both paths eventually lead to an end event, so there is no need to merge them back to a common flow. However, if the dispatch activity is seen as being exactly the same in both paths, then the process can be redesigned as shown in Fig. 11.8. Here, if the product is available in the warehouse then the process proceeds immediately to "Dispatch product"; otherwise, the product must be ordered first and only then dispatched to the employee.

This process follows a nested block structure because the splitting gateway initiates a block that is closed by the merging gateway. The same principle must be obeyed for other types of gateways, including the parallel, the inclusive, and the complex gateway, where the merging also plays a synchronization role.

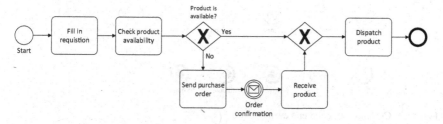

Fig. 11.8 An alternative design for the purchase process

The inclusive gateway is an unusual type of gateway in the sense that it allows an arbitrary number of branches to be followed. If only one branch is followed, then it is equivalent to an exclusive gateway. If all paths are followed, then it is equivalent to a parallel gateway. Finally, if any number of branches between one and all is activated, then these exact same branches will be synchronized at the end.

The complex gateway is used when the splitting and/or merging condition cannot be appropriately described by any of the previous gateways. It is included in BPMN for completeness, but its use can hardly be recommended since it does not convey a precise idea of the execution semantics. A more useful type of gateway, which is driven by events, will be discussed in Sect. 11.1.7.

11.1.5   Start and End Events

The process in Fig. 11.1 begins with a start event and eventually finishes with an end event, regardless of which path is actually taken after the exclusive gateway. Here such events have been drawn as generic start and end events, but BPMN allows these events to be more specific, namely to have a certain trigger (for start events) or result (for end events). Figure 11.9 shows a subset (but not all) of the start and end events defined by the BPMN standard. These are the types of start and end events that can be used in top-level processes. For subprocesses, there are additional event types, some of which will appear later in this chapter. For the moment, we focus on the most common event types.

With regard to start events, there are several event types that are meant to specify how such event can be triggered (and hence, since the start event is the first element in a BPMN process, this also says how the process itself is triggered). The start event with a message trigger means that the process begins when a certain message is received. In practice, this plays the same role as an activating receive, since it creates a new process instance. However, we have seen in Sect. 11.1.1 that there is also a special type of activity that plays a similar role: the instantiating receive. It is possible to use either one or the other. In general, an event conveys the idea that "when something happens..." whereas an activity places more focus on the idea that "something needs to be done." The start event with a message trigger is probably the most common way of marking the beginning of a BPMN process.

Fig. 11.9 Common start and end events

Other options include a timer, a condition, or a signal:

- The use of a timer means that at a certain date and time (or after a certain period of time) the process is triggered. The timer event can also be used for processes that need to be triggered periodically, after a certain amount of time has elapsed.
- The condition trigger is used for processes which begin when a certain condition becomes true, such as e.g., "temperature is below zero." The condition is usually an expression based on some data that is accessible to the process.
- The signal is similar to a message, but it works in broadcast mode, i.e., it does not have a particular recipient associated with it. When a signal is thrown, every process with a start event that is triggered by that signal will start to run. The concept of signal can be better understood by a physical analogy such as a sound alarm which goes off and is sufficiently strong for everyone to hear. When a signal occurs, it indicates that something has happened and everyone knows about it, so any number of processes can start as a reaction to that signal.

The last two start events in Fig. 11.9—multiple and parallel multiple—represent a combination of any of the previous event types. For example, a process which is triggered either when a message is received or when a condition is true has a start event with multiple triggers. If the occurrence of *any* of such events is enough to start the process, then the multiple trigger should be used. On the other hand, if the occurrence of *all* such events is required in order to start the process, then the parallel multiple trigger should be used. In this case, the process will start only after all of the required events have occurred.

As for the end events in Fig. 11.9, these represent the different kinds of results that a process may produce. In case of a message result, this means that the process will end by sending a message to some recipient. In case of a signal result, this means that the process will end by broadcasting a signal. In case of an event with multiple results (e.g., a message and a signal, or multiple messages, or multiple signals), *all* of those results will be produced at the end of the process. Here there is no need to distinguish between multiple and parallel multiple since an end event with multiple results has, in effect, multiple "parallel" results.

It is interesting to note that, at least in some cases, the type of end event is the logical counterpart of a certain type of start event. For example, the end event with a message result means that the process ends by *sending* a message, whereas the start event with a message trigger means that the process begins by *receiving* a message.

In a similar way, the end event with a signal result means that the process ends by broadcasting a signal, whereas the start event with a signal trigger means that the process begins when a certain signal occurs. This same duality between events that produce some output and events that consume some input also exists in connection with intermediate events, as we will see in the next section.

Before we proceed, however, there is an end event that finds no match in terms of start event, and that is the *terminate event*. This means that if the process flow comes to this event, then the process instance will terminate immediately. In particular, all branches that may be running in parallel will also be terminated. Also, if there are some loops or multiple-instance activities, these will be terminated as well.

11.1.6 *Intermediate Events*

Intermediate events are events that occur somewhere along the flow of the process. These events can be used either to wait for some input or to produce some output. In Fig. 11.1 there is an intermediate event to wait for an order confirmation from the supplier. At this point, the process waits for an incoming message before proceeding to the next activity. It is also possible to have intermediate events to produce outgoing messages. In this case, the process does not wait, it just produces the message and proceeds immediately to the next activity.

Figure 11.10 illustrates the graphical notation that can be used to represent these different kinds of intermediate events. In BPMN, an intermediate event that produces some output is said to be "throwing," while an intermediate event that waits for some input is said to be "catching." In Fig. 11.10 it becomes clear that there are several types of both catching and throwing events, and that these events have a similar rationale to the start and end events shown earlier in Fig. 11.9 (except for the terminate event, which is clearly an end event).

As such, the timer event in Fig. 11.10 is an intermediate event that waits until a certain deadline has been reached, or until a certain amount of time has passed; the condition event waits until a certain condition is true; the signal event waits for a certain signal; and the multiple event can wait for multiple things to happen (such as, e.g., a message and a condition, a message and a timer, etc.). As with the start events discussed above, there are two variants for an intermediate event with multiple triggers: the parallel multiple requires *all* triggers to occur before the process can proceed, whereas the simple multiple will allow the process to proceed after *any* of those triggers has occurred.

As for the throwing events, the first thing to be noted is that there is no graphical distinction between a throwing event and a catching event if the type of result that is being thrown is not specified. Throwing events have a more limited set of choices (just like end events in comparison with start events). A throwing event can either "throw" a message or a signal, or multiple messages and/or signals. It is interesting to note that for every intermediate event that throws a message or signal there is probably another intermediate event, in another process, to catch that message or

Fig. 11.10 Common intermediate events

signal. However, it could also be the case that the message or signal that is being thrown will be caught by the start event of another process!

One last issue to be mentioned is the fact that, along with intermediate events, BPMN includes special activity types to send and to receive messages, as described in Sect. 11.1.1. Again, the use of intermediate events is preferred to represent the fact that "something happens," whereas the use of activities is recommended when there is some action that needs to be done in order to send or to receive the message. An interesting example is provided in Fig. 11.1, where the process sends the purchase order by means of an activity, but receives the order confirmation by means of an event. This is because someone needs to actually prepare and send the order, while there is nothing to do while waiting for the confirmation.

Alternatively, the "Send purchase order" activity could have been replaced by a "Prepare purchase order" activity followed by an intermediate (throwing) event to send the purchase order to the supplier.

11.1.7 Event-Based Gateways

In Sect. 9.1 on page 234 we have introduced the listen shape, which is basically a decision with multiple branches, but where the decision of which branch to follow is deferred until the occurrence of some event. Each branch is associated with a particular event (such as a message being received, or a timer being elapsed) and the path to be followed is one associated with the event that occurs first.

In Sect. 10.3.4 on page 293 we have seen a similar BPEL construct, called <pick>, which has exactly the same behavior. The <pick> element contains one or more <onMessage> and <onAlarm> events. Each <onMessage> event represents the arrival of a message through a given partner link, and each <onAlarm> event represents a timer that waits for a certain deadline or duration. In turn, each <onMessage> or <onAlarm> event contains a block of orchestration logic that represents the branch associated with that event.

Given that such kind of construct often appears in practice, it is natural that BPMN should include a graphical notation for such behavior. This is represented in the form of an *event-based gateway*, as illustrated in Fig. 11.11.

Fig. 11.11 Event-based gateway

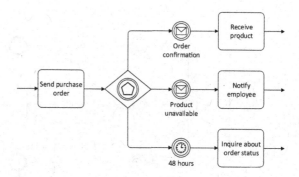

The event-based gateway has a special symbol in it, which is similar to an intermediate event with multiple triggers. In fact, each branch coming out of this gateway has an intermediate (catching) event, which means that every branch will wait for some event to occur. The event that occurs first will determine the branch to be followed, and the remaining branches will be skipped.

Figure 11.11 shows an example where the purchase order is sent to the supplier and then the process waits for one of several outcomes. Either the supplier sends an order confirmation, or it sends a message saying that the product is unavailable. As a third option, if the supplier does not respond within 48 h, then the process will proceed with some action to inquire about the status of the purchase order.

It is interesting to note that although the event-based gateway is typically associated with message and timer events, other types of trigger can be used as well. In particular, any intermediate (catching) event shown at the top of Fig. 11.10 can be used. This is different from the listen shape and the <pick> element in BPEL, which accept only message and timer events. Another possibility is to replace the intermediate events that have message triggers with receive tasks (see Sect. 11.1.1), although this is rarely done in practice.

In BPMN 2.0, the event-based gateway was extended to support additional behaviors. In particular, BPMN 2.0 introduced the possibility of an event-based gateway being the first element in a process (or subprocess). Such event-based gateway will instantiate the process and it represents the fact that the process may begin in one of several possible ways. Figure 9.3 on page 237 already introduced this possibility with the listen shape, and in BPEL it is possible to use the <pick> construct with the attribute createInstance="yes" (in this case, only <onMessage> events are allowed). In BPMN, the instantiating event-based gateway has two different versions, which can be represented as illustrated in Fig. 11.12.

At the top of Fig. 11.12 there is a subprocess (could be a top-level process as well) which begins with an exclusive event-based gateway. This means that the process will begin in one of the possible ways shown in the diagram, i.e., either by a message, a condition, or a timer. The first event to occur instantiates the process, determines the branch to be executed, and all other branches are disregarded.

At the bottom of Fig. 11.12 there is a curious possibility of allowing all branches to be executed. The first event to occur instantiates the process, but the remaining

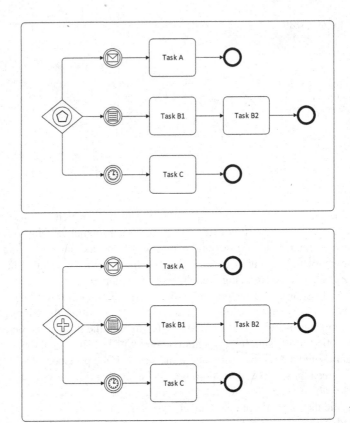

Fig. 11.12 Instantiating event-based gateways (exclusive and parallel versions)

branches will be kept alive and listening for their respective events. The process will be complete when all branches have been executed. Naturally, only the first event instantiates the process, the remaining events will just trigger additional branches within the same process instance.

11.2   Exception Handling

In BPMN there are several different ways to represent exceptions, and there are also different ways to include behavior that is specifically targeted at handling those exceptions. The most commonly used constructs to represent exceptions are intermediate events attached to the boundary of activities. Typically, if such an event occurs, the activity is interrupted and the process follows a different path. These attached events are very useful when modeling business processes, but it is not always easy to map them to an execution language such as BPEL, since the flow that is associated with attached events may not follow a nested block structure.

A more traditional solution to the problem of representing exceptions in BPMN are *error events*. This is a special type of event that, like other intermediate events, can be either thrown or caught, and therefore it is possible, with relative ease, to map these error events to the exception handling mechanisms of BPEL.

The BPMN 2.0 standard introduced additional options to deal with exceptions, namely the use of *escalation events* and of *event subprocesses*. Basically, event subprocesses are similar in concept to the use of event handlers in BPEL, whose purpose is to react to events that occur in parallel with the orchestration flow (see Sect. 10.4.4). An event subprocess can also be triggered by some event that occurs in parallel with the main process flow.

On the other hand, escalation events can be seen as a different form of error event. In fact, they do not represent an error in the sense of a system error, but a condition (i.e., a business problem) that occurs during the execution of a business process, and that requires some special handling. In particular, an escalation event means that someone with higher responsibility (such as, e.g., a supervisor) will be called to intervene, or at least will be notified. This is quite useful when modeling business process in organizations with some form of hierarchical structure. However, the semantics that are associated with escalation events do not have much impact from an execution point of view. In this regard, an escalation event is not much different from an error event, except that it can be non-interrupting.

The following sections provide a brief overview of these different constructs.

11.2.1 Attached Intermediate Events

Figure 11.13 shows the types of events that can be attached to an activity boundary. In every case, the occurrence of the specified event interrupts the activity and takes the process through another path. The graphical notation for the event itself is the same as for intermediate (catching) events (compare with Fig. 11.10). In particular, the trigger may be a message, a timer, a condition, or a signal. As before, there is also the possibility of specifying an event with multiple triggers (i.e., any combination of messages, timers, conditions, and signals). In this case, there are two possible versions: either *any* of the triggers will fire the event, or *all* triggers are required to occur in order to fire the event (i.e., parallel multiple).

Unfortunately, process modelers often make use of such attached events in a way that makes it difficult both to understand the model and to translate it into an executable language such as BPEL. Figure 11.14 shows two possible uses for the exception flow that comes out of the attached event. In both cases, task A is interrupted and the flow proceeds to task B. However, in the first case the exception flow ends after task B, whereas in the second case the exception flow merges back into the main flow, through the use of an exclusive (merge) gateway. This practice is perfectly legal in BPMN but can be hardly recommended, since it breaks the nested block structure that the process should adhere to.

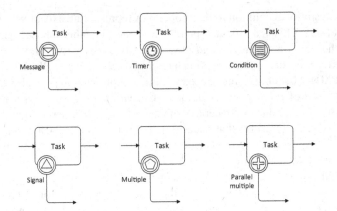

Fig. 11.13 Interrupting intermediate events

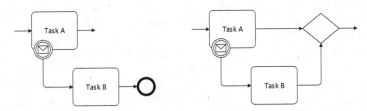

Fig. 11.14 Possible routings for the exception flow

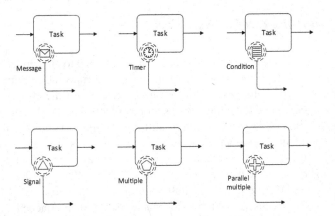

Fig. 11.15 Non-interrupting intermediate events

The attached events described above are interrupting events in the sense that their occurrence interrupts the execution of the activity they are attached to. However, BPMN provides also the possibility of having non-interrupting attached events. These are shown in Fig. 11.15. They are represented as intermediate events with a dash border. This means that their occurrence triggers the exception flow, but it does not interrupt the main flow, so the activity keeps running.

Fig. 11.16 Possible uses of the error event

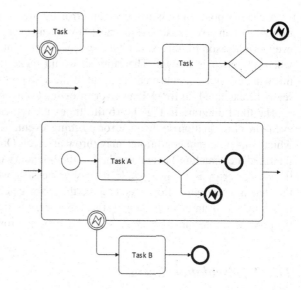

It is hard to see that such non-interrupting events will find much use in practice, except in some very particular scenarios. An example is when someone sends an inquiry while the activity is running. In this case, the use of a non-interrupting message event allows the inquiry to be handled and a response to be returned without interrupting the activity. Another example is the use of a timer: after some time it may be necessary to do something or to notify someone without interrupting the activity. Curiously, these are the two cases which can also be supported in BPEL through the use of event handlers with <onEvent> or <onAlarm> elements (see Listing 10.26 on page 302). However, besides messages and timers, BPMN allows for signals and conditions, as well events with multiple triggers.

11.2.2   Error Events

The error event is a special kind of event that can take the form of an intermediate event (if the error is being caught) or an end event (if the error is being thrown). Figure 11.16 illustrates the typical uses of error events. One possibility is to use an error event as an intermediate (catching) event attached to the boundary of an activity. This means that, in case an error occurs during execution, the event interrupts the activity and takes the process through an exception flow. In case of an error trigger, the attached event is always interrupting (i.e., it cannot be non-interrupting as some intermediate events discussed in the previous section). The reason for this is that if an error occurs then it is because something went wrong, and therefore the normal flow must not be allowed to proceed. In fact, the normal flow may have been already interrupted due to occurrence of the error.

A second possibility is to throw an error by means of an end event. Here, the throwing of an error must be represented by an end event, and not as an intermediate event. The reason for this is that the throw of an error interrupts the flow at the point where the error is thrown. Therefore, it would make little sense to use an error-throwing event as an intermediate event, if the activities that come after that cannot really be executed. In BPMN, an error-throwing event can only be an end event.

The third diagram in Fig. 11.16 illustrates the typical use of an error-throwing event in combination with an error-catching event. Here there is a subprocess which, under certain conditions, may throw an error. On the other hand, there is an intermediate (catching) event attached to the boundary of the subprocess, meaning that if the error is thrown inside the subprocess, it will be caught and handled through an exception flow. As before, the error-catching event is interrupting, meaning that if an error is caught, the subprocess is interrupted. In this example, the process is interrupted anyway, since the error is thrown by an end event.

11.2.3 Escalation Events

Escalation events are somewhat different from error events, in the sense that their main purpose is to alert someone else—particularly, someone who is above in the hierarchical structure of the organization—of some problematic situation that occurs in the business process. Escalation events can be used just like error events, but with the specific semantics that is associated with "escalation." Figure 11.17 shows an example. Here, the flow is identical to that shown earlier in Fig. 11.16, with the difference being that the error events have been replaced by escalation events.

Although the behavior is exactly the same as before, the escalation events are used here to denote the fact that the problem must be handled by someone with a higher degree of responsibility in the organization. This is represented in Fig. 11.17 by having task B performed by a supervisor. In other words, should a problem arise in the subprocess that is being performed by the employee, an escalation event will be thrown (as an end event), and this will be caught by an intermediate event and handled by having the supervisor perform task B.

A significant difference between error events and escalation events is that escalation events may be thrown by intermediate events, and they may also be caught by non-interrupting attached events. This is illustrated in Fig. 11.18. Here, the escalation event is not meant to interrupt the subprocess. Rather, if a problem arises then the escalation event is thrown as an intermediate event and the subprocess is allowed to continue. However, for this to happen it must be ensured that the catching event is non-interrupting. Such is indeed the case in Fig. 11.18, where the intermediate (catching) event is drawn with a dash border. This follows the same convention as for other non-interrupting events, as shown in Fig. 11.15.

At first sight, it could seem that the same behavior as in Fig. 11.18 could be obtained by simply replacing the intermediate, escalation-throwing event inside the subprocess with task B, and this would avoid the need for the escalation-catching

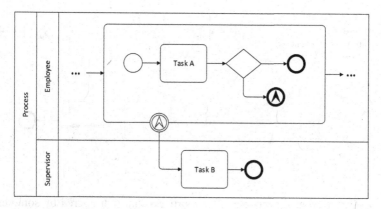

Fig. 11.17 Use of escalation events

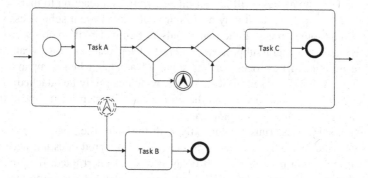

Fig. 11.18 Escalation with an intermediate throwing and a non-interrupting catching event

event as well. However, this is not the case. First, there is no guarantee that in case the escalation event occurs, task B will be performed before task C. Second, task B is intended to be carried out by a different participant, in another swimlane, as in Fig. 11.17. And third, BPMN models are intended to be as expressive as possible, and the substitution of the escalation events would hide the fact that such behavior is to take place only if there is a problem with the business process.

11.2.4 Event Subprocesses

The behavior associated with error and escalation events—in particular, the concept of throwing and catching these types of events—can be used to represent mechanisms of exception handling in BPMN processes. These mechanisms have been described in detail in Sects. 9.3 and 10.4.1. In addition to these, Sect. 10.4.4 described the possibility of listening to and reacting to events in parallel with the main orchestration flow. In BPMN 2.0, a new concept was introduced to support these mechanisms: the concept of *event subprocesses*.

Fig. 11.19 Use of event subprocess with a non-interrupting start event

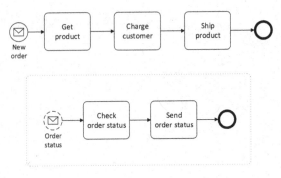

Basically, an event subprocess is a subprocess that is triggered by some event that occurs in parallel with the flow. This event may occur at any point during the process, and the subprocess will be run immediately as a reaction to that event. In fact, the event may occur or it may not occur at all, so an event subprocess should be regarded as some process logic that is only to be invoked if some special event occurs. Because an event subprocess is able to keep listening for events during the entire duration of a process, it has some advantages when compared to the intermediate events discussed in Sect. 11.2.1, which can only be attached to some particular activity or subprocess, and therefore cease to listen for the event trigger once the activity or subprocess completes.

An event subprocess runs concurrently with the main (i.e., parent) process. In other words, the fact that an event subprocess gets triggered does not necessarily imply that the parent process will get delayed or even interrupted. Imagine, as in Sect. 10.4.4, the scenario of an online bookstore. As the order is being processed, the customer may inquire about the order status. When this happens, the bookstore must be able to inform about the order status in parallel with the order processing. In this scenario, the activities that take place when the customer inquires about the order status could be represented as an event subprocess, as in Fig. 11.19.

The event subprocess is represented with a dot border; this is the graphical notation for event subprocesses in BPMN. Also, the start event for the event subprocess has a dash border; this means that the event is non-interrupting. Therefore, the customer may inquire about the order status without interrupting the parent process, and the event subprocess will run in parallel with the order processing.

Instead of starting the event subprocess with a non-interrupting event, as in Fig. 11.19, it is possible to start an event subprocess with an interrupting event. Here, the use of an interrupting event means that the parent process will be stopped when the event subprocess is triggered. In the above scenario this could mean, for example, that instead of inquiring about the order status, the customer just cancels the order, so the main process is interrupted.[2] Figure 11.20 expands the

---

[2]In practice, once the product has been shipped, the process may have ended already and the customer may be unable to cancel it. However, in this example we do not consider such problem.

Fig. 11.20 Use of event
subprocess with an
interrupting start event

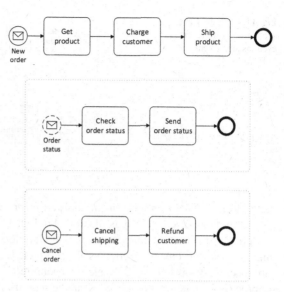

scenario of Fig. 11.19 by including an additional event subprocess to deal with order cancelation. The main difference is that the new event subprocess is interrupting, as indicated by the solid border of its start event.

Figure 11.20 also illustrates the fact that a process may have several event subprocesses. In this example, the event subprocess that has been introduced to support order cancelation can be seen as a form of *fault handler* as described in Sect. 10.4.1. On the other hand, the event subprocess that was introduced to respond inquiries about the order status can be regarded as an *event handler* as described in Sect. 10.4.4. The use of an interrupting start event versus an non-interrupting start event is what makes the distinction here. In general, it can be observed that event subprocesses are a flexible mechanism to implement different sorts of event handling, be it exceptions or concurrent events.

Also, it should be noted that it is possible to use different types of start events in these subprocess. For example, in Fig. 11.20 each event subprocess has a start event with a message trigger. Alternatively, the start event can be a timer, a signal, or a condition, as depicted at the top of Fig. 11.9 on page 326. It can also be a start event with multiple (and possibly parallel) triggers. For event subprocesses, all of these start events have an interrupting version (with a solid border) and a non-interrupting version (with a dash border).

An interesting feature of event subprocesses is that the error event, which has been introduced in Sect. 11.2.2 as an intermediate (catching) event and as an end (throwing) event, can actually be used as start event in an event subprocess. However, for this kind of start event there is only the interrupting version (i.e., the error event, when used as the start event for an event subprocess, can only be used as an interrupting event, but not as a non-interrupting one). This makes of an event subprocess with an error event (as start event) a true exception handler, in the sense

Fig. 11.21 Use of event subprocess with an error event as start event

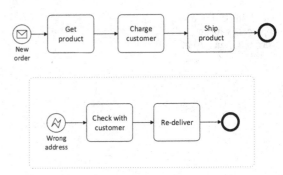

that it listens for errors and, in the case an error occurs, it interrupts the parent process and handles the error, as illustrated in Fig. 11.21.

Here, a third event subprocess is included to deal with the case when shipping fails because the customer address is incorrect. (For simplicity, the other event subprocesses from Fig. 11.20 have been omitted.) The start event for the event subprocess is an interrupting one, as can be seen from the use of a solid border.

Similar to the error event, the escalation event introduced in the previous section can also serve as the start event for an event subprocess, and in this case both the interrupting and the non-interrupting versions are allowed.

11.3   Transactions and Compensation

In Fig. 11.20 there is an event subprocess for order cancelation, which basically does a rollback of the shipping and charging activities. Such scenario could be thought of as a transaction involving those two activities. When the customer sends a message canceling the order, the transaction would roll back to a previous state. However, in Sect. 9.4 we have seen that, in orchestrations and business processes, transactions work in a different way from the traditional transactions in database systems. In particular, in a business process there are long-running transactions, where work is committed in a stepwise fashion instead of being held until the very end of the transaction.

For example, at a certain step in Fig. 11.20, the process charges the customer for the product that was ordered. At this point the product has not been shipped yet, but the assumption is that the shipping activity is part of the same transaction. However, this transaction is actually performed in two steps that commit separately. When the company charges the customer, the effects of this activity are immediate: a certain amount has been charged to the customer's credit card. If, for some reason, the product cannot be shipped, then the "Charge customer" activity will need to be *compensated* (but not rolled back, since it has already committed). Here, the compensation consists in giving a refund to the customer.

Fig. 11.22 Use of
compensation handler in
activity

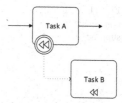

The BPMN language provides several constructs to represent transactions and compensation in business processes. In fact, compensation may appear in a process model without an explicit reference to an enclosing transaction. However, the use of compensation implies that the activity or subprocess where compensation is being used is transactional. This is somewhat equivalent to the use of the scope shape or the <scope> element in BPEL. A scope with a compensation handler implies that the scope is transactional, and that its compensation can be triggered by some event or exception that occurs after the successful completion of that scope.

In BPMN, a scope can be represented as a subprocess, or as an activity if its internal behavior is unknown or is not being modeled. The next sections explain how to use compensation in each of these constructs.

11.3.1 Compensation Handlers

In a BPMN process model, any activity that may need to be compensated can be represented as in Fig. 11.22. In this diagram, there is an association between task A and task B, and in particular this association means that task B is the *compensation handler* for task A. In other words, task B may never end up being executed; however, it will be executed if the need arises to compensate task A. Naturally, such need may only arise *after* task A has been successfully executed.

The fact that task B is a compensation handler is indicated by the compensation marker inside it. Such marker effectively precludes task B from being used in the normal flow of the process. It can only be used as a compensation handler that is connected to the boundary of some other activity through an *association*. The association is represented as an arrow with a dotted line, as opposed to an arrow with a solid line that represents a sequence flow.

On the boundary of task A there is something similar to an attached intermediate event (see Sect. 11.2.1). In fact, it is an attached intermediate event with a compensation trigger. Such triggering may occur in different ways. It may occur because the enclosing subprocess that contains task A failed, and therefore its inner activities need to be compensated. Alternatively, it may happen that the compensation of task A—specifically of task A—is invoked explicitly from somewhere else in the process, as will be explained in Sect. 11.3.3. In any case, when compensation for task A is triggered, task B will be executed.

Fig. 11.23 Use of
compensation event
subprocess

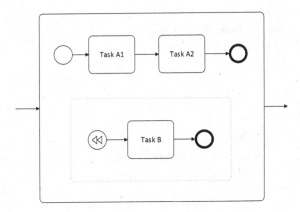

Another way to specify a compensation handler is through the use of an event subprocess. In the previous section, we have seen that a subprocess may have a number of event subprocesses, and each event subprocess has a start event with a specific trigger. For the purpose of compensation handling, it is possible to use an event subprocess with a start event that has a compensation trigger. This possibility is illustrated in Fig. 11.23. Here, the event subprocess will be triggered if there is a need to compensate the enclosing subprocess. Again, such need may only arise *after* the enclosing subprocess has completed successfully.

In the previous section we have seen that the start event for an event subprocess can be either interrupting (solid line) or non-interrupting (dash line). In Fig. 11.23 the compensation event is drawn with a solid line and therefore appears to be an interrupting start event. However, since compensation can only be triggered after the enclosing subprocess has finished, the property of being interrupting or non-interrupting does not apply here. For an event subprocess that serves as a compensation handler, the convention is to draw its start event with a solid line.

11.3.2   *Transactional Subprocesses*

In Sect. 11.1.3 we have seen that there are several types of subprocesses, namely loop subprocesses, multi-instance subprocesses, and ad-hoc subprocesses. Another type of subprocess available in BPMN is the *transactional subprocess*. In essence, the transactional subprocess can be regarded as a transactional scope that serves as a container for other activities or subprocesses. The transactional subprocess has the distinctive feature that it can be *canceled*, meaning that its inner activities will have to be compensated.

Figure 11.24 illustrates the use of a transactional subprocess in a scenario that is somewhat similar to the order fulfillment process used as an example before. The fact that the subprocess is transactional is indicated by the double-line border. Here, the activities "Charge customer" and "Ship product" have their own compensation

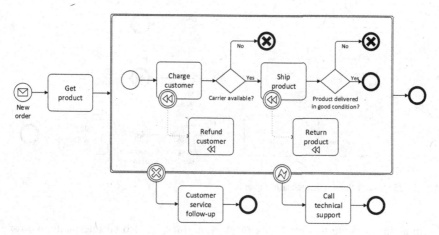

Fig. 11.24 Use of a transactional subprocess

handlers so, if the subprocess fails, these compensation handlers will be invoked. As explained in Sect. 9.4.2, compensation always takes place in reverse order of execution, so if both activities need to be compensated, "Ship product" will be compensated first, and then "Charge customer" afterwards.

When we say that the subprocess "fails," we mean that the transaction that is delimited by the subprocess could not be completed successfully. This can be due to a number of reasons, and Fig. 11.24 illustrates two of them. On one hand, if a carrier is not available then the product cannot be shipped and therefore the transaction cannot complete. On the other hand, if the product is shipped but does not arrive in good condition then the transaction cannot be said to have completed successfully. In both cases, the subprocess ends with a *cancel event*.

The cancel event is a special type of event that can take the form of an end event or an intermediate event attached to the boundary of the transactional subprocess. These events work in a similar way to the end event which throws an error and to the attached intermediate event which catches an error, as explained in Sect. 11.2.2, and as shown in Fig. 11.16 on page 333. However, cancel events can only be used in transactional subprocesses, and they have special semantics in the sense that the occurrence of a cancel event automatically triggers the compensation of all activities contained in the transactional subprocess.

In the example of Fig. 11.24, if a carrier is not available then the subprocess is canceled, and in this case only the activity "Charge customer" is compensated. On the other hand, if the product does not arrive in good condition, then the subprocess is canceled and both activities are compensated, in reverse order of execution. In addition, if any of these cancelations occurs, then the cancel event will be caught by the intermediate cancel event attached to the boundary of the subprocess, and this will be followed by an activity that involves the customer service getting in contact with the customer, as shown in Fig. 11.24.

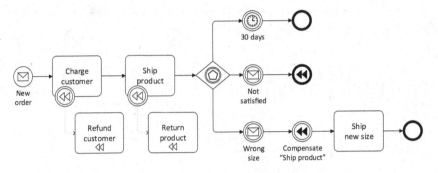

Fig. 11.25 Use of throw compensation events

In addition to the intermediate cancel event, there is also an intermediate error event attached to the boundary of this transactional subprocess. However, it should be noted that this intermediate error event is used for a completely different purpose when compared to the intermediate cancel event that is attached to the boundary of the same subprocess. Here, the intermediate error event is being used to specify the behavior of the process in case an unexpected error occurs. In particular, such error means that something went terribly wrong, to the point that the subprocess can no longer be completed or canceled in a proper way. In this scenario, the subprocess is interrupted abruptly and *no compensation takes place*. The situation then needs to be handled in some other way, and that is why Fig. 11.24 specifies that the technical support team should be called immediately.

11.3.3 Using Compensation Events

In the previous sections we have seen how compensation handlers can be specified and how they can be triggered implicitly by the cancelation of a transactional subprocess. In this section, we will see that compensation handlers can also be triggered explicitly through the use of compensation events. These events can take the form either of an end event or of an intermediate (throwing) event.

Figure 11.25 illustrates the use of compensation events. This model represents the order fulfillment process of an online shop that sells clothes. The shop has a customer satisfaction policy that allows 30 days for the customer to try the product at home and then decide whether to keep it or to return it and get a refund. A third possibility is the product not having the correct size, and in this case it can be returned and a new product will be sent to replace it (however, this can be done only once for a given purchase). In the model of Fig. 11.25, these scenarios are supported through different forms of compensation.

When a new order arrives, the shop charges the customer's credit card and ships the product to the customer address. After this, there is an event-based gateway (see Sect. 11.1.7) to wait for one of several possible events. If within 30 days the customer does not say anything, then it is assumed that the customer is satisfied with the product and the process ends, i.e., after this point there is no longer the possibility to return or to change the product. This is represented in the top-level branch with an intermediate timer event followed by an end event.

If the customer is not satisfied with the product, then it is possible to send a message through the company Web site to inform about the intention of returning the product. This is represented by an intermediate message event in the middle branch that comes out of the event-based gateway. If this event is the first to occur, then the company will trigger the compensation of the whole process by means of a special end event. This end event indicates that compensation is necessary and, since nothing else is being specified, this means that compensation is to be applied to all activities in the process (in general, it is applied to all activities in the enclosing subprocess). Here, compensation of the activities "Charge customer" and "Ship product" will be carried out, in reverse order of execution.

The third and last branch coming out of the event-based gateway represents the scenario in which the clothes are the wrong size, and the customer uses the company Web site to send a message about this fact. In this case, the product must be returned and replaced by another, but there is no need to compensate the "Charge customer" activity. Therefore, only the "Ship product" activity needs to be compensated. This is achieved by means of a compensation event which specifies which activity in particular is to be compensated. In addition, this is not an end event, but an intermediate (throwing) event, since there is more to do after the product has been returned. Namely, a new size must be shipped to replace the previous one.

This scenario illustrates that it is possible to throw a compensation event from either an end event or from an intermediate event. In addition, each of these events may specify a particular activity that is to be compensated, or it may not specify any activity to be compensated and in this case it means that all activities in the enclosing process or subprocess should be compensated. These two possibilities are equivalent to the use of <compensateScope> and <compensate> in BPEL, as described in Sect. 10.4.2. The <compensateScope> construct has a target attribute which specifies which scope should be compensated, whereas the <compensate> construct has no such attribute and triggers compensation of all inner scopes.

11.4 Conclusion

In this chapter we have explored the wide range of elements that BPMN provides to create business process models. Also, we have seen that most of these elements are conceptually similar to the BPEL constructs described in the previous chapter. However, the two languages have different purposes: while BPMN is a graphical notation for modeling business processes, BPEL is an XML-based specification for implementing service orchestrations. In fact, BPMN cannot be used as a graphical representation for BPEL, since several authors have shown that there are certain mismatches between both languages [22, 24, 33]. Still, the notation of BPMN is sufficiently clear to describe process behavior in a way that can be translated into an executable form, even if this requires some ingenuity in the use of BPEL constructs. From a conceptual point of view, the two languages are sufficiently similar to ease the gap between the design of business processes and the implementation of service orchestrations to support those processes. Using BPMN, business analysts can describe organizational processes in a way that can be understood by developers and system integrators, and that can serve as a blueprint for implementing the services and orchestrations required to support those processes.

But BPMN is not restricted to the internal business processes of an organization. As we will see in the next chapter, BPMN can also be used to model the interactions between and across organizations, where each organization has its own internal processes. The interconnection between processes running at different organizations is also a form of integration, and one that brings additional concerns and requirements to the integration platforms that aim to support inter-organizational processes. From a technological point of view, this new form of integration can be addressed with existing technologies, with the possible addition of some security mechanisms, so that is not where the main problem is. The main problem is in ensuring compatibility from a behavioral point of view, i.e., in making sure that the state of an inter-organizational process is kept consistent across all business partners, in order to avoid situations where, for example, one organization is waiting for a message that another organization will never produce. Using BPMN, it is possible to describe in a precise way the inter-organizational process—more precisely, the *choreography*—that takes place across multiple business partners, in order to ensure that each partner will implement its own internal processes in a compatible way.

Chapter 12
Inter-Organizational Processes

In Sect. 11.1 we mentioned the concept of autonomy, which allows an organization to define and implement its own internal processes. Namely, a process can be defined using a modeling language such as BPMN, and it can be implemented through an execution language such as BPEL, provided that the necessary services are in place. These services may be the lowest-level services that represent the underlying systems and applications, or they can be higher-level services that are built as compositions of lower-level ones, and these compositions can also be implemented through BPEL. For business analysts, BPMN provides a convenient way to express the behavior of a process, and if the process involves interacting with external partners, then these interactions can also be represented as message flows between pools, as in Fig. 11.1 on page 317.

In Fig. 11.1, each pool represents a different entity. These entities have their own internal processes and, at a certain point, these processes interact. There is a purchase order that is sent to the supplier, and there is an order confirmation that comes back as a response. Between sending the purchase order and receiving the order confirmation, the supplier is doing something which is not represented in this model, because it is up to the supplier to define its own internal process. As long as the supplier is able to receive the purchase order and return an order confirmation—i.e., as long as the supplier is able to comply with the expected message exchange—then it does not matter how its internal process is actually designed.

In other words, it is impossible to extend the control of a process beyond organizational boundaries, but it is still possible to interoperate with external partners through a set of well-coordinated message exchanges. This set of message exchanges can be defined independently of the way each organization implements its own internal processes, and it is referred to as a *choreography*, which defines the behavior that is expected to take place between a number of business partners. A choreography can also be referred to as a *public workflow*, as opposed to the *private workflows* that represent the internal processes within each organization [3].

Figure 12.1 shows an abstract example of a choreography involving two organizations. Here, organization A has an internal process, and organization B has its own internal process as well. These are the private workflows in this scenario. On

D.R. Ferreira, *Enterprise Systems Integration*, DOI 10.1007/978-3-642-40796-3_12,   345
© Springer-Verlag Berlin Heidelberg 2013

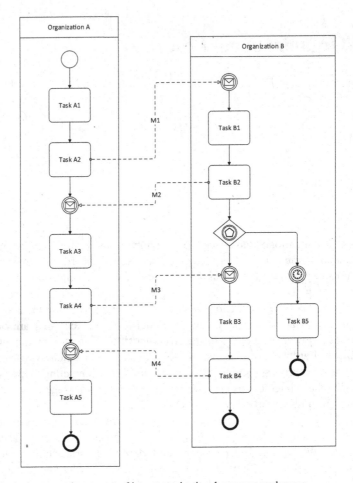

Fig. 12.1 A choreography as a set of inter-organizational message exchanges

the other hand, there is a public workflow that consists in the following message exchanges: M1 from A to B, M2 from B to A, M3 from A to B, and M4 from B to A. This sequence of message exchanges is the choreography between these two organizations, and their internal processes have been designed in such a way as to comply with the role of each organization in the choreography.

Naturally, the internal process of each organization may contain *more* behavior than what is specified in the choreography. For example, tasks A3 and A5 in organization A, as well as tasks B1 and B3 in organization B, do not appear to contribute directly to the choreography; rather, they are private activities that have to do with the purpose of each internal process. Also, the internal process at organization B includes an additional possibility: the possibility that M3 is not received within a certain time frame, as indicated by the intermediate timer event to the right of the event-based gateway. In this case, task B5 will be performed, and the process of organization B will end without waiting further for M3. After that point, if organization A tries to send M3, organization B will no longer be ready to receive it. This illustrates just how a choreography may not work properly if partners do not have a precise agreement as to what is their expected behavior.

In addition to the choreography, there are other concerns that must be taken into account in an inter-organizational scenario. One of such concerns has to do with the format or structure of the messages to be exchanged. Within an organization, it is possible to define the message schemas to be used in a given orchestration, according to the services and applications that are to be invoked in that orchestration. However, in an inter-organizational setting it becomes very difficult to achieve an agreement on the message format, since each business partner will have its own processes and requirements. For example, consider message M1 in the choreography of Fig. 12.1: who should define its format, is it organization A which produces it, or is it organization B who consumes it? Organization A can argue that it can only produce the message in certain format, while organization B can argue that it cannot handle the message unless it is in another, different format.

The solution to this problem is to rely on well-accepted standards. Fortunately, there are standards such as EDI (Electronic Data Interchange) which specify the format for a wide range of documents (such as invoices and purchase orders) that are typically exchanged between organizations. Rather than trying to impose some proprietary format on business partners, it makes more sense to ask for compliance with a common standard such as EDI. This way an organization that goes through the effort of implementing a standard message format will at least know that it will become interoperable not only with the current business partners but also with any potential partner that adheres to the same standard. In general, having the message formats defined by an independent third party facilitates business relations by relieving organizations from having to set up their own formats.

Another important concern that applies to inter-organizational processes is security. When business partners exchange messages over the network, they would like to ensure that such messages are authentic, that they have not been modified while in transit, and also that they have not been read by anyone else other than the intended recipient. This is usually attained through the use of digital certificates and public-key cryptography [28]. Here, too, the role of a trusted third-party—specifically, a *certification authority* (CA)—is essential in order to provide each business partner with its own digital certificate, and to allow a message recipient to check that the incoming message comes from a trusted source.

Naturally, these security mechanisms can also be used within an organization to protect against eavesdropping and impersonation. In this case, every user or system involved in message exchanges, either as sender or as a receiver, should have its own certificate. However, it is in inter-organizational scenarios that these security mechanisms become absolutely fundamental. In this chapter, we begin with the topic of security in Sect. 12.1; then we will move to EDI and related standards in Sect. 12.2; finally, Sect. 12.3 describes the special kind of diagrams that are available in BPMN in order to model choreographies.

12.1 Security

At the lowest level of an inter-organizational exchange there is the need to establish a secure connection between both ends. In particular, the message that flows across such connection should be encrypted so that it cannot be read or tampered with by anyone else except the receiver. In addition, the message should be signed by the sender, so that the receiver can verify that the message is authentic, i.e., that it comes from the supposed source. Both of these features can be achieved through public-key cryptography, with the advantage that public-key cryptography, as opposed to symmetric-key cryptography, does not require that both parties have met or exchanged some encryption/decryption key before.

In symmetric-key cryptography, the same key is used for both message encryption and decryption. Both parties have access to this key and they trust each other in keeping that key—i.e., their *shared secret*—as safe as possible. During message exchange, the sender uses the key to encrypt the message, and the receiver uses the same key to decrypt it. However, for this to work, both sender and receiver must have previously exchanged, by some means, the symmetric key that they will use for encryption/decryption. This creates a problem that must be solved through some other security mechanism, and it is also an obstacle to initiating an interaction between two business partners who have not met before.

In public-key cryptography, every entity that is to engage in some exchange has a pair of keys: one is the *public key* and the other is the *private key*. The private key, as the name indicates, is to be kept private and not to be shared with anyone. The public key, on the other hand, can be shared with everyone else, and it can even be published on some central repository. Each pair of public and private keys works in such a way that whatever is encrypted with the public key can only be decrypted with the corresponding private key, and vice versa (i.e., whatever is encrypted with the private key can only be decrypted with the corresponding public key). This is why the public and private keys are called a "pair," i.e., because they work in combination and they do not work with any other private/public key.

12.1.1 Encryption, Authentication, and Digital Signatures

In practice, there are at least two parties in any exchange, and each party will have its own pair of public and private keys. Therefore, there are two pairs of keys at play, and each party has access to three keys, namely: its own private key, its own public key, and the other party's public key. These keys can be used as encryption or decryption keys in different scenarios and for different purposes, as follows:

- The sender can encrypt the message with the receiver's public key. In this case, only the receiver's private key can decrypt the message. Since the receiver's private key is known only to the receiver, only the receiver can decrypt the

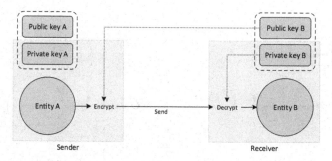

Fig. 12.2 Encryption with the receiver's public key

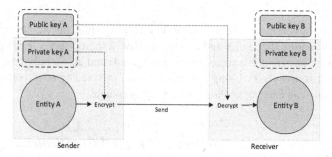

Fig. 12.3 Authentication with the sender's public key

message. This scenario is illustrated in Fig. 12.2 and it can be used as a security mechanism to protect the message against eavesdropping (i.e., reading by others).

- The sender can encrypt the message with its own private key. In this case, only the sender's public key can decrypt the message. But the sender's public key is accessible to everyone. Therefore, anyone can decrypt it. However, if the message is successfully decrypted with the sender's public key, then this means that only the sender could have encrypted the message, with its own private key. No one else could have produced such encrypted message. Therefore, this scenario can be used as a form of authentication and as a protection against impersonation (i.e., false identity). The scenario is illustrated in Fig. 12.3.

The second scenario above is the principle behind *digital signatures*. In essence, the sender can use its own private key to create a *hash* of the message content, to be sent together with the message. Then the sender's public key can be used to verify that hash. Such verification will simply fail against any other public key.

The two mechanisms above can also be combined together to create a message that is simultaneously signed and encrypted. First, the sender signs the message with its own private key, and then encrypts the whole message (signature included) with the receiver's public key. At the receiving end, the receiver decrypts the message with its own private key and verifies the signature with the sender's public key. This procedure is illustrated in Fig. 12.4.

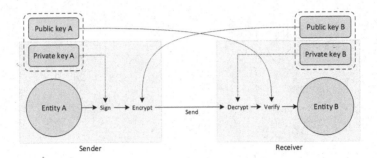

Fig. 12.4 Signing and encryption

Therefore, in contrast with symmetric-key cryptography, public-key cryptography does not require the sender and receiver to have a shared secret. Each party has its own private key (that is a secret, but is not shared) and also a public key (which is shared, but is no secret). Using either one's own private key or the other party's public key, one can encrypt and authenticate all messages.

12.1.2 Certification Authorities and Digital Certificates

The mechanisms described above rely on a fundamental assumption—that any given public key actually belongs to its alleged owner. Otherwise, anyone who (falsely) claims to have a certain identity and presents a valid public key will be able to impersonate that identity and exchange messages while posing as someone else. In particular, consider the following examples:

- Suppose that an entity X claims to be entity B in Fig. 12.2 and registers itself as being entity B together with its own public key in a central repository. Then entity X will start receiving and decrypting messages (with its own private key) that were originally intended for entity B.
- Suppose that an entity X claims to be entity A in Fig. 12.3 and registers itself as entity A together with its own public key in a central repository. Then entity X will start signing messages (with its own private key) as if it were entity A.

Clearly, there must be some way to determine that a given public key actually belongs to the entity that is registered as the owner of that public key, and not to someone else who is posing as that entity. This is why *certification authorities* are needed. A certification authority, or CA for short, certifies that a given public key belongs to certain entity. This is achieved by means of *digital certificates*. Basically, a digital certificate asserts that a given public key (included in the certificate) belongs to a certain entity (also specified in the certificate).

To ensure that a digital certificate is actually authentic and has not been forged, the CA signs the certificate with its own private key. This way, everyone can verify the certificate using the CA's public key.

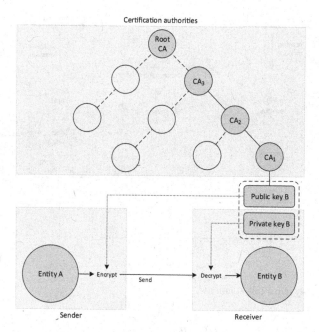

Fig. 12.5 Tree of certification authorities

Through digital certificates, the problem of trusting the public key of a given entity has now been turned into the problem of trusting the CA that signed the digital certificate for that public key. For example, when entity A in Fig. 12.3 encrypts the message with the public key of entity B, it trusts the CA that signed the digital certificate for this public key. It could be the case that this CA is the same who certified the public key of entity A. In this case, the CA is trusted by both parties and they can communicate with each other without further concerns.

However, if the CA that certified the public key of entity B is unknown to entity A, then the scenario gets more complicated. In general, the trustworthiness of a given CA can only be asserted by a higher-level CA. Trustworthiness is granted to a CA (let us call it CA_1) by having a higher-level CA (let us call it CA_2) sign the public-key certificate for CA_1. If CA_1 is unknown to entity A but CA_2 is trusted by that entity, then entity A can safely send the message to entity B. Otherwise, if CA_2 is not trusted by entity A, then there may be an even higher-level CA_3 which is trusted, and entity A can still safely send the message to entity B. .

This chain of verifications across a tree of digital certificates issued by different CAs, who have certified one another, is a usual procedure to determine the validity of a given public key. If entity A reaches the topmost root certificate (Fig. 12.5) without finding along the way a single CA that it can trust, then the public key cannot be trusted. Otherwise, as soon entity A finds a CA in that chain that it can trust, then the public key for entity B has been validated. Ideally, there should be some higher-level CA that is trusted by both entity A and entity B, so that the two parties can safely communicate with each other.

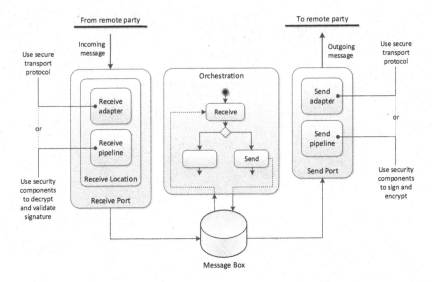

Fig. 12.6 Security in BizTalk solutions

12.1.3   *Security in Integration*

Public-key cryptography is the basis for many secure communication protocols available today. For example, SSL and it successor TLS are commonly used protocols for the exchange of data between a Web server and a Web browser (i.e., a client), and both of these protocols use public-key cryptography (with server authentication and possibly client authentication as well) during the initial setup of a session between client and server. Besides the Web, these security protocols can also be used in other scenarios, for example to secure the communication between an e-mail client and an e-mail server, or between e-mail servers.

In practice, there are implementations of SSL, TLS, and other security protocols available for general use, so many integration platforms already include those protocols. For the systems integrator, incorporating security mechanisms in an integration solution is often as simple as selecting the appropriate transport protocols, or including some predefined components for message encryption and authentication. Figure 12.6 illustrates how security mechanisms can be incorporated in an integration solution, using BizTalk as an example. In Sect. 2.3 we had already seen that each port includes an adapter and a pipeline, and optionally a transformation map as well. In Fig. 12.6, only the adapter and the pipeline have been represented in each port, since this is where security mechanisms can come into play.

Basically, communication with a remote party can be made secure in two different ways: either at the level of the adapter or at the level of the pipeline. At the level of the adapter, a port can be configured to use a secure transport protocol. For example, instead of using HTTP for communication, the adapter can use HTTPS (i.e., HTTP on top of SSL/TLS). This approach applies equally well to receive

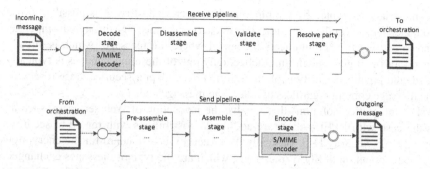

Fig. 12.7 Security components in BizTalk pipelines

ports and to send ports, since SSL/TSL provide encryption and the possibility of authenticating both ends through the use of digital certificates. This is also the approach that requires less changes to the integration solution, since it is essentially a matter of port configuration. However, it should be noted that an adapter can provide security only while the message is in transit; to secure the actual content of the message, it is necessary to perform some processing at the level of the pipeline.

As described in Sect. 2.3, particularly in Fig. 2.3 on page 21, a pipeline has several stages of processing. By default, the pipeline is empty and does nothing, but it is possible to insert some special, predefined components in these stages for custom processing. One of such components is the S/MIME encoder (for a send pipeline) or S/MIME decoder (for a receive pipeline). Basically, S/MIME is a standard for message encryption and authentication based on public-key cryptography. In a send pipeline, it is possible to use an S/MIME encoder to sign and encrypt the message; conversely, in a receive pipeline it is possible to use an S/MIME decoder to decrypt the message and validate its signature. This is the same sequence of operations as shown earlier in Fig. 12.4.

Figure 12.7 illustrates the use of S/MIME components in BizTalk pipelines:

- In a receive pipeline, the S/MIME decoder is placed in the decode stage, which is the first stage of processing. Once the message has been decrypted and its signature validated, other stages of processing may follow, such as disassemble (i.e., parsing and possibly breaking the message into multiple parts), validation (i.e., XML validation of the message or of each of its parts), and party resolution (i.e., mapping of the sender to a local party identifier).
- In a send pipeline, the S/MIME encoder is placed in the decode stage, which is the last stage of processing, when the message gets signed and encrypted. Before that, there is the pre-assemble stage (where custom processing can be applied to the message through some custom-developed components) and the assemble stage (which can be used to convert the message XML to flat file, or to add an envelope to the XML message).

Naturally, the use of the S/MIME components in pipelines dispenses with the need for transport security at the adapter level, since the content of the message has been already encrypted by the pipeline. However, if desired, it is possible to use both mechanisms at the same time, i.e., to encrypt the message through the pipeline, and to encrypt the communication channel where the message (which is already encrypted) will go through. In practice, only one of these mechanisms is typically used, and pipeline security is often preferred over adapter security, since it secures the message content regardless of where the message ends up.

For integration solutions that involve the invocation of Web services—such as is the case with BPEL—there are additional possibilities with regard to security, namely WS-Security [18]. Basically, WS-Security is a standard for the encryption and authentication of SOAP messages, which are the type of messages exchanged between a Web service and its clients, as explained in Sect. 6.4.2. However, the signing and encryption of each message at the sender, and the subsequent decryption and signature validation at the receiver, impose a significant performance overhead, especially when multiple exchanges are to take place. Therefore, other standards have been proposed, such as WS-SecureConversation [20]. The idea of WS-SecureConversation is to use WS-Security only in an initial setup phase, to establish a shared secret between parties. This shared secret can then be used to secure all subsequent exchanges between those parties in a more efficient way.

12.2 Electronic Data Interchange

Assuming that security concerns have been addressed by the mechanisms and technologies described above, the next issue to be considered in an inter-organizational scenario has to do with the actual content or structure of the messages to be exchanged. In particular, the problem of who defines the message format for an inter-organizational exchange becomes an especially sensitive issue, since each business partner will have its own requirements, and in the worst case there may be no consensus as to what format should be used. This can become a major obstacle to setting up the interaction between processes running at different organizations.

Within an organization, when there is a message to be exchanged between a sender and a receiver, it is possible to decide whether it is the receiver who will have to adapt to the message schema produced by the sender, or whether it is the sender who will have to adapt to the message schema consumed by the receiver. Also, there could be a third possibility, which is to have a transformation map between the two schemas. However, none of these options are very practical in an inter-organizational environment, because this would require the development of a new adapter or a new transformation map for every new business partner.

Inter-organizational relationships are supposed to be dynamic. For example, if a company has a supplier for a certain commodity, but suddenly finds that it can buy the same commodity at a lower price from a different supplier, then the company will want to switch to the new supplier immediately, without having to go through the effort of setting up new message schemas, new adapters, or new transformation maps just to be able to interact with the new supplier. Ideally, the trade of a given product or service should be standardized in such a way that it is possible to establish relationships with new business partners without having to introduce significant changes either in the processes or in the supporting infrastructure.

In general, the trade of any product or service involves the exchange of certain business documents such as, for example, a request for quote (when a customer asks for the price of a certain product), a purchase order (when the customer orders the product from the supplier), a delivery note (where the supplier says when the product will arrive), and an invoice (when the supplier requests payment for the product). These and many other types of business documents are well known to any business organization. The problem is that, in practice, each organization has its own internal representation for these documents, and this makes it difficult to automate the exchange of such documents in an inter-organizational scenario.

In an effort to devise a solution to this problem, several standards have been proposed for the representation of business documents. These standards were meant not only to provide a uniform format, but also to facilitate the automated exchange of those documents between systems running at different organizations. Because of this focus on automated processing, such standards are collectively known as EDI (Electronic Data Interchange), and they include the EDIFACT standard by the United Nations, which is used in Europe and Asia, the X12 standard which is used in North America, as well as some other standards that are used in specific industry sectors. Here we will be focusing mainly on the UN/EDIFACT standard.

12.2.1   Message Format in EDI

As of November 2012, the UN/EDIFACT standard (version D.12B) includes 196 different message types that can be exchanged between business partners.[1] Each message type is basically an EDI representation of a certain business document.

For example, in the process of Fig. 11.1 on page 317 there is an interaction between two organizations: a customer (the company whose purchase process is being modeled) and a supplier. At a certain point, the customer sends a purchase order to the supplier, and the supplier returns an order confirmation to the customer. Both of these messages have their EDI-equivalents: the purchase order corresponds to the ORDERS message type in the UN/EDIFACT standard, and the order confirmation corresponds to the ORDRSP (order response) message type.

In general, each message type defined in the UN/EDIFACT standard is identified by a six-letter acronym (e.g., ORDERS, ORDRSP, and INVOIC). In contrast, in the X12 standard these documents are identified by a three-digit number instead, e.g., 850 for a purchase order, 855 for a "purchase order acknowledgment," and 810 for

---

[1]For a complete list of these message types, see: http://www.unece.org/trade/untdid/d12b/trmd/trmdi1.htm.

Fig. 12.8 Paper-based
purchase order

```
From:
Customer Name
Customer Street
Customer City
Postal Code
                              To:
                              Supplier Name
                              Supplier Street
                              Supplier City
                              Postal Code

Order no. 123456
Date: March 8, 2013

Contact person: ...


Ref.       Description            Quantity      Price

68454      Bycicle Rockrider 6.0      1       250,00 €

57063      Helmet Procycle V          1        30,00 €

                                 Order total:  280,00 €


All prices with VAT 20% included.
Payment terms: as previously agreed.
Delivery: customer will pick up the goods.
```

an invoice. There are also some slight differences with respect to the content of these messages in both standards, although they are governed by the same principles.

Figure 12.8 shows how a purchase order could look like when printed on paper. This example is somewhat inspired in the bike store scenario of Chap. 5. In particular, the order is being placed by a certain customer, to a certain supplier; it has a number and a date; it has a contact person; it has two items that are being ordered, namely a bicycle and a helmet; for each item, there is a product reference, a description, a quantity, and a price; there is the order total amount; and finally there are some details concerning taxes, payment terms, and delivery conditions.

All of the information contained in this purchase order—the customer info, the supplier info, the product info, and even the payment and delivery details—can be represented as an EDI message. When represented as an EDI message, the purchase order can be transmitted electronically and processed by a remote system (i.e., the supplier's system) in an automated way. In particular, Listing 12.1 shows how the purchase order in Fig. 12.8 would look like when represented as a UN/EDIFACT purchase order message (i.e., a message of type ORDERS).

Clearly, the EDI message in Listing 12.1 is not intended to be human-readable; rather, it is a machine-processable representation of the purchase order. In any case, it is still possible to make sense of this message by referring to the specification of the ORDERS message type in the UN/EDIFACT standard.[2] Although here we will

---

[2]The D.12B version of this specification can be found at: http://www.unece.org/trade/untdid/d12b/trmd/orders_c.htm.

Listing 12.1 UN/EDIFACT purchase order message

```
 1  UNA:+.?*'
 2  UNB+UNOA:3+CUSTOMER:ZZZ+SUPPLIER:ZZZ+20130308:1430+1234'
 3  UNH+001+ORDERS:D:12B:UN'
 4  BGM+220+123456'
 5  DTM+137:20130308:102'
 6  NAD+BY+++CUSTOMER NAME+CUSTOMER STREET+CUSTOMER CITY++POSTAL CODE'
 7  CTA+AC+CONTACT PERSON'
 8  NAD+SU+++SUPPLIER NAME+SUPPLIER STREET+SUPPLIER CITY++POSTAL CODE'
 9  TAX+7+VAT+++20'
10  CUX+1:EUR:9'
11  PYT+18'
12  TOD+4'
13  LIN+1+1+68454:SK'
14  QTY+21:1'
15  FTX+AAA+1+DESCRIPTION+BYCICLE ROCKRIDER 6.0'
16  PRI+AAA:25000:PE'
17  LIN+2+1+57063:SK'
18  QTY+21:1'
19  FTX+AAA+1+DESCRIPTION+HELMET PROCYCLE V'
20  PRI+AAA:3000:PE'
21  UNS+S'
22  MOA+86:28000'
23  CNT+2:2'
24  UNT+22+001'
25  UNZ+1+1234'
```

go through some of the details of this particular message type, this is meant as an illustrative example of the general structure of EDI messages.

Basically, an EDI message comprises a series of *segments*, where each segment is identified by a three-letter code (e.g., QTY in line 14). Usually, there is one segment per line (as is the case in Listing 12.1) but this is not mandatory, since each segment is explicitly terminated by an apostrophe ('), after which another segment may follow immediately, on the same line. However, it is common practice to introduce a line break, as a "suffix," after each segment.

Each segment may have several *data elements*, which are separated by a plus sign (+). For example, the QTY segment in line 14 has a single data element, but the LIN segment in line 13 has three data elements. In some cases, there are several consecutive plus signs; for example, in line 9 there is a TAX segment which, at a certain point, has three plus signs (+++). This is the result of two data elements being left empty. When a data element is not used, its separator must be kept anyway, because each segment has a fixed number of data elements.

The EDI standards define the meaning of each data element according to its position in the segment. Therefore, when data elements are skipped, their separators must be kept anyway to ensure the correct position of the remaining elements. An exception is the data elements that are skipped at the end of the segment; in this case, there is no need to keep their separators, because no other nonempty element will follow until the terminating apostrophe.

Each data element may contain a single value, or it may have multiple *components*. In case there are multiple components, these are separated by a colon (:). For example, the QTY segment in line 14 has a data element with two components, which are represented by the values 21 and 1.

Now that the basic syntax of the EDI message has been explained, its actual content can be described as follows:

- The UNA segment specifies the special characters that will be used as delimiters.

  - The first character (:) is the component separator and the second character is the data element separator (+).
  - The third character (.) refers to the decimal notation, i.e., it is the character that will be used as a decimal point.
  - The fourth character (?) is an indicator to prevent misinterpretation when a data element happens to contain one of the characters that are being used as delimiters. For example, if a data element contains an apostrophe, then this should be preceded by the indicator (?').
  - The fifth character (*) can be given different interpretations. In earlier versions of the UN/EDIFACT standard, it was a reserved character for future use (in this case it must be a space character). In recent versions, it is interpreted as a repetition separator, to be used when a data element has multiple, consecutive occurrences inside a data segment (which is actually quite rare). In this case, an asterisk is used to separate those occurrences (rather than a plus sign, which would indicate the end of the data element).
  - The sixth character (') is the segment terminator, and if this is followed by a suffix (i.e., some form of line break) then it is assumed that every segment in the message will be followed by the same suffix.

  The UNA segment is optional. If it is not included in the message, then the default separators will be used. These default separators are exactly the same as the ones that are being used here, so the UNA segment in line 1 of Listing 12.1 is actually redundant. It has been included here in order to illustrate that it is possible to adjust the syntax of EDI messages.
- The UNB segment is mandatory and it works as an envelope for the EDI message. It is matched by a UNZ segment which closes the envelope at the end (line 25). Such envelope may actually contain more than one message, but in this case a single message is being transmitted. The envelope defined by a UNB segment and a UNZ segment is referred to as an *interchange* in the EDI terminology, where an interchange may contain several messages.

  In particular, the UNB segment specifies:

  - The character encoding for the interchange (UNOA version 3 refers to an encoding which is similar to ASCII but does not allow lowercase letters).
  - An identification for both the sender and the receiver of the interchange. The qualifier ZZZ in each of these elements specifies that the identifiers are user-defined.
  - The date and time when this interchange was prepared.
  - A unique reference number that the sender assigns to the interchange.

On the other hand, the UNZ segment comprises:

- The number of EDI messages contained in this interchange. In this case, there is only one message being transmitted.
- The reference number assigned to the interchange, as in the UNB segment.

- The UNH segment represents the message header. It is matched by a closing UNT segment (i.e., the message trailer) in line 24. The UNH segment has a unique reference number that the sender assigns to the message (in this case, 001) and also it specifies the message type (ORDERS), the version number (directory version D.12B), and the agency that specified this message type (UN for UN/EDIFACT). On the other hand, the UNT segment specifies the number of segments in the message (including header and trailer) and also includes the reference number assigned to the message in the UNH header.
- The BGM segment marks the beginning of the message. The first data element contains a code for the document name, which in this case indicates that it is some type of "order" (220). The second data element is an arbitrary document identifier (123456), which corresponds to the order number in Fig. 12.8.
- The following segment (DTM) contains the order date. The data element has three components. The code 137 indicates that this is the date when the order was issued, and the code 102 specifies that the date format is YYYYMMDD.
- The NAD segment in line 6 specifies the name and address for the "buyer" (this role is identified by the code BY). Not every data element is being used here, since this depends on how the party is being identified and how the address is being specified. Also, there is a country code at the end of the NAD segment that is not being used in this example.
- The CTA segment in line 7 specifies the name of the contact person as in the purchase order of Fig. 12.8. In this context, AC is a function code that specifies that the contact person is the person responsible for accepting the goods.
- The NAD segment in line 8 specifies the name and address for the "supplier" (SU), and it follows the same structure as the NAD segment in line 6.
- The TAX segment is used to include tax information. In this case, code 7 indicates that it is a general tax (as opposed to special taxes such as customs duties for imported products). The tax type is VAT, and the fifth data element specifies the applicable tax rate.
- The CUX segment in line 10 specifies that the prices are in Euros. Code 1 indicates that this is the currency for payment, and code 9 indicates that this currency is being used in an order.
- The segment PYT refers to the payment terms. In particular, code 18 means that payment will be carried out "as previously agreed."
- The segment TOD refers to the terms of delivery. Code 4 means that the goods are to be picked up by the customer, as specified in Fig. 12.8.
- Lines 13–20 contain the list of ordered items:

  - The LIN segment contains a line item identifier, an action code (1 for "add") and a product reference number in the form of a "stock keeping unit" (hence the code SK).

- The QTY segment refers to the "ordered" quantity (code 21).
- The FTX segment contains a free text description of the product. The code AAA indicates that this description is intended for customs or transport purposes. Code 1 means that this text is not relevant for order processing (because the item has already been clearly identified in the LIN segment).
- The PRI segment refers to the price for each item. The code AAA indicates that this is the net price, i.e., it includes all charges. The PE code means that the price is "per each" unit, so this price must be multiplied by the quantity specified in the QTY segment.

- Finally, we enter the summary section for the order:

  - The UNS segment is a general separator segment. Here it is being used to mark the beginning of the summary section for this order.
  - The MOA segment refers to the total monetary amount associated with this order. Basically, it is the sum for all items in the order plus any additional charges, if applicable. The code 86 means that this segment contains the total of all amounts mentioned in the order.
  - The CNT segment is a control count. Here, it is being used as a checksum for the number of line items in the order (as indicated by code 2). There are two line items, so the value is, coincidentally, 2. The data element in this segment contains 2:2, where the first component denotes the type of control count and the second component is the value for the count.

It should be noted that these segments are not exclusive to the ORDERS message. In addition to the fact that every EDI message has a header and trailer (UNH and UNT segments), many of the inner segments are also shared across multiple message types. For example, the QTY segment appears in 102 out of the 196 message types defined by the UN/EDIFACT standard (version D.12B).

Because the same segment may appear in different messages, there are several codes to specify how the segment relates to the current message. For example, the QTY segment in Listing 12.1 is used with code 21 to denote an "ordered quantity," but in other message types the same segment is used with different meanings, such as the number of returned items, the number of pieces delivered, the number of goods that are on back-order, a number of hours, a number of job vacancies, or even a number of livestock (i.e., live animals). There are about 500 different codes to characterize the type of quantity being specified in a QTY segment.

There are many data elements in other segments that need to be properly qualified as well (e.g., the codes associated with PYT and TOD in Listing 12.1). In essence, the UN/EDIFACT standard consists in the specification of the message types, the segments within each message type, the data elements within each segment, and the components within each data element. Where applicable, the standard also specifies the codes that can be used in a given data element or component.

12.2.2   Integration with EDI

The EDI standards specify the rules and basic syntax for EDI messages, but there are several settings that are left up to business partners to define. For example, a party may want to use different separators (to be specified in the UNA segment), or to use a character encoding that allows lowercase letters (to be specified in the UNB segment). In addition, each party has to decide how it will be identified in the EDI messages to be exchanged (UNB segment). Other terms, such as payment and delivery conditions, may also have to be settled beforehand.

Naturally, such settings—which govern the interaction between two parties—cannot be defined unilaterally by one of the parties alone. The terms, conditions, and parameters that are to be established before the interaction takes place must be the subject of an agreement between both parties. Such agreement is called a *trading partner agreement* (TPA). Typically, a TPA is valid within a certain time frame. If at the end of that time frame both parties are happy with the current TPA, they may decide to extend, renew, or renegotiate its terms.

A TPA may include business terms (such as pricing, payment, and delivery conditions) and also technical specifications that apply to the message exchanges between both parties. It is these technical specifications that we will be most interested in, since they have an impact on the integration between both parties. In an inter-organizational scenario, the TPA is an integral part of any integration solution that aims at connecting the parties at both ends, because it has important details concerning the format and transmission of messages between parties.

From a technical point of view, producing and consuming EDI messages are not very difficult. The message format may be rather elaborate as there are a lot of segments and data elements for different purposes, but the EDI standards are fairly clear with respect to the structure and use of such elements. Therefore, an EDI message can be regarded as being essentially a flat file with special delimiters (see Sect. 5.3.1 for a discussion of flat files, in particular delimited flat files).

While business partners may exchange messages in an EDI format, internally they will probably want to use XML in order to take advantage of modern integration solutions based on orchestrations, message transformation, and service invocation. In the BizTalk platform, the conversion of flat files to and from XML can be done through the use of special pipeline components, as shown in Fig. 12.9.

For a receive pipeline, the disassemble stage may include a flat file disassembler component which converts an incoming text message into an XML representation. Similarly, for a send pipeline, the assemble stage may contain a flat file assembler component that converts an outgoing XML message into a text message. In both cases, a flat file schema for the message must have been previously defined, and this schema is provided as input to the flat file disassembler component in the receive pipeline, and to the flat file assembler component in the send pipeline.

However, when using EDI the situation is slightly different because some of the information that is required to parse an EDI message may come from the technical

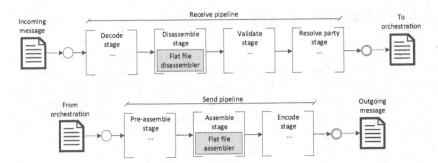

Fig. 12.9 Flat file components in BizTalk pipelines

specifications that can only be found in the TPA established between both parties. Therefore, to receive an EDI message it is necessary to use a special component in the receive pipeline that is able to parse the message (and convert it to XML) according to the specifications in the TPA. Conversely, to send an EDI message it is necessary to use a special component in the send pipeline that is able to produce the message (from XML) according to the specifications in the TPA.

In the case of BizTalk, this platform already includes special-purpose pipelines for sending and receiving EDI messages according to a given TPA. The use of these pipelines is illustrated in Fig. 12.10. Basically, to receive an EDI message, one must use the EDI receive pipeline in the corresponding receive port, and to send an EDI message one must use the special-purpose EDI send pipeline in the corresponding send port. Both of these pipelines are able to fetch the TPA and check the technical specifications that have been agreed between partners with regard to the separators, character encoding, and envelopes to be used with those messages.

As shown in Fig. 12.10, the TPA itself is kept in a separate module called "trading partner management." The TPA can be changed on-the-fly and its settings will be immediately applied to the next EDI message that is sent or received.

In practice, setting up a TPA in BizTalk involves the following steps:

- First, it is necessary to define the *local party* and the *remote party*. This means setting up an identity (i.e., a name) for each party, and optionally a digital certificate as well, to be used for party resolution purposes (i.e., the last stage in the receive pipeline of Fig. 12.9).
- Second, each party may be configured as having one or more *business profiles* (i.e., organizational units, divisions, or subsystems) which are able to engage in EDI exchanges. Each business profile may use a different EDI standard. For example, a global company with branches in Europe and North America may have two business profiles, one which uses the UN/EDIFACT standard and another that uses the X12 standard, respectively.
- Third, assuming that there is a business profile from the local party and a business profile from the local party which use the same EDI standard, it is possible to create a TPA involving both parties. In this context, the TPA is essentially a set

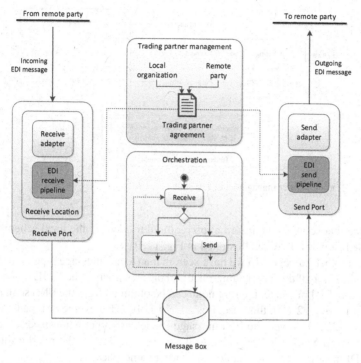

Fig. 12.10 EDI pipelines in BizTalk

of configurations regarding the separators, character encoding, and envelopes to be used in the actual messages to be exchanged.

Figure 12.11 illustrates how a TPA is set up in BizTalk according to the three steps above: first, the identities for the local party and for the remote party are defined; then their business profiles are created; and finally the messages to be exchanged are specified together with a set of configurations regarding special characters, encoding, etc. In the example of Fig. 12.11, the settings apply to a bidirectional exchange where an ORDERS message (i.e., purchase order) is sent from the customer to the supplier, and an ORDRSP message (i.e., order response) is to be returned from the supplier to the customer.

Each party will have to ensure that its local system is properly configured according to its own role in this exchange. Specifically, for the customer the ORDERS message is an outgoing message and the ORDRSP message is an incoming message, whereas for the supplier it is the other way around.

Another important feature of TPAs in BizTalk is that they specify how an incoming EDI message can be mapped to a local XML schema. In Fig. 12.9 we have seen that the flat file disassembler component in a receive pipeline must be provided with the local XML schema that the incoming message will be disassembled into. A similar requirement applies to the special-purpose EDI receive pipeline, with the

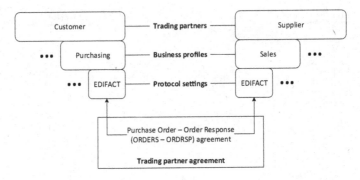

Fig. 12.11 Trading partner management in BizTalk

difference that some of the information required to identify the local schema must be fetched from the TPA, as illustrated in Fig. 12.10.

In Sect. 6.5.1 on page 176 we have seen that a (local) message type is identified by a combination of the target namespace and the root node of the XML schema. For an incoming EDI message, the root node can be obtained from the UNH segment, as shown in Listing 12.1. In this case, it is a UN/EDIFACT message of type ORDERS, version D.12B. However, the EDI message carries no target namespace, so one of the configurations that it is possible to include in the TPA is the relationship of a given EDI message type and version to a target namespace.

This way, when an EDI message arrives, the EDI receive pipeline retrieves the EDI message type and version from the UNH segment in order to identify the root node (for the message in Listing 12.1, the root node will be EFACT_D12B_ORDERS). On the other hand, the EDI receive pipeline verifies in the TPA which target namespace should be associated with such EDI message type and version. As a result, the EDI receive pipeline is able to obtain a fully qualified message type (in terms of target namespace and root node) that can be used to determine the local XML schema that the incoming EDI message must be disassembled to.

12.2.3 Security in EDI

Originally, the EDI standards were designed to be independent of any particular communication technology, i.e., an EDI message can be transmitted using any transport protocol agreed between the sender and the receiver. However, as more business partners started using the Internet for transmitting EDI messages, it became clear that it would be useful to have some predefined communication standards. In particular, those standards should address the security concerns of business partners, especially the need for encryption and authentication of EDI messages.

Initially, some business partners started exchanging EDI messages through e-mail in order to take advantage of the security features of S/MIME. This led to

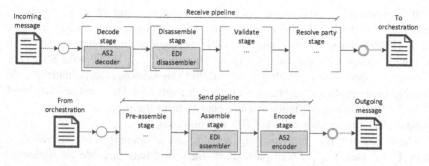

Fig. 12.12 EDI pipelines with AS2 support

a specification known as AS1 (Applicability Statement 1) [13] which is based on SMTP and S/MIME. However, soon it was realized that HTTP would be more convenient as a transport protocol, which led to a new specification known as AS2 [17] based on HTTP and S/MIME. Despite the fact that additional standards have been developed, namely AS3 based on FTP and AS4 based on Web service protocols, AS2 is still perhaps the most popular standard used in connection with EDI.

Using AS2, the message is transmitted to a remote party within an HTTP request. This HTTP request will have a special set of headers, which are referred to as AS2 headers. These headers identify the sender and the receiver, and also indicate whether a message acknowledgment is being requested by the sender. In AS2, the acknowledgment is referred to as a "Message Disposition Notification" (MDN), and it serves as a confirmation that the message reached its destination. If the MDN is requested by the sender, the receiver is obliged to produce it regardless of whether the AS2 message has been successfully processed or not.

The actual content of an AS2 message (i.e., the payload of the HTTP message) is the MIME-encoded version of an EDI message. In particular, the use of S/MIME allows the EDI message to be encrypted and digitally signed. As explained in Sect. 12.1.1, if the message is to be signed then it will be signed with the private key of the sender, and if the message is to be encrypted then it will be encrypted with the public key of the receiver. For a message that needs to be simultaneously signed and encrypted, it will be first signed and then the whole message (with the signature) will be encrypted, as illustrated in Fig. 12.4 on page 350.

In the BizTalk platform, AS2 is supported by means of a special pair of pipelines. Basically, these are similar to the EDI pipelines discussed in the previous section, with the difference being that AS2 pipelines have an additional component in the decode/encode stage to support the AS2 protocol.

As illustrated in Fig. 12.12, an AS2 receive pipeline has an AS2 decoder in the decode stage that precedes the disassemble stage (i.e., the EDI message will be first decoded and only then converted to a local XML schema). Conversely, an AS2 send pipeline has an AS2 encoder in the encode stage that follows the assemble stage (i.e., the EDI message will be first generated from a local XML schema, and then encoded before being sent out via HTTP to the remote party).

It is important to note that every port has a pipeline and an adapter (see, for example, Fig. 12.10). If the port uses an AS2 pipeline, then it must also use the HTTP adapter since, by definition, AS2 messages are transmitted over HTTP. Alternatively, the port may use the HTTPS protocol (i.e., HTTP with SSL/TLS) since AS2 supports this possibility as well, but this is somewhat redundant if the message content has already been encrypted through S/MIME. On the other hand, if the message has been signed but not encrypted in the pipeline, then the use of transport-layer encryption with HTTPS will make sense.

These options for implementing security have already been discussed in Sect. 12.1.3 (see Fig. 12.6 in particular). Basically, it is possible to implement security either at the pipeline level or at the adapter level, but pipeline-level security is preferred because it is aimed at securing the message content, whereas adapter-level security aims at securing the communication channel between both ends. Therefore, when an EDI exchange needs to be secured, this is best done through the use of a pipeline that is able to securely encode the message content according to some standard protocol, as is the case with AS2.

12.3 Choreography Modeling

In Sect. 12.2.2 we have seen that a trading partner agreement (TPA) contains important configurations with respect to the message exchanges that will take place between the two business partners, in both directions. In particular, the TPA in Sect. 12.2.2 concerned the exchange of an ORDERS (i.e., purchase order) message sent from customer to supplier, and the exchange of an ORDRSP (i.e., order response) message returned from the supplier to the customer. If there would be other exchanges between these business partners, these additional exchanges could be the subject of separate TPAs. Also, if there would be more business partners in this inter-organizational scenario, then there would be a separate TPA to govern the exchanges between each pair of business partners.

This means that, typically, a TPA is intended to govern a specific pair of exchanges, and such pairs of exchanges are the basic building blocks of inter-organizational processes, or *choreographies*, as described at the beginning of this chapter. This concept is perhaps better illustrated by means of an example. Figure 12.13 shows an inter-organizational scenario with four business partners. Basically, this scenario can be described as follows:

1. The buyer sends a request for quote to the supplier, in order to obtain the price for a certain product (and possibly other details as well, such as payment and delivery conditions).
2. The supplier replies with a quote for the product.
3. If the buyer keeps an interest in acquiring the product, it sends a purchase order to the supplier. Besides the product being ordered, the purchase order contains additional info, such as the delivery address and payment details.

Fig. 12.13 A
business-to-business (B2B)
scenario involving four
partners

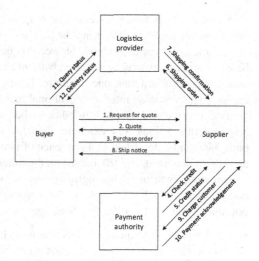

4. For its own protection, the supplier may inquire about the credit status of the buyer before proceeding with the order fulfillment.

5. An external payment authority (e.g., the buyer's bank or the supplier's bank) will provide information about the customer's credit status.

6. Assuming the credit status is alright, the supplier proceeds with the order fulfillment by sending a shipping order to an external, third-party logistics provider.

7. The logistics provider confirms that it will be able to deliver the package to the final destination and also provides an estimate for the arrival date.

8. The supplier informs that the product has been dispatched by sending a ship notice to the buyer. In addition to the estimate for the arrival date, the ship notice contains information about the logistics provider and the package identifier so that the buyer may track its progress.

9. After some time, the supplier charges the buyer for the due amount. In this example, the payment takes place through the payment authority, as if the buyer's credit card or account balance is being charged.

10. A payment acknowledgment is generated when the operation is complete.

11. If, in the meantime, the product is taking longer than expected to arrive, the buyer may inquire the logistics provider about the delivery status.

12. Upon receiving the query, the logistics provider returns a response with the current location or stage of processing for the incoming package.

In this scenario it is possible to see that virtually every exchange is part of some request–response pair. For example, the buyer sends a request for quote and receives a quote as a response; the supplier inquires about the credit status and receives the corresponding information as a response; the supplier also sends a shipping order to the logistics provider and receives a confirmation as a response; the supplier charges the customer and receives a payment acknowledgment; the buyer queries the logistics provider and receives the shipping status as a response; and even the ship notice, which does not seem to be directly related to a previous request can be interpreted as result of submitting the purchase order to the supplier.

Naturally, the correspondence between requests and responses does not need to be exact, since there may be a request without a response, and there may be a request which triggers more than one response. In any case, the most common message exchange pattern in an inter-organizational scenario is the request–response and, in general, every choreography can be described as a sequence of multiple request–response interactions. For example, the choreography depicted in Fig. 12.1 on page 346 can be described as a sequence of two request–response interactions (M1 and M2 on one hand, and M3 and M4 on the other hand).

However, even in a choreography—as in any process—there may be several possible behaviors. For example, in the scenario above (Fig. 12.13) there are several possible deviations from the described sequence of exchanges, namely:

- After receiving the quote, the buyer may no longer be interested in the purchase, and therefore the choreography ends prematurely.
- If payment is due in advance (i.e., before shipping) then the supplier may skip the credit check and charge the customer immediately after receiving the purchase order, or after receiving the confirmation for the shipping order.
- If the supplier checks the credit status for the buyer, and that status is negative or non-advisable, the supplier may decide not to continue with the order fulfillment, or it may require advance payment.
- If the logistics partner is unable to deliver the product to the buyer's location, then the supplier may be unable to proceed with the order fulfillment.
- The product may take long to arrive, and in the meantime the buyer may inquire the logistics provider several times. For each query, the logistics provider must respond with the current location of the package.

These are just some examples of what can happen as the choreography between these business partners is taking place. The informal diagram of Fig. 12.13 lists the message exchanges and provides an idea of their sequence, but this is clearly insufficient to serve as a precise model for the behavior of the choreography. As we will see in the following sections, it is possible to use BPMN to describe the behavior of a choreography in a more precise way. In fact, one of the major improvements in BPMN 2.0 was the introduction of special diagrams for modeling choreographies— namely conversation diagrams and choreography diagrams. Previously, if one would like to model a choreography, the only option would be to use a collaboration diagram based on message flows between pools, as in Fig. 12.1. However, as we will see in the next section, these are also unable to capture the behavior in a precise way. Therefore, although choreography diagrams are a new feature in BPMN, they will have an important role to play in inter-organizational integration.

12.3.1 Collaboration Diagrams

Figure 12.14 shows a collaboration diagram for the B2B scenario of Fig. 12.13. In this diagram, each business partner is represented as a separate pool, and these

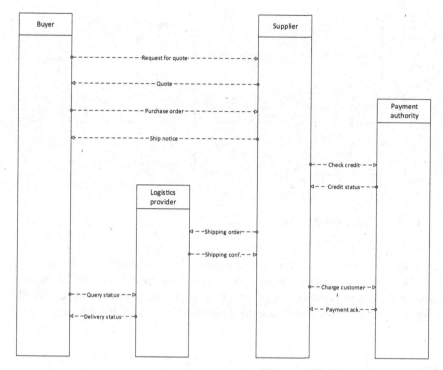

Fig. 12.14 A collaboration diagram

pools are empty of any detail since the main focus is on the choreography, i.e., on the message exchanges between partners. The use of message flows between pools indicates the sender and receiver for each message. However, a collaboration diagram does not specify the exact sequence in which these message exchanges take place. The order in which the message flows appear in the diagram provides a rough indication of the sequence of exchanges, but it cannot be taken for granted that the messages will be exchanged in that order.

For example, according to the scenario description, the ship notice is sent *after* the supplier has received the shipping confirmation from the logistics partner. However, the arrangement of elements in the collaboration diagram of Fig. 12.14 is such that the message flow for the ship notice is drawn *above* the interaction with the logistics partner. As another example, the interaction between the buyer and the logistics provider has been drawn at roughly the same level as the payment interaction between the supplier and the payment authority. However, this does not mean that these exchanges will take place at the same time; instead, one may happen before the other, or both may happen to be intertwined.

Some additional problems can be recognized within this sort of diagram. For example, it may be the case that the supplier does not actually check the credit status of the buyer; however, such pair of messages exchanges with the payment

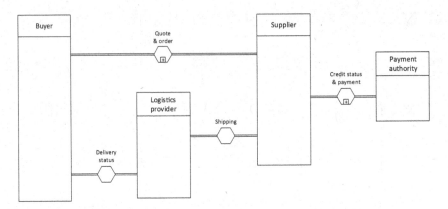

Fig. 12.15 A conversation diagram

authority is drawn to show that it *may* happen. Also, the interaction between the buyer and the logistics provider (i.e., the query about the delivery status) may not occur at all, it may occur only once, or it may occur multiple times; there is hardly a convenient way to represent these possibilities in a collaboration diagram.

12.3.2 Conversation Diagrams

The conversation diagram is a new type of diagram introduced in BPMN 2.0. It is meant to provide a quick overview of which partners collaborate in which phase of the choreography. Figure 12.15 illustrates a conversation diagram for the choreography shown above as a collaboration diagram in Fig. 12.14. In fact, there is an interesting relationship between conversation diagrams and collaboration diagrams: basically, a conversation diagram can be "expanded" into a collaboration diagram, where each conversation is expanded into a set of message flows. For example, the conversations "Shipping" and "Delivery status" in Fig. 12.15 can be expanded into the corresponding set of message flows in Fig. 12.14.

A conversation can also be expanded into a set of other conversations, which in turn are expanded into a set of message flows. In this case, the parent (i.e., topmost) conversation is referred to as a *sub-conversation* much in the same way that an activity which can be expanded into multiple activities is referred to as a *subprocess* (see Sect. 11.1.3). In Fig. 12.15 there are two examples of sub-conversations: "Quote & order" and "Credit status & payment." Each of these sub-conversations is expanded into separate conversations in Fig. 12.16. Each of these lower-level conversations (i.e., "Quote request," "Order submission," "Credit status," and "Payment") can then be expanded into a set of message flows, as in Fig. 12.14.

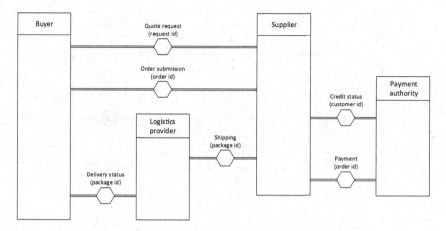

Fig. 12.16 Expansion of the sub-conversations in Fig. 12.15

But why should a conversation (actually, a sub-conversation) be expanded into a set of lower-level conversations rather than being expanded directly into a set of message flows? The answer is that, within a conversation, all messages exchanges are related by a correlation id which is present in every message (for a discussion on the important concept of correlations in business processes, see Sect. 9.2). In the case of "Quote request" and "Order submission" in Fig. 12.16, and the same applies to "Credit status" and "Payment," these conversations have different correlation ids, and therefore they cannot be represented as a single conversation. However, they can be grouped into a higher-level sub-conversation, as in Fig. 12.15.

The correlation id associated with each conversation is shown in parenthesis in Fig. 12.16. This is a standard notation in BPMN 2.0. In particular, "Quote request" uses a request id as correlation id, whereas "Order submission" uses an order id. This is the case in this scenario because the two conversations are somewhat independent: on one hand, a request for quote may not lead to an actual order and, on the other hand, an order id only exists when an actual order is submitted. This means that, for example, the "Quote request" and the "Order submission" conversations could be implemented by separate orchestrations at the supplier:

- The "Quote request" conversation is analogous to querying a product catalog. The buyer sends the request for quote with a certain request id, and the supplier returns a quote (i.e., the price for the product) with the same request id. An orchestration running at the supplier is activated by the arrival of the request for quote. The same orchestration queries the product catalog and returns the quote to the buyer, after which it ends. This interaction may or may not be followed by an order from the buyer. In any case, the supplier is left in a consistent state (i.e., no orchestration instance is running).
- If a subsequent order is received from the buyer, then this triggers a separate orchestration for order fulfillment. In this new orchestration, all messages

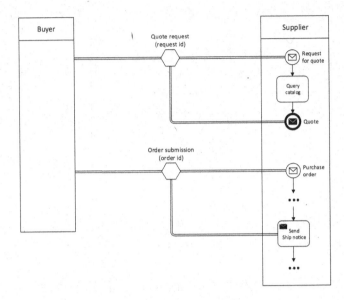

Fig. 12.17 Conversation links to events and activities in a process

exchanged between buyer and supplier will have a unique order id. However, the same orchestration may use a different correlation id for interacting with other partners, such as a package id when interacting with the logistics provider.

This idea of having two separate orchestrations at the supplier—i.e., one to handle the request for quote and another to handle the actual order—is illustrated in Fig. 12.17. This diagram also shows that the conversation links (drawn with double lines) can be extended to the events and activities in an internal process. For simplicity, only the events and activities that pertain to the "Quote request" and to the "Order submission" conversations have been represented, but the same diagram could be extended to include the conversations with the logistics provider and with the payment authority as well.

In fact, a similar scheme could be used for the two conversations that take place between the supplier and the payment authority (see Fig. 12.16). Here, too, it would be possible to have these conversations implemented by two separate orchestrations at the payment authority: one to handle the credit status request, and another to handle the actual payment. These two interactions have been separated into distinct conversations because they use different correlation ids. In particular, the "Credit status" conversation uses a customer id, whereas the "Payment" uses the order id. The use of customer id in the first conversation does not make perfect sense, because the same customer may have multiple orders being processed; in this case, there would be multiple instances of the order fulfillment process with the same customer id, and therefore this property would be inadequate to identify the correct process instance which the credit status response should be sent to.

Nevertheless, the customer id property was used here for illustrative purposes only, in order to show another example of an interaction between two parties that comprises multiple conversations. If the correlation id would be the same across these two conversations, then the two conversations could be represented as a single one, which could then be expanded into the four message exchanges shown on the right-hand side of Fig. 12.14.

12.3.3 Choreography Diagrams

The conversation diagrams described in the previous section have some of the same inconveniences as the collaboration diagrams discussed earlier. Namely, a conversation can be expanded into a set of message exchanges, but the order in which these exchanges take place cannot be specified in a precise way. Also, some conversations, or parts of conversations, may not actually occur, depending on how the choreography unfolds at run-time. For example, if the buyer does not have a good credit status, then the supplier may decide not to proceed with the order fulfillment. Clearly, there should be a way to specify the behavior of a choreography as if it would be a process with a sequence of steps, decisions, etc. However, there are some important differences between a process and a choreography, namely:

- The unit of work in a process is an activity or task, whereas in a choreography the unit of work is the exchange of a message (or pair of messages, in case of a request–response) between two partners.
- A choreography, even if modeled as a process, has only a descriptive purpose. In contrast with a process, which can often be implemented as an orchestration, a choreography is outside the control of any single organization, and therefore cannot be implemented in a centralized way. Rather, a choreography arises as the combined behavior of processes running at different organizations.
- A choreography is the public view of an inter-organizational process. Internally, each organization may have to perform many other (i.e., private) activities in order to produce the messages that are to be exchanged in a choreography.

These differences require the use of modeling constructs that are somewhat different from the activities in a process. However, there are certain features in a process model that would be desirable to have in a choreography as well. For example, the control flow in a process specifies an exact order of execution, and there is also the possibility of having decisions, parallel branches, etc. It would be useful to have these features in a choreography, since they would allow specifying the sequence of exchanges, as well as possible deviations to that sequence. To address these requirements, BPMN 2.0 introduced a new type of model—the choreography diagram—which combines message flows with control-flow elements in order to provide a precise description for the behavior of a choreography.

As explained before, the basic building block of a choreography is a message exchange between two business partners (or pair of message exchanges, in case of a

Fig. 12.18 Representation of
a pair of message exchanges
as a choreography activity

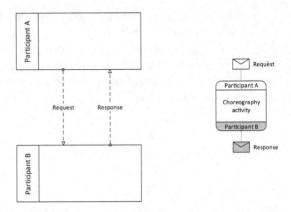

request–response interaction). Therefore, it is not surprising that the basic building
block of a choreography diagram in BPMN is a modeling construct that represents
such message exchange (or pair of message exchanges). That modeling construct is
shown in Fig. 12.3, and it is known as a *choreography activity*.

Basically, a choreography activity is represented as a rounded rectangle with two
bands to represent the two participants in the message exchange. The white band
represents the partner who initiates the exchange with a request message, whereas
the shaded band represents the partner at the receiving end, who may or may not
produce a response. The request message and the response message, if it exists, are
drawn as envelopes connected with association links to their respective bands (i.e.,
the band that represents the partner who produces the message). Again, the white
envelope represents the message that initiates the exchange, whereas the shaded
envelope, if present, represents the response (Fig. 12.18).

Now, the interesting feature of choreography activities is that it is possible to connect them to one another with sequence flows, something that one would not expect
to see in a choreography, but here those sequence flows are actually specifying a
sequence of message flows. In addition, it is possible to use some particular types of
events and gateways in that sequence flow. Figure 12.19 illustrates a simple example.
Here, the choreography activities are used in a collaboration diagram to specify the
sequence of exchanges between a buyer, a supplier, and a logistics provider. The
choreography begins after the start event, with the "Quote request" activity, and
then follows a sequence with three other activities, until the end event.

In summary, the first activity in the choreography is a pair of exchanges where
the buyer sends a request for quote to the supplier, and the supplier responds
with a quote message. The second activity contains just a single exchange, and it
consists in the buyer sending a purchase order to the supplier. The third activity
is a pair of exchanges where the supplier sends a shipping order to the logistics
provider, and the logistics provider replies with a shipping confirmation back to the
supplier. Finally, the fourth and final activity in this choreography consists in the
supplier sending a ship notice to the buyer. Here, the message flow has to go around
the diagram in order to reach the buyer's pool; the point at which this message

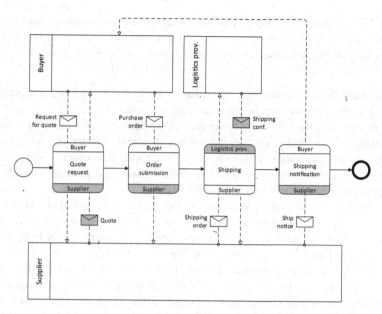

Fig. 12.19 Use of choreography activities in a collaboration diagram

flow connects to that pool is irrelevant, since the sequence of messages is clearly established by the sequence flow shown in the center of the diagram.

The use of choreography activities in a collaboration diagram, as in Fig. 12.19, is allowed by the BPMN standard, but it is somewhat redundant. Since a choreography activity already specifies the sender and the receiver for each message exchange in the white and shaded bands, it becomes unnecessary to include the actual pools for those parties (at least in the type of collaboration diagram shown in Fig. 12.19, because in collaboration diagrams where the pools are not empty, i.e., when they contain internal processes, it becomes possible to connect the message flows to specific activities inside those processes). Therefore, if the pools are to be kept empty, then they can be simply omitted without loss of information.

Another reason for omitting the pools is that they may create problems in the layout of the diagram, if it includes more than two interacting partners. In the example of Fig. 12.19, it was necessary to draw a message flow that goes around the diagram in order to reach the buyer's pool. This could get even worse if there would be additional exchanges between these partners. For example, if there would be a fifth choreography activity to represent an interaction between the buyer and the logistics provider, then the diagram would become significantly more complicated, because it would be necessary to rearrange the position of the pools and also route the sequence flow of the choreography around and between those pools.

For these reasons (i.e., redundancy and possible difficulties in placing all pools in the same diagram), a choreography diagram is usually drawn separately from a collaboration diagram, as a flow of choreography activities on their own.

Figure 12.20 shows an example of a choreography diagram for the scenario shown earlier in Fig. 12.13, with the inclusion of some possible deviations through the use of control-flow elements such as events and different types of gateways.

In particular, the choreography can be described as follows:

- The choreography begins with an exchange where the buyer sends a request for quote to the supplier, and the supplier returns a quote.
- After receiving the quote, the buyer may or may not submit a purchase order. It is impossible to predict whether the buyer will submit an order, but in any case it can be safely assumed that if the buyer does not submit an order within 30 days, then it has lost interest in the purchase (and, anyway, the quote provided by the supplier may not be valid for more than 30 days).

  These possibilities are represented in Fig. 12.20 by means of an event-based gateway. As explained in Sect. 11.1.7, an event-based gateway represents a decision based on events (i.e., the first event to occur determines the branch to be executed). In Sect. 11.1.7, we have seen that each branch contains an intermediate event that represents the trigger for that branch. In a choreography diagram, a choreography activity can serve as the trigger for a branch in an event-based gateway, meaning that if the message exchange that is represented by that activity occurs, then the branch to be executed is automatically chosen.

  In Fig. 12.20 the event-based gateway contains a branch with a timer event and another branch with a choreography activity. The first event to occur decides the branch to be followed. In other words, if a purchase order is not submitted within 30 days, then the choreography just ends at that point.
- If the purchase order is submitted by the buyer, then the next steps in the choreography will depend on whether payment has to be done in advance or not. In general, in a choreography diagram the branching conditions of a gateway can only be based on the content of messages exchanged earlier, so the payment conditions must have been specified in a previous message, possibly in the quote that the supplier sent to the buyer.
- If payment is due in advance, the choreography follows the upper branch, where payment is requested immediately to the payment authority. Assuming that payment is successful (the choreography does not specify what happens otherwise), this is followed by the exchange of a shipping order and a shipping confirmation with the logistics partner. After that, the ship notice is sent to the buyer, and then the choreography will enter the order tracking phase.

  In the original scenario of Fig. 12.13, the buyer may query the logistics provider multiple times in order to find out the current location of the package. This is done by sending a "query status" message to the logistics provider, who will then return a "delivery status" message, as depicted in the last choreography activity in the upper (i.e., rightmost) branch of Fig. 12.20.

  Because this "Order tracking" activity can be carried out an arbitrary number of times, it is represented with a loop marker. When the number of times that a choreography activity will run is known in advance, it is possible to use a multi-instance marker instead, as in Fig. 11.3 on page 321.

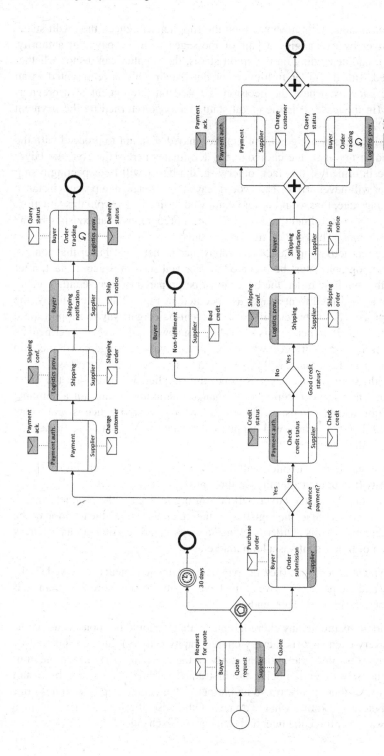

Fig. 12.20 A choreography diagram (rotated)

- If payment is not due in advance, then the supplier will check the credit status of the buyer by exchanging a pair of messages with the payment authority. After that, and depending on the credit status, the supplier can decide whether to proceed with the order fulfillment or not. Again, this is represented as an exclusive gateway, where the decision is based on the content of a previous message (in this case, it is the credit status message returned by the payment authority).
- If the credit status is not good, the supplier may decide not to proceed with the order, and in this case the choreography terminates here. However, the buyer should be informed of this fact; otherwise, the buyer will be expecting a ship notice that will never arrive. This would leave the buyer with a process instance in a pending state, that would never be allowed to finish. To avoid this situation, there is a "Non-fulfillment" activity in the choreography that consists in the supplier sending a "bad credit" message to the buyer.

  Having this activity in the choreography means that every buyer that adheres to this choreography must be prepared to received such message. In fact, after sending the purchase order, the buyer must be prepared to receive either a ship notice or a "bad credit" message, as specified in Fig. 12.20. Most likely, the internal process at the buyer will have an event-based gateway to support these possibilities. Each branch in this event-based gateway will have an intermediate event with a message trigger, where one branch will be triggered by the ship notice and the other branch will be triggered by the "bad credit" message.
- If the credit status of the buyer is good, the supplier proceeds with the order fulfillment and the next step is to exchange a shipping order and a shipping confirmation with the logistics partner. After this, the ship notice is sent to the buyer, and then two things will happen independently of each other (hence the use of a parallel gateway):

  - On one hand, the supplier will take care of payment with the payment authority (top branch after the parallel split).
  - On the other hand, the buyer will be waiting to receive the products and, if needed, it may contact the logistics partner in order to track the location of the package. Again, this "Order tracking" activity can be carried out an arbitrary number of times, so it has a loop marker.

After payment is complete (i.e., the payment acknowledgment is received by the supplier) and the products arrive at the buyer's site (i.e., no more tracking needs to be done), the choreography ends.

An important feature in any choreography is that it should be "consistent" in the sense that every exchange (i.e., every choreography activity) must be initiated by a partner who was either the initiating party or the receiving party in the previous exchange (the only exception being the first activity which is preceded by a start event). This way, there is always some partner in the choreography who has done something before and knows what to do next. Otherwise, if this is not the case, then there is no way to enforce the intended sequence of exchanges.

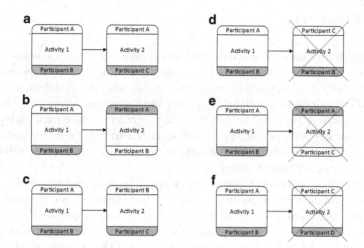

Fig. 12.21 Consistent vs. inconsistent sequences of choreography activities

Figure 12.21 illustrates this point with a few examples:

- In case (a) the sequence of activities is consistent because it is participant A who initiates the exchange in both activities. Participant A will know that it must initiate Activity 2 after having performed Activity 1.
- In case (b) the sequence of activities is consistent because participant B, who initiates the second activity, was the recipient in the previous exchange, so B will know that it must initiate Activity 2 after receiving a message from A.
- In case (c) the sequence of activities is consistent because B, again, is both the recipient of the first exchange and the initiator of the second exchange.
- In case (d) the sequence of activities is inconsistent because there is no way for participant C to know when it should initiate Activity 2. Unless someone tells participant C that Activity 1 has been done, there is no way to guarantee that C will initiate Activity 2 at the right moment. For this to work, there should be an intermediate activity (between Activity 1 and Activity 2) where either A or B inform participant C that it can initiate Activity 2. With such intermediate activity, the sequence of exchanges would become consistent.
- Cases (e) and (f) are inconsistent for the same reason as case (d). Since the initiator of Activity 2 is neither the initiator nor the recipient of Activity 1, there is no way for participant C to know when it should initiate the exchange.

Therefore, besides requiring business partners to implement their processes in a compatible way, a choreography must be consistent by itself, so that one exchange follows naturally another, without leaving the participants uncertain about what to do next. As illustrated in Fig. 12.21, the proper sequencing of a choreography can be guaranteed by ensuring that the initiator of a given exchange is either the initiator or the recipient of the previous exchange. The interested reader may check that this is indeed the case for all exchanges in Fig. 12.20.

12.4   Conclusion

In this chapter we have discussed the problem of inter-organizational integration at three different levels. At the lowest level, organizations need security mechanisms to ensure that the messages they exchange are authentic and confidential. This is achieved through the use of digital signatures and encryption, respectively. Both of these mechanisms are based on public-key cryptography, where each partner has both a public key and a private key. A third security artifact is the digital certificate; this is issued by a trusted certification authority and it asserts that a given public key actually belongs to its alleged owner.

Once these security mechanisms are in place, business partners will have to agree on a common format for the messages to be exchanged. A compromise can be difficult to achieve because each partner has its own preferred schemas, and also it is impractical to set up common formats for each interaction with a new business partner. Instead, business partners can rely on EDI standards, which specify the format for a wide range of documents that are typically exchanged between business organizations. Although the syntax of these standards predates the use of XML, it is not difficult to transform EDI messages into XML through the use of appropriate pipelines. These pipelines also play an important role in securing the message exchanges through the use of encryption and digital signatures.

Finally, the third level of inter-organizational integration consists in defining the choreography of message exchanges between partners. Just like a process defines the sequence of activities that are to be performed by different resources in an organization, a choreography defines the sequence of message exchanges that are to take place between a set of business partners. However, in contrast with a process, which can be implemented within a single organization, a choreography is the combined result of the internal processes running at different organizations. In particular, those internal processes must implement the message exchanges that are required to comply with the role of each organization in the choreography.

Naturally, for a choreography to work out correctly when all partners come together, the expected behavior for each business partner must be made absolutely clear from the start. This explains why it is important to have appropriate models to define the behavior of choreographies with the same rigor as in the case of business processes. In practice, both kinds of models will have a key role in shaping the orchestrations and integration solutions in each organization.

References

1. van der Aalst, W.: The application of Petri nets to workflow management. J. Circ. Syst. Comput. **8**(1), 21–66 (1998)
2. van der Aalst, W., ter Hofstede, A., Kiepuszewski, B., Barros, A.: Workflow patterns. Distr. Parallel Databases **14**(3), 5–51 (2003)
3. van der Aalst, W., Weske, M.: The P2P approach to interorganizational workflows. In: Advanced Information Systems Engineering, Lecture Notes in Computer Science, vol. 2068. Springer, Heidelberg (2001)
4. Allweyer, T.: BPMN 2.0: Introduction to the Standard for Business Process Modeling. Books on Demand GmbH, Norderstedt (2010)
5. Alonso, G., Casati, F., Kuno, H., Machiraju, V.: Web Services: Concepts, Architectures and Applications. Springer, Heidelberg (2003)
6. Beynon-Davies, P.: Information Systems: An Introduction to Informatics in Organizations. Palgrave Macmillan, Basingstoke (2002)
7. Booch, G., Rumbaugh, J., Jacobson, I.: The Unified Modeling Language User Guide, 2nd edn. Addison-Wesley, Boston, MA (2005)
8. Curbera, F., Duftler, M., Khalaf, R., Nagy, W., Mukhi, N., Weerawarana, S.: Unraveling the Web services web: an introduction to SOAP, WSDL, and UDDI. IEEE Internet Comput. **6**(2), 86–93 (2002)
9. Edwards, J.: 3-Tier Client/Server at Work. Wiley, Chichester (1999)
10. Erl, T.: Service-Oriented Architecture: Concepts, Technology, and Design. Prentice Hall, Upper Saddle River, NJ (2005)
11. Erl, T.: SOA: Principles of Service Design. Prentice Hall, Upper Saddle River, NJ (2007)
12. Ferreira, D.R., Szimanski, F., Ralha, C.G.: A hierarchical Markov model to understand the behaviour of agents in business processes. In: Business Process Management Workshops, Lecture Notes in Business Information Processing, vol. 132, pp. 150–161, Springer, Heidelberg (2013)
13. Harding, T., Drummond, R., Shih, C.: MIME-based secure peer-to-peer business data interchange over the internet. Doc. no. RFC 3335, IETF (2002)
14. Henning, M.: The rise and fall of CORBA. Comm. ACM **51**(8), 52–57 (2008)
15. Hohpe, G., Woolf, B.: Enterprise Integration Patterns: Designing, Building, and Deploying Messaging Solutions. Addison-Wesley, Boston, MA (2003)
16. Hollingsworth, D.: The workflow reference model. Doc. no. TC00-1003, Workflow Management Coalition (1995)
17. Moberg, D., Drummond, R.: MIME-based secure peer-to-peer business data interchange using HTTP, applicability statement 2 (AS2). Doc. no. RFC 4130, IETF (2005)
18. OASIS: Web Services Security: SOAP Message Security 1.1 (2006)
19. OASIS: Web Services Business Process Execution Language Version 2.0 (2007)

D.R. Ferreira, *Enterprise Systems Integration*, DOI 10.1007/978-3-642-40796-3,
© Springer-Verlag Berlin Heidelberg 2013

20. OASIS: WS-SecureConversation 1.4 (2009)
21. OMG: Business Process Model and Notation (BPMN), Version 2.0 (2011)
22. Ouvans, C., Dumas, M., ter Hofstede, A., van der Aalst, W.: From BPMN process models to BPEL web services. In: IEEE International Conference on Web Services (ICWS 2006), pp. 285–292 (2006)
23. Papazoglou, M., Traverso, P., Dustdar, S., Leymann, F.: Service-oriented computing: State of the art and research challenges. IEEE Comput. **40**(11), 38–45 (2007)
24. Recker, J.C., Mendling, J.: On the translation between BPMN and BPEL: Conceptual mismatch between process modeling languages. In: 18th International Conference on Advanced Information Systems Engineering. Proceedings of Workshops and Doctoral Consortium, pp. 521–532. Namur University Press, Luxembourg (2006)
25. Richardson, L., Ruby, S.: RESTful Web Services. O'Reilly, Sebastopol, CA (2007)
26. Scheer, A.W.: ARIS: Business Process Modeling, 3rd edn. Springer, Heidelberg (2000)
27. Silberschatz, A., Korth, H.F., Sudarshan, S.: Database System Concepts, 5th edn. McGraw-Hill, Boston, MA (2006)
28. Stallings, W.: Cryptography and Network Security: Principles and Practice, 5th edn. Prentice Hall, Upper Saddle River, NJ (2010)
29. Vinoski, S.: CORBA: integrating diverse applications within distributed heterogeneous environments. IEEE Comm. Mag. **35**(2), 46–55 (1997)
30. W3C: Web Services Description Language (WSDL) 1.1 (2001)
31. W3C: XML Schema Part 2: Datatypes, Second Edition (2004)
32. Weerawarana, S., Curbera, F., Leymann, F., Storey, T., Ferguson, D.F.: Web Services Platform Architecture. Prentice Hall, Upper Saddle River, NJ (2005)
33. Weidlich, M., Decker, G., Großkopf Alexander andWeske, M.: BPEL to BPMN: The myth of a straight-forward mapping. In: On the Move to Meaningful Internet Systems: OTM 2008, Lecture Notes in Computer Science, vol. 5331, pp. 265–282. Springer, Heidelberg (2008)
34. White, S.A., Miers, D.: BPMN Modeling and Reference Guide. Future Strategies, Lighthouse Point, FL (2008)
35. Wollrath, A., Waldo, J., Riggs, R.: Java-centric distributed computing. IEEE Micro. **17**(3), 44–53 (1997)

Index

D.R. Ferreira, *Enterprise Systems Integration*, DOI 10.1007/978-3-642-40796-3,
© Springer-Verlag Berlin Heidelberg 2013

Work item, 200
Workflow, 200
   client application, 200
   engine, 200
   pattern, 214
Worklist, 200

Wrapper, 172
Wrapper WSDL file, 274
WSDL, 166

XML, 103, 120. *See also* Schema

Printed in the United States
By Bookmasters